War in the Tribal Zone

The advanced seminar "Expanding States and Indigenous Warfare"
was sponsored by the Harry Frank Guggenheim Foundation.

The Advanced Seminar Series is published with generous support
from The Brown Foundation, Inc., of Houston, Texas.

War in the Tribal Zone
Expanding States and Indigenous Warfare

Edited by

R. Brian Ferguson and
Neil L. Whitehead

With a new preface by the Editors

School of American Research Press
Santa Fe, New Mexico

James Currey
Oxford

School of American Research
Advanced Seminar Series
Douglas W. Schwartz, General Editor

Contributors

Thomas S. Abler
Department of Anthropology
University of Waterloo
Waterloo, Ontario, Canada

Michael F. Brown
Department of Anthropology
and Sociology
Williams College
Williamstown, Massachusetts

R. Brian Ferguson
Department of Sociology,
Anthropology, and Criminal Justice
Rutgers University
Newark, New Jersey

Eduardo Fernández
Lima, Peru

R. A. L. H. Gunawardana
Department of History
University of Peradeniya
Peradeniya, Sri Lanka

Ross Hassig
Department of Anthropology
University of Oklahoma
Norman, Oklahoma

Robin Law
Department of History
University of Stirling
Stirling, Scotland

D. J. Matttingly
Department of Classical Studies
University of Michigan
Ann Arbor, Michigan

Andrew Strathern
Department of Anthropology
University of Pittsburgh
Pittsburgh, Pennsylvania

Neil L. Whitehead
Department of Anthropology
University of Wisconsin
Madison, Wisconsin

School of American Research Press
Post Office Box 2188
Santa Fe, New Mexico, 87504-2188

James Currey Ltd
73 Botley Road
Oxford OX2 0BS

Library of Congress Cataloging-in-Publication Data:
War in the tribal zone : expanding states and indigenous warfare / edited by R. Brian
Ferguson and Neil L. Whitehead.
p.   cm. — (School of American Research advanced seminar series)
Includes bibliographical references and index.
ISBN 0-933452-79-9. — ISBN 0-933452-80-2
1. War and society—Cross-cultural studies. 2. Warfare, Primitive—Cross-cultural
studies. 3. Territorial expansion—Cross-cultural studies. 4. Indigenous peoples.
I. Ferguson, R. Brian. II. Whitehead, Neil L. III. Series.
GN497.W28 1992
303.6'6—dc20
91-39599
CIP

British Library Cataloguing in Publication Data:
War in the tribal zone : expanding states and indigenous warfare.—
(School of American Research advanced seminar series)
1. War and society—Cross-cultural studies. 2. Military art and science—
Cross-cultural studies. 3. Indigenous peoples—Cross-cultural studies.
I. Ferguson, R. Brian. II. Whitehead, Neil L.
303.6'6
ISBN 0-85255-913-5

Cover: Two boy soldiers, members of the government-allied Kamajor (civil defense forces
in the south), at a training center run by the Christian Brothers, a local NGO that works
with unaccompanied, abused, and street children, as well as former child soldiers, in Bo,
Sierra Leone. Copyright © 1998 UNICEF/HQ98-0569/Giacomo Pirozzi.

Contents

Illustrations

Preface to the Second Printing

The time was right for *War in the Tribal Zone*. By the late 1980s the anthropology of war had grown into a large, cacophonous field, surging with conflicting theories that attributed war to one or another aspect of indigenous society and culture. At the same time, the growth of historical anthropology had increasingly revealed the fundamental changes that the colonial encounter had wrought, and various studies had shown that the practice of war was particularly sensitive to changes brought on by Western contact. Ferguson (1990) and Whitehead (1990) both recognized that this fact needed to be incorporated better into anthropological theory. In *War in the Tribal Zone*, our goal was to map out the main dimensions of state expansion and its effect on warfare as practiced by indigenous peoples, and to that end the concept of the "tribal zone" was advanced. As we indicated in our introductory essay, "The Violent Edge of Empire," a tribal zone is that physical and conceptual space that radiates out from the borders of the intrusive state system. This zone beyond the state's immediate control has a dynamic effect on developments within the colonial enclave and profoundly influences the social and cultural life of the independent peoples within its scope.

The term "tribal" was chosen to express the very particular effects on social structures and cultural proclivities that this kind of proximity to a colonizing state appears regularly to induce. Interestingly, but at that moment unknown to the editors, research in the field of colonial literature and history by Mary Louise Pratt (1992) had resulted in a similar notion—that of the "contact zone"—to describe the transcultural reconstruction of indigenous and colonial ideas and practices in that ambiguous space that lies at the margins and borders of direct political control by the metropolitan states. Since then there has been an increasing recognition that the nature of borders and boundaries in such contexts is highly permeable, constantly breached and put into question by the symbiotic and mimetic processes that belie the colonial discourse of difference and distinction (Taussig 1995; Whitehead 1997a, 1997b). In addressing these issues, *War in the Tribal Zone* also represents a bridge between humanistic and social scientific approaches to violence and warfare.

As summarized in the volume Introduction, material circumstances, patterned social interactions, and structured ways of thinking are in countless ways disrupted and recast by this process of culture contact. In most cases, the direct and indirect result of this was to worsen levels of collective violence among indigenous peoples. Whereas imperialists have long justified their mission as bringing peace to bloody savages, prior to any pacification the expansionist impact was quite the opposite, and the heightened violence the encounter produced has distorted the image of tribal peoples for centuries. Contrary to the straw man position a few critics set up to attack (e.g., Keeley 1996:20; and see below), we never suggested that war among nonstate peoples was nonexistent or benign until the arrival of the state—or of Western states in particular—but rather proposed that indigenous warfare was generally transformed, frequently intensified, and sometimes generated in the cauldron of contact. To understand war as observed and recorded, these changes must be foregrounded.

A tribal zone perspective has been accepted by, or has directly influenced, theoretically diverse students of war, including those working on
contemporary "ethnic conflict"—a subject to be discussed below
(Abbink 1993; Besteman 1996; Fukui and Markakis 1994:2–3; Hall et al.
1996; Hoskins 1996:3; Knauft 1992:400; Peregrine 1996:493; Sponsel
1997:621; Tainter 1998:185–88; Van der Dannen 1995:94, 495; cf.
Otterbein 1994:213–17, 1997:266–68; and see special issue of
Ethnohistory 46:4, *Warfare and Violence in Ethnohistorical Perspective*).
Some authors (Bamforth 1994:95–97; Shankman 1991:299–300) have
challenged Jeffrey Blick's (1988:654–55) categorical distinction between
traditional patterns of restricted feuding driven by revenge, and a post-
contact pattern of genocidal killing motivated by new economic goals—a
distinction we too would dispute, but not without recognizing the
importance of Blick's general argument to developing the perspective of
War in the Tribal Zone.

On the other hand, Lawrence Keeley (1995) bases his trade book, *War
before Civilization*, on the premise that scholars such as ourselves are
blinded to reality by political correctness and that we maintain that no
war existed before the Europeans arrived on the scene. Napoleon
Chagnon's (1996:207) response to documentation that Yanomami warfare is related to Western contact (Ferguson, this volume, 1995) has been
to compare the idea to the film "The Gods Must Be Crazy," in which
"Bushman" society is disrupted by a bottle tossed out of a passing airplane: just "substitute the words 'machete' or 'steel tool' for 'Coke bottle.'"
Psycholinguist and evolutionary psychology popularizer Steven Pinker
echoes this view, dismissing the idea that war was intensified by Western
contact as "romantic nonsense" (Pinker 1997:509).

THE TRIBAL ZONE PERSPECTIVE AND THE
ANTHROPOLOGY OF WAR

As we discussed in the Introduction to this volume, bringing history into
the analysis does not rule out, but may enhance, efforts to link war to various aspects of social and cultural life such as ecology, social organization,
politics, and cosmology. We believe that increased historical awareness
would lead to more accurate and realistic assessments of each of these
areas (see, for example, the editors' contributions to a volume on historical ecology: Ferguson 1998; Whitehead 1998c). Rather than deal with
particular theories here, we will instead briefly consider the implications

of a tribal zone perspective on war for four different research domains: ethnography, ethnohistory, archaeology, and primatology.

The basic idea to be applied to ethnographic studies of war is that the fighting, and any sociocultural variables used to explain that fighting, must be situated in its real political context, a context that involves people and forces from, or linked to, wider regional and even global processes. The discomfiting part of this perspective is that anthropologists must acknowledge that they are part of an outside intrusion, and that their own impact on the events they observe must become part of our discipline's theoretical reckoning. The impacts of outside impingement may be very little or may be great, but any study that does not properly consider them is weakened by that oversight. There is fertile ground for reconsideration of earlier anthropological portrayals that rest on the idea of an "ethnographic present" not yet "contaminated" by outside contact. A critical region for the application of the concept of the tribal zone is Highland New Guinea (see Strathern, this volume), where reports by early observers and careful reconstructions of indigenous histories provide the best information available about war practices that predate colonial contact (Knauft 1990; Meggitt 1977; Robbins 1982; Schieffelin and Crittenden 1991; Weisner and Tumu 1998). Nevertheless, our images of early conflicts in this area stand in clear need of careful historicizing in relation to the first direct and indirect effects of state penetration. When that has been accomplished we will have a quite different, and much better, understanding of Highland New Guinea warfare.

For ethnohistory the value of a tribal zone perspective is illustrated by the individual chapters of this volume. A couple of broad points might be emphasized. Although we sought to include information on how war was transformed, intensified, or generated in tribal zones around ancient states, our work here was only preliminary. Comparison of ancient and medieval states shows that they uniformly encounter militaristic "barbarians" at their fringes, and sooner or later incorporate them into their own armies (Ferguson 1999:439–41). Typically, however, historians of ancient states have assumed that this martial development is just an expression of the way barbarians are, and they have left unasked whether or not these peoples' martial valor is related to living on the edges of an imperial state. A similar bias pervades frontier studies, as of the North American West, and anthropology has generally been complicit here. Ethnohistorians in particular should treat critically what earlier anthro-

pologists wrote about war by tribal peoples: that it was a feature of func-
tionally self-contained complexes that persisted—as in days of old—
until finally brought to heel by Western might. There is a whole new
world to explore in the historical symbiosis and military interaction
across the fluid frontiers of the tribal zone.

Archaeology has already taken up the challenge of the tribal zone perspective, especially in studies of the Americas (Lambert 1997:80;
Redmond 1994:1; Maschner and Maschner 1998:19; Milner, Anderson,
and Smith 1991:581; Wilkinson 1997:22). It is also in archaeology that
both controversy and confusion are the most intense. Keeley (1995)
implies that the global archaeological record shows serious warfare going
back in time. Others who have carefully studied the archaeological
record come to a very different conclusion; that war leaves archaeologically recoverable traces, and that with few exceptions, evidence is consistent with the relatively recent development of war as regular
practice—substantially after the transition to sedentary existence
(though not necessarily agriculture), or, to put a date and place on it,
around 6000 B.C. in Turkish Anatolia (Ferguson 1997, n.d.a; Ferrill
1995; Haas 1993; O'Connell 1989; Roper 1969, 1975). After that date,
war develops in and spreads out from more, and new, locations, such that
by A.D. 1500 it had become quite common around the world, in all kinds
of societies.

But war still did not reach the pitch brought to it by European expansionism. A good illustration of this point is found in Debra Martin and
David Frayer's (1997) volume, if we compare Carol and Melvin Ember's
(1997) ethnographic statistics on war with all the archaeological studies.
Even though those archaeological case studies were assembled specifically to illustrate prehistoric violence, they reveal situations that are
starkly less violent than the bloody ethnography of the past few centuries. How is it, then, that Keeley can paint such a sanguinary picture of
the archaeological record on war? By using a method at least as old as
Herbert Spencer (Holsti 1913:78): report the worst as if it were typical.
Polemical arguments aside, it is clear that archaeology can play a key role
by focusing on indicators of ancient violence, and even more so by providing a record of violence that spans the time from before contact
through eventual pacification by state powers.

Finally, it is in primatology, which might seem the least promising area
for it, that it is perhaps most important to raise a tribal zone perspective.

Recent speculations about humanity's warlike nature have been fueled by observations of "warfare" among chimpanzees and other nonhuman primates (Ghiglieri 1999; Wrangham and Peterson 1996). These very influential views have reportedly reached even into the White House (Fukuyama 1998:39). But in fact, the chimpanzee comparison is based on two defective premises: that there has been continuous warfare throughout humanity's evolutionary past, and that the record of recent ethnography is a valid reflection of those past levels of violence (Wrangham 1999:19–20). If certain primatologists claim that to understand human warfare we must look at chimpanzees, they must recognize that it is a two-way street and that anthropological theory on collective violence must be considered regarding chimpanzee violence. Margaret Powers (1991) has argued that both the collective violence and the extreme hierarchical behavior observed among some chimpanzee communities is a manifestation of change brought on by an intensifying human presence. There is much to recommend her conclusion: Gombe is a chimpanzee tribal zone. Primatologists have asked to have it accepted on faith that similar chimpanzee violence occurs in the absence of major human disruption (see Wrangham and Peterson 1996), but these situations are very inadequately described. As with tribal warfare, if their defenders want such claims to be taken seriously, they must publish thorough, detailed descriptions of any human activity in these areas. It is not enough merely to assert that trooping chimpanzees *seem* to be unaffected by this growing presence. After all, cultural anthropologists made similar claims from the beginning of ethnographic fieldwork, claims that seemed quite plausible until others began to focus on history.

Consideration of primatology provides a bridge to the remaining two sections of this preface. Antedating but reinforced by primatologists' recent claims, sociobiologists and evolutionary psychologists and, indeed, Social Darwinists before them (Sumner 1960:27–30; Van der Dennen 1990:150–55) claim that our evolutionary heritage has endowed— or cursed—us with an inherent tendency for in-group amity and out-group enmity. This tendency to cling to those close to us and react with unreasoning hostility against those who are different is then taken to explain "ethnic violence" in the modern world (Reynolds, Falger, and Vine 1986; Shaw and Wong 1989). These views in fact often propound naive caricatures of contemporary conflict, as with Ghiglieri's (1999) suggestion that such conflict is based on a three-way association of cultural difference, genetic distance, and readiness to use violence between groups.

War in the Tribal Zone provides an entirely different frame of reference, one in which identity and violence are historically and culturally constructed. "Ethnic conflict" as it appears in this book is a problematic category of emergent, complex, and highly variable processes—anything but the eruption of some primitive and fixed group loyalty. Since completing this volume, both editors have gone on to deal with different aspects of such violence: Ferguson considering large-scale social structures, Whitehead the cultural processes of war and ethnic conflict. As will be evident, these perspectives are by no means exclusive, and integration of the results of this continuing research is crucial to advancing debate on the causes and meanings of violent conflict.

"ETHNIC VIOLENCE" AND COLLAPSING STATES

The end of the Cold War was followed by an upsurge of civil war along what appeared to be cultural divides, sometimes to the point of demolishing the structure of state polities. The frequent and denigrating use of metaphors of "tribal violence" cried out for a more sophisticated and more accurate tribal zone perspective (Whitehead and Ferguson 1993). An initial attempt to develop that, for a conference on violence in Africa, stressed the global-level processes that structured and conditioned local political fields and antagonisms, concluding that there is no such thing as a "purely local" war (Ferguson n.d.b). A more comprehensive effort was made at a 1994 conference organized by Ferguson titled "The State under Siege: Political Disintegration in the Post–Cold War Era." The basic question behind this gathering was this: If expanding states could engender so much local violence, was a weakening of the global system of states responsible for the recent carnage? Papers from this conference are still wending their way toward publication, and what follows here are lessons drawn from that collective effort, considered in relation to *War in the Tribal Zone*.

One dramatic contrast between the conflict situations of the last decade and those of expansionist periods of the past is that metropolitan powers are not directly organizing wars between local peoples: there is no (or very limited) use of ethnic soldiers in pacification campaigns, in slave raids, or even, since the end of the superpower rivalry, in waging proxy wars for imperial giants. Nevertheless, global forces, in continuous interaction with local realities, have directly shaped recent violence in a historically nested series of contexts. Most immediately, the end of the USSR and the Cold War brought a sudden enabling of disintegration, as both military and economic support for client governments dried up. Going back a decade or two, the superpower rivalry capitalized political factions and poured weaponry into unstable areas, while a general economic immiseration left many countries even more marginalized in the global economy and forced by debt to accept supervision by global financial institutions that prevented their governments from responding to critical material needs. Even before that, the interstate system imposed on former colonies after World War II and the Soviet model of creating ethnic republics and other political divisions gave us the set of polities that have only recently broken down. Earlier still was the age of imperial expansion—described in so many variations in *War in the Tribal Zone*—which generated many of the identities and inequalities that shape those current breakdowns.

Thus, basic parameters of political confrontation today cannot be understood without a strong grounding in the history of local-global interaction. But today, as in the past, potential confrontations are actualized by local agents in pursuit of power and wealth. Unlike many of the historical contexts covered in *War in the Tribal Zone,* recent struggles occur in a context in which the superordinate issue is which local actors will control, or be controlled by, the *state.* As noted in the Introduction to this volume, the meaning and significance of this term is disputed in social theory. In 1992 we sidestepped those debates by focusing on specific manifestations of states, but that is not so easy to do when considering recent violence. Even the concept of a tribal zone could be challenged by asking what constitutes "direct rule" by a government. At what points do indigenous peoples make the transitions we note from independence to encapsulation to incorporation? The territorial-hegemonic distinction that we conclude may be impossible to separate on the ground, merges into another distinction very prominent in the comparative study of ancient and medieval states: that between centralized and decentralized rule (Ferguson 1999:439). *When* is a state?

All this theory becomes highly political when global power centers assume the responsibility for preventing what is seen as state collapse. Until recently, it was an article of faith unquestioned by "East", "West," or "nonaligned" that the international system was constructed out of independent states, with established governments ruling over clearly bounded territories (Ruggie 1993; Taylor 1995). Wherever that was in question, state building would be commanded and underwritten from above. This is one major reason why, especially in the poorest areas, so much blood has been shed over who gets to be recognized as the government: the winners tap into the main channel of power and wealth (Villalon 1988:11–14; Fukui and Markakis 1994:8–9; Herbst 1990). But to seize and consolidate power—and international recognition—contenders must have a nationalist vision, a symbolic matrix that mobilizes support, legitimizes rule, and, ostensibly, binds the people of a country together (Anderson 1991; Hobsbawm 1994; Smith 1983). For decades, it was assumed that economic development, modernization, and nationalism would do away with those messy cultural identities, which is why the extremely problematic elision of "nation" and "state" could be overlooked for so long. But just as they were created or reworked and rigidified in colonial times, ethnic and other counter-identities have only intensified in response to nationalist agendas. The current "ethnic revival," which began after World War II and picked up steam in the 1960s, has roots that go back to the creation of relatively fixed European states by the 1648 Treaty of Westphalia (Geertz 1963:120; Guidieri, Pellizzi, and Tambiah 1988; Horowitz 1985:5; Smith 1981:18–20).

In this volume's Introduction, we suggest that it is useful to restrict "ethnic" to groups with perceived cultural distinctiveness, as opposed to "tribe," which suggests a degree of political coherence. Ethnicity is an enormous industry in academia. In the current literature, one finds three different perspectives, often combined at different weights: the instrumentalist, which stresses the use of ethnic categories in political competition; the constructionist, which highlights the shifting and dialogic character of ethnicity; and the primordialist, which emphasizes the emotional power of the social givens of personal identity (Gurr 1993:3–5; Smith 1983:xxviii–xxiii; Turton 1997:6–14; Young 1993:23–25). Unfortunately, "primordialist" is often used in a different sense—one that is incompatible with instrumentalist or constructionist approaches—to denote a fixed, bounded group attachment and rejection of all others, which supersedes any calculation of interests; what might be called the "ancient loyalties and hatreds" perspective. But as originally, and more usefully, formulated, the operative word regarding identities in primordialism is not "ancient" but "given" (Geertz 1963:109; Stack 1986:1).

War in the Tribal Zone illustrates all three perspectives on ethnicity.

Ethnic identities rise and fall in historical process (and see Hill 1996). They gain strength from above as state agents try to map peoples for purposes of rule, from below by brokers seeking their own or their group's advancement, and in struggle as categories for the application of violence (see Brown and Fernández, Strathern, this volume). Yet this contingent character in no way minimizes the analytical or historical significance of culturally specific phenomenologies, as Whitehead stresses in the following section of this Preface (and see Nordstrom and Martin 1992; Warren 1993). Distinctive systems of meaning affect how people perceive their situation and act on it. Group identity is defined by attachment to common symbols, among the most potent of which are constructions of "our history." Symbols, of course, mean many things to many people and are well suited to manipulation by self-aggrandizing ethnic entrepreneurs, as has been witnessed again and again in recent years. But to focus too exclusively on the machinations of leaders would be as serious an error as to believe that ethnic conflict bubbles up out of cultural difference itself. Culture at the level of the grass roots and the pavement must be grasped to understand how local peoples take culturally calibrated propaganda against a demonized other and either resist it, or internalize it with terrible ferocity (see Hinton 1998a, 1998b).

Yet "ethnic violence" itself is a misleading label, a late-twentieth-century pejorative that primitivizes conflicts that are every bit a part of the modern world. Used loosely, the label denotes little, and obscures practically everything we need for explanation (Bowen 1996; Gantzell 1997). The reader of this book could ask what would be gained or lost if the myriad struggles described herein which somehow involve cultural differentiation were categorized in that way. We maintain that there is no necessary link between cultural difference and intergroup violence. Anthropology provides countless examples of peoples with highly distinctive cultures getting along symbiotically, and just as many examples of people who are culturally identical inflating trivial distinctions to divide "them" from "us." When one examines closely the so-called ethnic groups that are involved in recent struggles, as in the projected volume "The State under Siege," it is clear that the identities of peoples who are successfully mobilized for confrontation are never merely (and sometimes not at all) ethnic. Calls to arms are heard differently by people with different mixes of interest and identity, as these are structured by gender, generation, age, geography (including region and location in the gradient from city to countryside), class position (inclusively defined), and—if applicable—caste, race, religion, language, tribe, clan, and ethnicity. All of these elements tend to merge and morph into one another, as do interest and identity, and in their unstable compounds they largely determine which individuals rush to the center of a movement, which stay on the sidelines, and which try to fight it. The "ethnic" divisions that grow into conflict are in reality entirely new constructions, shifting constellations of compound identities and interests that, in their politically potent actuality, never existed before. Until the categorical killing begins, that is. Then whatever group label has been fixed on each side may overwhelm all other distinctions.

"ETHNIC CONFLICT" AND THE CULTURE OF VIOLENCE

In the years since the first publication of *War in the Tribal Zone* there has been a dramatic and continuing expansion of collective and community violence, which often appears to defy attempts at outside interpretation and so hampers an effective political response by institutions of governmental control, both internal and external. Yet such conflicts, as witnessed in Rwanda, Bosnia, Sri Lanka, or India, are clearly meaningful and significant to the communities involved, even though they are often enigmatic to the Western media, government policymakers, and academic specialists (Whitehead and Ferguson 1993).

The reasons for this, however, become more apparent once we begin to examine our own cultural prejudices and assumptions with regard to the violence and savagery of others, and when we bring a historical appreciation of the roots of conflict to our analysis of contemporary situations. This approach broadly defines a hermeneutic for warfare and community violence, and it was the purpose of *War in the Tribal Zone* to highlight the close articulation between external and internal socioeconomic forces in the production of such conflict. Less directly addressed in this volume, though clearly implicit in its arguments, was the related task of interpreting the cultural forms of violence that develop from this symbiosis of antagonists. It is this aspect of the burgeoning ethnic and community conflicts of the last decade or so that has confounded most commentators.

In place of real cultural context, there is a tendency to give commentary, policy, and direct intervention a pseudo-ethnological spin by reference to the "tribalism," "savagery," and "primitiveness" of the participants in contemporary conflicts. Such discourse mimics the evolutionism of past anthropological thinking and endows such judgments with a spurious aura of academic authority. These images are deeply deceptive, for while no one disagrees that instances of extreme violence occur, the motives for this are not the upwelling of atavistic, even biological urges, which are then somehow harnessed by the cynical (and often Western-educated) leaders of the benighted "primitives"; rather, they are a complex product of culture and history which the notion of the tribal zone was designed to make more apparent.

The tribal zone does this by emphasizing the episodic, symbiotic, mimetic, and hybrid nature of conflicts that emerge at the margins of state power; this being understood to mean both the physical and geographical placement at a distance from state centers, but also situations in which the state itself has become marginalized within a globalized ranking of political and governmental institutions. In this way the tribal zone speaks not only to the ancient contexts of imperial expansion, such as the Roman, Aztec, and Sri Lankan, and to the moment of global colonial expansion out of Europe, but also to the implosion of state structures and the reconfiguration of political boundaries that mark the postcolonial present.

Just as with the notion of "modernity," so too the idea of the *post-colonial* might be taken as referring to a historically unique conjuncture. But although *War in the Tribal Zone* very much emphasized historical contingency, it was grimly evident that certain forms of politico-military strategy were transcendent in their utility. Massacre, mutilation, and rape are transcultural and transhistorical forms of violence that express a cultural meaning that appears simple to interpret; it is what other meanings these acts involve that is important in making an adequate interpretation—that is, one that does not deny radical difference by constructing that difference as simply a monstrous aberration.

War in the Tribal Zone identified a systematic effect in the production of warfare and conflict, as expansive state systems encountered socially distinct and smaller-scale political communities. The theoretical principles by which we did this may be extended to a consideration of postcolonial violence in the context of the collapse of state structures and, most importantly, the threat (or promise) of external intervention. In this way, we can address critical aspects of human violence that many scholars and other commentators ignore: principally, how violence may be an expression of fundamental cultural practice and a sanctioned means of collective communication and exchange, such that the "enemy" becomes integral to cultural identity. By offering this framework for understanding the genesis and dynamics of ethnic violence and its burgeoning challenge to national and individual security, we hope to stimulate debate and contribute to better-informed policy with regard to the causes and development of collective conflict.

Although the analysis of human violence is relevant to many academic disciplines in both the humanities and social sciences, such analyses have usually been undertaken without questioning the possibly divergent cultural meanings of "violence" itself. This is not to suggest that violence can be "deconstructed," or that with closer cultural contextualization it will be revealed as somehow less brutal or destructive. Nor is it to suggest that the ethical evaluation of violence may simply be relative cross-culturally and so beyond the critical analysis of the external observer. Rather, the guiding principle of *War in the Tribal Zone* is that the manner in which violence is enacted is not simply instinctual, psychopathological, or the result of sociocultural primitiveness ("tribalism"), but that it is also a cultural *performance* whose logic may be quite alien to Western cultural experience. This would imply that a careful comparison of those local cultural contexts in which violence has an accepted, positive, and radical role in social practice can lead to a more developed understanding of this fundamental human capacity and its role in social and cultural relationships between communities, ethnicities, and nations. This comparison and understanding might range from the "ethnic cleansing" in Bosnia to the recent frenzy of witch-killings and interreligious rioting in Indonesia, the conflict between Hindu and Christian communities in India, or the ethnocide in Rwanda.

At the same time, we must also take account of the way in which we culturally represent the collective violence of others and, by contrast, how violence in the West is categorized as individually criminal or delinquent rather than as an aspect of wider cultural patterns. The analytical interplay between these ideas of external (other) cultures of violence and the violence of our own (internal) culture is, we believe, a key aspect of analysis that has been missing from other studies of violence, which ignore the way in which cultural classification is fundamental to *how* acts of violence are committed. This is as true for the serial killer or gangbanger as it is for the ritual assassin or agent of genocide.

Equally, our conception of what constitutes "violence" remains largely unexamined (Riches 1986). We all feel that we know what it is, and it may well be that gross physical acts of harm are relatively unproblematic to identify. However, there have been few attempts to map how cultural conceptions of violence are used discursively to amplify and extend the cultural force of violent acts, or how those violent acts themselves can generate a shared idiom of meaning for violent death. In short, the ways in which persons are killed or mutilated is not arbitrary, haphazard, or simply a function of perceived instrumentality. The manner of killing and injury may be used to delineate ethnic difference and identity, to construct ideas of sexuality, or to assert of ideas of tradition and modernity (Appadurai 1996; Bataille 1986; Eller 1998; Tambiah 1996; Trexler 1995). Therefore, while it is evident that the cultural meanings of violent acts vary cross-culturally and historically, it is far from clear how that variation affects the representation of others, how it affects the form of violent acts, or the ways in which violence itself might define cultural practice (Whitehead 1998a, 1998b).

Ethnographic research by Whitehead in Guyana and Brazil over the last decade (1994, 1996a, 1999), for example, has closely investigated the ways in which ideas of tradition and modernity are mediated through violence of a very particular cultural form known as *kanaimá*. A killing or mutilation in the manner of *kanaimá* involves highly specific kinds of violence that have exact symbolic and ritual meanings, and it is precisely the *form* of that violence that marks a death as *kanaimá* rather than murder or political assassination. A *kanaimá* killing therefore sets up a field of sociocultural significance that speaks not only to the immediate relations of the victim, but also to the wider community, other ethnic groups in Guyana and Brazil, and the institutional structures of the nation-state. This cultural force is engendered not just by the vivid physicality of what is done, but also by the ways in which such acts recall the history and traditions of an indigenous war against the colonial occupation, and so suggest the fragility of postcolonial nationalisms and their institutions throughout the region. This becomes all the more evident through the lack of any effective police or military response to such *kanaimá* killings, even when the perpetrators are easily identified.

In such a context, the violence of the capture, killing, and consumption of enemies is itself a ritual form understood by both perpetrator and victim. It can be seen as expressive of consensus or harmony over the broader questions of sociocultural reproduction, since both allies and enemies share the cultural quest for human body parts to become, in their cosmologies, killer-gods or man-jaguars. In such cases, violence and war actually come to represent intercourse, communication, and exchange (Viveiros de Castro 1992), which prompts the question as to the semiotics of the combat, capture, and death that constitute the forms of that communication (Basso 1995; Hendricks 1993). In this autorepresentation of violence we must accept that violence appears as both appropriate and valuable, even if it is enigmatic and shocking to us, and is not necessarily understood as something at all dysfunctional or pathological by its practitioners and victims.

In anthropological thinking, more widely traditional forms of violence such as cannibalism (Combès 1992; Whitehead 1995, 1998b; Zheng 1996), witchcraft (Geschiere 1997), and head-hunting (George 1996; Hoskins 1996) have recently begun to be reconceptualized in a similar light, as violent discourses as much as violent acts. It is therefore the interaction between acts and discourses that also needs our close attention, since these have tended to be studied separately: the former as a matter for the social sciences, the latter as more properly the domain of the humanities. We certainly intend to cross these, and other, disciplinary boundaries in the search for a better conceptualization of human violence as a cultural expression and in order to develop better interpretive strategies for warfare and violent acts as closely linked to the changing socioeconomic conditions of modernization, democratization, and development. The discursive practice of violence, the ways in which such cultural idioms may become a shared historical legacy, and how forms of killing and mutilation are carefully proscribed culturally and so achieve their own semiotic force, are among the key issues that have to be addressed if a well-rounded understanding of ethnic violence is to be achieved.

Through this cross-cultural and historical examination of the discursive role of violence and its representations from regions of the world where issues of modernity and tradition have likewise engendered collective violence of a specific cultural form, it will be possible to address a theoretically broader field than has been tackled by previous commentators. Such examination will also permit the development of a general framework for the analysis of violence that does not reduce violent acts to the cultural primitiveness or individual psychopathology of its practitioners. It is to be hoped that better interpretation then can be made of what otherwise is relegated to the "mindless," the "psychotic," and the "savage."

For lack of such a framework, many violent contexts, including those internal to the societies of the "First World," appear to us as cultural enigmas, such that we have no culturally particular understanding of the forms and/or intensities of violence. As a result we are apt to fall back on unexamined cultural categories, however inadequate, as a form of explanation. Recent anthropological research clearly confirms this proclivity in the way in which both scholars and media commentators have presented the Rwandan and Burundian massacres (Lemarchand 1996; Malkki 1995; Taylor 1999), African witch-killings (Geschiere 1997), and Bosnian ethnic cleansing (Sudetic 1998). Close ethnographic engagement with such situations strongly suggests that it is the cultural meanings of the violence that is performed, not just the empirical fact of the act itself, which is a key element in advancing our understanding of these human capacities. The performance of violence, how it is enacted according to cultural codes, is therefore as relevant to our understanding as is the appreciation of its sociopolitical consequences and causes, with which *War in the Tribal Zone* principally dealt.

Accordingly, even careful analyses of Western forms of violence, such as the Nazi genocide, are not necessarily relevant to the understanding of postcolonial ethnic violence, such as the genocide in Cambodia or Rwanda, precisely because the act of "genocide" is here mediated through cultural forms with which we are often unfamiliar. Unless the meaning of the mode of violence is itself understood, we unnecessarily limit policy options—other then the application of even greater violence, as in the case of Kosovo. As a result, commentators now contemplate the paradoxical possibility that "a peaceful, humane world is not going to be built with good-governance programs... [F]orce may be necessary" (B. Crossette, *New York Times* 1/24/99). However, this conclusion ignores another possibility: that through a better understanding of violence as a cultural form, political responses might become more effective—especially since that violence is often engendered not simply by adherence to globalized ideologies, such as communism or Islam, but by the regional and subregional disputes whose origins are in the complexities of local political history and cultural practices. This is so even where such global ideologies do come into play, since it is the local meaning of those ideologies that drives community and ethnic conflicts. Thus, critical to effective policy toward those who advocate and organize extreme violence is an appreciation of the degree to which perpetrators should be considered as enactors of a cultural "norm" rather than as individual psychopaths. If it is shown that violence may be a culturally enjoined and acceptable mode of political conduct, then it follows that it cannot effectively be suppressed or eradicated by treating it simplistically as a form of behavior that needs to be punished, even if on a collective scale. Moreover, the violence deployed to punish the brutality of others may itself be perceived as a validation of violence as a cultural form, in which case it may only serve to license the further use of that violence it intended to suppress. We can come to see that sustained violent engagement with others may even go on to produce a symbiotic sociocultural practice, such that those who would hold the moral high ground are themselves degraded through the ethical and political necessity of their own violent practices (Zolberg, Suhrke, and Aguayo 1989).

As *War in the Tribal Zone* illustrates, any adequate hermeneutic strategy must emphasize the mimetic and mutual meanings produced by cultural opposition and ethnic conflict, not the static and monolithic confrontation of primordial biologies, cultural identities, and social norms that has often been the intellectual starting point for previous examinations of these conflicts (Crawford and Lipschutz 1998; Ghiglieri 1999; Wrangham and Petersen 1996). We would suggest that the answer to the perennial conundrum of how we should picture ethnicity—either as an instrumental, almost cynical ideological manipulation or as a deep atavistic and primordial form of human attachment—would be partly clarified through closer attention to how and when such ethnicity is performed. Lethal violence is an apt expression of ethnic sentiment because of the compelling force such a cultural performance entails and because it simultaneously is effective in physically restructuring kin and community (Whitehead 1996b, 1997a).

The theoretical principles that were developed in *War in the Tribal Zone* can be extended in these ways to meet the interpretative challenge of burgeoning inter- and intra-community violence and the ways in which these phenomena might be connected, for it is our conception of how violence is produced that drives the political, economic, and military interventions our governments make. The criminalization of internal violence, be it derived from ideologically motivated terrorism or the political and economic alienation of survivalists, militiamen, or school-shooters, thus feeds off and is used to picture the external violence of the "savages," "tribal" peoples, "cannibals," and "butchers" at the political and economic margins of Western capitalist interests. But those "margins" exist as such only when perceived from a notional "center," and—just as *War in the Tribal Zone* illustrated how a symbiosis of military enemies might produce profound change not only among those "savage" tribals but within the expansive state system itself—so too massacres in Bosnia, Rwanda, or Indonesia are expressive acts that are culturally meaningful in those contemporary centers, and this may become an aspect of such violence even as it is directed toward the immediate victims. Institutions of military and politico-economic intervention—the UN, NATO, World Bank, IMF, and their attendant NGOs—are themselves predicated on the existence of crisis and conflict and so have a vested interest in its discovery. This may be well known to the agents of genocide and community violence, just as the panoptic eye of CNN, BBC, and other global media are sometimes unwilling or unknowing participants in the performance of the violence they so readily deplore as beyond explanation. Such violence *is* beyond the explanation of these institutions for the very reason that they are entangled in the circumstances of its production, just as the monstrous ethnic killer is lost not in his own pathological political fantasy but in our collective one.

In sum, by critically evaluating diverse aspects of the cultural representation and practice of violence, we can demonstrate more clearly the ways in which close attention to cultural forms improves our interpretation of shocking and troubling instances of conflict and killing. We may also highlight the ways in which those interpretations may themselves contribute, or be mimetically linked, to the ways in which violence is performed on the bodies and minds of others. By these means, the arguments and case studies in *War in the Tribal Zone* strongly suggest that more adequate attention to the cultural genesis and dynamics of violence will enhance the possibility for greater human security, in the face of what appears (and what is designed to appear) as unpredictable and uncontrollable manifestations of ethnic and community violence.

R.B.F. and N.L.W.

Works Cited

Abbink, Jon
    1993   Ethnic conflict in the 'tribal zone': The Dizi and Suri in Southern Ethiopia. *The Journal of Modern African Studies* 31:675–82.

Anderson, Benedict
    1991   *Imagined Communities*. London: Verso.

Appadurai, Arjun
    1996   *Modernity at Large: Cultural Dimensions of Globalization*. Minneapolis: University of Minnesota Press.

Bamforth, Douglas B.
    1994   Indigenous people, indigenous violence: Precontact warfare on the North American Great Plains. *Man* 29:95–115.

Basso, Ellen
    1995   *The Last Cannibals: A South American Oral History*. Austin: University of Texas Press.

Bataille, Georges
    1986   *Erotism: Death and Sensuality*. San Francisco: Harbor Lights.

Besteman, Catherine
    1996   Violent politics and the politics of violence: The dissolution of the Somali nation-state. *American Anthropologist* 23:579–96.

Blick, Jeffrey
    1988   Genocidal warfare in tribal societies as a result of European-induced culture conflict. *Man* 23:654–70.

Bowen, John R.
    1996   The myth of global ethnic conflict. *Journal of Democracy* 7(4):3–14.

Chagnon, Napoleon A.
    1996   Chronic problems in understanding tribal violence and warfare. In *Genetics of Criminal and Antisocial Behavior*, G. R. Bock and J. A. Goode, eds., pp. 202–32. New York: John Wiley and Sons.

Combès, Isabelle
    1992   *La Tragédie cannibale chez les anciens Tupi-Guarani*. Paris: P.U.F.

Crawford, Beverly, and Ronnie D. Lipschutz, eds.
    1998   *The Myth of Ethnic "Conflict": Politics, Economics, and "Cultural" Violence*. International and Area Studies, University of California at Berkeley.

Eller, Jack David
    1998   *From Culture to Ethnicity to Conflict: An Anthropological Perspective on Ethnic Conflict*. Ann Arbor: University of Michigan Press.

Ember, Carol R., and Melvin Ember
    1997   Violence in the ethnographic record, results of cross-cultural research on war and aggression. In *Troubled Times: Violence and Warfare in the Past*, D. L. Martin and D. W. Frayer, eds., pp. 1–20. Langhorne, PA: Gordon and Breach.

Ferguson, R. Brian
    1990   Blood of the leviathan: Western contact and warfare Amazonia. *American Ethnologist* 17:237–57.
    1995   *Yanomami Warfare: A Political History*. Santa Fe: School of American Research Press.
    1997   Violence and war in prehistory. In *Troubled Times: Violence and Warfare in the Past*, D. L. Martin and D. W. Frayer, eds., pp. 321–55. Langhorne, PA: Gordon and Breach.

1998   Whatever happened to the Stone Age? Steel tools and Yanomami historical
        ecology. In *Advances in Historical Ecology*, W. Balée, ed., pp. 287–312. New
        York: Columbia University Press.
1999   A paradigm for the study of war and society. In *War and Society in the Ancient
        and Medieval World*, K. R. Haflaub and N. Rosenstein, eds., pp. 409–58.
        Cambridge, MA: Harvard University Press.
n.d.a   Anthropological perspectives on war. In *The Study of War*, Richard Kohn and
        Alex Roland, eds. In preparation.
n.d.b   Dangerous intersections: The local and the larger in African violence. In *Paths
        of Violence*, G. Bond and J. Vincent, eds. New York: Gordon and Breach. In
        press.

Ferguson, R. Brian, and Neil L. Whitehead, eds.
1992   *War in the Tribal Zone: Expanding States and Indigenous Warfare*. Santa Fe: School
        of American Research Press.

Ferrill, Arther
1985   *The Origins of War: From the Stone Age to Alexander the Great*. New York: Thames
        and Hudson.

Fukui, Katsuyoshi, and John Markakis
1994   Introduction. In *Ethnicity and Conflict in the Horn of Africa*, Katuyoshi Fukui and
        John Markakis, eds., pp. 1–11. Athens: University of Ohio Press.

Fukuyama, Francis
1998   Women and the evolution of world politics. *Foreign Affairs* September/October:24–40.

Gantzel, Klaus Jürgen
1997   War in the post–World War II world: Some empirical trends and a theoretical
        approach. In *War and Ethnicity: Global Connections and Local Violence*, David
        Turton, ed., pp. 123–44. Republic of San Marino: Center for Interdisciplinary
        Research on Social Stress. Rochester: University of Rochester Press.

Geertz, Clifford
1963   The integrative revolution: Primordial sentiment and civil politics in the new
        states. In *Old Societies and New States: The Quest for Modernity in Asia and Africa*,
        Clifford Geertz, ed., pp. 107–57. London: The Free Press.

George, Kenneth M.
1996   *Showing Signs of Violence: The Cultural Politics of a Twentieth-Century Headhunting
        Ritual*. Berkeley: University of California Press.

Geschiere, Peter
1997   *The Modernity of Witchcraft: Politics and the Occult in Postcolonial Africa*.
        Charlottesville: The University Press of Virginia.

Ghiglieri, Michael P.
1999   *The Dark Side of Man: Tracing the Origins of Male Violence*. Reading, MA: Perseus
        Books.

Guidieri, Remo, Francesco Pellizzi, and Stanley J. Tambiah, eds.
1988   *Ethnicities and Nations: Process of Interethnic Relations in Latin America, Southeast
        Asia and the Pacific*. Austin: University of Texas Press for Rothko Chapel.

Gurr, Ted Robert
1993   *Minorities at Risk: A Global View of Ethnopolitical Conflicts*. Washington, D.C.:
        Institute of Peace Press.

Haas, Jonathan
1993   The origins of war and enemies. Paper presented at the 146th Annual Meeting
        of the American Psychiatric Association, San Francisco.

Hall, Thomas, Christopher Bartalos, Elizabeth Mannebach, and Thomas Perkowitz
    1996   Varieties of ethnic conflict in global perspectives: A review essay. *Social Science Quarterly* 77:445–52.

Hendricks, Janet Wall
    1993   *To Drink of Death: The Narrative of a Shuar Warrior.* Tucson: University of Arizona Press.

Herbst, Jeffrey
    1990   War and the state in Africa. *International Security* 14(4):117–39.

Hill, Jonathan, ed.
    1996   *History, Power and Identity: Ethnogenesis in the Americas, 1492–1992.* Iowa City: University of Iowa Press.

Hinton, Alexander Laban
    1998a   "Why Did You Kill?" The Cambodian genocide and the dark side of face and honor. *The Journal of Asian Studies* 57:93–122.
    1998b   A head for an eye: Revenge in the Cambodian genocide. *American Ethnologist* 57(25):352–77.

Holsti, Rudolf
    1913   *The Relation of War to the Origin of the State.* Helsinki: Annales Academic Scientarium Fennicae XIII.

Hobsbawm, Eric J.
    1994   *Nations and Nationalism since 1780.* Cambridge: Cambridge University Press.

Horowitz, Donald
    1985   *Ethnic Groups in Conflict.* Berkeley: University of California Press.

Hoskins, Janet, ed.
    1996   *Headhunting and the Social Imagination in Southeast Asia.* Stanford: Stanford University Press.

Keeley, Lawrence H.
    1996   *War before Civilization.* New York: Oxford University Press.

Knauft, Bruce M.
    1990   Melanesian warfare: A theoretical history. *Oceania* 60:250–311.
    1992   Warfare, Western intrusion and ecology in Melanesia. *Man* 27:399–400.

Lambert, Patricia M.
    1997   Patterns of violence in prehistoric hunter-gatherer societies of coastal Southern California. In *Troubled Times: Violence and Warfare in the Past*, D. L. Martin and D. W., Frayer, eds., pp. 45–75. Langhorne, PA: Gordon and Breach.

Lemarchand, Reni
    1996   *Burundi: Ethnic Conflict and Genocide.* Washington, D.C., New York: Woodrow Wilson Center Press, Cambridge University Press.

Malkki, Liisa
    1995   *Purity and Exile: Violence, Memory and National Cosmology among Hutu Refugees in Tanzania.* Chicago: University of Chicago Press.

Martin, Debra L., and David W. Frayer, eds.
    1997   *Troubled Times: Violence and Warfare in the Past.* Langhorne, PA: Gordon and Breach.

Maschner, Herbert D. G., and Katherine L. Reedy-Maschner
    1998   Raid, retreat, defend (repeat): The archaeology and ethnohistory of warfare on the North Pacific Rim. *Journal of Anthropological Archaeology* 17:19–51.

Meggitt, Mervyn
    1977   *Blood Is Their Argument.* Palo Alto, CA: Mayfield.

Milner, George R., Eve Anderson, and Virginia G. Smith
    1991   Warfare in late prehistoric west-central Illinois. *American Antiquity* 56:581–603.

Nordstrom, Carolyn, and JoAnn Martin, eds.
    1992   *The Paths to Domination, Resistance, and Terror.* Berkeley: University of California Press.

O'Connell, Robert L.
    1989   *Of Arms and Men: A History of War, Weapons, Aggression.* New York: Oxford University Press.

Otterbein, Keith
    1994   Ethnic soldiers, messiahs, and cockalorums. *Reviews in Anthropology* 23:213–25.
    1997   The origins of war. *Critical Review: An Interdisciplinary Journal of Politics and Society* 2:251–74.

Peregrine, Peter N.
    1996   Archaeology and world-systems theory. *Sociological Inquiry* 66:486–95.

Pinker, Steven
    1997   *How the Mind Works.* New York: W. W. Norton and Co.

Power, Margaret
    1991   *The Egalitarians—Human and Chimpanzee: An Anthropological View of Social Organization.* Cambridge: Cambridge University Press.

Pratt, Mary Louise
    1992   *Imperial Eyes: Travel Writing and Transculturation.* London: Routledge.

Redmond, Elsa M.
    1994   *Tribal and Chiefly Warfare in South America.* University of Michigan, *Memoirs of the Museum of Anthropology* 28.

Reynolds, Vernon, Vincent Falger, and Ian Vine, eds.
    1986   *The Sociobiology of Ethnocentrism: Evolutionary Dimensions of Xenophobia, of Discrimination, Racism and Nationalism.* Athens: University of Georgia Press.

Riches, David, ed.
    1986   *The Anthropology of Violence.* London: Blackwell.

Robbins, Sterling
    1982   *Auyana: Those Who Held onto Home.* Seattle: University of Washington Press.

Roper, Marilyn
    1969   A survey of the evidence for intrahuman killing in the Pleistocene. *Current Anthropology* 10:427–59.
    1975   Evidence of warfare in the Near East from 10,000–4,300 B.C. In *War, its Causes and Correlates,* M. A. Nettleship, D. Givens, and A. Nettleship, eds., pp. 299–344. The Hague: Mouton.

Ruggie, John Gerard
    1993   Territoriality and beyond: Problematizing modernity in international relations. *International Organization* 47:139–74.

Schieffelin, Edward I., and Robert Crittenden, eds.
    1991   *Like People You See in a Dream: First Contact in Six Papuan Societies.* Stanford: Stanford University Press.

Shankman, Paul
    1991   Culture contact, cultural ecology, and Dani warfare. *Man* 26:299–321.

Shaw, R. Paul, and Yuwa Wong
    1989   *Genetic Seeds of Warfare: Evolution, Nationalism, and Patriotism.* Winchester, MA: Unwin Hyman.

Smith, Anthony D.
    1981   *The Ethnic Revival.* Cambridge: Cambridge University Press.
    1983   *Theories of Nationalism.* New York: Holmes and Meier Publishers.

Sponsel, Leslie E.
    1997   Comment on Headland's revisionism in ecological anthropology. *Current Anthropology* 38:619–22.

Stack, John F., Jr.
    1986   Ethnic mobilization in world politics: The primordial perspective. In *The Primordial Challenge: Ethnicity on the Contemporary World*, John F. Stack, ed., pp. 1–11. New York: Greenwood Press.

Sudetic, Chuck
    1997   *Blood and Vengeance: One Family's Story of the War in Bosnia.* New York: Penguin Putnam Inc.

Sumner, William Graham
    1960   *Folkways.* (Orig. 1906) New York: Mentor.

Tainter, Joseph A.
    1998   Competition, expansion, and reaction: The foundations of contemporary conflict. In *The Coming Age of Scarcity: Preventing Mass Death and Genocide in the Twenty-First Century.* M. N. Dobkowski and I. Wallimann, eds., pp. 174–93. Syracuse: Syracuse University Press.

Tambiah, Stanley
    1996   Leveling Crowds: Ethnonationalist Conflicts and Collective Violence in South Asia. Berkeley: University of California Press.

Taussig, Michael
    1995   *Mimesis and Alterity: A Particular History of the Senses.* New York: Routledge.

Taylor, Christopher C.
    1999   *Sacrifice as Terror: The Rwandan Genocide of 1994.* New York, Oxford: Berg Press.

Taylor, Peter J.
    1995   Beyond containers: Internationality, interstateness, interterritoriality. *Progress in Human Geography* 19:1–15.

Trexler, Richard C.
    1995   *Sex and Conquest: Gendered Violence, Political Order, and the European Conquest of the Americas.* Ithaca: Cornell University Press.

Turton, David
    1997   Introduction: War and Ethnicity. In *War and Ethnicity: Global Connections and Local Violence.* David Turton, ed., pp. 1–45. Republic of San Marino: Center for Interdisciplinary Research on Social Stress, Rochester: University of Rochester Press.

Van der Dennen, Johan M. G.
    1990   Origin and evolution of "primitive" warfare. In *Sociobiology and Conflict: Evolutionary Perspectives on Competition, Cooperation, Violence and Warfare*, J. Van der Dennen and V. Falger, eds., pp. 149–88. London: Chapman and Hall.
    1995   *The Origin of War.* Groningen, Netherlands: Origin Press.

Villalon, Leonardo A.
   1998   The African state at the end of the twentieth century: Parameters of the critical juncture. In *The African State at a Critical Juncture: Between Disintegration and Reconfiguration*, Leonardo A. Villalon and Phillip A. Huxtable, eds., pp. 3–25. Boulder, CO: Lynne Reiner.

Viveiros de Castro, Eduardo
   1992   *From the Enemy's Point of View: Humanity and Divinity in an Amazonian Society*. Chicago: University of Chicago Press.

Warren, Kay
   1993   *The Violence Within: Cultural and Political Opposition in Divided Nations*. Boulder: Westview.

Weisner, Polly, and Akii Tumu
   1998   *Historical Vines: Enga Networks of Exchange, Ritual, and Warfare in Papua New Guinea*. Washington, D.C.: Smithsonian Institution Press.

Whitehead, Neil L.
   1990   The Snake Warriors—Sons of the Tiger's Teeth. A descriptive analysis of Carib warfare: 1500–1820. In *The Anthropology of War*, J. Haas, ed., pp. 146–70. Cambridge University Press.

   1994   Assassination and incorporation in Amazonia: The symbolism and praxis of internal violence and external threat. Paper prepared for the AAA panel "The Anthropology of War: New Directions," American Anthropological Association, Atlanta.

   1995   The cannibal trope in the semiotics of colonial process: Convergence and mimesis in symbolization and praxis. Paper prepared for the AAA panel "The Metapragmatics of Socio-Cultural Discourse," American Anthropological Association, Washington, D.C.

   1996a *An Oral History of the Patamuna, Yawong Valley, Guyana*. Georgetown: Walter Roth Museum.

   1996b Ethnogenesis and ethnocide in the settlement of Surinam. In *Ethnogenesis in the Americas*, J. Hill, ed., pp. 20–35. Iowa City: University of Iowa Press.

   1997a White Tupis, Black Caribs and Civilized Indians: The rhetorics of ethnic transgression in the colonial possession of South America. Paper presented at the 20th Burdick-Vary Symposium, Institute for Research in the Humanities, University of Wisconsin, Madison.

   1997b Monstrosity and marvel: Symbolic convergence and mimetic elaboration in trans-cultural representation. *Studies in Travel Writing* 1:72–96.

   1998a Kanaimá: The cultural practice and political morphology of ritual death in the Pakaraima Mountains, Guyana. Paper for the AAA panel "Violence and population: Bodies and the body politic in indigenous Amazonia," Philadelphia.

   1998b Mayden America and Manlie Europe: Sexuality, violence, and colonial discovery in the New World. Paper presented at the 21st Burdick-Vary Symposium, Institute for Research in the Humanities, University of Wisconsin, Madison.

   1998c Historical ecology and ecological history: Diachronic modeling versus historical explanation. In *Advances in Historical Ecology*, W. Balée, ed., pp. 30–41. New York: Columbia University Press.

   1999   *Tales of the Patamuna*. Georgetown: Walter Roth Museum.

Whitehead, Neil L., and R. Brian Ferguson
   1993   Deceptive stereotypes about tribal warfare. *The Chronicle of Higher Education*, November 10:A48.

Wilkinson, Richard G.
  1997   Violence against women: Raiding and abduction in prehistoric Michigan. In
         Troubled Times: Violence and Warfare in the Past, D. L. Martin and D. W. Frayer,
         eds., pp. 21–43. Langhorne, PA: Gordon and Breach.

Wrangham, Richard
  1999   Evolution of coalitionary killing. *Yearbook of Physical Anthropology*, pp. 1–30.
         In press.

Wrangham, Richard, and Dale Peterson
  1996   *Demonic Males: Apes and the Origins of Human Violence*. Boston: Houghton-
         Mifflin Co.

Wright, William
  1998   *Born that Way: Genes, Behavior, Personality*. New York: Alfred Knopf.

Young, Crawford
  1993   The dialectics of cultural pluralism: Concept and reality. In *The Rising Tide of
         Cultural Pluralism: The Nation State at Bay?*, C. Young, ed., pp. 3–35. Madison:
         University of Wisconsin Press.

Zheng, Yi
  1996   *Scarlet Memorial: Tales of Cannibalism in Modern China*. Boulder, CO: Westview
         Press.

Zolberg, A., A. Suhrke, and S. Aguayo
  1989   *Escape from Violence*. Oxford: Oxford University Press.

Preface

THE anthropology of war has come a long way in the last decade. As recently as 1980, it was routine for anthropological discussions of war to begin with an apology for the discipline's lack of attention to the subject. At present, though, it is difficult to keep up with the steady output of new work. Research interests have deepened and diversified, case studies have proliferated, and geographic coverage has become more global. There is every reason to expect that this growth will continue in future decades. Moreover, the need for an anthropological understanding of war becomes more acute as existing tribal, ethnic, and national conflicts continue and intensify.

The present volume is the result of an advanced seminar held at the School of American Research in April 1989, and sponsored by the Harry Frank Guggenheim Foundation. That seminar was the outgrowth of

another advanced seminar held in March of 1986, under the same spon-
sorship, in which both editors of this volume participated. The 1986 seminar on "The Anthropology of War" (Haas 1990a) sought to cover all major
approaches to the subject. One theme that emerged was the need to examine the role of European colonialism in generating or transforming
warfare among non-Western peoples around the world (Gibson 1990;
Whitehead 1990a). In November of 1987, Karen Colvard, of the Harry
Frank Guggenheim Foundation, and Jonathan Haas, then of the School
of American Research, approached the editors with the proposal of organizing an advanced seminar on that topic.

Although there is abundant empirical evidence that European expansionism has had a tremendous impact on indigenous warfare, this fact has
not been appreciated theoretically and extraordinarily little has been done
to explore its ramifications. Many anthropologists interested in war continue to discuss conflict patterns as if they were pristine manifestations of
indigenous cultures. The organizers of this seminar had two basic objectives in mind: first, simply to force attention to the possible impact of
state expansionism on observed and recorded warfare; second, and more
ambitiously, to conceptualize this area of study, to map its significant
dimensions in a way that will encourage future research.

From the perspective of current interests in the anthropology of war,
the key question is the effect of European expansionism since the fifteenth
century on the warfare of nonstate peoples around the world. The organizers, however, felt that too narrow a focus on that topic would be self-
defeating. To understand the impact of the recent expansion of European
states, one must place it in a broader context, a context that includes
expansionist efforts of ancient states and even pre-state polities. It is necessary to establish the significant parameters and major variations of expansionism, and consideration of other cultural situations highlights what
is general and what is particular about the European cases.

This point merits special emphasis here. The relationship between expanding states and indigenous warfare is, in a sense, that of independent
and dependent variables: our interest is in explaining the latter, but as a
prerequisite it is necessary to develop first a fuller understanding of the
former, to clarify what it is that states do when they expand. Thus, the
reader will find that the initial chapters of this volume deal more with
the dynamics of state expansionism than with tribal warfare itself. These
cases deal both with state-to-state conflicts and with conflicts between
states and nonstate peoples. There is not as radical a disjuncture between
the two situations as might be imagined. We had hoped initially that these
case studies might include more discussion of warfare among nonstate

peoples on the peripheries of non-Western states, but that information remains very limited. Our hope now is that this volume will stimulate further investigation of the topic.

It should also be clarified that although the central question for current anthropological debates on warfare may be the impact of European expansionism on the warfare of nonstate or tribal peoples, it would be unwise to restrict the field of inquiry to those cases. On general principles, a robust theoretical understanding should apply across the range of polities that Europeans encountered. Moreover, a major point of these studies is that the political structures of non-Western peoples are transformed by the process of contact. A very frequent result is the creation of distinct tribes, but another consequence can be the creation of a "secondary state," which itself may set off new tendencies toward tribalization. Thus, the chapters by Hassig and Law deal with European encounters with non-Western states.

Given the vast scope of this project, seminar participants found useful the idea of a "rolling focus." Taken separately, an early and a late chapter might seem virtually unrelated, but taken in sequence, the chapters together form a continuum of interests, covering the diverse aspects of expanding states and indigenous warfare with a completeness and global range that no single study could attempt. A guide to those successive interests will be found in the introductory chapter.

One other point merits emphasis at the start. Our intent has been to inject history into the anthropology of war. That does not place the organizers, or this volume, in opposition to cross-cultural comparison and analysis of war. This is no essay in "particularism." Rather, the idea is to develop a new and more powerful approach to explanation, studying peoples and societies in motion, and transcending the unreal stasis of imagined "ethnographic presents." The concepts developed in these papers, and summarized in the introductory chapter, are steps toward an analytic history of war.

Finally, the editors wish to express gratitude to a number of institutions, programs, and individuals. All of the seminar participants approached the discussions in an open and constructive spirit, and all have shown an unusual alacrity in responding to editorial deadlines. Melburn Thurman is the one seminar participant whose paper, part of a much larger reconsideration of Great Plains ethnohistory, could not be included here, but his insights on ecological change as a consequence of Western contact are felt at several points in the volume. David Turton was unable to attend the seminar, but did submit a report about recent violence in the Horn of Africa which was discussed during the meetings. That too could not be included, but it did direct our attention to several important issues concerning contemporary warfare.

The Harry Frank Guggenheim Foundation not only sponsored the seminar, but has supported both Brian Ferguson and Neil Whitehead with research grants and has provided additional funding to bring the volume quickly to completion. At the Guggenheim Foundation, program officer Karen Colvard has been consistently helpful. The seminar could not have taken place without the support of former Guggenheim president Floyd Ratliff, support that has continued under James Hester. At the School of American Research, Jonathan Haas both helped arrange the meeting and participated in several seminar discussions. Douglas Schwartz provided enthusiastic support; and Jane Kepp and Joan O'Donnell have been model editors. The staff at the Seminar House, Jane Barberrouse, Sarah Carson, and Jennifer McLaughlin, made our stay in Santa Fe most pleasant.

War in the Tribal Zone

Chapter 1

The Violent Edge of Empire

R. BRIAN FERGUSON AND NEIL L. WHITEHEAD

T HIS book is about the transformation of indigenous patterns of warfare brought about by the proximity or intrusion of expanding states. The primary concern is changes associated with European colonial expansionism since the fifteenth century, and more recently with the expansion of independent Third World states. To put these epochs of state expansion in perspective, the scope of comparison is broadened to include studies of more ancient expanding states. The indigenous peoples discussed here as affected by European or other state expansionism are themselves organized in a range of political forms from bands to empires, although a dominant concern in the volume is the tribal form of organization. Though the focus here is warfare, to place war in an analytic context it is considered along with all the social transformations associated with state contact.

The impact of colonial states on indigenous warfare has not been recognized as a topic for cross-cultural investigation in the past. The School of American Research advanced seminar that preceded this volume was organized in order to define and explore this new theoretical domain, itself created by the intersection of two broad currents in recent anthropological research.

The first of these currents is anthropology's general shift away from synchronic theory and toward diachronic, historical analysis (Cohn 1980; Ortner 1984; Roseberry 1989; Wolf 1982). The once-pervasive assumption that societies tend toward equilibrium, and the associated research orientations of one or another type of functionalism, created a bias against history. Western contact was perceived as a source of contamination that obscured and disrupted the integrated, pristine cultural system. The ethnographic objective, then, was to reconstruct that pristine culture, and the study of contact was consigned to the neglected area of acculturation studies. That situation is changing, with increasing attention being paid to the colonial context of most ethnographic situations (Asad 1973; Bodley 1982; Cooper and Stoler 1989; Rodney 1972; Willis 1972). Now, the idea of the timeless primitive is good only for postmortem dissection (Kuper 1988; Rosaldo 1980; Stocking 1987); Levi-Strauss's ambiguous distinction between "hot" and "cold" societies is rejected (Douglas 1989; Friedman 1975; Hill 1988; Leach 1989); and the possibility of reconstructing a precontact "ethnographic present" is challenged (Dobyns 1983; Ramenofsky 1987). The common premise of the papers collected here is that the study of culture must always recognize its changing historical circumstances.

The other relevant research current is the burgeoning anthropological literature on war and peace (Ferguson 1984a; Ferguson with Farragher 1988; Haas 1990a). Most studies, however, especially the older ones, give little attention to history and the effects of Western contact. That neglect is even more pronounced in general theoretical formulations and textbook discussions. "Warfare among the so-and-so" usually is depicted and analyzed as part of a stable and long-standing cultural system, and the major role attributed to expanding states is that of pacification (Ferguson 1990a).

But pacification occurs rather late in the process. As the late Klaus-Friedrich Koch, one of the leading theorists on war in the 1970s, commented in one of his last publications,

> many accounts of warfare among tribal peoples were written after these peoples had suffered the direct or indirect conse-

quences of foreign intrusion, and we know very little about the
stimulating and aggravating effects of this intrusion on indigenous modes of violent conflict. (Koch 1983:200–201)

In our view, the frequent effect of such an intrusion is an overall militarization; that is, an increase in armed collective violence whose conduct,
purposes, and technologies rapidly adapt to the threats generated by state
expansion.

That area continuously affected by the proximity of a state, but not
under state administration, we call the "tribal zone." Within the tribal
zone, the wider consequence of the presence of the state is the radical
transformation of extant sociopolitical formations, often resulting in "tribalization," the genesis of new tribes.[1]

By bringing together the historical and the military, this volume also
connects with theoretical developments in historical sociology and political science, in which a growing body of literature (Giddens 1985; Knutsen
1987; Mann 1986; McNeill 1982; Tilly 1975, 1985) seeks to incorporate
collective violence as a topic within the mainstream of social research.
Military factors are given analytic attention comparable to that traditionally devoted to economics, politics, and ideology. That perspective is implicit in this volume, since the objective is to discover how differential
involvement in armed conflict in the contact situation produces observed
historical trajectories.

While the importance of history and the role of violent conflict may
be readily seen, it is more difficult to know what that recognition implies:
at the very least, it involves the need to revitalize our ideas about the
ethnographic universe, going beyond the rejection of untenable notions
of self-contained, stable local societies, and instead developing a conceptual framework for understanding conflict and change as part of the historical process underlying observed ethnographic patterns.

How, then, do we get beyond the analytic anomie that has resulted
from the collapse of old paradigms and led to the conceptual impasse of
deconstructionism? We approach the great number of factors involved,
and the enormous range of variation they present, through the device of
an analytically and temporally progressive focus. Thus, the chapters in
this volume are ordered by four complementary criteria: (1) chronology,
following the passage from ancient to modern cases; (2) evolutionary
complexity, beginning with empires and ending with localized bands and
villages; (3) relative position during state expansion, starting with the
perspective of the center and concluding with that of the periphery; and
(4) the level and units of analysis, early papers dealing with properties of

empires and states, the final papers considering the organization of small groups.

This is the "rolling focus" mentioned in the Preface, the organizing device by which this vast subject matter is handled. This shifting analytic focus will be evident throughout the Introduction, which considers a series of interrelated topics in an order which roughly parallels the changing emphasis of discussion throughout the chapters. In this introductory chapter, however, the contextual material, the varying circumstances of state expansionism, and aspects of contact other than war, are discussed prior to the topic of war itself. We also attempt here to relate these topics to recent developments in anthropological theory.

WORLD SYSTEMS AND EXPANDING STATES

Our interest in the consequences of an expanding Europe may lead some to categorize this volume as an application of world system theory (Wallerstein 1974, 1980), and clearly, there is a degree of affinity. But the papers presented here support the standard criticism of that theory: that it overemphasizes determination by the center and underrates the active role of peripheral peoples. In this sense, these essays are more closely aligned with an approach that focuses on "anthropological subjects at the *intersections* of global and local histories" (Roseberry 1988:173; see also Steward et al. 1956; Ferguson 1988a; Whitehead 1988).

A second difference from world system theory responds to a criticism leveled at political-economic approaches in general: that they are "too economic," or "not political enough" (Ortner 1984:142; e.g., Rowlands, Larsen, and Kristiansen 1987). In contrast, the contributors to this volume focus on military articulation and the political patterns through which it occurs. This focus does not, however, imply any necessary contradiction of existing world systems (or structural Marxist) theories on the nature and transformative effect of capitalist penetration of noncapitalist societies. The contributors to this volume are simply looking at another side of the process of articulation, one that may complement more economically oriented analyses.

A third difference from the standard world system approach is that this volume, while placing great stress on the significance of European expansion, also seeks in its early chapters to fit this epoch into a larger, global perspective. From their inception on the planet, states have developed and existed within a broader matrix involving the flow of people, products, and ideas (Chang 1986; Claessen and Skalnik 1978; Claessen and van de Velde 1987; Curtin 1984; Kipp and Schortman 1989; Nissen

1988). In the long view, the *modern* world system is as much a creation as a creator of connections (McNeill 1982).

From the time of the first urban centers, the networks that engender states also have connected them to nonstate peoples, and the connection has had a great impact on the latter (Algaze 1989). In the ensuing millennia, the regions of state-nonstate contact (i.e., "tribal zones") have expanded along with the global expansion of states. As a result, some form of contact with states has been very common for nonstate peoples (Curtin 1984; Headland and Reid 1989; Khazanov 1984; Kopytoff 1987a; Wolf 1982).

The scope of such contacts can be seen by considering the cases examined in this volume, an exercise that serves the additional function of introducing individual papers. The first four chapters following this introduction are concerned largely with the dynamics of state expansionism, and they call attention to huge areas of state-nonstate interaction. The Roman empire, whose North African presence is discussed by Mattingly, was of course in contact with "barbarians" all over Europe, and its land and sea trade to China passed through territories of many nonstate peoples (Randers-Pehrson 1983; Rowlands, Larsen, and Kristiansen 1987: pt. 4). Those east-west sea-lanes became secondary centers of state formation. The succession of states in Sri Lanka and South India discussed by Gunawardana thrived on this trade, especially after the rise of Byzantium, at the same time that they transformed the political structure of nearby nonstate peoples (and see Gibson 1990; Warren 1981). Hassig describes a similar pattern of interaction with nonstate peoples for the Aztecs, the last in a long series of Mesoamerican empires. In West Africa, the European slave trade discussed by Law built upon an earlier trade which crossed the Sahara to the Arab Mediterranean (Lovejoy 1983; Reyna 1990), and which, as Mattingly shows, extends back to Roman times.

Crossing over to the New World and to a more tribal focus, Whitehead notes the existence in Guyana and Amazonia of complex polities and extensive trade systems before the European arrival (see also Whitehead 1989). This emphasizes a point raised by Gunawardana, that political expansionism of some form antedates the rise of states. The Yanomami discussed by Ferguson may have been within the sphere of one of these extinct and virtually unknown centers. The ancestral Iroquois, for all of the interpretive controversies noted by Abler, were clearly part of a broad, even continental trade system, and were enmeshed, in a peripheral way, in the processes leading to the rise and fall of complex societies in the Mississippi Valley (Dincauze and Hasenstab 1989). Similarly, the Asháninka (or Campa) discussed by Brown and Fernández were one of many non-state peoples (Salomon 1986) with established connections to the Inca empire. Highland New Guinea, the site of Strathern's account, is about as remote as can be from all centers of state activity, and seems to offer some of the best material for relatively pristine warfare (Connolly and Anderson 1988). Yet even there, the subsistence base observed at "first contact" was reliant on cultigens introduced from the New World in the last three hundred years (Feil 1987).

Documentary information about the consequences of these connections between state and nonstate peoples usually is very limited prior to the epoch of European expansion, but there is no justification for assuming that social transformation and human innovation did not produce historical change at the periphery as much as at the center. Constant change seems a more realistic expectation than the old assumption of timeless stability (see Bloch 1986:194). In our view, all societies have the same amount of history behind them. European explorers only step into local history, they do not set it in motion. The uniqueness of European contact is thus taken not as a given, but as a question, a topic to be investigated. It is to an examination of the dynamics of that historical process that we now turn.

Anthropologists familiar with the debate over the use of the term "tribe" may not know that a similar debate has been and is going on in other social sciences about the term "state" (Brown 1989). "The state" had virtually disappeared from comparative historical studies. Recent efforts to "bring the state back in" (Evans, Rueschemeyer, and Skocpol 1985) have met with strong opposition (Ferguson and Mansbach 1989). Anthropology may have avoided this debate because the state, as a centralized, institutionalized, authoritative system of political rule, is in obvious evolutionary contrast to nonstate societies, especially when state and nonstate are thrown together by the establishment of new colonial states. But besides indicating this contrast, "the state" is also useful for understanding contact.

Using "the state" in a narrow sense—as the institutions of political control, the government—we find support for Skocpol's (1985:3) view of "states as weighty actors." When it comes to surrounding nonstate peoples, governments have *policies*, policies that affect if not control the behavior of state agents,[2] and policies that change over time. Such changes are described throughout this volume (and see Fitzhugh 1985; Washburn 1988). But "the state" can also be taken in a broader sense, as a society that includes the particular mix of social agents and interests present within its borders at any given time. As Ribeiro (1970; and see Henley

1978) emphasizes, the dominant economic enterprises in state expansion will strongly condition all social relations along the contact "front." So too, in the political sphere, changes in sovereignty and policy or shifts in borders can have a tremendous impact on the lives of proximate nonstate peoples. This is dramatically illustrated, for example, in the rapid passage of the North American Southwest from Spanish to Mexican to United States territory (Kroeber and Fontana 1986; Spicer 1962).

Thus, contact situations can be broadly compared by the strategic posture and degree of territorial advance of the state. One distinction is whether the state seeks territorial or hegemonic control (Luttwak 1976): that is, conquest and direct control over defeated lands and peoples (territorial), or establishment of military superiority and indirect control through local authorities (hegemonic). This contrast is considered prominently in the chapters by Mattingly, Gunawardana, and Hassig, and was discussed extensively at the seminar. Our conclusion was that the distinction works best when applied to studies of imperial policy "from the center"; at the peripheries, the territory versus hegemony distinction is too broad, since there are always blends of direct and indirect control. Even from the perspective of a state, territory and hegemony are not the only possible strategic objectives. As Law points out, West African states wanted neither, their relation with nonstate neighbors being one of predator and prey.

In the seminar discussions we found an alternative distinction to be of greater utility in understanding the dynamics of the tribal zone, that of "coercion" versus "seduction." The primary means of coercion are military threats; those of seduction are gifts, trade opportunities, and pledges of political support. These tactical alternatives also occur in some kind of blend or mix, but unlike the territory/hegemony distinction, specific elements of the mix are clearly identifiable in peripheral situations.

Finally, the process of state intrusion can be characterized by degree or intensity of contact. Four broad phases are identified: indirect contact, direct contact, encapsulation, and incorporation. This is a logical progression, and not necessarily a generalization about actual process, as annihilation of native peoples can occur early in the sequence, as sometimes happened in the Americas and the Pacific through the impact of epidemics. Furthermore, even the logic of the progression may not apply to all situations of state expansion. European expansionism differs from that of Rome or Anuradhapura in Sri Lanka, in that the incessant outward drive of the developing world capitalist order virtually foreclosed the possibility of long-term coexistence with tribal groupings around the state frontiers. The Aztecs had their own internal dynamic requiring unending wars of expansion, but these were directed against other city-states rather than at tribal peoples on the state peripheries. Thus, ancient states offered long-term coexistence as a major alternative to the annihilation or incorporation of tribal peoples.[3]

THE TRIBAL ZONE

When it comes to the analysis of specific situations, these broad categories are of less value, as the state disappears into a welter of specific "factors and actors" (a phrase introduced by Strathern). This is so whether one focuses on the dynamics of state expansionism itself or on its articulation with indigenous warfare patterns. Consideration here will begin with the factors associated with an intrusive state which can spread beyond the direct observation of state agents (indirect contact) and whose changing parameters continue to shape situations throughout later phases.

First among these factors is disease. The impact of disease is a critical marker separating state contact situations. The introduction of new diseases for which indigenous people have little or no resistance apparently was not a characteristic of ancient state expansion, since such expansion was typically into immediately adjacent areas. Thus, we note that the population of North Africa actually increased during the Roman period. By contrast, in the European epoch, introduced epidemic diseases had a tremendous impact in those situations involving New World and Pacific peoples long isolated from Old World diseases.[4] On this point, the Slave Coast of West Africa is in sharp contrast to the New World cases that follow it. A different sort of contrast is presented by Highland Papua New Guinea, where modern medical technology and the political will to make it available have reduced the consequences of disease, with the result that the area's population has grown substantially in the post-contact period.

Dobyns (1983), Ramenofsky (1987), and Purdy (1988) document some of the catastrophic consequences of Old World diseases in North America, and argue that their introduction led to rapid and massive population decline, frequently if not always prior to direct observation by Europeans. In this volume, Abler and Whitehead consider the impact of early epidemics, but conclude that massive losses probably did not occur until well into the period of direct contact. One general implication of these cases is that settlement patterns and social networks must be taken into account when deriving estimates of the rate and extent of disease transmission. In northeastern South America, for example, it was only the permanent establishment of the mission complex in the eighteenth century that brought regular epidemics to the Orinoco Basin. More recently among the Yanomami, disease has been carried into remote areas by Yanomami men who have journeyed downriver to acquire newly accessible Western manufactures.

These and other cases (Crosby 1986; Fitzhugh 1985) leave little question, however, that when epidemics occur among nonresistant populations, the effect is devastating, leading to fundamental changes in population density; settlement size, duration, and location; and age profiles. Ferguson describes how the loss of so many people at one time tears apart the fabric of social relations and contributes to various kinds of violence among the Yanomami. The Iroquois exhibit an even more direct connection between war and disease in their unusual practice of capturing adult men to integrate into their society. And it is interesting to note that both the Carib and the Iroquois only rose to political and military prominence after the virtual elimination by disease and other factors of once more powerful, but more exposed, neighbors (Brasser 1978a; Whitehead 1989). The same circumstance is true for other notably warlike peoples, including the Cherokee (Perdue 1979:20) and the warriors of the Amazon River (Hemming 1987).

Another set of influential factors relates to ecological change, the modification of the physical environment by the introduction of new plants and animals. This phenomenon is not unique to European colonization, as diffusionist studies of the Old World show, but Europe accelerated and globalized the process. The most massive impact is seen in areas that Crosby (1986) calls Neo-Europes, areas environmentally suitable for the spread of a European plant-and-animal complex but without an evolved state production system. The rapid spread of this biological complex facilitated settlement by European colonizers (and see Cronon 1983; Super 1988). But the picture is even more complicated, as European expansionism has brought important "lateral transfers" of domesticants, often from tropic to tropic. Manioc and corn were brought from the New World to West Africa, for example, allowing for population growth even during the period of the slave trade (Smith 1988:4; Wolf 1982:204).

The spread of introduced plants and animals also was involved in the development of new cultural patterns among indigenous peoples, some of whom obdurately resisted European settlers. The role of the horse on the Great Plains is the classic example. Thurman (1989), in a seminar paper that could not be included in this collection, emphasized that this introduction led to the florescence of a new and vital culture pattern (and see Ewers 1980; Lewis 1970; Secoy 1953). New World sweet potatoes were introduced to New Guinea, touching off, some say, an "ipomoean revolution" that transformed Highland societies (Feil 1987).

The *effective* environment (physical surroundings as they are significant for human use) also changes in response to changes in the economic reasons for state expansion. Furthermore, human activity leads to modification of the physical environment itself. Such changes are not related to state contact only, since recent research suggests that indigenous peoples have effected long-term modification of huge areas of Amazonian forest (Posey and Balee 1989), but European contact certainly intensifies the process. Subsistence resources are depleted (Ferguson, this volume; Thomas 1985:154; Whitehead 1988:30–32), fur-bearing animals are wiped out (Abler, this volume; Ferguson 1984b), or a wholesale transformation takes place, as in the current assaults on the rain forests of the world. Even less catastrophic interventions can lead to ecological impoverishment and the limitation of future use possibilities (Bunker 1988). Such major changes in the relationship between a people and their environment will be accompanied by a restructuring of labor patterns, and thereby lead to substantial modifications of the rest of social life.

A third set of factors is technological change. The ability to manufacture utilitarian and luxury goods beyond the productive capabilities of nonstate peoples may be one of the key factors in the development of the first states (Algaze 1989; Nissen 1988; Szynkiewicz 1989), and the circulation of these items beyond state borders has been a basis of state-nonstate interactions ever since. But the development of its mass-production technology made Europe different. Considering cheap metal tools alone (guns will be considered below), there has been a tremendous impact in areas that did not have local metalworkers, since steel cutting implements have been calculated as being three to nine times more efficient than stone (Carneiro 1979a; Colchester 1984). Scattered exceptions notwithstanding, the rule is a tremendous demand for metal among nonstate peoples (Whitehead, Brown and Fernández, Ferguson, this volume; Fitzhugh 1985; Rodman and Cooper 1983). As one of the first French traders among the Ottawa put it, "The savages love knives better than we serve God" (quoted in Turner 1977:32). Certainly, the metals worked by the artisans of Rome and ancient Sri Lanka would have been highly valued by nearby peoples with lithic technology, but it is doubtful that these metal implements could have been supplied in sufficient quantities or low enough costs to become routine means of production.

Metal tools circulate widely in indigenous trade networks (Whitehead 1988:160–63) and typically have replaced stone tools before any trained observers arrive (Carneiro 1979b; Ferguson 1990a). These trade networks are intimately involved in war and alliance, as will be discussed later. But beyond those direct links to war, there is the question of what happens to a society when its basic technology is suddenly replaced. The well-known studies by Salisbury (1962) and Sharp (1974), which indicate the magnitude of expectable changes, stand out dramatically in a literature that glosses over the presence of steel.

The impact of disease, ecological transformation, and technological change will vary. It is apparent, for instance, that these factors have had a much more acute effect in the Americas than in Africa. The question must be approached empirically. In some cases, no impact will be found. But often, singly or in combination, these factors radically transform the basic orders of social life, as has occurred with the Yanomami (Ferguson, this volume; and see Fitzhugh 1985). Moreover, all these factors typically, though not always, travel far ahead of observers. They are the media of indirect contact; their extent defines the scope of the tribal zone, which thus, by definition, becomes a very dynamic field. Therefore, we should be very cautious about accepting even "first contact" reports as representing societies unaffected by Europe.[5]

Turning now to the actual presence of state agents, the "actors" in our formulation, we generally encounter a very heterogeneous group. In this, European states are probably no different from ancient states. The first order of sorting depends on whether there is only one expanding state present or multiple states are present and in competition. Other things being equal, the existence of competition among the Europeans gives native people more autonomy and a better rate of exchange for products. But as Whitehead and Abler (this volume) show, there is a price: more bloodshed, as indigenous people are drawn into European wars. A variation on this theme occurs when a European society is divided into hostile factions, with their own ties to native allies as in the British North American colonies in the 1630s (Fausz 1985:226).

Underneath these "national" divisions, the analyst encounters a multiplicity of types of actors: government administrators, soldiers, priests, traders, settlers, felons, scientists (including anthropologists), and so forth, all with their own circumstances and interests.[6] The interactions of these actors with each other and with indigenous people thus produce historical process on the local level. For indigenous people, state actors may seem tremendously fickle, rearranging themselves frequently and quickly in response to many factors. What may seem a small change from a distance, such as the relocation of a trading post or the replacement of a captain at a fort, can have a tremendous impact on the lives of indigenous people, creating political crises and worse (Fitzhugh 1985; Rodman and Cooper 1983; Whitehead 1988). Many of the chapters that follow show that such small-scale changes have strongly influenced the pattern of warfare.

TRIBALIZATION

Beyond these particular interactions linking state agents and indigenous peoples, there is a larger process of structural articulation. The restructuring of indigenous forms of social organization as a result of connecting to European colonizers has been the subject of a great deal of work. Dependency theory, world system theory, and structural Marxism all focus on economic articulation. Some structural Marxists have attempted to expand their framework to encompass political articulation (e.g., Reyna 1990), but they have been more concerned with the development of models than with the historical process. Wolf (1982) opens up a new area of research into ideological articulation and struggle. Without implying any necessary criticism of these previous and largely complementary efforts, in this volume we focus on military and political articulation. This brings us to the issue of tribe.

Many uses of the term "tribe" can be found in the literature (Helm 1968), but two meanings are most relevant here. Service (1962) uses tribe to designate a general stage in sociocultural evolution. Sahlins (1968) elaborates on the tribal stage, stressing the role of institutions such as age-grades and clan systems which integrate bands or villages into a larger polity. Fried (1967, 1968, 1975) pays little attention to integrative structures, focusing instead on the matter of uniformity and bounding; that is, on the distinction of one tribe from another (see Haas 1990b:174). Fried rejects tribe as a stage in evolution and sees it instead as a "secondary" phenomenon, the product of contact with a more complex society, and particularly, with a state. All of these authors associate the emergence of tribes with an increase in warfare (Fried 1975:71–72; Sahlins 1968: 5–7; Service 1962:113–15). In this volume the evolutionary questions are left largely unexplored (see Haas 1982, 1990b), although Whitehead discusses some of the theoretical implications of differing evolutionary perspectives for the historical analysis of Amerindian societies.

Whether or not tribes evolved in the pre-state past, the main issue here is that of the relationship between state expansion and the formation of tribes. That issue is clouded by an ambiguity in Fried's position. The theory is that a tribe is a political unit brought into being, in various ways, by contact with a state—any state. The tribe-creating capacity of ancient states is noted by Fried (1968:18), and he calls attention to the great expanse of tribal peoples across central Asia from the fifth century B.C. to the seventeenth century A.D. (Fried 1975:72).[7] But except for this and a few other passing references, this classic area of tribalism is not scrutinized by Fried, and neither is another center of tribalism, the Middle East (Crone 1986:55).[8] Instead, Fried pays most attention to tribalization associated with European expansionism (e.g.; Fried 1979:4), and the message that seems to have had the widest hearing in anthropology is that "Europe created tribes." In other statements, however, Fried makes it seem as though tribes have *never* existed (Fried 1975:1), and most of his illustrations puncturing holes in tribal theory are taken from areas of European colonialism, precisely where one would theoretically expect to find tribes.

The papers collected here in one sense underscore that ambiguity (and see Fitzhugh 1985). Although many tribes will be seen to emerge in response to state expansion, the reader will also encounter a variety of other political forms in the tribal zone: secondary states, open-ended alliance networks, autonomous villages, clan segments and extended families, specialized bandit groups, and so on (see Whitehead, this volume, for discussion). Tribes may be the most prominent political feature of the tribal zone, but they remain only one of many possible outcomes of contact. Resolution of this ambiguity is possible, but it requires that we look first at the forces at work in the tribal zone that create or modify political groupings among indigenous people.

States have difficulty dealing with peoples without authoritative leaders and with constantly changing group identity and membership. All expanding states seek to identify and elevate friendly leaders. They are given titles, emblems, and active political and military support. The status of state-identified leaders is also increased by their central position in trade relations with the state, because of both their control of basic technology and their privileged access to prestige items (Menezes 1977; Szynkiewicz 1989; Washburn 1988; and see Kipp and Schortman 1989). At the same time, however, a leader must exist within the constraints of local social organization. Breakdown of old patterns may undermine authority, as described by Strathern, but an increase in warfare can refocus support of tested leaders. The kind of authority that actually emerges also depends on the prior political organization of the native people and the nature of the contact process. When states connect with chiefdoms, and the contact allows a period of indigenous autonomy, secondary states (Price 1978) may form rather than or in addition to tribes, as happened in West Africa (Law, this volume; and see Kopytoff 1987a, 1987b).

State agents, whether they be Roman governors in North Africa or Roman Catholic missionaries on the Upper Amazon, also seek to identify or, if need be, to create clear political boundaries ("polity") in place of the multilayered and constantly shifting allegiances they actually encounter ("anarchy"). Tribal identification then becomes a means of relating to the political apparatus of the state. This lesson has been taught by the recent history of tribalism in Africa (Vail 1989), it is manifest in contemporary developments in Highland New Guinea (Strathern, this volume), and it looks to be the future, as it has been the past, of indigenous people in Amazonia (*Cultural Survival Quarterly* 1989; Whitten 1981). So it is that the needs and policies of states create tribes.

This is not the whole story, however. Where do the groups that become tribes come from? State contact changes the patterning of social relations, sometimes reinforcing existing patterns, sometimes reorienting them, sometimes shattering them and rebuilding from scratch. Two primary forces that structure the new patterns are trade and war. In European contact situations especially, trade in manufactures creates new networks of connections. Built as they are upon a flow of critical means of production, these are very strong connections, and connections that carry a tendency toward unequal political status. The political and military aspects of trade are even more pronounced if trade includes a flow of captive labor.

War does several things to indigenous groups. It reduces numbers, as does disease, and so may force previously separate peoples to come together, if only to increase the pool of marriage partners. War forces alliances: deliberate efforts to draw peoples together and cement their relationships. And war crystalizes oppositions: it separates peoples into clearly identifiable groups. Generally, war leads to the differential survival of ethnic formations and political organizations. In these ways, Western contact forces new political alignments and oppositions, generating the groups which the state can elevate to the political status of tribes.

But trade and war patterns are linked to a state presence that is continuously redefining itself, and the nature of political groups is also connected to other simultaneous social transformations occurring in the tribal zone. In European cases these transformations may be especially destabilizing because of, along with everything else, the rapid and radical changes associated with capitalist penetration. This general instability in European contact situations can explain why European contact typically does not produce the evolved forms of tribalism described by Sahlins. While the genesis of group identities and boundaries can occur rapidly in the conflict situations typical of the European tribal zone, the creation of socially integrative mechanisms and structures, such as sodalities and age-grades, cannot occur while the world is being turned upside down (see Szynkiewicz 1989).[9]

The importance of historical time in the process of tribalization can be appreciated by looking across the frontier of the northern United States—from a situation of virtually complete breakdown of larger political structures related to the colonial presence in New England (Brasser 1978b:85; Thomas 1985), to the Iroquois and other loose confederacies which were elaborated on top of village polities at the fringes of early European contact (Abler, this volume; Engelbrecht 1985), to the distinctively tribal organization that developed on the Great Plains during the time of indirect contact (Biolsi 1984; Hanson 1988; Hoebel 1978). Of course, it was only a matter of decades before the classic Great Plains tribes were forcibly incorporated into the United States, a development that highlights the fact that European expansion was inimical to the enduring linkages that connected ancient states and tribes.[10]

A similar argument applies to ethnicity. Since "tribe" and "ethnic group" are often used interchangeably by anthropologists, Fried's polemic against the former may be taken to apply to many assumptions about the latter. Nonetheless, we would argue that a useful and important distinction may be made between these concepts, hinging on the idea that tribes are bounded and/or structured political organizations, while ethnic groups are a cultural phenomenon with only latent organizational potential.[11]

The papers collected in this volume provide examples, from both ancient and European state expansions, of ethnic groups being created in response to the same forces involved in tribalization. The creation and significance of ethnic divisions responds to the efforts of state agents and the patterns of conflict and cooperation existing in the tribal zone. As these change, so does the structure and meaning of ethnicity (Brown 1989; Fardon 1988; Gonzalez 1989; Whitten 1976; and see Barth 1969; Moerman 1968). Whitehead's concept of "ethnic formation" calls direct attention to this historical specificity. Thus, even if it is not linked to one political group, an ethnic formation is inherently political, shaped by and shaping the politics of "us versus them" in political systems ranging from egalitarian bands to empires.

These processes are not confined to the indigenous side of the encounter. From the time of the *Reconquista* to the imperial rivalries of the twentieth century, Europe's dealings with non-Europeans have affected the crystallization of European national identities. At the same time, another level of cultural identification is involved. Europe's expansion is a unique event in global history in that it involved simultaneous contact with so many culturally, politically, and physically diverse peoples. Despite the often intense interstate struggles between colonizing Europeans, there was a degree of commonality in culture when seen against this global diversity. Christianity often provided the ideological expression of this unity, as did racialist systems of classification, and hierarchies based on the idea of social evolutionary progress (Adas 1989; Berkhofer 1978; Kiernan 1972; Pearce 1988). Such ideologies allowed the development of a self-perceived identity as Europeans, in addition to the development of "colonial" and "national" identities (Canny and Pagden 1989; Hulme 1986). As Whitehead discusses, these identities connect to the larger ideological opposition of civilization versus barbarism or savagery, which for centuries has been part of the myth charter of European state systems (Bronson 1988; Hobbes 1651; Pagden 1982; and see Garraty and Gay 1981:727).[12] European states may not be unusual in this ideology: the elite of ancient Sri Lankan states (Gunawardana, this volume) had their own traditions of noble and ignoble savages.

STRUCTURE, AGENCY, AND HISTORY

The previous section focused on changes in large-scale social organization, the articulation of expanding states with the broad patterning of indigenous societies. Underlying these macroscopic changes are the actions of indigenous peoples, the behaviors that actually produce process. Just as the state dissolves into a variety of factors and actors when one "gets down to cases," so too do tribes and ethnic formations give way to native people and their circumstances.

Usually, especially when contact involves relatively egalitarian societies, indigenous people do not exhibit the same kind of functional specialization as state agents (soldiers, settlers, and so on), although these begin to emerge at higher levels of political complexity. But there is still a great deal of diversity in individual situations and interests, based on differences in tribal, ethnic, or other social identity, on position within political hierarchies, and on the overall context of contact-related changes in social organization and ecological adaptation. All of these have major implications for the life of any person, and will affect all perceptions and decisions.

Nevertheless, the most salient issue for anyone in the tribal zone often is the question of relationship to the agents of the state. Cases collected here indicate that ambivalence may be the rule, as it certainly was regarding European colonizers. Against the seductive lure of manufactured goods and powerful political backing, there is the coercive and unpredictable behavior of the colonizers, the dependency and loss of autonomy that comes with cooperation, and in many parts of the world, the virtual certainty of epidemic disease.

All of these circumstances and possibilities can change rapidly. Together, they present to any individual a political field that can be complex, dense, obscure, and shifting. Evaluations and decisions must be made. The three basic options in regard to state agents are resistance, cooperation, and flight. Often a result of being faced with this persistent matrix of choice is factional division among the natives, centering on how to deal with the intruders. Some leaders advocate attack, others conciliation; some take followers closer to the frontier, others lead into the wilderness; some assimilate, while others valorize local traditions.

Specific circumstances determine what kinds of decisions can be made, what options are possible, the probable consequences of any action, and the likelihood of a given behavior becoming more or less widespread. But within those constraints, there may be great latitude for action and innovation, and the understandings and agreements worked out by individual leaders play a crucial role in patterning war and alliance. Here then we see "agency," in an appreciation of the fact that social processes exist only in the actions of individual persons, and that people are active subjects in the creation of their own history. A decision to escape into unknown lands, a dream that becomes a prophecy, a political marriage, a successful surprise attack are thus the individual behaviors that determine the particular course of the historical processes at the local level and within wider social constraints.

Participants in this seminar differ in how much of the indigenous perspective they bring into focus and what characteristics they ascribe to it. But the overall thrust of the papers is very similar to that found in other collections about European contact (Fitzhugh 1985; Rodman 1983:19–21): that indigenous peoples make pragmatic responses to changing conditions in order to maintain tolerable living conditions and prevent military losses. It thus contradicts a currently popular assumption that indigenous behavior in contact situations will appear enigmatic to Westerners because native actors respond to conditions with a radically different cultural logic.

Obviously, native beliefs and values will be necessary to explain specific historical trajectories. As authors in this volume show, native categories such as religious doctrines (Gunawardana, Hassig), ethnic oppositions (Whitehead), prophecies (Abler; Brown and Fernández), the valorization of violent aggression (Ferguson, Strathern), witchcraft beliefs (Ferguson), and rules of war (Strathern) are very relevant to the explanation of historical events. Nevertheless, in all these cases, existing cultural patterns are reshaped and employed practically, and in ways that show substantial cross-cultural uniformity. The compelling reason for pragmatism is not difficult to fathom. Those who lose in the often violent conflicts of the tribal zone may cease to exist, as persons or as cultural units.

MILITARIZATION IN THE TRIBAL ZONE

Up to this point, this essay has outlined the major dimensions of the encounter between expanding states and indigenous peoples, what is involved when states move into new territory, and what happens to nearby nonstate peoples when they do. This has been done in order to develop a context in which to situate an understanding of warfare. In the following section, war itself is the focus. Discussing war in the tribal zone requires some form of classification. Here, war will be classified according to its basic relationship to state agents, in the following three categories: (1) war by indigenous people directed against the state presence, that is, wars of resistance and rebellion; (2) war by indigenous people carried out under the control or influence of state agents, that is, ethnic soldiering; and (3) war between indigenous peoples responding to their own perceived interests in the changing circumstances of the tribal zone, or internecine warfare.

Under these headings, other more functional divisions are discussed. But it must be emphasized that these three categories are for purposes of exposition only, and in reality one would find many overlapping, ambiguous, and anomalous cases. A fourth and final discussion deals with the changing conduct of warfare in the tribal zone.

WARS OF RESISTANCE AND REBELLION

The form of warfare most directly related to state expansion is that which puts state agents in direct combat with indigenous people. This involves attacks by the intruding state on the natives, their settlements, and their provision grounds; alternating with native attacks on state outposts, such as forts, watering places, or sites of resource extraction (Belich 1989; Bodley 1982; Crowder 1971; Utley and Washburn 1985). Raids by either side can be directed at removing an unwanted presence, accompanied by other motives, such as slave taking by the state, or the plundering of manufactures by natives. The most disastrous scenario for indigenous people occurs when the state seeks to exclusively occupy new territory. When conditions are right, state systems have shown a ferocious ability to sweep away indigenous inhabitants, as in the "winning of the West" in North America (Utley and Washburn 1985), the British occupation of Tasmania (Moorehead 1967), or the invasion of the Brazilian forests (S. Davis 1977).

This kind of fighting may be very localized, involving a single village or band, or even a single leader with a personal following. As conditions in the tribal zone deteriorate, however, a basis is created for formerly disparate peoples to join in pan-ethnic coalitions against the intrusive state.[13] Broad movements of resistance are often inspired in such contexts by prophecies of a millennium, as discussed here by Brown and Fernández; although, as Thurman stressed in seminar discussions, prophetic leadership of this sort may arise when conditions have already thrown different peoples together. Occasionally, armed rebellions have been successful at driving out invaders, as with the Jívaro in 1599 (Harner 1973), the Puebloans in 1680 (Sando 1979; Terrell 1973), or the Carib in 1684 (Whitehead 1988). In all these cases, however, the state sooner or later returned to establish control.

Ancient and European states are both similar and different in their ability to successfully wage war against tribal peoples. They are similar in that the primary military advantage of any state is its ability to authoritatively direct and sustain massive force against a target. Even if indigenous fighters are able to repel state forces in open field combat, a state can send more men, and keep sending them, until native forces are routed. This makes state armies most effective against fixed targets, and thus against the more sedentary and centralized indigenous polities (Hedeager 1987: 126). European colonial and modern state armies have the additional advantage of being independent of labor demands for subsistence production, a major constraint on nonstate and ancient state forces, such as the Aztecs (Hassig, this volume; and see Belich 1989).

Indigenous peoples, on the other hand, often have a major advantage in mobility. The effectiveness of state armies is limited by logistical considerations (Hassig, this volume; Goldberg and Findlow 1984; Mann 1986). Protracted campaigns against people without any central authority, living in small and mobile settlements, are very costly, if not logistically impossible. The advantages of mobility are greatly magnified if indigenous people are mounted, as with the nomads of central Asia and the Middle East (Barfield 1989; Crone 1986), the (postcontact) horse warriors of the Great Plains (Biolsi 1984), or their Paraguayan counter-parts, the Guaicuru (Hemming 1978). States may opt for a hardened perim-eter defense at the point where they lose effective superiority, sometimes leaving walls as the high-water mark of their control (Goldberg and Find-low 1984; Jagchid and Symons 1989; Lattimore 1940; Luttwak 1976). However, such a balance of forces is most apparent in ancient states. European expansionism since 1500, in contrast, has proceeded rapidly and globally, rarely being halted for long on a tribal frontier, once suffi-cient resources have been committed to expansion. The economic motor of this expansion often has been the relentless pursuit of profit. But the ability to expand has depended on other factors, corollaries of the devel-oping system of industrial capitalism.

One major factor in this expansion is weaponry. Contrary to popular notions, early firearms usually did not have a decisive advantage over native weapons in terms of range, accuracy, or rate of fire (Hassig, this volume; Townsend 1983), and in wet climates, they often did not work at all (e.g., Medina 1988). Nevertheless, they clearly had some advantage, since native peoples often went to great lengths to obtain muskets. Abler (this volume; and 1989a) suggests that lead shot deprived the enemy of one of the primary defensive techniques of arrow warfare: dodging the projectile. Also, in some cases at least, guns could penetrate armor or shields that would stop arrows. Law's study of western Africa indicates that the military implications of firearms existed only in relationship to the organization and professionalism of the army (a general point em-phasized by Turney-High [1971]), and that the transformation of army structure was part of a broader process of sociopolitical centralization. Cannons and swivel guns, however, did provide a less ambiguous advan-tage. These could both destroy fortifications and seacraft and be used as effective antipersonnel weapons from either (McNeill 1982:95–101).

The relative effectiveness of sidearms, and so Europe's battlefield ad-vantage, took a great leap after 1850 with the development of rifling and repeating weapons (McNeill 1982:231ff.; O'Connell 1989:200). The contrast lives on today in the New Guinea Highlands, where crude locally made shotguns and high-powered rifles both draw blood, but the latter make the bigger impact (Strathern, this volume). A comparable if not greater leap occurred in stages beginning in 1862, with the development of machine guns. Long before they were used widely on other Europeans, Maxims and Brownings were making possible conquests in Africa, as well as other colonial exploits (Ellis 1975:79–103). The seminar paper by Turton on violence in the Horn of Africa added a contemporary and hor-rifying perspective on this point, reporting that wholesale slaughter replaced individual killings when one side in a local tribal conflict was provided with automatic weapons.

A second technological consideration giving increasing advantage to the Europeans was transportation and communication. The transportation system developed by the Spanish in Mexico enabled them to intensify control and exploitation beyond anything the Aztecs could accomplish (Hassig, this volume). Over the centuries, larger, stronger, and faster ships, and the spreading networks of roads, railroads, and telegraph lines, made it possible to bring force to bear more quickly, at greater distances, and at less cost. In the twentieth century, motor launches, bush airplanes, and helicopters have enabled imperial and Third World states to strike at resistant indigenous peoples far from centers of state control.

Organizationally, European armed forces were being qualitatively transformed, in a gradual "military revolution" which began virtually contemporaneously with the start of Europe's expansion (Headrick 1981; McNeill 1982; Parker 1989). Over its first three centuries, the balance of destructive power shifted in favor of the colonialists. By the start of the nineteenth century, this tragic evolution produced the bureaucratized and thoroughly drilled modern military. Only at this relatively late date did Europeans attain a usually decisive edge over the forces of non-Western states.

Nevertheless, European dominance was built only partly on military abilities. In those areas where there was little resistance to Old World diseases, epidemics could do as much damage as armies. Certainly, newly introduced pathogens took more lives than bullets. The case of the Aztecs also illustrates another advantage often held by the Europeans, that of being the new contender entering into an extant conflict situation. European support leads to one side's victory, but the victors themselves are soon overwhelmed by the increasing European presence. This brings us to the next category of warfare in the tribal zone, in which expanding states induce indigenous people to make war on other indigenous people.

ETHNIC SOLDIERING

The second broad category of warfare involves indigenous people who fight under the control or influence of state agents. Ethnic soldiers and martial tribes have been an aspect of state expansionism from earliest times. Ancient states of the Middle East regularly maintained separate units of ethnic fighters (Faulkner 1953; Saggs 1984; Schulman 1964), and similar direction of native forces is one of the recurrent points in this volume. Indigenous peoples are employed to attack forces of other states, native allies and auxiliaries of rival states, and independent native peoples. They are drawn into the service of state agents by varying combinations of coercive and seductive measures. The extent of state control also varies greatly, in a range running from independent native polities with negotiated alliances (Whitehead, this volume), to hired tribal raiders (Murphy 1960) and regular tribal auxiliary units (Hemming 1978), to ethnic groups disproportionately incorporated into state armies (*Cultural Survival Quarterly* 1987a, 1987b, Mazrui 1977), to a standing army of ethnic mercenaries, upon whose sometimes questionable loyalty the state depends (Gunawardana, this volume).

Ethnic soldiers may be used as raiders to procure something the state needs, but more usually they are used to further the colonial and geopolitical interests of the metropolitan state. Whitehead and Abler provide clear illustrations of this with the general alignment of different ethnic groups with different imperial powers, although they also show that it was never quite that simple. This kind of fighting caused tremendous destruction of native peoples all along the early North American frontier (Fitzhugh 1985; Perdue 1979; Utley and Washburn 1985). Recent cases seem more complicated. In East Africa, as described by Turton (1989; see also Gamst 1986; Markakis 1990), global East-West polarization is refracted through the political structures of independent Third World states and extends down to capitalize indigenous warfare with sophisticated new weaponry. But that is only one possibility among many (see Nietschmann 1987).

Ethnic soldiers are also used in violence within states. As indigenous peoples become more integrated into national political and economic systems, the strains of those systems ramify throughout indigenous societies. So in Papua New Guinea (Strathern, this volume) we see traditional oppositions and new conflicts on the local level intertwine with power struggles of national economic and political elites. Brown and Fernández show that indigenous peoples may be drawn into externally led revolts against a national power structure, and Whitehead shows that they can be used to perform the functions of police (see also Whitehead 1990b).

In all of these situations, but more so in cases of greater indigenous autonomy, there may be a mix of incentives to raid: those of the state agents, and those of the native people. In early phases of direct contact, it may be more a case of indigenous people using Europeans than the reverse, as certainly was the case in West Africa (Law, this volume). But more than just a mix of incentives, there is a dialectical interaction. Native peoples play off European interests to pursue standing grievances; Europeans stir up strife and factionalism to encourage natives to attack each other. And with time, native interests and conflicts themselves become a product of the interactions of the tribal zone.

INTERNECINE WARFARE

The third category of warfare encompasses wars carried out by politically autonomous native peoples, pursuing their own perceived interests under the changing conditions of the tribal zone. This category includes wars related to the control of trade. Control of trade is, of course, a major impetus to war between states, as described in this volume by Gunawardana. Military conflict related to state trade into or through nonstate territory is suggested by the earliest archaeological evidence of war (Roper 1975), and probably has been a major cause of war among nonstate peoples ever since. But the sudden arrival of European agents produced a dramatic rearrangement and militarization of trade networks.

Three often interrelated aspects of this trade merit special note. One is the flow of Western manufactures, from basic tools to prestige items, for great distances beyond their source. As discussed earlier, trade in these items often is a primary political concern for indigenous peoples. A second aspect, actually a subtype in the manufactures trade, is the trade in guns. The demand for guns often leads to more fighting, as on the Northwest Coast of North America (Ferguson 1984b) or among the Maori of New Zealand (Vayda 1960, 1976), where in different ways war captives became a means for obtaining weapons, or among the Jívaroan groups of the Andean piedmont, where rifles were traded for shrunken heads (Bennett Ross 1984). Furthermore, the unequal acquisition of effective firearms by one side in an ongoing conflict can dramatically lower their risk in war, and so encourage them in new attacks (Ferguson, this volume; Todd 1979; Vayda 1976).

The third aspect is trade in captive laborers, which of all indigenous "products" implies a high level of force as a necessary accompaniment to trade. The slave trade supported the elaboration of militaristic states throughout West Africa, a result which Law calls "indigenous subimperialism" (see also Warren 1982). That is an apt characterization, even when, as in northeastern South America, the raiding was carried out by nonstate peoples (Whitehead, this volume; Ferguson 1990a).[14] In North America as well, extensive areas far beyond the frontier were disrupted by native peoples raiding to capture slaves for the Europeans (Bailey 1973; Deagan 1985; Lewis 1970:186; McNitt 1990; Perdue 1979; Turner 1977:9).[15]

Law also observes that the production of slaves through war must be distinguished from the control of the trade in captive workers, which involves its own kind of conflicts. Thus, control of the flow of semi-free workers for the Australian plantations played an important role in military developments in the Solomons and nearby islands (Rodman 1983).

The control of trade brings wealth and power. Networks of alliance radiate outward from Western centers, built upon flows of precious commodities. Patterns of opposition likewise develop, reflecting tensions related to unfavorable positions in the trade. Those who are able seek to maximize the political, economic, and military advantages of trade control by establishing themselves as monopolists; not in production, usually, but by controlling some middleman position which cannot be circumvented (Brasser 1978b; Ferguson 1984b; Fitzhugh 1985; Griffen 1988; Milloy 1988; Rodman and Cooper 1983; Whitehead 1988). The possible extent of trade-related conflicts is indicated by MacDonald's (1979, 1980) excavations of Northwest Coast forts, showing intensified militarism along interior trade routes with the introduction of European items from the east, 75 years or more before direct contact along the Pacific coast (and see Jablow 1950; Lewis 1970; Mekeel 1943).

In addition to wars related to middleman control, there are wars of plunder. Abler describes how Hunt's (1940) view on Iroquois war as an effort to become middlemen has given way to a perspective that sees their wars as an effort to plunder pelts and control new trapping lands. Plunder, however, is a high-risk, high-cost way to obtain the benefits of trade with Europeans, and may be used only when more monopolistic control is not militarily possible (Ferguson 1984b). Ferguson (this volume, and 1990a) describes a different situation, in which those without access to Western manufactures obtain them by plunder.

Conflict related to trade extends outward from the European frontier, and so is often beyond direct observation. Moreover, indigenous interests and European interests in the control of trade are often antagonistic, as traders or missionaries may want nonviolent, open access to their posts. Analysts should be sensitive to the possibility that recorded native explanations and accounts of wars have been tailored to manipulate European trade behavior. As a result of these obscuring conditions, only the most obvious cases tend to be reported, as when a certain tribe or chief has a tight, enforced monopoly on certain trade (Jablow 1950; Whitehead 1988:165–70), or when large-scale fighting is associated with a distant or disadvantaged group seeking less restricted access to trade (Maybury-Lewis 1974:18–22; Murphy 1960:29–30). But the Yanomami case (Ferguson, this volume) indicates that strains associated with Western trade can ramify through the dendritic connections of exchange, fostering antagonism, factionalism, and war even among closely related people.

In addition to trade-related conflicts, autonomous warfare by indigenous people also includes conflicts related to territorial displacements. When an expanding state frontier pushes out previous occupants, dislocated people may move into uninhabited areas. Many of our current "most primitives" may have this origin (Fox 1969; Kloos 1977; Stearman 1984). Alternatively, displaced people may be able to disperse and assimilate into other populations, as Turton described for East African refugees. But they may also enter into war with previous occupants or other refugees (Balée 1988; Biolsi 1984). This kind of fighting may be even more remote from Western observation than are trade conflicts, and details are correspondingly more obscure.

Considering all these processes of militarization in the tribal zone, there is reason to suspect that, in addition to the Yanomami, other classic anthropological cases of "pristine" warfare are related to European contact. In Highland New Guinea, Salisbury (1962) reports a great increase in warfare when steel tools began to come in through native networks (and see Blick 1988). Kelly's (1985) controversial reconstruction of Nuer history shows intense state militarism at their borders, and the florescence of a slave trade along rivers through their area, at least roughly coincident in time and space with the Nuer expansions (and see Holt and Daly 1979; Mercer 1971). These findings also suggest new perspectives on standing arguments about the role of European contact in generating the wars of the Zulu (Peires 1981) and Quechans (Forbes 1965; Kroeber and Fontana 1986).[16]

THE CHANGING CONDUCT OF WAR

Along with the causes of war, the way war is waged can also change with contact, and these changes can stimulate additional wars (Whitehead 1990a). An illustration of this concerns the introduction of guns. As noted earlier, even the early firearms were more difficult to dodge or to shield against than slings and arrows. In some cases, this seems to have led to a major shift in indigenous military tactics. As Abler describes for the Iroquois, in their first military encounter involving firearms, they prepared for battle by forming lines.[17] Champlaign's fire killed several men and routed the Iroquois, who henceforth relied more on the surprise attacks that American schoolchildren learn as "fighting Indian style." A similar pattern, of a line being decimated by gunfire, followed by a shift to mobile tactics, occurred on the northern Great Plains (Lewis 1970:183–84) and among the Carib of Brazil (Whitehead 1990a). Strathern also describes the vulnerability of lines to firearms, followed by a decline in open battles in favor of more individualistic violence. It may be that other peoples too gave up an indigenous tradition of set-piece projectile combats with the introduction of firearms.

While the introduction of guns may encourage a change in the conduct of war toward the use of guerilla tactics, other aspects of the situation may foster greater concentration of military force. Control over access to firearms can be a basis for increased political centralization and domination in both secondary state (Law, this volume; Goody 1971; Warren 1982) and nonstate systems (Abler, Brown and Fernández, and Ferguson, this volume; Rodman and Cooper 1983; Turner 1977). Dobyns (1972) described the "military transculturation" of Northern Pimans, who were trained in Spanish formations. The teaching of state military tactics is a very common practice in contact situations, part of the use of ethnic soldiers (Law, this volume; Whitehead 1990b; Hemming 1978).

In the ancient world, tribal peoples, often following a charismatic leader, converting to "civilized" forms of combat have dealt major blows to once-dominant empires (Delbruck 1990; Hedeager 1987; cf. Tainter 1988). More formidable tribal forces can lead to a shift in imperial strategy, away from hegemony to a more fixed territorial defense (Luttwak 1976; McNeill 1982:33–35; and see Mattingly and Hassig, this volume). In the long run, this may mark the beginnings of the dynamics of imperial collapse (Yoffee and Cowgill 1988; Ferrill 1986). The possibility of tribal peoples meeting and defeating state forces in set-piece battles was dealt a severe blow with the revolution in military technology of the nineteenth century; but that may be changing, as demonstrated by the Soviet experience in Afghanistan. It seems a real possibility that tribal peoples armed with modern weapons and using state military practices will pose a greater challenge to state armies in the future.

CONCLUSIONS

For a seminar intended to explore a new subject area, it is not realistic to expect the development of a general theory. The participants did take steps toward that goal, however, formulating tentative diagrams of key variables and relationships, which are included as an appendix to this volume. But the findings of these authors do support two basic conclusions: (1) that the effects of expanding states, and particularly of European colonialism, typically precede extensive descriptions of indigenous warfare, so that by far the greater part of our ethnographic information about nonstate warfare is postcontact; and (2) that very frequently the result of state impingement is to generate warfare and transform its conduct and purpose, rather than to suppress it. For the anthropology of war, these findings suggest the need to reconsider current assumptions and theories about the causes and practice of war in nonstate societies, which have been formed without reference to the contact-related variables identified here. What has been assumed to be "pristine" warfare now seems more likely to be a reflection of the European presence. This does not mean that nothing can be known about war outside of the influence of Europe or other state systems. Archaeological data and judicious use of early reports from some situations can provide such information. The point, rather, is that we cannot discriminate precontact war patterns without a theoretically informed sensitivity to the influences of contact even in its earliest phases.

The tribal zone can be a very violent place. At its worst, it can consume a population, leading to major demographic losses (Cook 1973; Turner 1985). Violence can saturate the fabric of social life, as with the Yanomami, in Highland New Guinea, or along the Connecticut River in the mid-seventeenth century (Thomas 1985). However, and this point merits special emphasis, this is not necessarily so. The purpose of this volume is to examine warfare in relation to state expansion. Were the focus on the tribal zone in itself, intense militarization would appear at one end of a range of possibilities, with peaceful contact at the other.[18] Our argument is not that all state expansion generates indigenous warfare, but that indigenous warfare in proximity to an expanding state is probably related to that intrusion.

In focusing on warfare, this volume deals with indigenous peoples who retain at least some degree of political autonomy. As the contact process proceeds from encapsulation to incorporation, warfare may be succeeded by new forms of violence. Under the right circumstances, the process of incorporation may be halted by broad rebellions against the state. But there can also be new individualistic forms of violence, as is occurring in Highland New Guinea (Strathern, this volume), and as was expressed with the *kanaima* assassination cult in highland Guayana (Whitehead 1990a). But those developments, and the process of pacification, go beyond the scope of this volume.[19]

Our conclusions on the militarization of the tribal zone, combined with other points on tribalization and ethnogenesis, can be applied to a central element in contemporary Western ideology. With astonishing frequency, in popular media and even scholarly tracts, one finds collective violence explained as an outgrowth of "tribal loyalties." With greater or lesser biologism, it is asserted that humans are fundamentally tribalistic in orientation, and that relations between tribes are inherently hostile. In other words, people tend to identify blindly with their own social group or "tribe," and to react with virtually instinctive animosity toward those belonging to other groups.

This Hobbesian image rests on a triple fallacy. First, that the warfare recorded among nonstate peoples is a continuation of pre-state warfare, rather than being a historical product of the state presence. Second, that the ethnic divisions and tribes which are observed making war are survivals of ancient forms of organization, rather than being configured, in the great majority of cases, in relatively recent historical time. Third, that when war does involve tribes, the relationship between tribes is automatically one of unreasoned hostility and violence, rather than exhibiting the entire range of diplomatic-military possibilities found among states during times of war.

Stereotypes of savages notwithstanding, it would be an extremely rare occurrence for members of one tribe to attack members of another simply because they are different, apart from any other source of conflict. Certainly nothing like that is suggested in any of the cases examined here. "Tribal loyalty" can indeed be fierce, with appropriate reinforcement, but it can be evanescent or nonexistent in other situations. Any idea that an innate sense of tribalism inclines people toward collective violence is sheer fantasy.

Our emphasis on the need for a historical perspective on indigenous warfare suggests one other general implication for the discipline of anthropology. The initial development of a historical approach in anthropology was associated with studies of local communities within states. Those studies also led to a recognition of the need to situate community studies in a larger social context (Ferguson 1988a; Roseberry 1988). These "part-societies" within state systems were and continue to be contrasted to indigenous nonstate societies. The latter were imagined to be largely self-contained, such that all significant cultural patterns could be directly observed in the locality of the ethnographer. In our view, this distinction is untenable, if not positively misleading. Indigenous nonstate peoples too live within, react to, and shape a larger complex social universe. Attempts to understand their behavior, institutions, and beliefs which do not take this wider and historically changing context into account may radically misconstrue ethnographic reality.

——— Notes ———

1. Haas (1990b:172) defines tribes as follows:

In simplest terms, a tribe is a bounded network of communities united by social and political ties and generally sharing the same language, ideology, and material culture. The communities in a tribe are economically autonomous and there is no centralized political hierarchy.

2. For our purposes, "state agent" designates any member of a state society operating in the tribal zone, regardless of the nature of his or her connection to the formal institutions of the state.

3. A study of a "classic" tribe of northern Europe or Asia would have been an appropriate addition to our seminar. The organizers opted for some less well-known ancient state-tribe situations.

4. It was not just "European" diseases that afflicted New World peoples, but "African" ones as well, such as malaria, hookworm, yaws, and leprosy (Deagan 1985:290; Whitehead 1988:23).

5. "First contacts" by sea may be a general exception to that caution.

6. Mann's (1986) formulation of four networks of social power—ideological, economic, military, and political—each with its own scope, constraints, and characteristics, could prove useful for approaching this range of actors, but his paradigm is not pursued in this volume.

7. Recent investigations of Eurasian nomads (Golden 1991; Khazanov 1984) place new emphasis on their long-term interactions with neighboring states.

8. Gottwald (1979) describes a process very consistent with Fried's views leading to the tribalization of the Israelites in the period of 1250 to 1050 B.C.

9. Turton's (1989) report at the advanced seminar noted the great difficulty in carrying out ceremonies essential to the functioning of an age-set system in the context of greatly escalated warfare. Eder's (1987) study of "detribalization" among the Philippine Bataak, while not a situation of warfare, also details the breakdown of cultural institutions in a rapidly changing tribal zone.

10. Haas (1990b) makes a similar argument for tribalization as a process rather than an event. However, his study of pre-state tribe formation among Kayenta Anasazi operates in the much longer time frame of in situ sociocultural evolution. The evolution of these tribes occurred in identifiable stages, over a period of about 750 years.

11. See Nietschmann (1987) for a relevant argument, asserting that "ethnic group" and related terms should be replaced by "nations."

12. The fact that so many "tribal" names are pejorative terms, assigned by neighboring indigenous peoples and indicating less than human qualities, suggests that states are not alone in this kind of classification. However, it was noted in seminar discussions that many of these assignations occur as those more in contact with state agents label those who are less in contact, with whom they may be in contact-related competition or actual warfare. Thus, it is not always clear that these negative labels represent precontact categories.

13. Many indigenous attacks on Europeans occur following a substantial reduction in the amount of manufactured goods crossing the frontier (e.g., Ferguson 1984a:294–95; Mekeel 1943:150; Utley and Washburn 1985:90–91; Sahlins 1987:68–71; and see Szynkiewicz 1989:154).

14. The east-west sea trade previously noted in regard to Sri Lanka also

engendered a series of Southeast Asian states. The Philippine Sulu state (Warren 1981, 1982) of the eighteenth and nineteenth centuries participated in this trade, largely through reliance on slave labor. Gibson (1990) shows how this demand for labor resulted in several broad types of local societies, distinguished by their ability to mobilize force and, inversely, by their degree of victimization by raiders.

15. On the Pacific Northwest Coast, the slave raiding which increased during the contact period served the interests of the newly wealthy and powerful indigenous trade controllers, and did not involve substantial supply to Europeans (Donald 1987; Ferguson 1984b; Mitchell 1984). This stimulated indigenous demand for slaves in turn stimulated raiding as far away as the upper Columbia River and into northern California (Ruby and Brown 1976:21–22).

16. On the other hand, Smith (1987) argues that Western Woods Cree did *not* embark on military expansion westward when they acquired guns, as previously had been thought. That finding should stand as a caution. It never can be assumed that any of these contact-related causes of war are operating in a given case. The matter must be investigated empirically, and the theoretical possibility kept open that indigenous warfare has not been greatly modified by contact.

17. Anthropologists often take the formation of military lines to indicate a "ritual combat," but as Turney-High (1971) emphasized, battle lines respond to the practical necessities of combat.

18. Especially noteworthy in this context are a number of distinct Southeast Asian societies, including the Buid, Semai, and Bataak, who were targets of slave raids from the Sulu sultanate. Their response was withdrawal into the forest and the elaboration of a remarkably similar ethos of nonviolence (Gibson 1990). It would be interesting to compare these people with other predated peoples, such as the Piaroa, Maku, or Akuriyo of northern Amazonia.

19. During the seminar discussions, Ferguson noted that many ethnographic reports of feuding which involve a high number of killings come from the partially incorporated peripheries of state systems, rather than from more autonomous peoples (e.g., Bennett Ross 1984; Boehm 1984; Goodwin and Basso 1971:178–85; Keiser 1986; Wilson 1981; and see Black-Michaud 1975:29–30). He suggested that there may be a pattern here, related to their fringe positions, involving: (1) subversion or elimination of native mechanisms of social control at the same time that the state is unable to exercise effective legal control; (2) breakup of larger social structures and increasing individualization of life chances; (3) sharp interpersonal competition relating to the demands of the state; and (4) as the culturally constructed response to such a perilous situation, an honor complex involving a sensitivity to insult and readiness to respond to any personal slight with violence. A fifth element is a prior history of warfare, which would carry over into a more pronounced ideology and sophisticated practice of violence. Where there is no prior history of war, conditions 1 to 4 may produce a high homicide rate, without the trappings associated with feud, perhaps like those discussed by Knauft (1987).

Chapter 2

War and Peace in Roman North Africa

Observations and Models of State-Tribe Interaction

D. J. MATTINGLY

T HE Roman empire was one of the most successful expansionist states of all time. Its army was remarkably efficient in the practice of warfare, and the history of Rome provides a wealth of examples of violent confrontation between state and tribe. Perhaps paradoxically, however, the imperial governance of Rome was commonly characterized as peace—the *pax Romana*. This dualistic aspect of the relationship between Rome and the peoples she came into contact with merits elucidation, particularly as the relative success of the Roman state in reconciling conquered peoples to her rule distinguishes it from many more recent imperial or colonial powers. The Roman case study is used here to address issues of state-tribe interaction (hegemonic versus territorial control), the divergent processes of resistance and encapsulation or assimilation, and the mechanisms by which states seek to limit or avoid warfare in a contact situation. My focus is primarily on the state (Cherry 1987), but it will be apparent that the tribes were by no means passive victims. Their decisions on retreating, resisting, collaborating, or accepting assimilation were vital elements in the dynamics of social, political, and military change in the frontier zone.

TRIBAL STRUCTURE, LEADERSHIP, AND WARFARE

The geographical focus of this chapter is Roman Africa, comprising modern Libya, Tunisia, Algeria, and Morocco. Although we lack a source to match Tacitus's *Germania* for this region and there is a dearth of relevant archaeological data on pre-Roman native settlement (cf. Todd 1975), a number of useful characteristics of its outwardly diverse peoples can be postulated (Bates 1914; Brogan 1975; Camps 1980, 1984:7–26; Daniels 1975; Desanges 1962; *Encyclopédie Berbère*, various entries; Fentress 1979: 18–60; Fentress 1982; Gsell 1913–29 (1):275–326, (5):82–120; Horn and Ruger 1979; Lassère 1977; Tissot 1884:385–437). These tribes were the forerunners of the medieval and modern Berber peoples, predominantly of Mediterranean rather than black African stock and speaking a common language of Hamito-Semitic type, though with numerous dialect variations. The ancient sources give comparatively little detailed information about the social organization of these peoples and are mainly concerned with establishing in broad terms their geographical location (Pliny *Natural History* 5.1.1–8.46; Ptolemy *Geography* 4.3, 4.6; Strabo *Geography* 17.3.1–23). Categorizing and sorting out the ethnic and political groups encountered is a major problem faced by many states in a contact situation, and when the positions allocated to the various tribes by different Roman sources are plotted on a map, there is overlap and contradiction. The solution to the apparent conflict of evidence lies in recognizing that not all the tribal names we encounter, even in a single source, were of equal importance. Roman administrators will have had to resolve the question on the ground, of course, but most ancient geographers and historians made little attempt at defining tribal peoples according to a standard classification. Indeed, it is clear that Roman usage of terms for defining tribal units (*gens, natio, populus,* and *tribus*) was highly inconsistent, even within a single source.

SEGMENTED STRUCTURES

The principal feature of modern Berber tribal organization is the segmented structure (Dunn 1977; Gellner 1969; Gellner and Micaud 1973). Tribes are composed of a hierarchy of units: individual people make up households, several households form a kin group, several kin groups constitute a regional clan, a union of clans makes a small tribe, and these small tribes will on occasion, and under well-established rules or customs, form larger confederations. The structure combines the advantages of dispersed and decentralized tribal systems with the military and political strength of much larger groupings. At the higher levels of confederation there is clear evidence for chiefs and elites exercising greater centralized control. To this extent the people of the Maghreb—the region of northwestern Africa with which this chapter is concerned—maintain elements of a purely tribal organization, within a structure which is at the upper level that of the chiefdom (cf. Creamer and Haas 1985). In the ancient world, the contact situation with Rome (and earlier Carthage) promoted the development of chiefdoms, but the poor quality of our data prevents detailed analysis of the process. So while I acknowledge the utility of the "chiefdom" concept, the term "tribe" is retained here for convenience to describe native groups whose organization ranged from small tribal bands to large chiefdoms, with aspects of both sometimes present in a single case.

Careful examination of the ancient evidence suggests that a similar pyramidical, segmentary structure was also a feature of tribal organization in antiquity. Pliny (*Natural History* 5.4.29–30) stated that there were 516 *populi* ("peoples," including 53 urban groups) in Africa Proconsularis (an area equivalent to eastern Algeria, Tunisia, and northwest Libya), but he referred to only 25 of the tribal groupings by name. For comparison, a recent catalog based on all surviving literary and epigraphic evidence for this region (Desanges 1962) contains less than 130 names. The discrepancy is best explained by assuming that a hierarchy of tribes and subtribes existed across much of the ancient Maghreb. We probably know the names of most of the major ancient tribal groups and a small percentage only of the subgroupings. Unfortunately, we cannot presume that Pliny, Ptolemy, and our other main sources were at all discriminating in their selection of tribal names. Hence the problem, already alluded to, of composing maps of tribal geography, since more than one name features in different sources at the same location. The solution must be to attempt to identify the major tribal names and assign other tribal ethnics the status of subtribes of one of the certain major groups. So, for example, in the Tripolitanian portion of Africa Proconsularis the major tribes or groups were the Garamantes, Nasamones, Macae, and Gaetuli (fig. 2.1). Other tribal names associated with this area should be subgroups. For instance, the Cinyphi, Elaeones, Mamuci, Muducivvi, Seli, Samamuki, Tautamei, and Zamucii are all to be identified as Macae subtribes (Mattingly 1984).

The principle is clear-cut in a number of other examples. Massinissa became king of a protostate, Numidia, with a good deal of Roman support

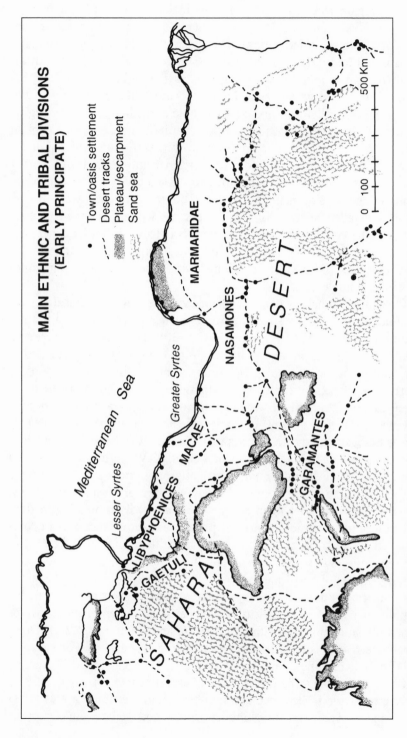

Figure 2.1. *The principal tribal groupings in Tripolitania. The Libyphoenices were the Punicized inhabitants of the coastal towns and their territories.*

during the extraordinary conditions of the Second Punic War at the end of the third century B.C. He had previously been king of one of the larger tribes of the territory, the Massyli, and under his rule the Numidii extended their control over numerous other tribes. The kingdoms of Numidia and Mauretania to its west demonstrate the capacity of the higher level chiefdoms of pre-Roman Africa to advance toward the status of civilized states, with towns, coinage, highly centralized economic controls, and military organization, though contact with the Carthaginian state had done much to foster this development (Buck 1984; Camps 1960; Leveau 1984). But in spite of the growing sophistication of the core territory of the Numidian kingdom, much of its extended zone of control was occupied by tribes of more traditional aspirations. The Musulames, for instance, covered a territory spanning the modern Tuniso-Algerian border in the region of Tebessa. They were a subtribe of the Numidii and were themselves composed of subgroupings of which at least three are known (Desanges 1962:83). Another good example of this stratification comes from northern Numidia, south of Bone, where three inscriptions show the existence of a *tribus Misiciri*. In this case *tribus* cannot signify clan, as no less than 62 Libyan inscriptions have been found in this broad area containing the ethnic *MSKRH* and also mentioning the further subdivisions *NSFH, CRMMH, NNBIBH, NFZIH,* and *NNDRMH* (Camps 1960: 248–50; Fentress 1979:45–46). In another example from Mauretania Tingitana (modern Morocco), a tribal notable and his son (both called Julianus) were given Roman citizenship as a reward for the loyalty displayed by their family group (*domus*) and clan (*familiae*). The elder Julianus was one of the notables (*populares*) of one of several subtribes (*gentes*) which made up the *gens Zegrensium* (Seston and Euzennat 1971; Sherwin-White 1973).

The exact mechanics of segmented tribal structures in antiquity will remain elusive, but it is apparent that we shall learn far more about the possibilities from modern anthropological work than from primary sources. The number of levels in my diagram (fig. 2.2) is hypothetical and to some extent unimportant. The crucial factor is that the tribal societies encountered by Rome in Africa were commonly fragmented into numerous subgroupings while retaining the organizational structures for confederated action in certain contexts.

LEADERSHIP AND BARAKA

The existence of elite elements within tribes and the development of higher-status forms of leadership can be demonstrated for some tribal groupings in Roman Africa. It is impossible, however, to assess the extent

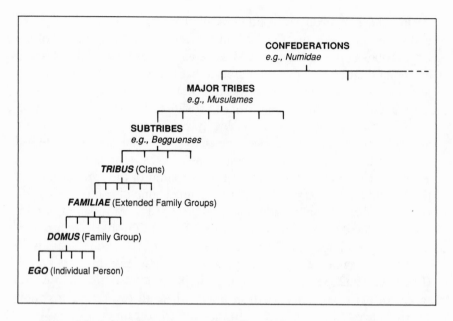

Figure 2.2. A diagrammatic view of tribal hierarchy.

to which these had come into being prior to extensive contact with Carthage or Rome. Nonetheless, suspicion can be voiced that the pre-Roman evolution of chiefdoms and protostates in the ancient Maghreb was greatly accelerated through contact with Carthage and other Punic centers. The Roman annexation of these African polities in the early years of expansion brought her next into contact with tribes that were, initially at least, at a less advanced stage in their development.

Tribal chieftains in Roman Africa were designated by various Latin tags—*rex, dux, princeps, tyrannus, praefectus, magistratus* (technically "king," "general," "leading man," "autocrat," "prefect," "magistrate")—but the application of these terms was frequently inconsistent. The broader tribal elites were sometimes defined as *populares* or *seniores* (Mattingly 1984). How chieftains came to succeed to, or to be imposed on, or elected by, or selected for particular tribes is unclear. There are hints that primogeniture succession was not the commonest form. Some leaders seem to have held power for their own lifetime, others to have been selected to deal with a particular crisis or military adventure. In some cases, chiefs may have been supported (overtly or otherwise) by Rome in their candidacy. The younger Julianus of the *gens Zegrensium* (see above) became chief (*princeps*), but his father, before the award of citizenship, had simply been one of the notables.

In another example from Mauretania Tingitana, we know the names of some of a long series of chieftains of the Baquates tribe. The general lack of family relations between them is striking: Aelius Tuccuda (A.D. 140), Ucmetio (A.D. 173–75), Aurelius Canartha (A.D. 180), Ilasene son of Ureti (who had also been chief at an earlier, unspecified date) (A.D. 200), Sepemazine (A.D. 245), Iulius Nuffuzi son of Iulius Matif (A.D. 277), Iulius Mirzil brother of Iulius Nuffuzi (A.D. 280). The two brothers who succeeded each other in A.D. 277 and 280 were distinguished by the title king (*rex*), while the other chiefs were simply *principes*. The Romans were always sparing in their use of the title *rex,* and in North Africa it was probably restricted to clear cases of dynastic succession (as with the kingdoms of Numidia and Mauretania before their abolition and annexation by Rome). It is certainly possible that the Baquates tribe was evolving into a more cohesive polity by the late third century A.D., with a concomitant shift in the balance of power in tribe-state relations. I do not intend to examine in detail the changing picture of the late Roman period in this essay, but it is worth noting that larger confederations of tribes reappeared in opposition to Rome at that time and that some of them were complex polities ruled by kings (Camps 1974:191–208; Camps 1980:117–28; Euzennat 1984; Warmington 1954:69–75).

A common basis for tribal or religious leadership among Berber communities in the Islamic Maghreb has been the possession of *baraka,* a sort of spiritual charisma which also commonly reflects perceived military or political prowess (Gellner 1969:31–34). Interestingly enough, a late Roman source describing wars with the renascent tribes bordering the African provinces focuses on the significance of the religious stature of the Libyan leaders in uniting disparate tribes into a large confederation (Corippus *Iohannidos*; Mattingly 1983). One of the leaders, Antalas, rose to prominence as a result of an oracle from Ammon (the most important Libyan cult), which predicted that he would be a unifying leader. Ierna, chief of the Laguatan confederation, was high priest of the cult of Gurzil, the bull-headed progeny of Ammon, whose effigy he carried into battle to enlist divine assistance in the struggle. Paradoxically, Ierna was killed when he was prevented from escaping from the scene of a defeat because of the encumbrance of this effigy, which he refused to relinquish. He was replaced by Carcasan, who was elected by the leading tribes of the confederation from among their chiefs. Carcasan consolidated his position by seeking a favorable oracle from Ammon.

The ultimate origins of a pre-Islamic version of *baraka* may be far earlier, as a general phenomenon perhaps even pre-Roman (see Camps 1960:279–95; Camps 1980:220–24 on the sanctity of Numidian kingship). Its potential role as the catalyst to spark higher levels of tribal confederation should certainly not be underestimated. The Numidian kingdom was dismantled in 46 B.C., yet over 60 years later a tribal revolt started up in a corner of its former territory. The Musulamian leader, Tacfarinas, succeeded in putting together a confederation that covered practically the entire area of the former kingdom (and in some points extended well beyond it) and which resisted a substantial Roman army for seven years (A.D. 17–24). Other examples could be given. Resistance on this scale is most clearly understood in the context of formal structures of tribal organization designed to facilitate confederation and a latent potential for high-level unity in support of a leader of extraordinary spiritual or religious prestige (cf. Brown and Fernández, this volume, for comments on messianic movements).

TRIBAL WARFARE

Tribal warfare in the Maghreb has been dominated down to the twentieth century by the horse (Bates 1914:144–52; Camps 1980:66–67; Daumas 1968, 1971:24–49). The indigenous populations who opposed or served in the armies of Rome and Carthage were renowned for their ability as cavalry (e.g., Caesar *Bellum Africae*; Livy *History* 29.34.4–7; 35.11.4–13; 45.13.13–14; Silius Italicus *De bello Punico* 1.215–19; 2.56–57; Lucan *Pharsalia* 4.677–883). A series of stelae from Algeria show bearded men on horseback, armed with two or three lances and a small round shield; these are normally interpreted as depictions of native cavalrymen in the immediately pre-Roman phase (*Encyclopédie Berbère* 1: s.v. Abizar). African cavalry were still much respected and feared in the Byzantine period (Corippus *Iohannidos*; Procopius *Wars* 4.11.20, 4.12.3–28). Their light armaments (javelins and other light missiles) and lack of body armor meant that the native cavalry and infantry were unsuited to large-scale pitched battles with heavily armored troops. But as swift-moving raiders, skirmishers, and ambushers they were most effective. This posed initial problems for the Romans, whose favored style of warfare was slow-moving infantry advance followed by pitched battles or sieges (e.g., Sallust *Jugurtha* 89–95). In order to bring the enemy to battle it was frequently necessary for the Romans to march deep into hostile territory and threaten their centers of habitation and production. Although this posed grave logistical problems, not to mention military risks, the conquest of Africa was achieved and defended with extremely small forces, estimated at approximately 30,000 men for the whole region shown on figure 2.3. For most of the time there was a single legion (the elite infantry) of about 5,500 men, with the rest of the force made up of auxiliary units—many of them wholly or in part detachments of cavalry.

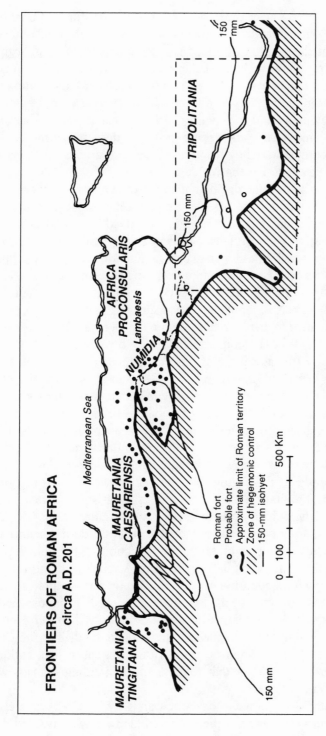

Figure 2.3. Map of the Roman frontier zone in North Africa showing the proposed zones of territorial and hegemonic control and the location of forts in relation to the desert margin (indicated by the 150-mm rainfall isohyet).

Although there is evidence of occasional revolts during the several centuries of Roman rule, these were not on the same scale as resistance to modern colonialism has been, though some commentators caught up in the colonial spirit have wished to believe otherwise (Rachet 1970). A good deal of modern debate has been based on the (mistaken) assumption that Rome was confronted, as modern European states have been, by implacably hostile nomads and mountain guerillas. That resistance has been denigrated by many scholars writing in the modern age of imperialism and subsequently glorified by the anticolonialists (Baradez 1949; Gautier 1952; Leschi 1942; cf. Benabou 1976).

There is an important distinction to be drawn here between long-range nomadism and fixed-base transhumance. Because transhumants follow the same routes year by year and have fixed bases and assets (frequently in the form of permanent centers and agricultural lands), they present greater possibilities for state control than do true nomads. Fixed-base pastoralism was far more common during the Roman period in Africa, with long-range nomadism probably a medieval development. The relative fixity of ancient populations has major implications for the analysis of the interaction between Rome and the peoples of the Maghreb (Louis 1975; Shaw 1981; Trousset 1980a, 1980b; Whittaker 1978).

Yet even with the advantage of modern firepower the garrison maintained by the French in Algeria and Tunisia was over twice the size of the Roman one, and rather shorter lived. The Maghreb is not an easy zone to conquer or to control. The military capabilities of its people are backed up by a difficult environment for outsiders to operate in (Dunn 1977; Horne 1977; Shaw 1987), so we should not underestimate the achievement of the Roman state in expanding into and holding its position for a protracted period in this region. But nor should we necessarily look to purely technical military reasons for Rome's success and eventual failure. Warfare is not the only or even necessarily the dominant form of contact between an expanding state and neighboring tribes. I do not believe that the tribes of late antiquity, who eroded large sections of the Roman provinces before and after their fall to invading Vandals, Byzantines, and Arabs, were much different in terms of military or demographic strength from their predecessors who had earlier vainly tried to oppose Rome's advance. Nor was Rome necessarily weaker militarily than her eventual conquerers; certainly we can rule out the popular myth that the camel was used as a shock weapon on the African frontiers in late antiquity (Mattingly 1983:104–5) or that rootless and marauding nomads were to blame (Trousset 1984a).

The question typically asked about war is "Why does war occur?" Perhaps equally significant is the question, "How is war avoided?" My contention is that the Roman state did attend to that question, and that the relative tranquility of the frontier regions, specifically that of Africa in the first to third centuries A.D., was a result not of chance, but of deliberate strategy. The ultimate failure of the frontiers may have been more the result of a breakdown in the mechanisms by which war was avoided than of declining military standards. It is to a broad view of Roman frontier policy that we now turn.

ROMAN FRONTIERS: FORM VERSUS FUNCTION

There are two divergent approaches to understanding Roman frontiers. Luttwak is well known for his application of modern strategic thinking (and jargon) to their study, and his ideas have invigorated debate among classical scholars. Luttwak's approach is illustrated by the following quotation:

> Innocent of the new science of "systems analysis," the Romans, nevertheless, designed and built large and complex security systems that successfully integrated troop deployments, road networks and signaling links in a coherent whole. In the more abstract spheres of strategy it is evident that, whether by intellect or traditional intuition, the Romans understood all the subtleties of deterrence, and also its limitations. (Luttwak 1976:3)

Mann, on the other hand, is typical of the body of scholars who remain unconvinced by Luttwak's arguments and his "grand strategy" (for example, Isaac 1990):

> Rome had no institute of strategic studies. In military matters as in government, within a broad framework of the simplest form, Rome tended less to act than to wait for things to happen and then react. Frontier development shows this admirably. Each developed as a local response to local circumstances. (Mann 1979:180)

Luttwak identified three main systems adopted by the Romans in the period from Augustus to Diocletian, and some aspects of his thesis have been rightly criticized. But it is undoubtedly true that traditional studies of the Roman army and its frontiers have concentrated overmuch on outward form and that much greater thought needs to be given to functional aspects. Although some of Luttwak's conclusions require modification, there is ample justification for persevering with conceptual approaches and seeking to build on his pioneering attempt (as Jones 1978).

Roman frontiers were not conceived and executed at a stroke, and any attempt to define general policy for broad time periods is problematic. Development and experimentation were continuous processes, but this as much as anything demonstrates a high level of awareness of and concern for tactical and strategic matters. Discussion here will be limited to two of Luttwak's arbitrary phases of frontier policy: first, the situation under Augustus and his immediate successors; and second, the radically changed perspective of the late first and second century A.D. Luttwak characterized the application of the first phase as a "hegemonic empire" and the second as a "territorial empire." Although I agree with much of his argument, I shall propose an alternative view of one vital point.

POWER AND FORCE

Before examining the Roman evidence, it is worth considering the implications of a crucial distinction which Luttwak raises, the difference between power and force. Power can be defined as the ability of states to affect the will and behavior of other states by armed coercion or by the threat of armed coercion. The essential difference between power and force is that power is a "perceived phenomenon," while force is a physical one. The active use of force, in warfare for instance, consumes itself (through casualties and the use of logistical resources). Power, on the other hand, can function without consuming force by eliciting a response to the threat of using force (Luttwak 1976:195–200). Expansionist warfare is a heavy consumer of force, and it is notable that in the Roman world, as in other periods of history, there was a tendency for this form of aggression, if pursued unremittingly for prolonged periods, eventually to incur serious military problems for the state. The emperor Augustus was perhaps the most expansionist of all Romans, yet late in his reign military disasters in Pannonia and Germany abruptly ended this phase of adventurism. The resources of Rome were not limitless, and awareness of the significance of the ageless distinction between power and force evidently played its part in curtailing ambition.

In modern assessments of the success or failure of Roman frontier policy, an incautious bias toward Clausewitzian offensive warfare (see the handy translation, Clausewitz 1968) has led to an undervaluation of defensive strategy and deterrence. What makes Luttwak's analysis so important is the way he illustrates Rome's operation of both expansionist and defensive strategies, balancing the use of power and force in a controlled manner. Different situations demanded different responses, not simply in terms of warfare, but also in the level of suasion or diplomacy attempted or in the spatial deployment of garrisons.

In the first century B.C. and early first century A.D. the limits set by

Rome on her expansion were those of the known world. The boundless empire (*imperium sine fine*) was not simply a dream of certain poets in the age of Augustus, it was a belief shared by their contemporaries in command of the Roman armies. Augustus practiced expansionist warfare in some areas, backed up by deterrent-based diplomacy in others (Luttwak 1976:7–50). There were in fact no formal frontiers at this date; the *termini* and *fines* were temporary halting places en route to world conquest, and these terms also had an even wider application to include the territories of all kingdoms, tribes, and peoples who had submitted to Roman hegemony—irrespective of whether their lands had ever been, or continued to be, occupied by Roman troops. Under this wide hegemonic definition of empire, Augustus could claim suzerainty over Britain, parts of India, and the Garamantes of the Sahara.

There was a clear change in this hegemonic view of the limits of the expanding state during the first and early second century A.D. Strategy became less expansionist and more overtly defensive. Frontiers were delineated and in some cases physical barriers erected. Luttwak characterizes this development as the creation of a territorial empire (1976: 51–126). According to him, the practice of indirect (hegemonic) rule through client kingdoms or client tribes was virtually ended and these territories incorporated into the provincial structure of the empire. Yet the annexation of these client kingdoms was, in territorial terms, one of the most expansionist phases of the Roman Principate. Furthermore, it is apparent that the use of the "friendly king" (or "friendly queen") was neither abandoned nor changed beyond recognition in the second and later centuries A.D. (Braund 1984).

Here then is my principal modification of Luttwak's thesis: the territorial empire differed from the hegemonic one primarily in terms of physical manifestation of boundaries (*termini, limites*), while continuing the earlier tradition of hegemonic control of people living outside those limits (on hegemony, cf. Hassig, this volume). In other words, Rome did not try to bring down the shutters on the "barbarian world" beyond her frontiers. Quite the reverse, in fact. There is good evidence for extensive Roman diplomatic activity beyond her boundaries, frequently spilling over into actual interference in local political or economic arrangements and occasionally into warfare (see, for example, Barrett, Fitzpatrick, and Macinnes 1989). Roman deterrence was used not simply to defend her territorial interests but her wider hegemonic ones as well. It was the continued operation of a hegemonic zone of control beyond the frontiers proper that allowed Rome opportunities for some further territorial expansion.

The reasons territorial expansionism was comparatively slight under the Principate post-Augustus are straightforward. First, the resources of the state were limited and any further conquest needed to offer something worthwhile in return: improved security, economic exploitability, cultural compatibility, and so on. Second, the question of cultural compatibility became ever more important the farther the empire spread away from its Mediterranean heartlands, with their relatively high degree of homogeneity of population, lifestyle, and shared cultural references (Braudel 1973; Davis 1977). As Lattimore (1940) has observed in the case of the Chinese empire, frontiers can be highly mobile up to the point where the expanding state reaches a zone that is totally alien to its culture and lifestyle, at which point the frontier becomes more static and potentially volatile. Dissemination of the dominant state's culture in the frontier zone may be protracted and partial, and its influence may be swamped by cultural importation in reverse. In some cases the cultural balance will favor advance of the frontier, but potentially the peculiar cultural fusion of the frontier region may also lead to the overthrow of the state (Lattimore 1940, 1962; cf. Bartel 1980; Bohannon and Plog 1967). There are certainly parallels here with the situation on the German frontier in the later Roman empire, with the hybrid Romano-German culture of the frontier zone eventually triumphing over the Mediterranean-style *romanitas*. Hegemonic control (or the attempt at it) of people beyond the formal frontiers could serve to narrow the cultural divide between Rome and her neighbors, but the successful conquest of the Mediterranean lands pitted Roman civilization against increasingly less familiar cultures dwelling beyond them, and this posed obstacles to their physical incorporation within the empire (Buck 1985).

A variant view of the effect of cultural contact is given by Kirk (1979: 51–52). He suggests that the impetus for further advance of frontiers frequently comes not from the central organs of the state, but from the commonality of interests developed between garrisons and their immediate neighbors beyond the frontier. Economic and cultural links across the frontier can in time turn hostile people into friends who actively seek state protection and even incorporation into its territory as defense against other tribal groups more distant from the frontier. The picture has relevance to the Roman situation, but the speed of assimilation will have varied according to the initial level of common culture.

The third factor, and by no means the least significant, was the nature of the Roman Principate: a military autocracy born out of bloody civil war between competing generals and several times endangered by contested succession (Millar 1977). Precedents were soon established to limit the opportunities for the personal aggrandizement of the emperor's generals.

Most major wars were conducted by the emperor (*princeps*) himself, or a member of his family or a particularly trusted associate. The actions of generals in command of large armies were circumscribed by the issuing of detailed imperial instructions (*mandata*), by the need to refer many issues back to Rome for a decision, and by the potential consequences of a governor being too independent (Campbell 1984; Isaac 1990; Millar 1982). The result was that the use of force (warfare) was very much at the discretion of the emperor, and was used for expansionist purposes as a means of boosting his prestige (as with the Claudian invasion of Britain). The armies were meanwhile more frequently employed for power-based deterrence and frontier policing.

THE OPERATION AND DEVELOPMENT OF ROMAN STRATEGY

Rome had no "institute of strategic studies," but her military traditions and the existence of shadowy ad hoc "foreign policy committees" (made up mostly of the foremost military figures of the age) to advise the emperors encourage the view that there was a broad strategic intuition which informed frontier policy and provided a lead from the center on many aspects. Rome did not simply wait for things to happen on her frontiers, and it was through the exercise of hegemony and forceful diplomacy that she gathered intelligence and took precautions.

During its evolution from the first century B.C. to the early third century A.D., Roman frontier strategy changed in various respects regarding warfare, diplomacy, and garrison deployment. Although Rome is notorious in history for the number of expansionist wars she fought in "self-defense," it is clear that by no means all such wars were waged for the purpose of territorial gain. The recognition of Rome's long-maintained hegemonic interests permits new interpretation of many attested campaigns outside of areas of direct rule. The nature of revolts against Roman rule varied also, though often they might affect both hegemonic and territorial spheres, and this could condition the severity of the state's reprisals (Dyson 1975). Interestingly enough, lenient treatment of rebels was much more common than their attempted annihilation under Rome, and in many cases implacable enemies were rapidly transformed into allies. Similarly, interference in tribal affairs—both inside and outside formal frontiers—was conditioned by Rome's perception of the receptiveness of the native peoples to either subtle diplomacy or brute force. Rome actively sought to fashion the frontier situations to her advantage: she gave technical and military assistance to favored allies, arbitrated in disputes, provided new rulers on occasion (from a pool of "hostages" sent to Rome for

education), and gave refuge to losers in intratribal coups (e.g., Appian
Proem 7; Suetonius *Augustus* 48; Tacitus *Annals* 2.62–63, 11.16, *Germania* 15). Much attention was focused on fostering good relations with elite
elements in the indigenous societies and in encouraging pro-Roman sentiment at that level in the tribes. We have noted already the case of a
Moorish notable and his son being granted Roman citizenship as a reward
for being loyal friends of Rome. The implications of Roman diplomacy,
then, spread beyond the question of mere suasion or coercion. At its most
developed, it entailed a complete system for the management and organization of subject and client peoples, with a scale of penalties and rewards to encourage compliance.

The military garrison played a wide range of roles in the frontier zone
(Rebuffat 1982). In addition to open war, it was the essential means of
policing the region and of controlling the transborder movement (particularly important in a major transhumance zone such as North Africa;
Trousset 1980a, 1984a, 1984b). In some cases it also seems to have operated as overseer of the linked processes of pacification, land delimitation, urbanization, and self-rule for those tribes considered ready for full
assimilation into the provincial structure.

SOME MODELS OF ROMAN FRONTIER INTERACTION

The following models attempt to illustrate these processes graphically for
the Augustan period (model 1; fig. 2.4) and for a later point in time after the development of a more formal separation between zones of territorial and hegemonic control with the creation of frontiers (model 2;
fig. 2.5). The principal difference between the models in terms of state-
tribe interrelations is one of complexity. The models are designed above
all to illustrate cycles of behavior (warfare, pacification, revolt) both inside
and outside the territory directly controlled by Rome. They also communicate the multidimensional aspect of the interaction in frontier zones and
some of the mechanisms by which Rome sought to avoid warfare and to
promote socioeconomic and political development, with an idealized sequence of events from the viewpoint of the state denoted in the figures
by the use of bold type. The models have been designed specifically with
the African example in mind, but ought to be applicable, with a certain
amount of adaptation, to other frontiers of the Roman world. The place
to start in each diagram is with the box marked "Roman expansionism,"
appearing near the top center in both figures. The incursion of an army
into tribal territory may be met with either resistance or submission: if
the former, then war results. The Roman army in its heyday was very

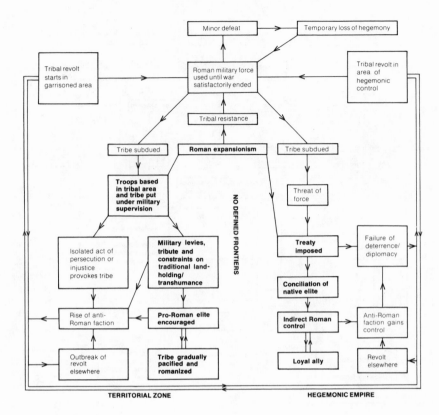

Figure 2.4. Frontier interaction model 1, first century B.C. *and early first century* A.D.

good at winning wars, though it not infrequently lost battles on the way. The assumption here is that the armed struggle between the expanding Roman state and the tribes of North Africa typically ended in victory for the former, though a considerable input of force might be necessary. Once subdued (or once submission was made without a fight), a tribe was either put under military supervision in territory that was garrisoned (encapsulation of the tribe) or subjected to a treaty under the more remote threat of renewed Roman force in the hegemonic zone (model 1; fig. 2.4).

In the early stages of establishing either hegemonic or territorial control, there was a high danger of revolt. Roman policy in garrisoned regions was designed to speed the work of pacification and full assimilation, while also carrying out sensitive tasks such as military recruitment, tax assessment, land delimitation, and so on. Over 55 percent of the Roman army was composed of units drawn from allies and subject peoples, although

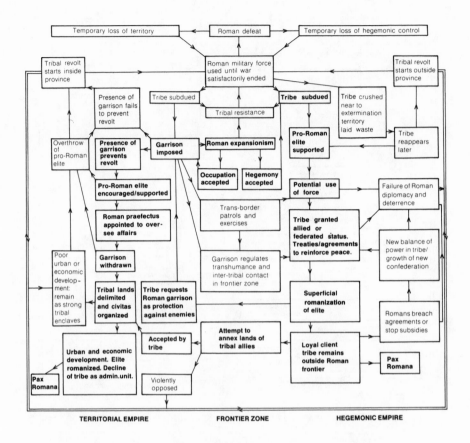

Figure 2.5. Frontier interaction model 2, later first century to early third century A.D.

the ethnic character of such units tended to be lost over time. Large-scale military recruitment of defeated tribesmen for service in other frontier regions had the dual effect of removing potential sources of armed resistance and of educating these people in the workings and opportunities of the Roman world. The "ethnic soldier" thus played a major role in the warfare of the Roman state during its expansionist phases. Military force was not adequate on its own to transform enemies into good subjects. The key factor was the conciliation and active participation of the native elites, but, as model 1 illustrates, with the frontiers totally fluid there was considerable potential for revolts in the hegemonic zone also affecting tribes under direct control, and vice versa.

Model 2 (fig. 2.5) represents not sudden and dramatic policy change, but rather steady accretion onto the practices outlined above. The system became more sophisticated, but its basic principles remained intact. Roman expansionism was rarer, though not unheard of, and the mechanisms for avoiding war more complex and more efficient. To take an idealized view, let us follow the process of pacification of a defeated tribe whose territory was incorporated within the frontiers of the empire (see the left-hand side of fig. 2.5: boxes with bold type, reading from top to bottom). The imposition of a garrison, frequently based at or close to a tribal center, might rapidly spark further resistance. But once accepted, there was ample scope for overt favoritism to be shown toward pro-Roman elements of the tribal elites. Some military commanders seem to have been given the additional title of tribal prefects. The duties of the *praefecti gentis* are somewhat obscure, but we may speculate that they may have extended to supervising the transformation of traditional tribal forms of organization, leadership, and government into "Romanized" self-governing *civitates* with their own urban centers and magistrates. In the best cases, the Roman garrison might be withdrawn within a generation or two, tribal lands delimited and reallocated (with significant increase in the degree of sedentary farming), and towns containing Roman-style amenities and offices created.

There were dangers of the process going awry at various points, but the further the tribe was taken down the road to full integration into the self-governing provincial organization, the weaker the old social structures became and the less the chance of mishap. Roman policy in individual cases had to take account, indeed was constantly reshaped by, the changes induced in those structures, and the length of time involved between encapsulation of tribes and their full assimilation could vary considerably. In the hegemonic sphere, the situation was more complex, because the success of the integration of the tribes within the province, and the relative Romanization of some of those outside it, did allow the frontier to advance over time, bringing fresh tribes into direct contact with the *limes* (frontier zone). Roman control of the tribes beyond the frontier was achieved by active diplomacy (treaties, economic measures, gifts, technical aid, and support for allies and pro-Roman elite groups), deterrence (patrols, military exercises, displays of force), and policing (regulation of cross-border movement for transhumance or seasonal labor, etc.). Adjustments to the frontier line could occur through the voluntary or forced imposition of a garrison on a loyal ally *or* through the subjugation of a tribe rebelling for other reasons against hegemonic control. Such ruptures of the hegemonic network might often occur as the result of Roman negligence or mismanagement, rather than because of wholly external factors. The principle of tribal confederation continued to pose the threat of minor revolts becoming large-scale ones and affecting both intra- and extraprovincial peoples.

In reality, the interaction between state and tribes seems to have been fairly skillfully managed on a divide-and-rule basis. The recognition of tribal *civitates* and the use of treaties was no doubt designed to cut across the traditional segmented structure of tribes below the upper level of confederation (fig. 2.2, levels 2–3), thus undermining the facility for united resistance. Roman treatment of defeated tribes, even rebels, was generally conciliatory, but even on the rare occasions that near extermination was allegedly practiced, the tribal name reemerged later.

Although there is a danger that this type of analysis will produce an overly schematic picture, there is surely utility in such a conceptual approach. It has been observed already that the Maghreb has never been an easy zone to conquer or govern and that the Roman state not only achieved this, but maintained it over several centuries with a small garrison. Compared to some other frontiers of the Roman empire, the African provinces were clearly considered to be under a "low intensity threat" (Luttwak 1976:69), but that does not detract from the achievement of the Roman state in avoiding warfare while exercising power. One reason for the success highlights an important distinction between Rome and many more recent colonial states. The Roman empire was very cosmopolitan, and its expansion was achieved by the progressive integration of conquered peoples, with their elites being able to share to a greater or lesser extent in the wealth, power, and resources of the empire. Roman Africa produced several emperors, but no Indian maharajah could have married into British royalty, and no prominent African could have held the higher state offices of colonial France or Italy. The racially enlightened (though highly elitist) assimilation of indigenous peoples by Rome is a distinctive feature of this particular interaction between an expanding state and tribal peoples. Rome's avoidance or limitation of war in her frontier zones was based on a policy that sought to identify and then satisfy the aspirations of the tribal elites within the framework provided by her own strategic interests. This was pragmatism not altruism, however, and the policy in operation was no doubt frequently exploitative and cynical.

STATE AND TRIBE: SOME APPLICATIONS

The provinces of Roman North Africa are not parts of a natural homogeneous geopolitical zone. Figure 2.3 shows the maximum extent of Roman territorial control circa A.D. 201. The 150-mm rainfall isohyet indicates

the approximate edge of the pre-desert zone and reveals the essential differences between the frontier deployment across the Maghreb (Trousset
1984a, 1986). Africa Proconsularis (including its later subdivisions Numidia and Tripolitania) was the most important military area because of
the legion based there (at Lambaesis from the second century A.D.). The
Tripolitanian frontier was essentially a desert, as were some sectors in
Numidia. But the major troop deployments in Numidia and in the two
Mauretanian provinces lay in better-watered areas confronted by regions
of high plains and fertile mountains (Daniels 1987). At one end of the
spectrum, then, Rome was dealing with Saharan tribes occupying major
oases centers, at the other by populous montagnard communities; but
similarities of organization, warfare, and transhumance patterns will have
lessened the importance to Rome of the geographical disparities (Rebuffat
1979). The techniques of control at both extremes, I would argue, were
similar to those outlined in the previous section. Territorial control was
achieved by a small fixed garrison and a good deal of encouragement of
political and socioeconomic development in the frontier regions. Beyond
the frontier lines (in part demarcated by linear barriers; Baradez 1949;
Trousset 1984b) extended a zone of varying depth within which Rome
sought to exercise hegemonic control. In the remainder of this chapter,
we shall seek some concrete examples to illustrate both the theoretical
framework outlined above and the key questions of this book.

STATE WARFARE AND TRIBAL WARFARE

The Augustan concept of an empire without physical limits and extending
to encompass the lands of allied kings and tribes makes sense of one of
the more extraordinary military escapades of his reign. In 19 B.C. Cornelius Balbus was awarded a triumph (the last person outside the imperial
family to be so honored) for African conquests. Pliny (*Natural History*
5.35–37) gives some details of the campaign(s) and the triumphal pro-
cession. It is clear that a major element had been the penetration of the
desert defenses of the Garamantes, the major tribal grouping of the Libyan
Sahara (fig. 2.1). This was a logistically problematic round trip of approximately 2,000 to 3,000 km, mainly through waterless desert, and the fact
that the exploit was repeated by Roman armies on later occasions illustrates the lengths to which Rome was prepared to go in order to create
and maintain hegemonic control. Several Garamantian centers were captured by Balbus, and the award of a triumph implies major native casualties. But Balbus seems to have campaigned on a broader front than the
Garamantian heartlands alone; some of the place-names recorded by Pliny

related to the Gaetulian Phazani, from the desert and semidesert lands to the northwest, and another group of names can best be reconciled to evidence from Algeria, about 500 km to the west and again in a pre-desert zone (Daniels 1970; Desanges 1957, 1978). It would seem, therefore, that Balbus's brief was to attack desert-dwelling tribes far in advance of the lands physically occupied by Rome at this date, and through violence and intimidation to persuade them to accept Roman hegemony and give up their own hegemonic aspirations.

There was a major tribal revolt across an even bigger zone in the period from about 3 B.C. to A.D. 6, and this may be interpreted as concerted resistance to Roman hegemony (Dio *History* 55.28.1–4; Velleius Paterculus *Compendium of Roman History* 2.16). One result of this war seems to have been the incorporation by A.D. 14 of additional tribal lands into the zone under garrison control, and this in turn led to a further major war in A.D. 17 to 24, a war that seems to have originated as a territorial revolt by the Musulames, whose lands were in the front line of Roman expansionism. The leader of the revolt, Tacfarinas, had been drafted into the Roman army and commanded an auxiliary unit before the condition of his tribe provoked disillusionment with Rome. A substantial confederation of tribes rallied around him and the Musulames, but an attempt to train them in the Roman manner led to a severe defeat in a pitched battle; Tacfarinas thereafter resorted with great success to hit-and-run tactics on a thousand-kilometer front. The length and difficulty of the war illustrate the problems posed by really large-scale tribal confederation around a charismatic leader and the way in which this could rupture the pattern of imperial control, both territorial and hegemonic. The final Roman victory was achieved by a major military and diplomatic offensive (with the offer of an amnesty to those tribes willing to abandon the rebel's cause; Tacitus *Annals* 3.73–74) and the substantial assistance of the client kingdom of Mauretania (Tacitus *Annals* 4.23–25). There was further campaigning at various points later in the first century A.D., but it is notable that these actions tended to involve smaller tribal groupings, perhaps reflecting Roman success at preventing major confederation. The heartlands of the Garamantes were again visited by Roman armies in A.D. 70 and circa 87, in the former case to punish Garamantian intransigence, in the latter perhaps simply to make a show of force and to campaign even further south toward the land of the Ethiopians (Desanges 1978). Through the second and third centuries A.D., Rome maintained her capability for long-range campaigning far in advance of her frontiers for the purpose of intimidation and deterrence, as a well-known inscription from Algeria demonstrates (*CIL* 8.21567, found some 500 km southwest of Lambaesis). At the turn of the second-third century, the emperor Septimius Severus initiated a phase of frontier advance, accompanied by longer-range action to ensure hegemonic suzerainty over more remote tribes (Birley 1988: 146–54). Such campaigning for purposes of hegemonic control was clearly a long-term concern of frontier policy.

The Mauretanian kingdom was formally annexed as two separate provinces following the assassination by Caligula of king Ptolemy in A.D. 39, though the Roman takeover was fiercely contested. After initial victories over the tribes and people of the Mauretanian heartlands (territorial expansionism), the campaigning was extended (hegemonic expansionism) to the remoter tribes of the Atlas Mountains and Moroccan deserts (Dio *History* 59.25.1, 60.9.1–6; Suetonius *Gaius* 35; De la Chapelle 1934; Fishwick 1971). The importance of hegemonic control is perhaps best illustrated by this Mauretanian example, where the necessary land route between the two provinces ran through ungarrisoned mountains (see fig. 2.3; Rebuffat 1971). There were sporadic revolts affecting the Mauretanian provinces thereafter, some internal, some external, some spilling over from one zone into the other. Morocco is a notoriously difficult region to control militarily from its northern plains (Gellner 1973; Hart 1973), but it is easy to be seduced by the few attested incidents of rebellion, and by the graphic accounts of the French and Spanish colonial experience in the Rif and Atlas mountains (Seddon 1973; Woolman 1969), into a false perspective, imagining the garrison living under a near permanent state of siege from implacably hostile tribes (Benabou 1976; Rachet 1970; Shaw 1987). However, there are signs that the situation was deteriorating in the later third century A.D., particularly in mountainous sectors where the policies of urbanization and assimilation had been least successful.

The pattern of warfare described above demonstrates an awareness by the Roman state of several differing strategic options open to it, of which seizure of territory was but one. The establishment and maintenance of military dominance over neighboring tribes was at least as important. Experience was to show that when respect for Rome's power broke down or her efforts to conciliate tribal leadership failed, revolts could be difficult to contain within a single tribal grouping. In the long term, Roman atrocities and massacres were unlikely to eradicate resistance, and Roman skill at warfare was inadequate to the task that near continuous hostilities would have presented. In Africa as elsewhere, Rome succeeded above all by translating her military prowess into power and combining forceful diplomacy with the politics of conciliation.

DIFFERENT TYPES OF CONTACT

Contact with tribes living outside the territorial limits of the province was not always violent or confrontational, though as we have seen Rome was prepared to travel enormous distances to inflict damage on recalcitrant tribes. Nor did the fact of defeat by Rome, and acknowledgment of her suzerainty, always carry the same conditions. Rome did not as a matter of course demand tribute from all her client kings and tribes (Braund 1984). In fact, the decision of whether to levy tribute for a period, continuously, or not at all will have been made with due care, weighing the economic benefits against potential political ones of a reduced level of imposition. In certain cases the tribute flow was reversed, with Rome actually prepared to provide subsidies and technical aid (cf. Shaw 1987:77). The terms of ancient treaties are lost secrets by and large, but we should be aware of the flexibility that Rome allowed herself in dealing with defeated enemies and that the conditions could have been renegotiated or reimposed over time.

Contact was not simply at the state-tribe level, and there were personal rewards and gifts which could be extended to individuals who proved helpful to Rome. We have already noted the case of the Zegrenses tribe in Mauretania, some of whose elite were courted by Rome in a long process of (presumably) gift exchange and mutual support, which culminated in an award of citizenship and a bronze plaque being set up to commemorate the event (Christol 1988; Seston and Euzennat 1971).

Another example involves the Baquates tribe, who feature in an important series of inscriptions from Volubilis, the major southern city in Mauretania Tingitana (*IAM* 2.348–50, 356–61, 384, 402). These inscriptions concern ceremonial altars erected at irregular intervals jointly by the Roman governor and the chief of the Baquates tribe in commemoration of meetings (*colloquia*) held between them and of reconfirmations of the peace treaty which resulted. The traditional interpretation of these events was that peace was being reestablished after revolts, but more recently the consensus has been that, on the contrary, they mark reaffirmations of a long-term treaty between Rome and the tribe (cf. Frezouls 1957, 1980; Rachet 1970; Romanelli 1962; Sigman 1977; Shaw 1987). Inscriptions survive of A.D. 169–75, 173–75, 180, 200, 223–24 or 233–34, 239–41, 241 (x2?), 245, 277, and 280, and there may have been more originally erected. An earlier *princeps* of the Baquates, Aelius Tuccuda, was evidently granted Roman citizenship in the reign of Hadrian and set up a dedication to Hadrian's successor, Antoninus Pius, in A.D. 140 (*IAM* 2.376). Even if the formal and precise *colloquium/ara pacis* ritual was not initiated until the A.D. 170s, what we know of Aelius Tuccuda implies some form of similar contact much earlier. The irregular periodicity of the altars of peace is best explained in terms of the accession of new leaders of the tribe, the *colloquium* with the Roman governor and confirmation of the treaty with Rome being an important initial step following their promotion (Shaw 1987). The A.D. 240s seem to have been a period of dramatic turnover of chieftains, perhaps indicating unrest among the subtribes who made up the Baquates and consequent problems for any candidate to maintain prestige and position. It does not necessarily imply that there was warfare between state and tribe. Indeed, the very intensity of Roman diplomacy at this stage is perhaps indicative of her desire to avoid resorting to force.

Some of the chieftains had clearly been granted Roman citizenship, and we know that the son of one of these men (Aurelius Canartha) died in Rome (*CIL* 6.1800; he was perhaps there as a hostage). Two of the treaties mentioned the Baquates in confederation with other major tribes, once with the Bavares and once with the Macennites. The territory of the Baquates is believed to have lain to the south and southeast of the province in the Middle Atlas, that of the Bavares to the east, and that of the Macennites further to the south. There seems no doubt that hegemonic control over allied tribes was being practiced well in advance of the territorial limits of this province and that the maintenance of the peace treaty was prominently advertised in the town that lay in the front line should a major tribal incursion occur.

Another possible example of this sort of extraterritorial control comes from Tripolitania. After Balbus's raid in 20 B.C., the Garamantes tribe was considered within Rome's hegemonical sphere, though several further military campaigns were necessary to reinforce the lesson that Rome could strike at the Garamantian oases centers if the tribe reneged on agreements. The dramatic sequel to Roman campaigns of A.D. 70 and 87 is apparent in the archaeological record from Fezzan. Although there is no sign of a Roman garrison ever having been installed at Garama, the tribal capital, neither was it left a smoldering ruin. Instead, large and architecturally ornate, part ashlar buildings of classical appearance were erected there in the late first century A.D. "Roman" style monumental tombs were constructed (probably for the Garamantian kings and their families), and many graves were filled with imported goods (wine and oil amphorae, fine pottery and glassware, etc.). Some of these goods may have arrived through trade, others as gifts to members of the Garamantian elite (Daniels 1970).

At some point in the late first century, a certain Julius Maternus

traveled south of Garama on a four-month mission with the Garamantian
king, who was conducting a campaign against some subject Ethiopian
tribes. It is generally assumed that Maternus was a trader, rather than a
soldier, and that this incident illuminates the increased possibilities for
developing trans-Saharan traffic in goods such as slaves, gold, ivory, and
wild beasts (Bovill 1970; Desanges 1978; Di Vita 1982; Law 1967). The
rapid transformation of the state-tribe relationship here from one of open
warfare to that of mutually assisting allies is striking, and the fact that
Rome's relationship with the Garamantes was peaceful for a considerable period thereafter was based, we may suppose, on a favorable treaty
backed up by good intelligence, regular contact, and diplomacy. For their
part, the Garamantes seem to have been left as middlemen on the trans-
Saharan trade route and to have been wooed with technical aid and material goods. The military campaign waged by the Garamantes against
their Ethiopian neighbors may well have been a slaving raid (if slaves were
an important element of trade with the Mediterranean world), and the
parallelism with the rise of the Dahomian state (Law, this volume) is striking in this respect. A cache of day lists and reports from the Roman fort
of Bu Njem, on one of the routes to Fezzan, shows that in the third century A.D. Garamantians moving through the frontier zone were carefully
scrutinized and issued with letters of passage, and on occasion Roman
soldiers may have gone on missions to Garama (Marichal 1979).

Border control and policing were important duties of the garrison of
Roman provinces. Roman frontiers of whatever type (walls, earthworks,
rivers, mountains, deserts, or road and fort networks) were not intended
to be lines of blockade or first defenses against invading forces. Rather
they were filters, designed to facilitate observation and supervision of
movement between the territorial and hegemonic zones. Customs control
of transhumants, migrant seasonal laborers, and traders was probably an
important aspect of their function (Rebuffat 1982; Trousset 1980a, 1984a,
1984b). It should be apparent that such policing, involving a thinly
spread garrison, would have been unworkable if imposed unilaterally on
hostile neighbors. Treaty relations with tribes dwelling beyond were essential to the recognition by those peoples of the existence and meaning
of the frontier.

Within the province itself, the pacification and partial demilitarization
of the frontier zone was pursued in a number of ways. Tribes were in
some cases affiliated to existing towns, as at Gigthis in Tripolitania, where
a tribal notable of the Gaetulian Cinithi was magistrate in the mid-second
century (CIL 8.22729; Christol 1988). In other cases, the role was played
by civilian settlements that grew up around forts (vici) and which occasionally achieved full urban status. At Rapidum in Mauretania Caesarien-

sis, the town was defended by a wall, erected jointly by veterans and native inhabitants (*pagani*), who seem to be identified in another inscription as the *Masat*[. . .]*ori gens* (Desanges 1962:61). Two unusually large and well-planned *vici*, Gemellae and Ad Maiores, in the Numidian predesert sector of the frontier achieved municipal status, their parent forts remaining in occupation long after the towns had been promoted to full urban rank (Mattingly 1986). Although we lack confirmation either way, it is likely that, being located adjacent to major oases, these towns were the result of tribal rather than veteran settlement. In these instances we see the successful integration of tribes into Roman style patterns of urban life and local government.

As already noted, there is evidence that some serving military officers were appointed as tribal prefects during the first century A.D. (Lepelley 1974; Leveau 1973:153). Their activities may have been wide-ranging, from supervising tribal decision making, resolving disputes, promoting Romanization among the elite, recruiting for the auxiliary units of the army, and collecting taxes to judging the right moment for a tribe to be accorded self-governing status. There is also a mass of evidence for the survey and delimitation of tribal lands, starting as early as A.D. 30 and continuing until the early third century at least (Benabou 1976:429–45; Fentress 1979:72–76; Mattingly 1984:177–79; Trousset 1978:159–63). The speed of progress made by some tribes toward full integration is impressive. The Nybgenii tribe, of the oases of the Nefzaoua at the western edge of Tripolitania, was organized as a *civitas* under Trajan and its territory delimited (Trousset 1978). Less than a generation later the chief town, Turris Tamalleni (the oasis of Telmine), was accorded the major honor of municipal status. There is no reason to suspect the presence of colonists here, and the promotion must have been due to the merits of the indigenous population. The impressive level of urbanization and many examples of rural development show the success of Rome's policies for integrating potentially troublesome tribes into the fabric of her empire. On the other hand, the first regions of North Africa to secede from Roman control by renewed resistance were precisely those where urbanization and concomitant development had been weakest.

LEVELS OF PACIFICATION AND ACCULTURATION: THE SURVIVAL OF TRIBES

It should be evident from the foregoing discussion that there were different levels of pacification and acculturation among the various tribes encountered within and beyond Rome's African frontiers. This was inevitable in a system that combined methods of territorial and hegemonic control. It was also a feature of Rome's eclectic attitude to her own culture and to that of potential rivals. The remarkable degree of religious syncretism between Rome and her subjects is but one facet. Roman civilization was in fact forever in the act of remodeling itself as a result of these cultural contacts. Moreover, there was no specific cultural or religious package which the empire wished to enforce on new subjects, and preexisting local traditions tended to remain highly significant. Thus the culture of much of Roman Africa was recognizably Punic or African in origin, with a gloss of *romanitas* particularly in the urban centers (Garnsey 1978; Mattingly 1987a; Millar 1968).

Nonetheless, Rome was interested in achieving a commonality of interests—at least at the elite level—between herself and the people she encountered. One way of eliciting such a response was to persuade the elite groups to identify with aspects of the dominant culture. The award of Roman citizenship carried prestige as well as material advantages in the Roman world. Beyond the frontiers, the judicial perks of being a citizen were less important, but the kudos was recognized and reinforced in the complexities of tribal politics. Similarly, it is unrealistic to argue that merchants or the state would have chosen to transport delicate ceramics and glass from the Mediterranean to the Saharan oases in anything but minute quantities had it not been the case that these goods had considerable status value there. The construction of Roman style buildings at the Garamantian capital is another example of the cultural acquisitiveness of even remote tribes. The superficial "Romanization" of tribes in the hegemonic zone was no doubt reinforced in ceremonial contexts, such as at meetings between Roman officials and tribal leaders, for we must not believe that what lay behind the Volubilis altars was an isolated phenomenon. Byzantine sources describe ritualistic confirmation of Moorish chieftaincy by the state, involving the presentation of "symbols of office according to the ancient custom" (Procopius *Wars* 3.25.3–7, 4.21.2–11). In the hegemonic zone Roman authority was achieved cheaply, but the level of acculturation was low and continued participation by native elites in the maintenance of the status quo did require rewards or periodic and forceful reminders of Roman power. Without deterrence and the bilateral participation of native elites, the frontier was an open door. In Mauretania, hegemonic cooperation seems to have ended by the end of the third century, with dire consequences for Roman control of the province. Elsewhere in Africa the frontiers proved somewhat more resilient, but ultimately no less vulnerable to the loss of hegemonic control and a resurgence of tribalism (Euzennat 1984; Matthews 1976; Mattingly 1983).

Within the province, the process of pacification was enhanced by political and economic changes favoring increased sedentarization and urbanization (Gascou 1972). In the urban context, tribes started to be submerged into the organizational structures of town life. L. Memmius Messius, the Cinithian notable and magistrate at Gigthis in the mid-second century, was proud of his ethnic association, but he also clearly had aspirations as a leading figure in the Romanized town, as Roman citizen, benefactor, magistrate, and priest. More commonly the native elite, once absorbed into the oligarchic networks of Roman government, were happier to forget their tribal ethnicity. The transformation of tribes inside the territorial limits of the empire could in ideal cases be complete, to the point that the tribe ceased to have any real meaning as a unit and the name fell out of use.

Rural development, especially in the form of increased sedentarization, is a notable feature all along the African frontier zone. Older studies attributed this to direct Roman colonization of the land (Baradez 1949), but it is now clear that it was due to indigenous efforts, no doubt encouraged and facilitated by Rome. To take but one well-published example, the pre-desert zone of the Tripolitanian frontier was brought into cultivation on an extraordinary scale during the Roman period, with a Mediterranean range of crops being cultivated by Libyan farmers of the Macae grouping (Barker and Jones 1982, 1984; Brogan and Smith 1985; Jones 1985; Mattingly 1985, 1987b; Veen 1985). Outside influence on this development could have come from the delimitation of lands in favor of the elite (eroding previous patterns of tribal or communal ownership?) and the economic opportunities afforded by the presence of a garrison and by the marketing networks of the Roman empire.

On the other hand, some tribes (especially those in the frontier zones remaining under military supervision) showed an intermediate level of development. Leveau (1984) identifies two distinct countrysides in Africa: one Romanized and dominated by towns and villas, the other comprising tribal "reserves." In the areas where urbanization and economic development had been far less successful, once Rome's power started to wane in the late empire there was a stong revival of tribalism and of an indigenous culture which had never really been submerged. The renascent tribes of the frontier land, nominally committed to its defense, may have shown a preference for alliances with the tribes living beyond the frontiers (Mattingly 1983:100–106, 1987a:88–93).

CONCLUSION

The history of Roman imperialism in North Africa is notable for the economy of force deployed to achieve impressive results in the first three centuries A.D. There were periods of concerted resistance to Roman expansionism, as during the reign of Augustus and his successor Tiberius, but after this initial hostile phase, Roman deterrence operated relatively efficiently for a century or more, preventing large-scale tribal confederation and allowing significant economic development of the provincial territory. The work of development and local administration of the province was carried out by and large by the indigenous population, not by colonists, and this illustrates a key component of Roman imperialism: the integration of local elites into the political and value systems of the empire. Close to the frontiers and in the hegemonically controlled extra-territorial zones, the processes of assimilation were taken less far and less fast. I have outlined a possible framework for analyzing the successful operation of a frontier policy in Roman Africa during the first two centuries A.D. Perhaps by understanding more about its ideal implementation, we shall be able to turn to the vexing questions surrounding its ultimate failure with a clearer perception of what had changed in the relationship between state and tribe.

Chapter 3

Conquest and Resistance

Pre-state and State Expansionism
in Early Sri Lankan History

R. A. L. H. GUNAWARDANA

I N the initial phases of pre-state and state expansionism in Sri Lanka, beginning in about the third century B.C., warfare was an essential element of a process leading to the emergence of the early state (Claessen and Skalnik 1978). In the later phases, however, especially during the ninth and tenth centuries A.D., indigenous warfare was decisively affected by the growth of trade and increasing military contact with the powerful kingdoms that arose in neighboring South India. The history of Sri Lankan warfare from the third century B.C. to the end of the tenth century A.D. has to be traced within the context of a complex process of social change and against the background of the expansion and rise into prominence of Buddhism in the island. The relationships between warfare and ideology and between warfare and ritual are crucial to our understanding of the changes taking place in Sri Lankan society.

The primary focus of this advanced seminar volume is the impact of European colonialism, to which the thirteen centuries of Sri Lankan history covered in this chapter provide an illuminating contrast, calling attention to the commonalities and variations in the general phenomenon of state expansionism. The scope of this history, beginning with pre-state polities (chiefdoms) and ending in an era dominated by South Indian empires, also suggests both continuities and change in the nature of political expansionism. Conquest and tribute seeking did not begin with the state, but preceded and in part gave rise to it. Moreover, the strategies and tactics of conquest and resistance described here in regard to state-to-state conflicts are comparable in many ways to those described later in this volume in regard to state-tribe interactions.

PRE-STATE EXPANSIONISM
AND THE EMERGENCE OF THE STATE

Inscriptions and literary works that reflect conditions in the earliest phase of Sri Lankan history indicate the presence of a large number of pre-state polities which are best described as chiefdoms, scattered over a wide area within the island (Gunawardana 1982). The conflicts among these chiefdoms, which culminated in the emergence of the early state, constitute the earliest phase of recorded warfare in Sri Lanka. Food production in these polities was primarily based on the cultivation of a rice crop irrigated by small-scale reservoirs; these reservoirs were constructed with the communal labor of the village and owned by the village as a whole. Raising of livestock, especially cattle, and swidden farming existed side by side with irrigated agriculture. Some craft specialization was also known, especially in pottery production and metallurgy involving copper and iron.

The physical setting introduced an element of inequality in the access that different polities enjoyed to certain basic resources. The chiefdoms located at Kälani, Yaṭahalena, Ämbul-ambē, and Kirimakulgolla were close to areas where iron-bearing ores like hematite, limonite, and goethite were found close to the surface. Similarly, in the area where the chiefs of Tittavela and Ranagirimaḍa held sway, there were deposits of nodular ironstone or ferricrete very close to the surface (Gunawardana 1982). A few of these polities, namely those at Yaṭahalena, Kirimakulgolla, and Kolladeniya, had access to some of the most important sources of precious stones in the island. Such differences would have stimulated specialization in production and exchange. Long before the emergence of a state that wielded power over a unified island, linkages of marriage and trade had developed between these polities. In fact, trade had linked the island even with other parts of South Asia, and some sailors from Sri Lanka were reaching points as distant as the mouth of the Indus River as early as the fourth century B.C. (McCrindle 1901:20).

Clearly, this was an economy that had the capacity to produce a surplus, part of which was evidently collected as irregular tribute (*bali*) by the chiefs, while another part was channeled through kinship ties to heads of compounds (*gahapati*) and leaders of clans (*parumaka*). Such conditions provided incentives for raids to plunder mobile wealth as well as to displace the better-off communities from their favored ecological niches and from irrigation facilities. Apart from Sri Lankans, armed migrants from South India evidently participated in these raids.

Tribute was another motivation behind military activities leading to struggles for hegemony among the large number of chiefdoms within the island. It was these struggles that set in motion the process of the expansion of power of the chiefdom at Kusalānkanda. The account preserved in the chronicle *Dhātuvaṃsa*, combined with the earliest Brāhmī inscriptions, gives an idea of the initial stages of this process. Originally a junior branch of another chiefly line, the ruling house of Kusalānkanda, which dominated the valley of the river Mundeni Āru with its rich hydrological resources, embarked on a vigorous policy of expansion which continued unabated over three generations. Begun in the time of Goṭhābhaya, it culminated in the unification of most of the island by Duṭṭhagāmaṇī and the shifting of the seat of this lineage to Anurādhapura. For more than a millennium, Anurādhapura would be the foremost center of power in the island.

Though war was the primary mechanism utilized in the expansion of the power of the Kusalānkanda lineage, intrigue and diplomacy were also of crucial importance. The winning over of formidable foes through cunning stratagem (*mantayuddha*), including actual matrimonial alliances or hinting at the possibility of future alliances, was one means used by leaders of expanding polities to prevent formidable combinations of foes, as well as to gain political ends without battle (*Mahāvaṃsa* 25.9, 49). Without allies, an isolated defender frequently had little choice but to accept the hegemony of a powerful invader. If a weak ruler decided to resist, often his only viable option was to use a band of daring fighters to cleverly force their way to the presence of the invading ruler, and try to capture or kill him (*Mahāvaṃsa* 25.58–66).

In some instances in the expansion of the Kusalānkanda polity, the defeated rulers were put to death, but more commonly the strategy of the victor was to transform rivals into clients of subordinate status who paid tribute and provided troops for his army whenever the need arose. The chronicle *Dhātuvaṃsa* (29) would have us believe that all the members of the ruling lineage at Kataragama were killed by Goṭhābhaya, but inscriptions from the area present a different picture. Even if their power had been broken, certain members of this lineage did continue to rule their chiefdom for quite some time (Paranavitana 1970: 42–44). The pace of the evolution of administrative arrangements conducive to centralization was very slow, and, in the absence of such arrangements, the elimination of local rulers was counterproductive. On the other hand, the existence of the tributary option encouraged weaker rulers to submit to, rather than fight, expansionism.[1] Thus, tangible political and economic advantages encouraged rulers of expanding polities to prefer the reduction of vanquished rulers to client status rather than their physical elimination, and imposition of hegemony to total destruction of polities. An expanding hegemonist polity would progressively encounter less resistance, and at the same time acquire new economic and military resources, which it could use for further conquest. Arresting the continued expansion of such a polity would indeed be a formidable task.

Although the extraordinarily violent and extensive military campaigns of Duṭṭhagāmaṇī in the second century B.C. constituted a catalyst of primary significance in the process leading to the formation of the Anurādhapura state, ritualized political aggression also contributed to the expansion of the early Sri Lankan polity, as it did in other parts of South Asia.[2] It is said in the chronicle *Dhātuvaṃsa* that Kākavaṇṇa Tissa of the Kusalānkanda ruling house decided to build a Buddhist monument, a *stūpa* enshrining "the relics of the Buddha," in accordance with the dictates of "a prophecy that had been made by the Buddha himself." What is most noteworthy about this pious venture was that the place where he was "destined" to build that monument according to the prophecy lay at a considerable distance from his polity and within the chiefdom ruled by Siva of the house of Seru. When Tissa arrived at the selected site with the relics—and accompanied by Buddhist monks as well as his troops—the choice before Siva was either to confront him militarily and disrupt what was ostensibly a pious act by a ruler who claimed he was carrying out a prophecy or to follow the more prudent course of acquiescence. Siva chose the latter. In the course of the construction of the monument, not only Siva but also other rulers from nearby polities, like Mahānāga of Lōṇa and Abhaya of Sōma, are found to have been reduced in status to individuals who carry out various orders issued by Tissa (*Dhātuvaṃsa* 70–72; Paranavitana 1959: 150). Here, ritual was utilized by an expanding polity as a means of demonstrating its power and thereby reducing potential rivals to client status without resorting to open warfare.

The *stūpa*-building activities of Kākavaṇṇa Tissa bring out the relationship between religion and political aggrandizement. A militarily powerful ruler utilized ritual to extend his hegemony without actually engaging in battle. Ritualized political aggression was a device that enabled the conversion of power into hegemony, and force displayed in the rituals was not "consumed" during the process. The extension of hegemonic domination in turn helped to enhance the power of the dominant polity.[3] The possibility of utilizing ritualized political aggression as an alternative to the actual application of force was generally limited to situations of struggle for hegemony, as distinct from aggrandizement of the territorial state. However, in the long run, the hegemonic relationship could be the precursor to territorial incorporation.

WARFARE UNDER THE EARLY STATE

The second century B.C. through the last few decades of the third century A.D. in Sri Lanka may be described as the period of the early state. In terms of irrigation technology, it saw the development of reservoirs capable of irrigating areas larger than a single village, canal systems that transcended the boundaries of village settlements, and sluices that enabled stricter control of the outflow of water from irrigation systems. The rulers of Anurādhapura were increasingly involved in this expanded irrigation activity, but some enhanced irrigation works were constructed and owned by powerful local lineages. In the growing trade between Rome and South Asia, Sri Lankan ports that were initially secondary to South Indian ports gradually gained greater prominence (Ptolemaeus 1966:127, 136–37, 148). Increasing commercial relations with the West, as well as within the South Asian region, promoted processes of monetization that were an important feature of this period. Paralleling these changes in the economy was the transformation of levies collected by the rulers from tribute to a tax (*kara*) on productive resources and to tolls (*suṅka*) on commodities.

This period also witnessed the evolution of administrative institutions which gradually supplanted rulers of local polities by taking over such functions as the collection of revenue and the administration of justice. By about the middle of the second century A.D., inscriptions reveal that orders issued at Anurādhapura were being implemented in the far south of the island (Paranavitana 1983:95–96). Thus, the transformation of hegemonic domination it had secured over most parts of the island into territorial incorporation appears to have been an important achievement of the early state.

The emergent Sri Lankan state reflected the changing balance of diverse forces and was a product of the interaction of multiple factors. Expansionism was one aspect or dimension of this complex interaction in an ongoing process that repeatedly redefined the very nature of the state. The early state was continually at war to maintain its hold over its territory, to suppress "rebellions" by local magnates and rival claimants to the throne, and at times to counter armed migrations from South India. In the first century B.C., an uprising in the southeastern parts of the island which remained unsuppressed for about twelve years, and a wave of armed immigrants from South India that led to the loss of the capital for some time, focused attention on the crucial importance of military preparedness. Even after the restitution of the ruling house, political disorder prevailed for a time and rebels remained at large.

In response to these conditions, the state made significant attempts to enhance its military capacity. Anurādhapura was fortified and developed into a circumvallated stronghold which was the most impressive symbol of military power in the island. The office of the commander of troops (*senāpati*) gained importance, and was reserved for the most trusted members of the ruler's kin group. The kings, who faced conditions of intense competition even within the ruling group, tended to avoid the creation of a large standing army of local draftees. In wars against foreign invaders they relied more on a militia mobilized through the mediation of nobles at the court and prominent men in the rural hinterland. Mercenary troops constituted a new element in the army of the early state. Valued later as palace guards and defenders of the city in case of attack, they were for the first time employed in campaigns against local contenders for power. The military arrangements proved to be effective. Only one South Indian invasion is recorded in the first three centuries of the Christian era, and the power of Anurādhapura over the unified island remained firm.

For comparison with other states represented in this volume, it is especially important to note that not all the pre-state peoples within the island of Sri Lanka were totally incorporated within the early state or the states that succeeded it. Several totemistic kin groups, whose subsistence practices varied from hunting and gathering to swidden cultivation, were within the territory claimed by the state, but remained virtually outside its control. Since these groups produced very little or no surplus, their military subjugation would not present a compelling economic attraction. Furthermore, exposure to irrigation agriculture and to the dominant language and religion in the state facilitated the continuous, voluntary assimilation of some of these people, while others apparently became attached to large settlements where there was a demand for their services as hunters. For instance, the hunters who were provided with a special quarter in the suburbs of Anurādhapura, and were expected to supply meat to the city dwellers (*Mahāvaṃsa* 10.95; *Vaṃsatthappakāsinī* 295), were probably drawn from among such groups.

The subsistence technology of hunter-gatherers could be carried over into combat (Ferguson 1990b), and, as such, was of military use to the state. It is very likely that warriors who used the central highlands as a base to conquer Anurādhapura, such as Vaṭṭagāmaṇī in the first century B.C., employed hunter-gatherers in campaigns. In the twelfth century, Parākramabāhu I recruited into his army hunters and other men of the forests who were skilled in following tracks in the mountains and forests even at night. They were also employed in missions to assassinate his enemies (*Cūlavaṃsa* 69.20, 72.208). Even as late as the seventeenth century, men from hunter-gatherer groups were being pressed into military service in the Kandyan army when it marched against the Dutch who had occupied the maritime provinces in the island (Knox 1911:100). Their performance impressed the Dutch, who considered them to be "brave fellows in the hunt and expert bowmen," and who later looked into the possibility of recruiting them into their own armed forces (Van Goens 1932:44). Hunter-gatherers were not always eager to serve the state, and Knox (1911:100) noted that their response to the increased demand for bowmen in the Kandyan army was to retreat deep into the woods and avoid contact with the king's men. Despite this reluctance, the hunter-gatherers did constitute a source of auxiliary bowmen for Sri Lankan states well into the nineteenth century (Sedaraman 1970:144; Pieris 1956:181). This military utilization was part of the process of assimilation of nonstate peoples.

Trade was another factor that facilitated closer contact, if not assimilation. The hunter-gatherers were compelled to seek opportunities to obtain metal arrowheads and cloth in exchange for such forest products as dried meat, honey, wax, and ivory. In the seventeenth century, when some of the trade between Kandy and the ports passed through their forests, they opted for brigandage and thus, for the first time, posed a threat to the state. The Kandyan king initially failed when he sought to protect the trade routes by attempting to relocate the brigands in other forest tracts, but later on, assisted by "the treachery of their own men," he succeeded in having their leaders killed.

It is probably the effects of contact with state society that led to some violent clashes among hunter-gatherers. Knox records that a dispute over territory between two such groups led to a fight with bows and arrows and left "twenty or thirty" dead. With the expansion of the influence of state society, a distinction began to be made between the "tame and settled" groups and the "wild ones" (Knox 1911:98–100). However, as Brow (1978:34) has pointed out with reference to the descendants of these groups, now known as the Väddās (*Skt vyādha*, "hunter"), assimilation was not a simple one-way process, and there have been at least some instances of the assimilation of outsiders into the Väddā group. The survival of the identity and culture of pre-state peoples into modern times is symbolic and reflective of their resistance to total subjugation and assimilation.

That the literati of the Anurādhapura state recognized the distinct status of the hunter-gatherers is evident from their use of the term "Pulinda" to denote all their varied kin groups within the island. Like the Amerindian terms *maku* and *poito* cited by Whitehead (this volume), the term Pulinda used by the Sri Lankan chroniclers was transethnic in its early connotations. It had wide currency in the Sanskrit literature of South Asia, denoting "wild and savage" people of the mountains and forests, or groups of hunters and gatherers occupying the marginal areas on the borders of kingdoms (Thapar 1971:422–24; Apte 1978:1035). In the ideology of the Sri Lankan state as reflected in the chronicles, Pulindas are categorized as a single group descended from a common ancestor, and this categorization is reminiscent of the connotations of the Aztec term "Chichimec" (Hassig, this volume). Unlike the Chichimecs, the Pulindas were not a "border people" in the strict sense of the term: they are presented in the chronicles as a group who occupied the central highlands "with the assent" (*anuññāya*) of the king of Anurādhapura (*Mahāvaṃsa* 7.68), though in fact they were at times mobile and their habitat does not appear to have been limited to the highlands.[4]

The case of the Pulindas provides an example of the creation of a new identity for pre-state peoples as a consequence of contact with a state, an identity that transcends the boundaries of their kin group. It supports Whitehead's hypothesis (this volume) that the process of "tribalization" he noted in relation to colonial contact situations in South America may be also found in precolonial contexts. It is particularly striking that the Pulindas were not considered "barbarians" (*mleccha, milakkha*) in the early Sri Lankan writings, as they are in ancient Indian and even more recent Sri Lankan usage. Although the hunters who served the city were assigned a low rank in the allocation of urban space, "the Pulindas of the highlands" were reputedly descended from the mythical founder of the Sri

Lankan dynasty, and thus they ranked well above the artisans of low caste status (Gunawardana 1979b). It is interesting to note that, in certain writings (*Sumaṅgalavilāsinī* 176), the term "barbarians" denoted "foreigners," including sedentary agricultural peoples with a developed culture such as the Damiḷas of South India, whose states posed a potential threat to the Sri Lankan polity. The term Pulinda and, at least in certain instances, the term "barbarian" seem to denote categories based as much on political as on technocultural criteria.

PROBLEMS OF EXPANSIONISM
IN COMPLEX STATE FORMATIONS

The Sri Lankan state from the end of the third to the middle of the ninth century was a trading state, and conflicting interests in long-distance trade were major factors behind warfare during this period. Diplomatic initiatives of Sri Lankan rulers helped to develop links with Byzantium and the court of the Early Sungs in China, enabling the island to benefit greatly from the revival of trade between the Mediterranean region and Asia in the fourth century. In the context of the growing importance of sea routes in this trade, the island's strategic location in the Indian Ocean proved a decisive advantage. The commercial importance of the island was at its height in the fifth century and in the early part of the sixth century, as noted by Cosmas Indicopleustes (1909:322) and Procopius (1961:193). According to these two writers, it was one of the main bases from which Persian traders operated to acquire Chinese silk for the Mediterranean markets. Persian as well as Ethiopian ships called at its ports, and Sri Lankans dispatched their own ships to commercial centers around the Indian Ocean. This extensive network of trade relationships elevated the ports in the island to centers of trade and transshipment involving such diverse merchandise as precious stones, pearls, aloe, sandalwood, sisam logs, pepper, cloves, musk, androstachya, brassware, horses, elephants, and cloth, including silk. Cosmas described the emporia in the island as "the greatest in those parts." While trade brought prestige goods such as horses, with which rulers could reward prominent supporters, and increased revenues in the form of custom dues, it also brought about the growth of a wealthy and influential group of merchants. The preceding outline draws attention to the fact that the perspectives and interests of rulers of individual states are shaped by a wide system of interactions, and that the modern European world system, whatever its unique qualities, is hardly the first global network. Shifts in ancient global networks were also responsible for changes in political and military patterns.

The growth of commerce in the Indian Ocean, while it linked South Asia with centers of trade as far apart as Byzantium in the west and Nanjing in the east, helped to draw the scattered South Asian centers closer, and added further content to the concept of cultural and geographical unity embodied in the term *Jambudvīpa*. Even if what emerged did not approximate a "world economy" as defined by Braudel (1977:83–84), it may be described as a nascent world economy or a proto-world economy. The unity represented by the proto-world economy of South Asia led to the acceptance of common standards of weights and currency. This proto-world economy differed from the true world economy of the post-eighteenth-century era in respect to centralization. It remained divided into several economic zones, with coexisting, competing centers. Tensions arising out of such conditions of competition, especially within the zones, were reflected in diplomatic efforts, in localized and limited conflicts, and in wars aimed at controlling or manipulating trade. Sri Lanka came to be deeply involved in the competition within the zone encompassing the Maldives and the states across the Palk Straits, located in the area occupied by the modern Indian states of Tamiḷnāḍ, Kerala, and Āndhra. Trade also generated competition within the island. Competition for the control of long-distance trade was to be one of the primary factors behind warfare during this period.

A persistent problem faced by the rulers of Anurādhapura was the threat posed by rebels in the south who sought to win for themselves a share of the long-distance trade. From about the late sixth century on, Persian and Arab traders from the western Indian Ocean increasingly sailed eastward beyond Sri Lanka to trade centers located around the Bay of Bengal, and sometimes as far away as China. These changes in the patterns of navigation in the Indian Ocean meant that the southern ports of Sri Lanka were becoming more attractive to foreign merchants (Gunawardana 1987:76). Compared with the northern ports, the southern ports also allowed easier access to gem-producing areas of the island. Consequently, rebels who succeeded in wresting control over the southern coastal region and resisting the power of Anurādhapura could draw considerable revenues from long-distance trade.

The inability of the Anurādhapura state to control Rohaṇa, the southern region, becomes a prominent feature of the political conditions during this period. For two centuries, Anurādhapura attempted to subjugate Rohaṇa through frequent invasions. It set up garrisons and sought to "protect the ocean" (*Cūlavaṃsa* 41.35), a euphemism that probably denoted naval activities, including patrols to dissuade foreign merchantmen from visiting southern ports. These means were ineffective. Even in the sixth century, Cosmas noted that the island was divided into two kingdoms. At that time the more important emporia were controlled by the northern ruler, but the gem-producing area was within the other kingdom (Cosmas 1909:322). Paradoxically, it was when Anurādhapura was captured by southern rulers like Mahānāga (ca. A.D. 573–75) and Moggallāna III (ca. 618–23) that the whole island was united within a single kingdom. But such unity was only temporary, and conditions had not improved appreciably at the time of the visit of Vajrabodhi in the eighth century. This Buddhist pilgrim found that the gem mines were still within the area under the rule of the southern kingdom (Lévi 1900:419–21).

By the end of the eighth century, it was clear to the rulers of Anurādhapura that it was not feasible to seek a solution to the problem of Rohaṇa by military means alone. Mahinda II (ca. 777–97) invaded Rohaṇa and ravaged the land, but instead of attempting reannexation, he entered into a treaty with the ruler of Rohaṇa. The latter agreed to pay tribute, and both rulers accepted the Gāḷha River as the boundary between the two kingdoms (Cūlavaṃsa 48.131–32). The agreement acknowledged that the southernmost part of the island, which had been territorially incorporated in the period of the early state, could no longer be held by Anurādhapura under that form of domination. The hegemonic form of domination had become more suited to the prevailing political conditions. The treaty brought about a semblance of political unity in the island at a time when Sri Lanka was coming under increasing pressure from the rising power of South Indian kingdoms. In later years, though there were instances when military force was used, as in the reigns of Sena I (ca. 833–53) and Udaya II (ca. 887–98), more typically the rulers of Anurādhapura played off rival claimants to power in Rohaṇa against each other, or used marriage alliances and other diplomatic means to influence the southern kingdom and obtain its cooperation.

The failure of the agriculturally more prosperous and densely populated northern kingdom to retain Rohaṇa within its territory becomes understandable when one notes that Anurādhapura itself was divided by intense struggles between rival claimants to the throne, and between the two leading clans, the Lambakaṇṇas and the Moriyas. These internal divisions kept Anurādhapura from effectively using its demographic advantages in warfare. On the other hand, neither the northern nor the southern kingdom had a clear advantage as regards the technology of warfare. Elephants and horses were available to both kingdoms, and both kingdoms had access to mercenaries. Under such conditions where the foes were more or less equally matched, the selection of the location of the battle was of decisive importance. Usually, it was the rebels rather than the rulers of Anurādhapura who determined the site of battle. Thus, though it was sometimes possible to ravage the land, it was rarely possible to capture a rebel leader alive.

The role that mercenary forces played in the frequent warfare of this period elevated them into positions commanding extensive economic resources and immense influence in the polity. Commanders of South Indian mercenaries were capable of extending patronage to the Buddhist clergy on a lavish scale by constructing mansions for their use, by endowing monasteries with income from irrigation works and villages, and by donating slaves (*Cūlavaṃsa* 46.19–24). Patronage brought returns in terms of influence. On the other hand, the use of mercenaries tended to severely affect the economic resources of contenders for power. Some rulers were reduced to dire straits and could meet the costs of warfare only by confiscating monastic wealth, despoiling Buddhist monuments, and melting down sacred images. If frequency of wars had made the permanent presence of a trained group of men bearing arms necessary, their very presence in turn created a need for warfare which provided occasions for booty capture. Though maintained at a cost that was not easy to bear, the mercenaries were capable of abruptly changing sides and turning against their erstwhile masters. In the reign of Kassapa II (ca. 650–59) they revolted and burned down the palace and the important shrine of the Tooth Relic. When Māna, the heir apparent, attempted to expel the mercenaries, they deposed him and placed a rival on the throne. After the death of Aggabodhi IV (ca. 667–83), Potthakuṭṭha, the commander of mercenary troops, arrested the heir apparent and carried on the administration on behalf of the two nominees he successively placed on the throne (*Cūlavaṃsa* 44.134; 45.11, 19–21; 46.39–46). These incidents demonstrate that a group which had been manipulated by the rulers of Anurādhapura as well as by those who resisted their power had now metamorphosed into a virtually independent political force.

DYNAMICS OF EXPANSIONISM AND RESISTANCE
IN AN AGE OF EMPIRES

The relative success of the early state and its successor in providing security from South Indian intervention perhaps owed as much to the comparatively slower processes of state formation in the southernmost parts of India as to the military capacity of Sri Lankan states. The situation was to change dramatically with the rise to power of the Pallava, Pāṇḍya, and Cōḷa states, which began to compete intensely to increase their own shares of the Indian Ocean trade. Their activities decisively affected warfare and political conditions in the island from about the seventh century onward. Thus the Anurādhapura state, which had been attempting to extend its control over the southern parts of the island, began in turn to feel the effects of other states trying to extend their power at its expense. Invasions dispatched by the South Indian states plundered and devastated cities on the island, probably seeking not only to collect booty but also to disrupt trade and divert foreign merchants to their own ports. In certain later instances, the invaders attempted to annex Sri Lankan territory and gain possession of important centers of trade.

The Sri Lankan rulers now faced a challenge of unprecedented proportions. Their South Indian adversaries controlled extensive military resources: at the height of their power, the Cōḷas were capable of mobilizing thirty-one regiments (Stein 1980:188). The South Indian rulers also had the support of mercantile guilds, who could supply horses and weapons. There appears to have been a close symbiotic relationship between guilds such as the Aiññūruvar and the Cōḷa state. While the guilds' activities facilitated the extension of Cōḷa power, the guilds themselves gained greater prominence in areas that came under Cōḷa control (Abraham 1988:86–87). The mercantile guilds also maintained armed retainers that the rulers could mobilize in times of need and could provide crucial assistance in the transport of forces and equipment over the Palk Straits. A major source of concern for the defenders was the constitution of the Sri Lankan army. Although their mercenary troops were generally effective in local warfare among Sri Lankan adversaries, they proved to be unreliable when the rulers of the island faced South Indian invaders. Thus the chronicles record that the South Indians living in the island crossed over to the side of the Pāṇḍya king when he invaded in the reign of Sena I in the ninth century (*Cūlavaṃsa* 50.14–15).

The Pāṇḍya invasion was a disaster for the Sri Lankan ruler. The chroniclers attribute the defeat of the Sri Lankan forces to disunity among the local military leaders, the skillful leadership of the invading army, and the desertion of the mercenaries (*Cūlavaṃsa* 50.13–19). However, the defeat appears to have directed the attention of the Sri Lankan rulers to a wider range of problems. While they were forcefully made aware of the need to strengthen their military capacity, they also seem to have grasped the vital role that ideology would play in this task. Equally important was the realization that their position could not be defended if they depended solely on their own military resources. Their state had become an element of a larger political system and, consequently, developments in South India would crucially impinge on war and politics in Sri Lanka. After the Pāṇḍya experience, Sri Lankan rulers responded to the new challenges they faced by making a deliberate move to extend the field of their diplomatic and military activities.

After the seventh century Buddhism and Jainism declined in South India, giving way to a resurgent and militant form of Hinduism, while in Sri Lanka Buddhism continued to be the dominant religion. Religion thus came to constitute an important cultural marker that distinguished Sri Lankans from the greater majority of South Indians. In their inscriptions, the Sri Lankan rulers claim that their dynasty was descended from the lineage of the Buddha. They also state that, as prophesied by the Buddha himself, it was the destiny of the island kingdom that every one of its kings would be a Bodhisattva, that is, a person destined to be a Buddha in the future. It was further maintained that kingship in the island was an office bestowed by the *sangha*, the Buddhist clerical community, for the express purpose of defending the Buddhist order. The implication of these assertions—namely, that rulers of the neighboring South Indian states, not being Buddhists, were unsuitable to rule over the island—was clearly specified in some inscriptions (Gunawardana 1979a:172–77).

Another element of the ideology that became dominant during this period was the concept of the Sinhala identity, which emphasized the bonds of common heritage and interests that linked the leading lineages of the island with the ruling dynasty. Initially this ideology was articulated through monuments built by the rulers and through the chronicles and other writings by the literati. It is very likely that it played an important role in mobilizing support for the resistance against expansionist South Indian states. Over time, the long confrontation with foes across the Palk Straits would have a "feedback" effect on the further evolution of ideology, creating a climate conducive to a redefinition and extension of the Sinhala identity to include all subjects of the kingdom (Gunawardana 1979b). In other words, conditions of war and the threat of war contributed toward furthering the processes of ethnogenesis.

Evidence from chronicles and inscriptions testifies to the widening sphere of political activities of the Sri Lankan rulers. It is likely that, even before the time of the Pāṇḍya invasion, they had begun to collect information on South Indian political developments. Their agents were active in South India, and Sena I is said to have directed the assassination of a rival claimant to the throne who was living in South India (*Cūlavaṃsa* 50.4). Similarly, South Indian rulers, too, were gathering intelligence about Sri Lanka. Merchants involved in long-distance trade proved to be a valuable source of political information for rulers on both sides of the Palk Straits (*Cūlavaṃsa* 55.13). The preservation of long-standing friendly relations with the Pallavas and the creation of new allies in South India were important objectives in the diplomatic effort of the Anurādhapura state. Mahinda IV (ca. 954–72) entered into a marriage alliance with the ruling house of Kaliṅga, the kingdom beyond the northern borders of the Cōḷa domain, and there is little doubt that this was designed to secure an advantage against the potential military threat from the Cōḷas (*Cūlavaṃsa* 54.9–10). When a struggle for power broke out in the Pāṇḍya kingdom not long after the Pāṇḍyas had invaded the island, the Anurādhapura ruler Sena II (ca. 853–87) cleverly made use of the situation. Allying himself with the Pallavas, he sent his forces to intervene in the Pāṇḍya struggle. At the battle of Ariśil, he succeeded in defeating the ruler who had earlier invaded Sri Lanka, and placed his own nominee, Varaguṇa II, on the throne.

The accession to power in the Pāṇḍya kingdom of a new ruler who owed his throne to the support of the Pallavas and the Sri Lankans meant that the neighboring South Indian state which had earlier been a powerful enemy of Sri Lanka was now a friendly power. By following a policy of close collaboration with the Pallavas and the Pāṇḍyas, the rulers of Anurādhapura took advantage of the opportunities offered by the struggles for power in the larger political arena of South India. This policy was one of the main factors behind their success in ensuring the security of their kingdom from foreign invasions for almost a century. However, the premises basic to this policy were being undermined with the expansion of the Cōḷa kingdom, which gradually displaced both the Pallavas and the Pāṇḍyas. While the rivalries between the Cōḷas and the large kingdom of the Rāṣṭrakūṭas further north sometimes worked to the advantage of the Sri Lankan rulers in the earlier part of the tenth century, the rise of the Cōḷa state, which was to be more powerful than any of its predecessors in the Tamiḷnāḍ area, was to shift the advantage slowly but decisively against the island kingdom.

Warfare between the Sri Lankan and the South Indian states reveals general patterns common to situations of interaction between states and pre-state polities. Sri Lanka was the weaker entity, facing the formidable South Indian challenge. During the tenth century the Sri Lankan rulers reduced their dependence on mercenaries, gave prominence to military leaders of local origin, and developed their army into an efficient fighting force. Their strategy also relied on preemptive action, designed to involve potential invaders in battles on South Indian soil. Thus Mahinda IV (956–72), who faced the threat of a Cōḷa invasion, helped leaders in territories conquered by the Cōḷas to assert their independence (Sastri 1955:171). When invasions did occur, one preferred option was a preemptive attack on the invader at or near the point of landing, soon after the invading forces had completed their travels by sea. It demanded anticipation and preparedness. During the successive invasions by the Rāṣṭrakūṭa king Krishna III and the Cōḷa king Parāntaka II, Mahinda IV attacked the invaders soon after they landed, without allowing them opportunities to secure their positions or to devastate the land (Cūlavaṃsa 54.14–16; Pūjāvalī 104). Both these invasions were repulsed, and South Indian inscriptions record the death of the Cōḷa general in Sri Lanka (Sastri 1925:367).

Often the only viable option for the Sri Lankan rulers was withdrawal. Threatened by a powerful invader, the Sri Lankan king would avoid open confrontation and withdraw into the forests of the central highlands or to the south, hoping to inveigle the enemy into difficult terrain and to attack the enemy's rear when he finally decided to retreat. Defeated by the invading army of the Cōḷa king Parāntaka I, Udaya IV (ca. 946–54) retreated to Rohaṇa, leaving his capital city open to plunder. When Parāntaka was forced to leave suddenly, probably owing to problems in his kingdom, Udaya seized this opportunity to attack the Cōḷas and win back the booty that had been taken away (Cūlavaṃsa 53.46–47). Withdrawal could also entail grave and debilitating consequences for the defenders. In irrigation societies, one of the most common tactics utilized by invaders was the destruction of reservoirs and canals. When used systematically, such tactics would effectively undermine the economic and demographic bases of the power of a state. According to the Arthaśāstra (377), the aim of the expansionist ruler was to ensure that the enemy's sources of wealth—including irrigation works, mines, roads, and the sources of elephants and timber—were destroyed or rendered unproductive. The resultant impoverishment would make the subjects migrate, thereby undermining the demographic advantages of the rival, or at least alienate the ruler from his subjects. Disruption of the production processes by destroying irrigation reservoirs was also common in South Indian warfare (Sumati 1984:37–39).

In Sri Lanka, the Cūlavaṃsa describes how contenders for power wrought destruction "by breaching reservoirs filled with water and by destroying everywhere all weirs and canals" (Cūlavaṃsa 61.64–65). In the core regions where the economy was heavily dependent on large-scale irrigation works, such destruction would create major setbacks which necessitated many years of reparative work involving massive diversions of labor and other resources. Despite these disadvantages, the strategic retreat, often used by the "rebels" of Rohaṇa in their struggle against the expanding state of Anurādhapura, was now being used by the rulers of Anurādhapura against the South Indian invaders. In fact, this was to be an important tactic of the Sri Lankan rulers of later times when they were confronted with the threat from the technologically superior European invaders.

Mahinda V attempted to use the same tactic when the Cōḷa ruler Rāja-rāja invaded the island in about 992–93. However, if in retreating to Rohaṇa, Mahinda intended to use the area as a base for a successful strug-gle against the invaders, events did not unfold in accordance with his plans. Rājarāja annexed the northern part of the island as a province of the Cōḷa kingdom, and his inscriptions show that his power over the area was very much intact almost twenty years after the invasion (Venkayya 1913:428). In acquiring control over some of the most important north-ern ports in the island, like Mahātittha, Gokaṇṇa, Jambukola-paṭṭana, and Ūrātoṭa, the Cōḷas gained one of their primary objectives for the first time. Mahinda remained confined to Rohaṇa for almost twenty-five years, until he was captured in 1017. Their success enabled the Cōḷas to expand their control over the seaborne trade in the region and to create the conditions for the extension of the activities of the South Indian guilds over a wide area within the island. The far south, which was beyond the grasp of Cōḷa military power, remained a base of resistance from which, more than half a century later, Vijayabāhu I launched his campaigns and reunified the island under Sri Lankan rule.

WARFARE IN PRECOLONIAL SOUTH ASIAN HISTORY

The long history of pre-state and state expansionism examined in this chapter is in essence a study of the role of force in the emergence and expansion of the state, in the resistance to state expansionism, and in the overthrow of the dominion of the state. The diverse factors behind these complex processes involved the interaction of local, regional, and global situations and of actors of different types (e.g., rulers, literati, mercenaries, and merchants) representing varied perspectives.

The objectives of expansionism are often multiple, and the relative importance of the "incentives" vary over time. Disputed succession and factional struggles provided South Indian and Sri Lankan states with op-portunities for intervention in each other's affairs. War was often accom-panied or caused by movements of people to new locations. Scarcity of subsistence resources, created by ecological or demographic constraints, or both (cf. Sartre 1960; Rappaport 1968; Cohen 1985), appears to have been an important factor behind movements of armed migrants and cer-tain instances of warfare in ancient Sri Lanka. The island owes its ethnic plurality and cultural diversity in large measure to immigrations during the period under discussion. The period of Cōḷa occupation marked an important phase in the immigration of settlers from South India. With the development of intensive techniques of food and craft production, the appropriation of the surplus, as tribute or plunder, became an important objective of expansionism. In certain instances, conquest provided opportunities for an expanding state to acquire services of specialists with valued skills and gain access to categories of technology that had reached higher levels of development in the conquered lands. Thus, after their conquest of Sri Lanka, the Cōḷas appear to have attempted to introduce to South India certain devices used in irrigation which they found in the island (Gunawardana 1984). War was usually accompanied by plunder, but overemphasis on plunder as "the first and foremost prospect" motivating the Cōḷa invasions of Sri Lanka (Spencer 1983:23) would shift attention from such important factors as trade which this chapter has sought to highlight.

While trade linked Sri Lanka closely with states around the Palk Straits, it also stimulated competition among them for a greater share in the wider network of trade in the Indian Ocean. These states utilized warfare as a means of controlling trade in the interest of their own local economies in two different ways. First, when directed toward the destruction of facilities like ports and the disruption of trade in the territories of rivals, warfare played the role of undermining existing trade networks and creating new networks that were more favorable to the expansionist state's economy. Second, warfare enabled such a state to incorporate places that had come to occupy strategic points in the trade network in consequence of their favorable location or the presence of highly valued natural products. Thus, warfare appears to have been a crucial mechanism that enabled one local economy to develop at the expense of another (Ritchey 1978:11). Trade, in such contexts, was not exactly an alternative to war, but a factor that led to war. As Ferguson (1990b) has noted, existing trade relationships are often crucial considerations for those initiating aggression.

Generally, trade took place in historical contexts of uneven distribution of power. The organization and terms of trade were, to a considerable extent, reflections of the prevailing balance of power. Hence trade itself created potentialities for conflict and war. The initiative to war could come not only from the dominant power seeking to preserve the status quo and to further strengthen its position, but also from alliances of small states which strive to change the prevailing conditions. Thus the constant struggle among South Indian and Sri Lankan states may be understood as much in terms of an "archaic imperialism" as in terms of a recurrent trend of alliance formation among the weaker powers to preserve and to increase their own shares in the lucrative trade of the Indian Ocean. The employment of military force was only one among several means adopted by these states to achieve their objectives. Ritualization of political aggression made it possible for expanding polities to extend their hegemony without engaging in actual combat, and thereby achieve an "economy of force" (Luttwak 1976:198–99). Among the other means adopted by the rulers of Anurādhapura in the pursuit of their objectives were diplomatic efforts to foster trade relations, the formation of marriage alliances, a resort to intrigue and even the assassination of foes, and the forging of political alliances to maintain a favorable balance of power.

The capacity of the state to apply force depended on its military organization. Conversely, the state's involvement in military activity affected its organization. Pre-state expansionism in Sri Lanka was a prominent factor in the emergence of the early state from the level of the chiefdom. Warfare also wielded a formative influence on certain aspects of urbanization in that defensive needs were given significant emphasis in the layout of cities. As in several other historical contexts (Cohen 1985:286), the development of circumvallation and fortification was the response of the Anurādhapura state to the needs of warfare.

The capacity of early Sri Lankan states to apply force was to a considerable extent dependent on the employment of alien armed men, drawn from distant communities and linked by bonds of personal allegiance to the ruler. The use of such fighting men was a feature common to many early states (Skalnik 1978b). The increasingly prominent role of mercenaries was a characteristic feature of warfare in state societies which distinguished it from warfare in the pre-state polities of Sri Lanka. The mercenary troops of the Sri Lankan states invite comparison with the "ethnic soldiers" described elsewhere in this volume. The mercenaries in Sri Lanka came from ethnic groups distinct from the local population in the militia, but unlike the tribal soldiers encountered by the Europeans, they were being recruited from South Indian states which, during the last three centuries under review, were growing, rather than diminishing, in power in relation to the Sri Lankan state.

Though mercenaries became ubiquitous in warfare, their services contributed to the power of both the Anurādhapura state and its adversaries. During the later state formations, they did represent an emerging "class" of professional warriors. Following Schumpeter's (1951:32–35) theoretical insights, one would expect that the long period of exposure to the threat of expanding South Indian states would create conditions for the further growth of this "class." Though mercenaries did develop into an independent group wielding considerable power, this trend could not continue—primarily because the mercenary force turned out to be an ineffective instrument for countering South Indian invasions. Being probably constrained by ethnic loyalties and religious considerations, the mercenaries were at best reluctant participants in such battles. On the other hand, their increasingly assertive role in local politics evidently made the kings apprehensive of the threat they posed to the prevailing political equilibrium, and they appear to have opted to continue to rely on a militia raised by the leading men of the kingdom and to use the mercenaries more as a countervailing force. The changed status of the mercenaries seriously affected the ability of the state to use them against its opponents.

Ideology was an important factor which could either inhibit or enhance the ability of states to deploy force. Theoretically, the influence of religions that espoused the cause of nonviolence would inhibit the military activities of a state, but the history of Buddhism in Sri Lanka reveals the transformation of a religious ideology within a state struggling for its survival under conditions of frequent warfare. In some Sri Lankan myths the Buddha is cast in a role that does not conform to his ideals of nonviolence. These myths present the message that violence, though generally abhorrent, is permissible in certain special situations, as when the survival of the Buddhist order is threatened (Gunawardana 1978). It is an irony of history that, in the ninth and tenth centuries, the rulers of the island did effectively utilize the Buddhist identity as a means of mobilizing local support for their military struggles against the expanding states of South India. Warfare was also a factor that promoted trends toward ethnogenesis. Thus Sri Lanka provides good examples for the transformation of ideology under the impact of warfare, as well as for the effective utilization of ideology for purposes of military mobilization.

Almost all the factors affecting warfare that have been cited above influenced the choice of tactics by the expanding state and its adversaries. Military expeditions dispatched by an expansionist state could vary from raids bent on plunder or the capture of a leader to invasions seeking systematically to undermine the economic base of the state by destroying its irrigation facilities. The most common responses to aggression were resistance or withdrawal. Problems of logistics that affected the deployment of force by South Indian invaders of Sri Lanka could be used to maximum advantage by the defenders, and preemptive attacks on invaders at the points of landing were generally a successful form of resistance. It is important to note that the significance of withdrawal would vary in accordance with associated conditions. Under hegemonic conditions, withdrawal would amount to a denial of hegemony, but under the territorial state, withdrawal was tantamount to cession of territory. Strategic withdrawal, on the other hand, was often used by the later Sri Lankan rulers in times of South Indian invasions. It was an effective device for conserving force for delayed resistance under more favorable circumstances. Cooperation, the third form of response recognized in this book, was pivotal to the system of hegemonic domination. Ritualized aggression provided an ideal means for a ruler of a weak state to begin cooperating with an expanding state without being subjected to a humiliating defeat. Cooperation between leaders of Rohaṇa and the invading armies of Anurādhapura became possible when the former realized how destructive the campaign could be and the latter grasped that it was not feasible to annex Rohaṇa. Here, too, cooperation led to hegemonic control. Marriage alliances often helped victors to create conditions for future cooperation with defeated rulers.

If the struggle for hegemony characterized pre-state expansionism, the transformation from hegemonic domination to territorial domination was the important achievement of the early state. This is not to suggest, however, that there was a clear transition from the hegemonic state to the territorial state in the manner that Luttwak (1976) proposed in the case of the Roman empire. Though it is analytically useful to distinguish the hegemonic and the territorial as two different forms of domination, most historical states were mixed types that represented a combination of both forms. The hegemonic form of domination, which appeared at an earlier time in history, has proved to be remarkably resilient and adaptable to varied stages of history, and it was revived as an important aspect of Sri Lankan political arrangements not long after the period of the early state. Despite the emphasis on territorial domination under the early state, the Pulindas were never brought under that form of control. The Pulindas and their descendants present a case similar to situations of tribalization under European colonialism but, unlike the tribals in contact with expanding imperial states of modern times, Pulindas were able to survive in contact with the Sri Lankan state for centuries. Their success at preserving their identity perhaps illustrates an important difference between the limited expansionism of ancient states and the pervasive expansionism of European capitalism.[5]

––––––––– *Notes* –––––––––

1. South Asian treatises on politics like the *Arthaśāstra* provide directions for rulers placed in situations of inequality of power. The weak ruler was to accept subordination: paying tribute, ceding his resources if forced to, and even providing hostages, the aim being to await an opportunity when the situation could be reversed (*Arthaśāstra* 298–301).

2. The best-known South Asian archetype of such ritualization is the *aśva-medha*, or horse sacrifice. The *aśvamedha* is mentioned as early as in the *Ṛgveda* (214–19), datable to the late second millennium B.C., and in its elaborate form it appears in later Vedic texts like the *Śatapatha Brāhmaṇa* (274–375) and the *Taittirīya Saṃhitā* (402–83), which may be assigned to the early first millennium B.C. The descriptions of the sacrifice in these texts are rich in multilayered symbolism. An important stage in this ritual, which sought to magically enhance the ruler's field of authority, was the period of about one year when the sacrificial horse was allowed to "roam freely," followed by troops who would ensure that its roamings were not hindered. While it is likely that the choice of the circuit was not left entirely to the whims of the horse, the troops were expected to fight any rival ruler who tried to bar the horse's progress or to capture it. The ritual was a risky undertaking, and rulers were advised that "whosoever performs the sacrifice without possessing power" would be swept away (*Śatapatha Brāhmaṇa* 274–375). The *aśvamedha* provides an illuminating example of ritual being substituted for violent assault. Chiefdoms which acquiesced, by not disrupting the ritual, thereby implicitly accepted the primacy of the polity of the performer of the sacrifice. The *aśvamedha* thus permitted the extension of political hegemony through demonstration of power without involving actual military combat and the destruction of life and property.

3. The "flower wars" of the Aztecs (Hassig, this volume) and the "pounding matches" of the Yanomami (Ferguson, this volume) appear to be devices similar to South Asian forms of ritualized aggression, though the former involved the deliberately controlled, and escalated, application of violence, while the latter was evidently a device for resolving intragroup competition.

4. Anthropological investigations in the early part of this century led to the view that the Väddās, who may be regarded as the descendants of the Pulindas, occupied the "triangular tract lying between the eastern slopes of the central mountain massif and the sea" (Seligmann and Seligmann 1911:vii). More recently, Brow (1978) has shown this view to be inaccurate by drawing attention to the existence of other groups in the Anurādhapura District in the north-central parts of the island.

5. The author wishes to record his gratitude to the participants in this advanced seminar, especially to Brian Ferguson and Neil Whitehead, for their comments.

Chapter 4

Aztec and Spanish Conquest in Mesoamerica

ROSS HASSIG

WARFARE is patterned by the social and political structures through which it is conducted. Although empires have no single structure, throughout history Mesoamerican[1] empires have been dominated by two fundamental structural alternatives: the territorial and the hegemonic (Hassig 1985:85–103; Hassig 1988:11–12, 17–25; Luttwak 1976). The hegemonic system was particularly suited to the Mesoamerican context, where the absence of wheeled vehicles and draft animals made long-distance interaction both costly and time consuming. Nevertheless, both territorial and hegemonic systems existed, producing distinctively different patterns of interaction with surrounding groups. The Aztecs offer a uniquely detailed glimpse into Mesoamerican empire building, and their complex relations with both incorporated and independent groups can be contrasted with those of the Spaniards after the conquest of Mexico.

HEGEMONIC VERSUS TERRITORIAL EMPIRES

In a territorial empire, land is conquered and political control typically is consolidated by replacing local leaders and armies with imperial governors and garrisons. This political restructuring of incorporated areas allows great extraction of tributary goods, but at a high political and administrative cost (particularly in maintaining troops). In a hegemonic system, however, the conquered government is left intact and rule is exercised through the existing system. This approach permits less extraction, but the cost to the conqueror is low because no troops remain in the conquered areas.

Each system has its own benefits and liabilities. A territorial empire ensures compliance through force—physical action—which permits direct political control, but it is spatially limited because the necessary imperial manpower is quickly exhausted. A hegemonic empire relies on power—the perception that it can achieve its ends—which offers only indirect control. The subordinates police themselves, allowing the empire to conserve its own forces and freeing imperial manpower for further expansion, thereby permitting a potentially larger tributary area.

The two systems relate to other groups very differently. Nomadic groups can flee even if conquered and are particularly unsuited to hegemonic systems, which seek control of populations rather than land and thus most easily incorporate state-level groups. Accordingly, geographical contiguity of the empire is not a primary concern. When goods are sought from areas lacking states, hegemonic empires enter into trade relationships or establish colonies.

Territorial empires are primarily concerned with consolidating an area that can be defended and exploited. Since contiguity is a major determinant of area defensibility, the sociopolitical development of the inhabitants has less effect on their likelihood of being conquered. In contrast to the hegemonic system, territorial empires can and do incorporate substate peoples.

Thus, the two types of empires differ radically in the ways they expand, the areas they dominate, and whom they incorporate. Hegemonic systems are potentially much larger, are often discontinuous, and primarily incorporate other states. They tend to deal with nonstate groups only when there are essential resources to be obtained, and then do so largely through colonization. Territorial systems are generally smaller and more compact, expanding into territorially contiguous areas to create a defensible boundary, and doing so without regard to the sociopolitical groups incorporated. Although territorial empires are effective under certain conditions, hegemonic empires emerged as the dominant model for imperial expansion in Mesoamerica.

CONQUEST AND THE AZTEC EMPIRE

Generalizations about relations between Mesoamerican empires and other polities can be formulated only in the broadest terms. Not only are data scarce and scattered, but the ways empires were structured varied as conditions changed. Thus, there is only partial comparability between earlier empires and the historically known and best-documented Aztecs, but the latter case offers some opportunity to assess imperial expansion involving the integrated use of projectile and shock troops. (For a fuller discussion of the mechanics of Aztec warfare, see Hassig 1988.)

Where the Aztecs expanded and whom they conquered were largely determined by practical considerations. Aztec armies moved slowly, averaging approximately 1.5 miles per hour, or 12 miles per day.[2] Because the roads restricted Aztec armies to traveling in double files, a *xiquipilli* (the standard Aztec command of 8,000 men) stretched out for 7.5 miles, increasing the total time en route so much that units marched one day apart so that each could complete its march by nightfall. To reduce the total time spent en route, the Aztecs frequently marched by several alternative routes simultaneously (*Crónica mexicana* 1975:307, 605; Durán 1967(2):319; Hassig 1988:70–71; Torquemada 1975–83(1):259).

Speed was crucial because the Aztecs and their accompanying porters carried enough food for only about eight days, giving the army a combat radius of three days or 36 miles: three days going, one day fighting, one day recuperating, and three days returning.[3] This logistical bottleneck was partially overcome by the practice of demanding food from tributary towns along the way. But food was not always available: the labor demands of the commoner farmer-soldiers during the summer and early autumn and the May-to-September rains (Vivó Escoto 1964:201) resulted in a campaign season that ran from early December to late April.

Marching speed, labor seasonality, and the availability of food largely patterned where and when the Aztecs fought, but *why* they fought is more complex. One reason for their wars was the Aztecs' precarious economic position: as the last major group to enter the populous Valley of Mexico, they settled on a barren island lacking sufficient arable land to support them. Basic subsistence was thus a persistent problem that the Aztecs partially solved through military expansion, tribute exaction, and expropriation of land.

New wealth largely accrued to the king, lessening his dependence on the commoners for either goods or political support. These circumstances provided greater economic stability to the nobility, but not necessarily greater political stability. Much of the empire's internal support grew from its ability to generate increasing amounts of tribute. This required continued imperial expansion, however, which meant the king had to be successful at war. The king's military prowess was not simply a matter of ideology or honor: if a weak leader became king, the perception of power could dissipate, and with it, the hegemonic empire. Failure struck directly at the interests of the nobility, undermining their support for the king and even threatening his physical safety. Consequently, both wealth and self-preservation were incentives for the king to avoid defeat.

In response to these pressures, the Aztecs did not simply expand outward in all directions, but followed a course of lesser (though not always least) resistance. To maintain continual expansion and relatively constant victories, easier targets were selected. Difficult targets that would not simply submit to their demands were dealt with through the famed "flower wars" (xochiyaoyotl).[4]

Flower wars were part of a long-term strategy, beginning with what were essentially demonstrations of military prowess in which equal numbers of soldiers from both sides fought in hand-to-hand combat to display their skills. If this failed to intimidate one side into surrendering, the wars escalated in ferocity, in the number of combatants, and in the use of weapons of indiscriminate destruction such as bows and arrows (Hassig 1988: 162, 171; for a full history of the flower war with Chalco, see Chimalpahin 1965). Even while ongoing, these wars pinned down dangerous enemies while their forces were decimated in these wars of attrition that the numerically superior Aztecs were bound to win, and they allowed Aztec expansion to continue elsewhere. Flower-war opponents were gradually encircled until, cut off from outside support, they were defeated. Not simply an exercise in religious or ritual warfare, flower wars were a logical part of Aztec expansion designed to deal with difficult opponents without endangering too many men or curtailing expansion elsewhere.

EXPANSION AND RESISTANCE

State and imperial expansion generates its own resistance. This is due partly to the spread of military technology associated with expansion, partly to the political stimulus of imperial contact, and, in the case of hegemonic systems, partly to their declining efficiency with distance.

Technology alone does not account for the rise and fall of Mesoamerican empires, but there are convincing patterns of imperial expansion in association with weaponry.[5] The general spread of innovative military technology was from north to south, particularly during the last millennium of Mesoamerican civilization. Some weapons, such as atlatls and spears, had been used for millennia, and some, such as quilted cotton armor, were uniquely Mesoamerican. But other weapons, such as the bow, were introduced relatively late from the desert north, and others, such as the broadsword (*macuahuitl*), were late developments in central Mexico.

The Aztecs' particular weapons complex spread with their empire. Some states probably had many of these weapons before Aztec encroachment, but the distribution of weapons in Mesoamerica indicates that the farther the Aztecs expanded, the less likely it was that the groups encountered possessed the full complement of weapon types. Proven effective, most of these weapons were spread by the Aztecs. Beyond the empire, they were often adopted as a counter to Aztec aggression.

Weapons alone did not guarantee significantly more effective opponents, however. Their importance lay in how they were integrated and used. The hand-to-hand weapons used by elite warriors, for example, required considerable training. But by expanding their educational system to ensure that every youth received training in the use of these weapons, the Aztecs greatly expanded the pool from which specialist warriors could be drawn. They then trained them rigorously, and fielded armies that were unsurpassed—organizationally, if not technologically. Thus, even when Aztec weapons were accepted into contact areas, they could only be absorbed by the local elites and not by untrained commoners who made up the bulk of that society (Acuña 1982–87; Paso y Troncoso 1905–48). So despite the diffusion of sophisticated arms throughout Mesoamerica, their concentration among the few elite in the main towns limited their military impact, although their importance in local control may have been significant.

Resistance aside, Mesoamerican empires created areas of unequal power and influence. Because the military is primarily lodged at the center of a hegemonic empire, power typically declines with distance. This produces a pattern in which competing powers are located at some distance from one another, all intervening contenders having been eliminated. How far away these centers are depends primarily on their military strength, which in turn determines the distance at which they can carry out successful conquests. Geography is also a factor, however, because rugged terrain adds defensive strength. The result is a series of powerful centers whose influence and allies decline with distance before the political

influence of adjacent centers is encountered. Mesoamerica, then, was not
uniformly integrated but varied in a pattern of rising and falling influence
around regional and imperial centers.

IMPERIAL INTEGRATION

Confined entirely within the bounds of Mesoamerica, Aztec expansion
was eased by the broadly shared traditions of the areas into which it
spread. Thus, the changes the Aztecs induced within subordinated groups
were often consistent with existing practices. Nevertheless, there were alterations in a variety of fundamental social patterns, including politics,
economics, religion, ideology, and social structure.

POLITICAL CONSEQUENCES

The political consequences of conquest can vary widely, but a major
determinant of those changes is the nature of the conquering empire.
Territorial empires mark boundaries more precisely than do hegemonic
empires, since the former conquer and control definite geographical areas
whereas the latter concentrate on the control of populations through existing social mechanisms. Territorial empires can easily regulate social,
political, and economic intercourse with other states, but within hegemonic empires local-level relations are concerned with internal activities
only to the extent that they affect imperial purposes.

Especially in the hegemonic case, however, the political sophistication
of the conquered group directly affects the way it is treated by the conqueror. As noted, the Aztecs retained local leaders in power and incorporated their states into an overarching political system, leaving internal
matters in local hands while subjecting external affairs to Aztec control
and manipulation.

In territorial empires, nonstate entities are dismantled and their people
incorporated into the empire. In hegemonic empires, nonstate groups are
not deliberate targets of expansion since they cannot maintain the internal
organizational and control functions of a state and cannot be controlled
in a hegemonic fashion. Nevertheless, such groups are occasionally found
both at the peripheries and between state-level groups, and they usually
meet one of two fates: either they quickly adopt state-level political structures and are assimilated in the same fashion as other tributary states, or
they are politically destroyed, their people dispersing among other, more
developed groups. In either case, the nonstate entities are reorganized in
ways compatible with hegemonic control.

The existing data are too fragmentary to allow us to be certain which, if any, conquered groups were stimulated to state development by the Aztecs. But this process certainly had occurred with earlier hegemonic systems, such as Teotihuacan, which spurred development in both highland and lowland Maya zones, and it is probable that the Aztecs stimulated similar developments. Dispersal of substate peoples is difficult to see archaeologically, but it is well represented in the Aztec case by the Otomies, who were spread throughout central Mexico and typically made up the lower segments of heterogeneous communities. The Otomies also settled on the borders of competing regional powers, such as Tlaxcallan, and were welcomed as buffers against Aztec incursions.

The internal structure of empires also affected their relations with external groups. The expansion of territorial empires, which creates relatively rigid borders, is not dependent on the political sophistication of the outside groups, but, barring hostilities from the outside, these empires have only indirect extraimperial political impact.

Hegemonic empires, however, are primarily concerned with control of peoples rather than territory, although their control is exercised through property. Possession of static goods, such as houses and irrigation works, ties the local populace in place where it can be controlled either directly or through the threat of return of imperial troops. But the Aztecs were also in contact with politically less sophisticated groups, including nomadic hunter-gatherers and horticulturalists (generically called Chichimecs) in the desert to the north. Without conventional armies to engage, large populations to supply foodstuffs en route, or roads to speed the march, these areas were difficult to conquer, and Aztec military expeditions into the north ultimately met with little success (Torquemada 1975–83(1):296, 312). In addition, the lack of a fixed political organization made these nomadic groups ill suited to Aztec control (Goldberg and Finlow 1984:378). Even when groups were not politically incorporated, however, contact often had disruptive consequences (see chapters by Law and Whitehead, this volume).

Because territorial contiguity is not a primary goal in hegemonic systems, other states as well as nonstates can exist in an area well within the greatest expanse of the empire. States may ultimately be conquered and controlled like the rest of the empire, but nonstates will probably be ignored because exploiting them requires direct control and administration—the very costs the hegemonic system is designed to avoid.

Some nonstate groups within central Mexico remained independent but adapted to state contact by exercising centralized control despite the lack of a suitable infrastructure. This phenomenon arose when an area produced little of interest to the state and the group living there lacked a social structure through which it could be controlled, as was the case with the Yopes of southern Guerrero (*Códice Tudela* 1980:74v; Gomez de Orozco 1945:60; Paso y Troncoso 1939–42(2):39; Sahagún 1961:187). Exploitation would have required an enormous Aztec investment in the region, an investment made even greater by the rugged terrain that would slow Aztec advances and work to the advantage of Yope hit-and-run tactics. The lack of material incentives and the presence of terrain that tilted the balance against the Aztecs combined to create a rough military parity between the two groups.

Nevertheless, even without conquest, Aztec pressure sparked political development. Leaders of substate polities typically lacked the ability to act in a decisive and binding way, but the dangers of provoking a hostile Aztec response were so great that Yope leaders were able to control their members through the use of force in a way that was usually alien to non-state societies. General recognition of the consequences for everyone of the actions of a few—however acceptable these may have been traditionally—provided the support the Yope leadership needed to command and carry them out. This statelike political control was not supported by an equally sophisticated internal political structure, but by the external pressure of the Aztec empire.

This development among the Yope did not create a secondary state (Price 1978:166), however, which entails internal infrastructural development capable of sustaining itself. Nor did it result from imitation of a more sophisticated system, as frequently happens with more developed substate groups. Rather, it was a situational response to external pressure that produced political control unsupported by institutional changes. Both leaders and populace were acutely aware of their political situation, and even in the absence of infrastructural support, traditional leaders exercised coercion against their own people, both to accede to imperial pressure and, at other times, to resist it. This pseudostate organization was fleeting, however, and could not be sustained without external pressure. With the Spanish conquest, Aztec pressure ceased and the Yope polity fell apart, devolving into a series of warring villages (Paso y Troncoso 1939–42(2):39).

ECONOMIC CONSEQUENCES

In the hegemonic case, economic interactions between independent states and imperial tributaries often continued, although political relations were severely reduced or severed. In many instances, market exchange between

independent states and imperial tributaries was relatively undisrupted because it was vital to the continued prosperity of the tributary, which was
of major concern to the empire. But in cases of exceptional hostility—
where independent states represented real military threats or were particularly obstinate opponents (*Colección de documentos* 1864–84(4):454;
López de Gómara 1965–66(2):127)—virtual trade embargoes were imposed to weaken their opposition.

The most immediate impact of incorporation, however, was the payment of imperial tribute. This siphoned off local wealth—usually from
the commoners as an additional burden rather than as a portion of the
tribute traditionally paid to their own king. Incorporation into the Aztec
tribute system had other consequences as well: the form of the tribute
was dictated by the Aztecs, and this sometimes stimulated production of
demanded goods and fostered greater regional market exchange. But political incorporation also gave tributaries access to goods available only
through the Aztecs, which often benefited the local elites (*Colección de
documentos* 1864–84(4):454).

Whatever political effects conquest had, economic ties between tributaries and nonimperial groups were not necessarily severed. And, in fact,
the demands of imperial tribute often fostered such links, effectively extending the Aztec economy beyond the empire's political borders.

Sophisticated trade goods reached beyond the empire, bringing dependency, economic ties (however tenuous), and probably cultural disruption (see Ferguson, this volume). Thus, Aztec expansion produced a
core area of exchange within the empire, but material demands extended
farther, producing a politically independent but economically linked
periphery.

RELIGIOUS AND IDEOLOGICAL CONSEQUENCES

Religion and ideology have been suggested as pivotal in Aztec expansion
(Conrad and Demarest 1984), but a distinction must be drawn between
religious and other ideological motivations, and between religion as a factor in imperial expansion and its use in imperial integration. Religious
orthodoxy in Tenochtitlan solidly supported the state and its imperial
aspirations, probably because the state was so successful and the various
cults and temples benefited economically (Chimalpahin 1965:192; *Códice Ramírez* 1975:51–52; Durán 1967(2):82–83). But the timing of ostensibly religious events that led to war strongly indicates that wars were
not primarily religiously motivated. Instead, religious mandates were manipulated by the state. Captives were indeed needed for religious festivals,

but their numbers turned on political considerations, with celebrations being emphasized or deemphasized accordingly. And religious events such as temple dedications were initiated when the king wanted to go to war, rather than the reverse.[6]

A case for religious motivation might also be made if the worship of victorious Aztec gods were spread through war. The likeliest supernatural beneficiary—and the only significant god that can be considered primarily or exclusively Aztec—was Huitzilopochtli, so spread of this god would point fairly conclusively to the spread of Aztec practices. However, worship of Huitzilopochtli was rare beyond the Valley of Mexico and, in the few places it is found, it is associated with Aztec rather than indigenous populations (Acuña 1982–87(6):76, 85, 144, 163, 173; (7):175, 233, 242; García Icazbalceta 1891:8; Paso y Troncoso 1905–48(6):8, 27).

Moreover, it is highly unlikely that the elite beliefs recorded in codices, art, and chronicles were shared uncritically by all classes and groups. Aztec commoners participated in the benefits of war and may have also shared the religious or ideological motivations of their leaders. But the likelihood of such unanimity between both commoner and elite soldiers elsewhere in the empire declines dramatically, since the Aztecs bestowed benefits disproportionately on the allied elites. Allied commoners did not benefit from the conquests the way their Aztec counterparts did, and widespread desertions among allied forces (Durán 1967(2):319–20) do not suggest strong religious motivations. What did motivate the Aztec armies was the taking of captives that led to social advancement (Clark 1938(1):93; Durán 1967(1):67; Sahagún 1954:76–77, 87). Social mobility through military success played a powerful ideological role: commoners could be elevated to the status of nobles, and hereditary nobles could achieve political advancement.

In sum, the Aztec empire expanded within an area that already shared basic religious beliefs, and there is little evidence of the spread of any specifically Aztec religious complex. Serving as a pretext for expansion rather than a rationale, religion did not spread with the empire. To the extent that Aztec expansion was motivated by ideology, the desire for social mobility was paramount.

Despite the lack of messianic expansion, Mesoamerican religion did have an impact beyond the empire—not among other states, since they already shared this tradition, but among nonstate groups. Borne by political, economic, and social contacts, Mesoamerican religion provided a basis for common understanding with non-Mesoamerican groups, such as those in the desert north, and was probably supported by material exchange. Adoption of Mesoamerican religious elements offered these nonstate groups such advantages as a more sophisticated calendar system, mathematics, writing, and new social ideologies that lay the groundwork for a progressive incorporation into the Mesoamerican system. And this religious influence ultimately repatterned these societies in ways more compatible with those of Mesoamerica, making them both more desirable and more feasible objects of imperial expansion. Although not part of a deliberate policy, in a hegemonic system conquest follows culture.

SOCIAL CONSEQUENCES

It is easier to explain Aztec expansion than to explain how their empire was integrated and maintained without institutional restructuring. One suggested mechanism for performing this integrative role is kinship (Smith 1986), specifically elite marriages that allied city-states.

The best-documented marital ties between rulers in Mesoamerica are in and around the Valley of Mexico. Dominant kings often gave daughters in marriage to dependent kings to reinforce alliances and establish relative political status. The practice of noble polygyny meant that a king could take numerous wives, thus cementing political ties with various rulers and producing even more numerous children with which further ties could be created. The king's successor was typically his son by his wife who was the daughter of the king's most important political ally (Carrasco 1984: 44, 48, 54–55). But who that successor would ultimately be shifted with the relative fortunes of the city-state and its allies, and an heir apparent whose mother came from the dominant city at the time of her marriage could be replaced by another son with maternal ties to a city that was more important at the time of the king's death. Multiple marital ties, then, provided political flexibility in the selection of an eventual successor.

Elite marital ties were an ancient and widespread phenomenon in Mesoamerica (e.g., Flannery 1983:290; Flannery and Marcus 1983a: 183; Flannery and Marcus 1983b:277; Grove 1987:436, 440; Marcus 1976:19, 39; Marcus 1983a:139, 143; Marcus 1983b:191; Marcus 1983c: 316; Marcus and Flannery 1983:220–22; Morley, Brainerd, and Sharer 1983:92, 101, 116, 136, 170–71, 224; Paddock 1966:201–2; Spores 1974, 1983:259; Spores and Flannery 1983:349). But the well-documented examples of marital alliances are predominantly local, where they could be augmented with other social, economic, and political ties, so it is unclear what part they played in integrating larger polities such as empires.

Empires encompass peoples without direct kin ties, so such relations must be created if they are to play a role in integrating the political system.

This is most readily accomplished through marital ties. But two factors affect the ability of marriages to unite an empire. First, the consequences of marital ties vary by the disparity in power between the two sides and by the proximity of the two cities, since power effectively declines with distance in a hegemonic system. Second, marital ties require time to consolidate. The political nexus of marital ties is not the relationship between the bride and groom, but between the dominant king and the offspring of the marriage who will eventually succeed to power. Thus, marriages produce eventual rather than immediate links between powers and, given the time lag involved in placing an heir on the throne, other integrative mechanisms are more significant, at least initially.

In Mesoamerica, local marital ties accommodated the constant shifts in relative power and status since these changes were relatively slow. But at the imperial level, the shift was often a radical departure involving a major reorientation to a new power, frequently entailing a sharp break with traditional allies.

Paradoxically, this new alliance, with the prospect of a new heir apparent, weakened the now-dependent local kings. Although local rulers typically remained in power after being conquered by the Aztecs, this did not mean the simple addition of a superior level to the existing local political hierarchy. The domestic political positions of conquered kings were often undermined by having been conquered, not simply because they were shown to be vincible, but because the entire political context of their rise—who supported them and who did not—changed.

Royal succession was predicated on the city's particular configuration of allies and enemies. But imperial conquest changed this, as old allies often found themselves outside the empire and now regarded as enemies. The alliances that had supported the reigning king were undermined, and existing political ties were disrupted, which weakened conquered kings even though the internal political structure of their towns remained intact. To the extent that they were dependent on other regional powers, the traditional power bases of conquered kings were weakened.

The Aztec empire appeared relatively nonintrusive because existing rulers retained their offices, but, in reality, Aztec expansion disrupted local political relations that determined who those officeholders should be. This altered the political support of both the local king and the other pretenders to the throne, often strengthening the latter at the former's expense. Conquest was, in effect, a radical acceleration of ordinary local power shifts that would change the probability of one son succeeding to the throne over his half brothers. The emergence of a pretender who now had more support than the reigning king led to local political instability.

Thus, while most local kings continued in power, many did so not by virtue of right—divine or otherwise—but by virtue of Aztec support, which was essential to their survival given the emergence of an altered configuration of internal competitors.

These local political upheavals often led to additional warfare as new coalitions of city-states formed in support of one side or the other. The Aztecs tolerated some internal wars while suppressing others, most likely reflecting the fortunes of the ruler or faction they supported.[7] Thus, rather than leading to a Pax Azteca, subjugation by the Aztecs increased conflict through both further imperial wars and increased internecine warfare.

The limits of Aztec expansion not only defined who was a tributary, but also typically undermined the political importance of the tributaries' marital alliances with polities outside the empire. No matter how significant these ties had been previously, they were now not only unimportant, but could be liabilities to some factions. The effects on the independent elites were the mirror image of those within the incorporated states: being cut off from part of their earlier political universe was even more disruptive of internal politics than it was for the incorporated tributaries.

Since royal marriages affected political relations, successor kings were selected at least partly because of their ties to major allies. If some of those allies were now conquered, the support for many of the royal contenders would significantly alter, and this was as true of the reigning king as of other pretenders. The loss of support from minor allies had little impact, but, in some cases, the loss to current rulers and to heirs apparent could be pivotal, leading to their overthrow or replacement, respectively. Thus, the shift in social ties within imperial tributaries had potentially devastating effects for independent polities beyond the borders.

Within the empire, the Aztecs compensated for local shifts in power by buttressing now-compliant local rulers. But no such support was available beyond the empire, and political disruption could continue for some time. The result was ultimately greater stability in the independent areas than among the imperial tributaries since, after the dust settled, the successful rulers would owe their positions to the combined support of their allies, many of them new. But it took time—often an entire generation—before an heir with kin ties to some new dominant partner could succeed to the throne. Meanwhile, the disruption of elite marital ties was enormously destabilizing, making the independent zones bordering the empire easily susceptible to continued imperial expansion. Whether or not war had existed previously between groups that found themselves on opposite sites of imperial borders, it now arose or continued as political coalitions altered radically.

THE SPANISH CONQUEST

Considering their success in dominating central Mexico, why did the Aztecs fall so quickly to the Spaniards? Spanish technology and military practices gave the conquistadors some tactical advantages, but not decisive superiority. And, in any case, the Aztecs were quick to adapt to Spanish tactics (e.g., Sahagún 1975:62); for instance, shifting battles from open ground to broken terrain to minimize the effectiveness of Spanish horses (Cortés 1971:178; Díaz del Castillo 1908–16(2):272; (4):19, 35, 75). But the Spaniards still maintained an advantage that rested on two factors.

The first factor was the ability to attract numerous Indian allies. The conquest of Tenochtitlan was carried out with the help of tens of thousands of Indian warriors, drawn from among many traditional Aztec enemies, such as the Tlaxcaltecs, and numerous tributary towns that defected as Aztec power eroded under the onslaught. Widely regarded as a Spanish triumph, the opportunity to create these new alliances actually appears to have been seized by the Indians, who could have defeated the Spaniards but did not because the latter were seen as potential allies against the Aztecs.

The second factor was the Spanish disruption of many traditional Mesoamerican patterns of warfare and alliance. As outsiders, some factors contributing to Aztec imperial stability, such as the perception of Aztec power, had no effect on the Spaniards. And since they were bent on appropriating gold and booty rather than controlling a functioning economy, the Spaniards fought without regard for seasonality and agricultural manpower demands, wreaking economic as well as military havoc.

At the same time, other events undermined the Aztecs. The death within 80 days of King Moteuczomah Xocoyotl and his successor, Cuitlahuah, left the empire without a leader able to consolidate control over its tributaries, particularly in the face of Spanish support for rebellious cities in the east. The Spanish ability to unite disaffected groups against the Aztecs during this time of weakness, and through precisely the same types of political alliance, proved decisive. Spanish technology did contribute to the Conquest—ships built and launched in the Valley of Mexico allowed the Spaniards to cut off canoe-borne supplies for the capital, and mobile horsemen interdicted Aztec reinforcements—but merely hastened the inevitable. In the final analysis, the Aztec empire fell because the Spaniards undermined the hegemonic organization upon which it rested.

SPANISH INCORPORATION OF INDIGENOUS GROUPS WITHIN MESOAMERICA

The fall of Tenochtitlan marked the end of major organized Indian resistance to the Spaniards. Over the next three to four years, the Spaniards pacified central Mexico and much of the Maya region, but they, in turn, faced many of the same problems experienced by the Aztecs in their imperial rule.

Although the Spaniards shared similar concerns with the Aztecs in the way they structured their empire, the ways in which they exercised this control were very different. The Spaniards did not operate through regional and local power structures, as had the Aztecs. Instead, political integration under the Spaniards was greater than it had been under the Aztecs (Gerhard 1972:64–69; Haring 1947:75–88, 119–78; Hassig 1985:262–67). Although native armies were disbanded, the Spaniards continued to rely on Indian auxiliaries, especially for expansion. But Spanish control of firearms, steel weapons, and the technology of their production tipped the power balance even further against the local communities than had been the case with the Aztecs. Maintaining significant local military strength was crucial in the Aztec system, but the Spaniards were spread throughout New Spain—albeit concentrated largely in cities, which facilitated greater control—and their rule was buttressed by horses, mules, and wagons that effectively shrank the region and permitted quicker military response from the center.

Although their nature and recruitment changed over time (Lockhart and Schwartz 1983:114–15), local rulers were retained not simply as a political expedient but to ease Spanish extraction of Indian goods and services, a process in which local rulers served as middlemen. Native goods were important, particularly for local sustenance, but the Spaniards were more concerned with Indian labor that they could turn to their own ends, such as the production of wheat or sugarcane or the construction of houses, mills, and irrigation works. This direct economic control yielded a greater return than the Aztec system, speeding the transfer of wealth from local producers to their political masters. And while the Conquest did create new economic opportunities and open existing ones to new participants—notably in the area of trade (Hassig 1985:240–41)—it relegated the Indians to the lower rung of an emerging two-tiered economy in which the Spaniards exercised national control.

In contrast to the Aztec case, religion played a crucial role in the creation and maintenance of this new political economy. Regular (religious

order) and secular (parish) priests penetrated native society to the local
level, where they exercised great political and economic, as well as religious, control (Gerhard 1972:66–69; Lockhart and Schwartz 1983:
108). Often, this was hastened through the religious conversion of the
indigenous elites, wedding sacred and secular control and linking it to the
national level (Haring 1947:203).

Spanish-Indian intermarriage occurred from the earliest days of the
Conquest, typically between Spanish men and Indian women, given the
extreme shortage of Spanish women in the New World. But this did not
perpetuate the importance of marital ties that had existed under the Aztecs. Although crucial for inheritance, the political importance of marital
ties declined drastically with the abolition of native imperial and regional
polities. Local rather than regional political support now determined local
politics, and the loss of these important political ties to other native rulers
was not offset by marriages to the Spaniards. However significant they
may have been on an individual and personal basis, marriages (and con-
cubinage) between women of native elite families and Spanish men were
simply that—and not significant political alliances. The Spaniards drew
very little on indigenous support for their political positions, and marital
ties to the Indians were correspondingly unimportant. Marital ties did
continue to be important among Indians locally, but their national and
regional significance atrophied.

The Spanish system differed from the Aztec in the depth of political,
economic, and religious control; in the modification of local economies to
suit Spanish ends; and in the dissolution of marital ties as politically significant variables. Within Mesoamerica proper, the Spaniards exercised
control by adopting existing polities as economic, political, and religious
units and often coopting native officials in their control and exploitation.
Although the Aztecs had also used existing systems, Spanish control differed in both nature and extent. Spanish extraction was much heavier:
land was taken and, though tribute was perhaps nominally no heavier,
the massive depopulation that followed the Conquest placed increasingly
heavy burdens on the survivors. Moreover, tribute was owed to local
Spaniards, to the king, and to the church, and the extraction occurred at
the local level. This pitted individual Indians against powerful Spaniards
and institutions: native rulers were greatly diminished, and local leaders
became little more than middlemen. In short, Spanish control within
Mesoamerica was much more direct. It extended to the lower levels of native communities, molding local institutions and directing their activities
in the Spanish interest, whereas Aztec rule had tapped local polities

only at the highest levels and played little or no local role beyond exaction of tribute. Beyond Mesoamerica, however, Spanish tactics changed considerably.

INCORPORATION OF INDIGENOUS GROUPS
BEYOND MESOAMERICA

With the discovery of silver in the desert north, the Spaniards expanded into unsettled lands peopled by hostile Chichimecs well beyond the confines of the Aztec empire (Naylor and Polzar 1986:34; Powell 1952:4–7). In contrast to their approach to central Mexico, the Spaniards saw the wealth to the north lying in valuable goods—in this case, silver—rather than in labor. But controlling the indigenous nomadic and seminomadic peoples was almost as far beyond Spanish capabilities as it had been for the Aztecs, since there was no native regional organization and few strong local officials (Naylor and Polzar 1986:34). Their push into the desert north therefore was aimed at displacing or eliminating native populations rather than exploiting them directly (Naylor and Polzar 1986:25; Spicer 1962:287). Spanish technology made this feasible, tying newly established mining outposts (Powell 1952:18–19) to New Spain's core area by wagon trains protected by mounted troops armed with European weaponry and Indian auxiliaries (Naylor and Polzar 1986:25).

The economic links to the rest of New Spain were fundamentally Spanish (Naylor and Polzar 1986:25). The Spanish economy gradually expanded to service the needs of mining communities and presidios and, although the indigenous population was much smaller than in central Mexico, some Indians were drawn into the system—largely as peasants and other dependent laborers—while others were pushed out.

Spanish control of Indian groups in the north was markedly less pervasive and successful than in central Mexico (Haring 1947:197). In the north, religion played a more prominent role (Haring 1947:196–97; Naylor and Polzar 1986:39), with priests establishing missions where Indians were congregated through a combination of inducements and coercion (Spicer 1962:287–92). Whatever the religious outcomes of these missionary efforts, their political and economic success was enormous; dispersed Indians were concentrated into more easily controlled groups and converted to enterprises more compatible with the growing colonial economy. Yet, for all that, the north emerged with an even more sharply divided political economy: largely Spanish towns and mines on the one hand, and local Indian communities on the other.

With little contact between Spanish settlements and Indians—and none at an elite level—the intermarriages that occurred (Spicer 1962: 301–2) had little or no political significance. Due to the absence of any indigenous regional organization, marital ties had never been important in the area, and with the Spaniards displacing rather than coopting the Indians, none developed.

COMPARISONS

The Aztec empire was restricted to Mesoamerica, where its expansion was built on common social, political, economic, and ideological perspectives, and it was based on the domination of existing social systems, extracting relatively modest levels of goods and services through established leaders. At the individual level, economic burdens increased for tributaries, but life was otherwise little changed. Most social practices and institutions remained undisturbed, with local rulers remaining in office, and much of the empire's strength was drawn from these tributaries who were important auxiliaries in Aztec expansion.

The Spanish system, however, differed significantly. Although the Spanish conquest owed much to the successful building of alliances on the Aztec model, this was largely true because the Indians, not the Spaniards, dictated their nature. Native allies based their participation on the political organization they knew and perceived the Spaniards in that light, as the nucleus of a competing hegemonic polity in opposition to the Aztecs. Despite their vastly different notions of political organization, the Spaniards did not, and could not, organize on a territorial basis during the Conquest itself. However, the Spaniards filled the political vacuum left by the Aztec defeat and, in very few years, converted their control to a territorially based system. In so doing, they removed or effectively limited native rulers to local matters, concentrating power at a national level and shifting it into Spanish hands.

Instead of drawing on native populations for their strength, as had the Aztecs, the Spaniards saw the Indians as threats or impediments. And, indeed, this was the case given the level of control and extraction the Spaniards sought. It is doubtful that the extent of exploitation exercised by the Spaniards could have been sustained under the Aztec system. A hegemonic system leaves too much power in local hands, so the Spaniards destroyed this and implemented a territorial system that largely freed them from such constraints.

Concerned with the control of lands and resources as well as labor, the Spaniards quickly spread beyond the confines of the Aztec empire into areas occupied by nonstate groups. Here, the Spaniards were little more successful in establishing control of these groups than were the Aztecs. But the Spaniards based their interests on the direct control of land and resources rather than tribute from the occupants.

Spanish expansion into the north was not territorial in the ideal sense: the conquistadors did not conquer all internal groups and erect fortifications to guard a frontier and control the interior. Clearly established boundaries were neither created nor maintained. Because they faced neither significant political competitors nor sufficiently serious threats to the security of their heartland, fortifications of their borders were an unnecessary expense. Instead, the Spaniards adopted a policy of colonizing hostile territory—a shift in tactics, though not of the fundamental territorial approach. Instead of conquering and/or excluding hostile populations, which was probably beyond their immediate capability, the Spaniards colonized important resource areas, fortified them, and gradually pacified the surrounding areas as their armed presence disrupted the movements of hostile groups until they left the area or were subdued. Despite bearing superficial similarities to the Aztec system, the Spanish imperial system disrupted indigenous systems and extracted from them, rather than building on them. As a result, its expansion was not limited to the culturally defined area of Mesoamerica that was necessary to sustain the Aztec empire.

——— *Notes* ———

1. Mesoamerica, defined prehispanically by the presence of state-level societies, includes Mexico south of the desert regions, Belize, Guatemala, and portions of El Salvador and Honduras.

2. Based on comparisons with United States Army march characteristics (U.S. Army 1971a:11, 16; U.S. Army 1971b:C-2) and those of preindustrial armies (Clausewitz 1943:275–77; Engels 1978:20; Maurice 1930:212; Neumann 1971).

3. Porters, called *tlamemes*, carried average loads of two *arrobas* (23 kg or 50 lb.) each. Calculated for one porter to every two warriors at 3,800 calories per day (*Boletín* 1940(11):16; Borah and Cook 1963:90; Cuevas 1975:52–53; Archivo General de la Nación, Reales Cédulas Duplicadas 3-17-9), or .95 kilograms (2.1 lb.) in maize, based on Benedict and Steggerda (1937:182).

4. The flower wars are typically described as ritual combat in which the goal is to take captives for sacrifice. This doubtless occurred, and, when flower-war battles are viewed as isolated events, little more of their purpose can be deduced. But this explanation is miscast. For more traditional interpretations, see Bray (1968:186), Brundage (1972:100), Canseco Vincourt (1966:101), Davies (1974: 96, 229), Hicks (1979:88), Isaac (1983), Katz (1974:168), Monjarás-Ruiz (1976:

254), Moriarty (1969), Peterson (1962:152–53), Soustelle (1970:101, 213), and Vaillant (1966:223–24).

5. Cipolla (1965), Creveld (1989), Headrick (1981), and McNeill (1982) discuss the role of technology in war, but it was not decisive in the Mexican case.

6. For example, King Moteuczomah Ilhuicamina used temple construction as a pretext to demand aid from surrounding cities: compliance tacitly acknowledged vassalage, while refusal led to war (Chimalpahin 1965:98; *Crónica mexicana* 1975:287–89; Durán 1967(2):133–35).

7. Previously, I suggested that the Aztecs permitted internal warfare where it destabilized larger, and potentially more troublesome, tributary regions and suppressed it among smaller polities (Hassig 1988:257–58). The addition of a political dynamic internal to the tributary groups refines that interpretation.

Chapter 5

Warfare on the West African Slave Coast, 1650–1850

ROBIN LAW

THIS chapter explores the changing character of indigenous warfare in coastal western Africa and its relationship to contact with Europeans during the period of the trans-Atlantic slave trade between the seventeenth and early nineteenth centuries. It focuses on the region known to Europeans as the "Slave Coast," corresponding in terms of modern political geography to the coastal portions of the republics of Togo and Bénin (formerly Dahomey). The inhabitants of this region belong to a single linguistic/ethnic group, nowadays usually called Ewe or Aja, though the use of these terms in this generic sense is a recent coinage, strictly anachronistic for the period dealt with here. During the eighteenth and nineteenth centuries much of this area was incorporated into the indigenous kingdom of Dahomey, whose population in the later nineteenth century was estimated to be between 150,000 and 200,000.

The most obvious innovation in West African military practice in this period was the introduction of firearms, which became available in the coastal areas (though not in the interior) through trade with Europeans from the seventeenth century onward (Kea 1971). The use of firearms is commonly held not only to have transformed the conduct of West African warfare, but also to have affected political structures. In particular, it has been argued that since the importation of firearms was relatively easy to control or monopolize, their adoption tended to favor the development of more centralized forms of political organization (Goody 1971; Law 1976). The significance of the impact of firearms has, however, sometimes been contested. Smith (1976), for example, in his general survey of precolonial West African warfare, asserts that firearms were "far from revolutionising warfare," though he does concede that their adoption tended to encourage the formation of standing armies of specialist soldiers.

The impact of firearms, and of the European contact more generally, upon indigenous warfare clearly varied in nature and intensity from area to area. A study of warfare in Angola during the sixteenth and seventeenth centuries, for example, tends to support Smith's emphasis on continuity rather than revolutionary transformation (Thornton 1988). Although firearms were adopted in Angola, they supplemented rather than replaced existing missile weapons (bows and arrows) and did not subvert existing tactical practice, which remained based principally upon close combat with swords, clubs, and stabbing spears, with missile weapons playing only a secondary role. Local patterns of military organization, based upon elite forces of specialist soldiers (the generality of the population being mobilized only as support troops and porters) likewise persisted essentially unaltered.

A very different picture is offered, however, in Kea's (1982) study of the seventeenth-century Gold Coast (i.e., modern Ghana, to the west of the Slave Coast), which posits a veritable "military revolution." In the early seventeenth century, warfare in the Gold Coast, as in Angola, was dominated by tactics of shock combat, employing spears (thrown at relatively close quarters or wielded as pikes) and swords, with missile tactics (namely archery) playing only a subsidiary role. Armies were normally small elite forces of specialist soldiers, mostly the retainers of nobles and professional mercenaries. In the second half of the century, however, missile tactics (initially archery, but later muskets) came to predominate. With the consequent shift of emphasis from individual skill in hand-to-hand fighting toward weight of firepower, elite forces were replaced by mass armies mobilizing the bulk of the adult male population. These changes were associated with an expansion of the scale of political organization, with the emergence of large empires, most notably Akwamu and later Asante (Ashanti), in place of earlier political fragmentation. This revolution is explained by Kea not merely (or even principally) as arising from the introduction of firearms, but as part of a more general socio-political transformation, in which an essentially urban and commercialized "mercantile" social formation (in which gold was the main export to the Europeans) gave way to a more militarized "imperial" social formation, geared to the export of slaves. The case of the Slave Coast presents a similar pattern of "military revolution," although it also offers important points of difference from Kea's analysis of the Gold Coast.

TRADE AND POLITICS ON THE SLAVE COAST

European contact on the Slave Coast was pioneered by the Portuguese, who first explored the area in 1472 and began trading there in 1553. The Dutch entered the trade in the 1630s, and the English and French in the 1660s. The principal commodity exported was always slaves (whence the name "Slave Coast"), who were sent mainly to the sugar plantations of the Americas. Initially this trade was on a modest scale, but in the second half of the seventeenth century the volume of slave exports rose dramatically. The Slave Coast remained a principal supplier of slaves for the trans-Atlantic trade down to the mid-nineteenth century, when slaves were replaced as the region's principal export by palm oil.

When Europeans first began trading on the Slave Coast in the sixteenth century, the region was divided into a number of indigenous polities which appear to have been largely autonomous, although speaking a common language (or at least closely related languages) and having traditions of a common origin. The most powerful of these polities was initially the kingdom of Allada (or Ardra), to which most of the other Slave Coast polities were originally tributary, but by the second half of the seventeenth century Allada's power was in decline. By the 1680s the kingdoms of Popo (Great Popo) and Whydah (Hueda), on the coast west of Allada, had broken away from Allada's authority. Whydah in fact competed successfully with Allada for control of the European trade, becoming the main center of trade in the area in the later seventeenth century. Allada's own coastal port, Offra, was also frequently in rebellion, supported by Whydah. The disorders arising from these developments were compounded by the intrusion into the Slave Coast of marauding bands of refugees and adventurers from the Gold Coast to the west, displaced by the expansion of Akwamu in the late seventeenth century. Groups of "bandits" from Alampo, on the eastern Gold Coast, were already infesting the western Slave Coast, raiding Great Popo, by the early 1680s (Kea 1986:119). Another group of refugees displaced by the Akwamu conquest of Accra (west of Alampo) settled in the 1680s at Little Popo, west of Great Popo. Besides raiding locally, the Accra of Little Popo intervened periodically in the wars between Allada and its former tributaries: in 1692, for example, they destroyed Offra and attacked Whydah, at the request of Allada.

Some degree of political order on the Slave Coast was eventually restored through the expansion of the kingdom of Dahomey, in the interior north of Allada. In origin, Dahomey was a minor tributary of Allada, whose authority it formally repudiated only in 1715. Under King Agaja (ca. 1716–40), Dahomey proceeded to overrun the coastal area to the south, conquering Allada in 1724 and Whydah in 1727. Dahomey thus extended its authority over much of the Slave Coast, although Great and Little Popo to the west resisted incorporation and a new independent state (and commercial rival) emerged at Porto-Novo to the east of Whydah. Dahomey itself, however, was attacked and defeated by the kingdom of Oyo, in the interior to the northeast (in modern Nigeria), in a series of wars between 1726 and 1748, and was forced to pay tribute. The superiority of the Oyo in these wars was due principally to their use of cavalry (cf. Law 1975). Dahomey attained its greatest military power and territorial extent under King Gezo (1818–58), who in particular defeated Oyo and ended the payment of tribute to it in 1823. Dahomey then remained the dominant power on the Slave Coast until it was itself conquered by the French in 1892–94.

Allada, Whydah, Dahomey, and the other Slave Coast polities have usually been regarded by historians as "states," but this perspective has been challenged. Ronen (1975) argues that they were not organized on a basis of territorially defined sovereignty, but comprised corporate kin groups or clans claiming descent from a common ancestor, whose "kings" had essentially ritual functions (related to the cult of the clan's founding ancestor) rather than exercising political authority. Although too complex to be regarded as "tribes," they were thus more tribelike than statelike in their organization. This analysis is, however, difficult to sustain empirically, at least with regard to Dahomey, which was clearly a heterogeneous community, comprising people of genealogically unrelated clans whose rulers had administrative as well as ritual functions. In Dahomey, in fact, royal authority was explicitly defined in terms of territory rather than consanguinity: the kings were held to "own" the land comprising Dahomey, which they had acquired either by conquest or by purchase from its original occupants, and their authority over its inhabitants was held to derive from their control of the land (Le Herissé 1911:243–45). Ronen's analysis might, however, be more valid for Allada and the other polities that preceded Dahomey. Akinjogbin (1967) argues that the rise of Dahomey represented a sort of revolution in political organization, involving the replacement of an earlier kinship-based (and decentralized) political structure by a territorially defined (and more autocratic) system based on effective military force rather than common descent. Although Akinjogbin himself does not formulate the process in these terms, this might be conceptualized as a transition from a "tribal" system to a territorial state. The stimulus for this transformation, it is suggested, was the disorders arising from the impact of the Atlantic slave trade, which the traditional political order was unable to contain. The rise of Dahomey thus reflected a process of militarization at least broadly analogous to that described by Kea for the Gold Coast (cf. Law 1986).

THE NATURE OF THE EUROPEAN IMPACT

Evaluation of the impact of the European contact upon indigenous warfare requires, first, a clear conception of the nature of that impact. This had a political and military as well as a purely commercial dimension, and the European trade on the Slave Coast, as on the Gold Coast, affected local warfare not only through the introduction of firearms, but also and perhaps more critically through providing an outlet for the sale of war captives as slaves.

THE EUROPEAN FORTS

For most of the period of the trans-Atlantic slave trade, the principal European nations maintained permanent establishments on the Slave Coast. The Dutch already had a trading lodge at Offra, the principal port of Allada, by 1660, and the English and French also established lodges there in 1663 and 1670, respectively. When the main center of the trade shifted from Offra west to Whydah in the later seventeenth century, the European trading factories were also removed to Whydah. The French were the first to move their lodge to Glehue, the coastal village of Whydah, in 1671, and they were joined there by the English in 1682, the Dutch in 1703, and the Portuguese in 1721. The Dutch presence in Whydah lapsed after the Dahomian conquest of that kingdom in 1727, but the other European establishments there were maintained throughout the eighteenth century, the French factory being abandoned in 1797, the English in 1812, and the Portuguese a few years later.

The earliest European factories at Offra in Allada were unfortified. This was at the insistence of the Allada authorities, who feared the military dominance which European forts might exercise: when the French in 1670 asked permission to build their factory "in their own manner" (i.e., apparently in brick or stone, rather than mud), the king of Allada refused, observing that "You would wish to build a house which would be much stronger than ours, then you would put two small pieces of cannon in it, the next year you would want to expand it, and put two more pieces of cannon in it; then you would build a Fort there which all the forces in my state could not take from you, as the Dutch have done at Elmina [on the Gold Coast]" (Delbée 1671:452). The factories established later at Glehue in Whydah were likewise initially unfortified. The vulnerability of these early European establishments was dramatically demonstrated in 1692 when the Little Popo army called in by Allada destroyed both the Dutch factory at Offra and the French at Glehue. The first of the European factories at Glehue to be made defensible was the English, which had been fortified by the construction of flankers, despite the king of Whydah's protests, earlier in 1692; these defenses were directed, it should be stressed, against the French, with whom the English were then at war, rather than against the indigenous Africans.[1] The French were permitted to build a fort at Glehue in 1704, and the Portuguese in 1721, though the Dutch continued to have only an unfortified factory. The official justification for the construction of these forts was to secure the Europeans' goods against theft, rather than for defense against military attack (Doublet 1883:255; Barbot 1732:454).

Despite the king of Allada's fears in 1670, these forts did not in fact exercise much effective power, and when put to the test, they proved *not* to be defensible against attack by the local Africans. When the Dahomians conquered Whydah in 1727, for example, they took and destroyed the Portuguese fort there and carried off its cannon (Van Dantzig 1978:222); the fort's governor explained apologetically to his superiors that "none of the forts built at the Port of Ajuda [Whydah] is capable of defending itself when the Blacks wish to attack it" (Verger 1968:146). The Dahomians also succeeded in storming the Portuguese fort a second time in 1743, their victory on this occasion being facilitated by fire igniting stores of gunpowder (Verger 1968:174–75). The only instance when a European fort played any sort of decisive military role was in 1763, ironically in *defense* of Whydah against external African attack, when the artillery of the English fort helped the Dahomians to repulse an attack by raiders from Little Popo (Dalzel 1793:103–4). Throughout the eighteenth century, indeed, the Europeans in Whydah were clearly under the dominance of the local Africans rather than vice versa. This dependence was most clearly demonstrated in 1703 when the king of Whydah, fearing that the intra-European war which had recently broken out would disrupt trade, insisted that the local representatives of the various European nations should sign a formal treaty guaranteeing the neutrality of the Whydah port (cf. Labat 1731(2):86–91). In 1715 the governor of the English fort, who was held to have broken this treaty by becoming involved in a fracas with his Dutch counterpart, was arrested and deported by the Whydah authorities (Akinjogbin 1967:44–45). There were, indeed, several other instances of European governors being deported by the local authorities; one English governor in 1729 was even executed by the Dahomians (Snelgrave 1734:130–34).

EUROPEAN INTERVENTION IN LOCAL WARS

The Europeans also occasionally intervened with mobile forces in the wars of the Slave Coast, in alliance with one African state against another. In a strictly military sense, this sort of intervention was also of only marginal significance, but it may have had some effect in familiarizing local Africans with new forms of military practice. The earliest attested instance of such intervention was in 1687, when a rebellion by Offra against its overlord Allada was disrupting trade, and the Dutch factor there brought in "a large party of Accra and Myna Negroes [i.e., from Accra and Elmina on the Gold Coast]" to impose peace; in 1691, when Offra was again in rebellion and supported against Allada by Whydah, the English in turn landed "40 fully armed Mina slaves and three field-guns" to assist the Whydah forces (Van Dantzig 1978:32, 35). It is noteworthy that on both occasions the Europeans employed African troops, brought from the Gold Coast, rather than European soldiers. In 1694 some French ships supported a campaign by Whydah against Great Popo, and French troops actually took part in the assault on the town, but the attack was decisively repulsed (Bosman 1705:335–36). In 1734 French ships with their cannon again supported a campaign against the Popo region, in this case by the Dahomians against Whydah refugees who had retreated there, and on this occasion they were held to have contributed materially to a Dahomian victory (Akinjogbin 1967:98).

European forces also played some role in internal factional fighting within the kingdom of Whydah during the later seventeenth and eighteenth centuries. Already in the 1670s, it is said that King Agbangla had been placed on the Whydah throne in preference to his elder brother, the rightful heir apparent, through the support of the Dutch, French, and

Portuguese traders in the kingdom, though what level of military intervention this involved is not made clear (Bosman 1705:366). Likewise in
1708, in another disputed succession to the throne, a force of 200 European soldiers was landed from French and English ships then at Whydah,
to assist in securing the installation of Agbangla's grandson Huffon (Barbot 1732:453).

In addition to such formal intervention by European forces, individual
Europeans were occasionally employed by African rulers as mercenaries
or advisers. In 1694, for example, the king of Whydah had a "Portuguese
negro" (perhaps from the island of São Tomé, off the West African coast)
called João Fernando at his court, who served as his "physician and gunner," though the cannon under his charge fulfilled a ceremonial rather
than a strictly military function (Phillips 1732:220). A more significant
figure was Etienne Gallot, an officer in the French fort at Whydah who
took service under King Agaja of Dahomey in the 1720s and taught the
Dahomians "how to dig trenches and raise crude fortifications, which was
unknown among these people": it was presumably through Gallot's in-
struction that the Dahomians were able, in 1728, to construct trenches
defended by cannon, in a partially successful attempt to resist the dreaded
cavalry of Oyo. A second French officer, on an official mission to Dahomey later in 1728, was also pressed into service as an engineer, constructing bastions to defend the king's palace.[2] Another pioneer of military
innovation on the Slave Coast was Antonio Vaz Coelho, a free Black from
Brazil settled at Porto-Novo in the 1780s, who introduced the use of brass
swivel guns in the war canoes used on the coastal lagoons (Dalzel
1793:169).

THE ARMS TRADE

It seems certain, however, that such direct military involvement by Europeans was of less importance in transforming the character of indigenous
warfare than was the impact of their purely commercial activities. The
rising importance of the European trade as a source of wealth was itself a
stimulus to warfare, as rival states fought to secure access to, or monopoly
control over, the new commerce. Wars between Allada and Whydah in
the late seventeenth and early eighteenth centuries, and between Dahomey and Porto-Novo subsequently, clearly had such a commercial dimension (Akinjogbin 1967). Beyond this, the European trade became a major
source of weapons used in local warfare. Several accounts mention the
sale by Europeans on the Slave Coast of swords, usually sabres or cutlasses
(i.e., broad-bladed slashing swords) (Delbée 1671:448; N***** 1719:

43; *Relation* n.d.:84; Labat 1731(2):195), but similar swords were also manufactured locally, so that in this respect the European trade was not introducing anything new. Greater interest clearly attaches to the importation of firearms and gunpowder, since this represented a military technology hitherto unknown in the region.[3]

The trade in firearms was slower to develop on the Slave Coast than on the Gold Coast to the west, where it was already well established by the mid-seventeenth century (Kea 1971). The earliest extant list of goods imported into Allada, relating to Dutch trade in the 1640s or 1650s, does not include firearms (Dapper 1668:491); but the Dutch had begun selling guns there, at least in small quantities (at an exchange rate of two guns for three slaves), by the 1660s (Leers 1665:311). A list of goods suitable for the Allada trade compiled by the French in 1670 also includes guns (Delbée 1671:448). The first cargo sent by the English Company of Adventurers to Allada, in 1663, included two pairs of pistols to be presented as gifts to the king and heir apparent, but no firearms in the cargo intended for the actual purchase of slaves. By 1678, however, the English were regularly including guns and gunpowder in their cargoes for Allada, guns now selling at five per slave.[4] The guns traded in this early period were normally matchlocks (or "firelocks"). In addition to handguns, small numbers of artillery pieces were also imported to the Slave Coast, though probably as occasional gifts to local rulers rather than as regular items of trade: the king of Whydah, for example, already had four small iron cannon at the gatehouse of his palace in 1682, and six (together, as has been seen, with a Black Portuguese gunner) by 1694 (Barbot 1732:334; Phillips 1732:220).

The quantities of firearms traded to Allada and Whydah during the 1670s and 1680s were still quite small: the English Company's cargoes for the Slave Coast in this period normally included only 25 to 50 guns and 10 to 20 barrels of gunpowder in each, well under 10 percent of their total value. The real takeoff of the arms trade to the Slave Coast occurred during the 1690s, when the English Company alone imported over 1,000 guns annually into Whydah (Kea 1971:194). During the same period, the matchlock guns of the early trade were replaced by the more reliable "snaphaunce" or flintlock muskets. In the early eighteenth century, as slave prices escalated upward, guns and gunpowder were traded in ever greater quantities: having been sold at five per slave in the 1670s, guns fell in value to six per slave in the 1680s, to 12 by 1713, and to 20 to 25 by the 1720s. The price of a slave in gunpowder during the same period rose even more drastically, from one barrel [30 lb.] for two slaves to 300 pounds per slave.[5] Not all of the guns and powder imported were destined for use in war, since guns were also commonly used for the firing of ceremonial salutes and for hunting, but by the early eighteenth century at least, the preponderant demand was clearly for military purposes.

Imported firearms were traded from the coastal kingdoms of Allada and Whydah in turn to states further in the interior. The traditions of Dahomey record that firearms first reached there in the time of Wegbaja, a late seventeenth-century or early eighteenth-century ruler, who instituted a head tax in cash (cowry shells, the local currency) upon his subjects to pay for their purchase (Le Herissé 1911:60, 84). It is claimed that the coastal middlemen perfidiously removed the guns' flints before selling them, so that the Dahomians had to carry lighted matches to fire them—perhaps a misunderstood recollection of the matchlock guns of the earliest phase of the trade. One of King Agaja's motives in his conquest of the coastal kingdoms of the 1720s appears to have been his desire for more secure access to supplies of firearms (Snelgrave 1734:21; Dalzel 1793:7-8).

THE EXPORT OF CAPTIVES

The volume of slave exports from the Slave Coast, although initially small, rose very rapidly and substantially in the second half of the seventeenth century. Dutch slave purchases at Allada during the 1640s amounted only to between 500 and 600 per year (Law 1986:239); but by 1670 slave exports from Allada, still virtually all taken by the Dutch, were estimated at no less than 3,000 annually (Delbée 1671:436–37). By the 1690s, when the center of the trade had shifted to Whydah, the combined purchases of the Dutch and other European nations were substantially higher again, Whydah being reported in 1698 to be able to supply 1,000 slaves a month, or 12,000 a year (Bosman 1705:343). Although the volume of slave exports fluctuated considerably from year to year, being subject to disruption both by interruptions in the supply of slaves from the interior and by European wars which inhibited the arrival of ships to purchase them, exports from the Slave Coast are thought to have averaged over 10,000 per year from the 1690s to the 1730s, and to have remained at over 7,000 per year down to the 1850s (Manning 1979).

The sources of the slaves exported from the Slave Coast were various: an account of Allada in 1670, for example, observed that they included captives taken by Allada's own army, people born into slave status within Allada, insolvent debtors, and people enslaved by judicial processes as punishment for serious crimes, as well as others purchased by Allada from states further in the interior (Delbée 1671:437–38). It is clear, however, that the great majority of those exported had become slaves through capture in war: an account of Whydah in the 1690s, for example, asserts explicitly that "most of the Slaves that are offered to us are Prisoners of War, which are sold by the Victors as their Booty" (Bosman 1705:364). The implications of the rapid expansion of overseas sales of war captives for indigenous warfare in Africa are debatable, and were indeed already the subject of debate in the eighteenth century. Abolitionist writers such as Benezet (1789) argued that the European demand for slaves inevitably served as an incentive for Africans to go to war to supply it, and that the growth of the Atlantic slave trade had therefore led to an increased incidence of disorder and violence in Africa. Anti-abolitionists such as Dalzel (1793), however, in a notable study of the particular case of Dahomey, maintained that warfare was endemic in Africa anyway, and that the slave trade merely drained off a portion of those captured who would otherwise have been put to death, so that the European demand for slaves had the effect of mitigating the brutality of traditional African warfare. In the case of the Slave Coast, the coincidence of the growth of the Atlantic slave trade with the growth of political disorder (with the disintegration of Allada's regional hegemony) in the later seventeenth century provides at least a strong circumstantial case in support of the abolitionist position (Law 1986).

The restoration of local political order through the consolidation of Dahomey as a new and more effective regional overlord after the 1720s modified the situation somewhat, since the kings of Dahomey enforced a prohibition on the sale overseas (except in judicial punishment for serious crimes) of all native Dahomians, including slaves as well as freemen (Law 1986:266–67). This prohibition, however, had the effect of relocating rather than reducing the violence involved in the slave trade, since slaves for export continued to be gathered by military means, but now principally through raids upon peoples around the periphery of the region. Disorder was thus suppressed within the boundaries of Dahomey, only to be transferred onto weaker and often politically fragmented neighboring countries.

THE MILITARY REVOLUTION ON THE SLAVE COAST

Assessment of the impact of European military and commercial involvement upon the practice of indigenous warfare is hampered by the deficiencies of the evidence. It is, virtually by definition, impossible to document conditions in the precontact period, since the available documentation consists more or less exclusively of records produced by the

Europeans. (Local oral traditions are not very informative or likely to be reliable on matters of detail relating to early military practice, and in any case do not appear to have a time depth extending back much beyond the seventeenth century.) There is, in fact, no serious detailed evidence relating to military matters in contemporary European sources for the Slave Coast earlier than the mid-seventeenth century, by which time the Europeans had already been trading there for a century. The indigenous military practice recorded in the earliest European accounts, during the late seventeenth and to some extent even the early eighteenth centuries, nevertheless shows little obvious sign of significant European influence and may reasonably be hypothesized to represent in essence a tradition deriving from earlier times. Since both the import of firearms and the export of war captives attained a really large scale only *after* the mid-seventeenth century, their effects can to some extent be traced in the available contemporary records. On this basis, it seems possible to reconstruct a "military revolution" on the Slave Coast which in its nature and origins was analagous to (though not identical with) that documented by Kea for the Gold Coast. Just as this "revolution" on the Gold Coast was linked to the emergence of new military states, such as Akwamu and Asante, on the Slave Coast it was associated with the rise of Dahomey.

ORGANIZATION: FROM MASS ARMIES TO ELITE FORCES

On the Gold Coast, as has been seen, Kea argues that the military revolution involved a transition from small elite forces of professional soldiers to large mass armies mobilizing the generality of the peasantry. On the Slave Coast, my own reading of the evidence suggests quite the reverse evolution, from mass armies to smaller specialist forces. The contradiction, however, may be more apparent than real, or at least a matter more of emphasis than of substance. In the seventeenth century, the contrast between the two regions was real and clear enough, with the much greater professionalization of military service on the Gold Coast probably reflecting the higher levels of commercialization of the economy and of social differentiation which had already evolved there. The early stages of the military revolution on the Slave Coast, in fact, comprised essentially a belated imitation of the tradition of professional soldiering that already existed on the Gold Coast. The end result in both cases was essentially similar, since the new states which emerged in the eighteenth century (Dahomey on the Slave Coast, Asante on the Gold Coast) both *combined* standing armies of specialist soldiers with a general obligation of military service. Rather than the supercession of elite by mass armies, this represented the incorporation of professional soldiering, hitherto largely autonomous and even anarchic, within a framework of central state authority.

The mass nature of military organization on the early Slave Coast is clearly documented. In Allada in the mid-seventeenth century, there is said to have been a general obligation of military service: "In time of war, nobody is exempt, except old people and small children" (Dapper 1668: 493). In Whydah in the early eighteenth century likewise, each provincial chief was obliged to lead "all his subjects" to join the national army (Labat 1731(2):189). This mobilization of the generality of adult males implies that armies were large, and this is corroborated by the figures offered for the military strength of both Allada and Whydah. The king of Allada in 1670 was said to command a force of between 40,000 and 50,000 (Delbée 1671:436, 558). The Allada army that opposed the Dahomian invasion in 1724 is also said to have numbered 50,000 (Snelgrave 1734:7). Whydah in the 1690s was said to be capable of mobilizing an even larger force, of 200,000 (Bosman 1705:396), but later accounts give the more modest figures of 100,000 (Snelgrave 1734:4) or 60,000 to 80,000 (*Relation* n.d.:82); the army actually mobilized to resist the Dahomian invasion of Whydah in 1727 is reported to have numbered over 40,000 (Law 1988: 327). Even if, as is very probable, these figures are exaggerated, they confirm, in an impressionistic manner, that these were mass armies rather than small specialist forces. As a corollary of this mass mobilization of ordinary citizens, standards of training and discipline were low. The Whydah army in the early eighteenth century, for example, was described as fighting "without station or order" (Labat 1731(2):189). European observers also regarded both the Alladas and the Whydahs as cowards, with no stomach for fighting (e.g., Bosman 1705:395).

From the late seventeenth century onward, however, the conduct of warfare on the Slave Coast began to be professionalized through the employment of mercenaries, who were recruited either from the Gold Coast to the west or from among the refugees and "bandits" who had been displaced from the Gold Coast into the western Slave Coast by the expansion of Akwamu. This use of Gold Coast soldiers on the Slave Coast was probably pioneered by the Europeans, since the earliest attested instances are the small forces imported to intervene in local wars by the Dutch in 1687 and the English in 1691. The superiority of these professional soldiers over the local forces was quickly evident. It was observed in the 1690s, for example, that ten of the Gold Coast men employed by the Europeans could beat "the best forty men the king of Whydah had in his kingdom," and that the entire strength of the Whydah army would not venture to take on 5,000 "well Armed Men" from the Gold Coast (Phillips 1732:216; Bosman 1705:394).

The idea was quickly taken up by local African rulers. The earliest attested example of such employment of mercenaries in the service of an indigenous ruler on the Slave Coast was the king of Allada's use of the displaced Accra at Little Popo to attack his rebellious port of Offra in 1692: the Popo commander, according to a contemporary account, was "bribed" by the Allada king to undertake this campaign (Van Dantzig 1978:52). The example was quickly followed by the king of Whydah, who after the failure of his attack (conducted with French support) on Great Popo in 1694 is said to have made no further attempt on the place with his own forces, but instead expended "large Summs" in seeking to "hire other Nations to engage in the Quarrel" (Bosman 1705:336). Likewise in the continuing conflict between Whydah and Allada, both sides by the late 1690s were employing mercenaries: "They never Fight against each other with their own Forces, but hire the Gold-Coast Negroes for that purpose," Akwamu being the principal source of such mercenaries (Bosman 1705:395–96). The military power of Whydah in the early eighteenth century, in fact, rested directly upon its preeminence in the European trade, since its commercial wealth provided the means to hire mercenaries: the Whydahs in particular used gold purchased from the Portuguese (who brought it from Brazil) for this purpose (*Relation* n.d.: 18, 77).

The rising power of Dahomey, according at least to traditions current in the mid-eighteenth century, had its origins in a group of "bandits" or mercenaries, who sold their services to the warring rulers of the region (Law 1986:253). King Agaja's attack on Allada in 1724 certainly originated as a mercenary venture, he being hired to support the claims of a pretender to the Allada throne (Snelgrave 1734:7). Only after his victory did Agaja decide to seize authority in Allada for himself. However this may be, the Dahomian military successes of the 1720s were clearly based upon the use of small professional forces, rather than the sort of mass armies deployed by Allada and Whydah. The army with which Agaja invaded Allada in 1724, it was reported, was "not very numerous," generally estimated at 10,000 (i.e., less than a quarter of the strength of the opposing Allada force), but they were "select troops, both brave and well disciplined" (Labat 1731(1):xi). The army that conquered Whydah in 1727 was even smaller, numbering no more than 3,000, of whom only half were combatants (Law 1988:327). A European who visited Dahomey later in 1727 noted that "the greatest part" of its army consisted of "regular soldiers," who were recruited as young boys and intensively trained.

In consequence, their standards of discipline and drill were much higher: they are described as organized into "Companies . . . [with] their proper Colours, and Officers," and "marching in a much more regular Order than I had ever seen before, even amongst the Gold Coast Negroes" (Snelgrave 1734:77–78).

The consolidation of Dahomey's authority over the conquered southern kingdoms after the 1720s, involving its transition from an essentially mobile military band into a territorially organized state, necessarily modified its military organization, but its dependence on an essentially professional army persisted. In the enlarged Dahomey state, as in Allada and Whydah, there was a universal obligation of military service, but this was in practice invoked only "on extraordinary occasions," and fighting was normally undertaken by a "standing army" which was kept permanently ready for mobilization (Dalzel 1793:x). In 1850 it was estimated that this "regular army" numbered 12,000, of whom 7,000 represented the king's private contingent (the other 5,000 being presumably the retainers of other senior chiefs). The total strength of the Dahomian army was put at 24,000 combatants, or around 50,000 including porters; this higher figure (around a quarter of the kingdom's estimated population) evidently included most of the adult male population (Forbes 1851(1):14). The standing army was recruited partly by conscription, each village in Dahomey being required to supply youths for military service (Pruneau de Pommegorge 1789:164). In addition, some of the captives taken by the Dahomian army were incorporated into it. A report of 1850 suggests, perhaps with some exaggeration, that the servile, non-Dahomian element predominated: "The officers are natives, the soldiery foreigners, prisoners of war, or purchased slaves" (Forbes 1851(1):19).

An unusual aspect of Dahomian military organization was the existence of a female component of the standing army, recruited from the female attendants in the royal palace (legally regarded as wives of the king), and generally called by Europeans the "Amazons" (d'Almeida-Topor 1984). This component already existed in at least an embryonic form in the 1720s, and had grown to a force of "several hundreds" by the 1770s (Snelgrave 1734:34; Dalzel 1793:xi). During the eighteenth century, this "Amazon" force normally served merely as the king's bodyguard within the palace: two recorded occasions on which the king led his female soldiers on campaign outside the capital, in 1729 and 1781, were clearly regarded as exceptional (Snelgrave 1734:126; Dalzel 1793:176). In the nineteenth century, however, King Gezo (1818–58) greatly expanded the Amazon force and turned it into a regular component of the Dahomian field army: in 1850 5,000 of the 7,000 troops in the royal contingent were women (Forbes 1851(1):14; (2):91). The reasons for this development are obscure, but it seems likely that Gezo, who had come to the throne irregularly by a *coup d'état,* was seeking to secure his position against internal opposition by creating a military force more closely under his personal control. The augmented Amazon force was recruited, again, by conscription, every leading family in the kingdom being required to offer its daughters for selection (Burton 1966:256). Despite the peculiarity of its sex, Gezo's Amazon army essentially represented a continuation of the Dahomian tradition of small elite forces of highly trained soldiers. To the end, Dahomey's military success depended upon the quality rather than the numerical weight of its forces.

ARMAMENT AND TACTICS: FROM SHOCK COMBAT TO MISSILE WARFARE

In mid-seventeenth-century Allada, a soldier's armament is said to have comprised a shield, spears (*assegais*), a bow, and arrows (Dapper 1668: 489); later evidence makes clear that swords (cutlasses) were also used (Delbée 1671:399). The same weapons remained in use, alongside imported firearms, in Whydah later; an additional item of traditional weaponry attested in Whydah was a form of throwing-club (Bosman 1705: 396; *Relation* n.d.:85; N***** 1719:43; Labat 1731(2):194–96). As to the tactical handling of this combination of weapons, the only source that offers any sort of detailed account relates to Whydah in the early eighteenth century (Labat 1731(2):190). By then conditions had been modified by the introduction of firearms, but these appear still to have played a very marginal role, being mentioned only as being discharged during the general hullabaloo that *preceded* the action, evidently more to reinforce the moral effect of the army's war cry than with any directly lethal intent. The action itself was opened by a barrage of arrows, after which the army advanced; as they came within range, the soldiers first threw their spears, and finally engaged at close quarters with swords and knives. This final stage, of close combat with swords, was the decisive one; it was normally at this point that one or the other of the opposing armies broke and fled.

Imported firearms were initially added to rather than substituted for existing indigenous weapons. An account of Allada in 1670 describes troops armed only with muskets and cutlasses (Delbée 1671:399), but these were a contingent of royal retainers and therefore probably untypical of the army, the bulk of which continued to be equipped in the traditional manner. In Whydah later, as has been seen, the traditional armament was substantially retained, with firearms playing only a sub-sidiary role. In the 1690s it was explicitly noted that the Whydah and Allada armies possessed only "a few Muskets," their "principal Weapons, and upon which they most depend," being their throwing-clubs (Bosman 1705:395). Even when they became more numerous, guns were not at first put to very effective use. Some sources suggest that the firearms sold to Whydah were inferior in quality, the Europeans deliberately withhold-ing the better models (N***** 1719:43; Labat 1731(2):194). The inef-fectiveness of firearms, however, was also due to lack of skill in handling them. One account states that the Whydahs did not aim their muskets, but fired them with their butts trailing on the ground, so that they nor-mally shot over the heads of their opponents: they were used "for show" rather than for inflicting serious casualties (*Relation* n.d.:83, 85).

The effective military use of firearms on the Slave Coast may well have been pioneered by the Gold Coast mercenaries who were commonly em-ployed there from the 1690s onward, since firearms had been in regular use on the Gold Coast since half a century or more earlier. At any rate, the earliest campaign on the Slave Coast in which firearms appear to have played a significant role was the attack by the Little Popo forces on Why-dah in 1692. In preparation for this attack the Little Popo obtained "a great deale [of] ammunition" from a Dutch ship.[6] They broke off the cam-paign and retreated, after initial successes, when a large convoy of gun-powder sent for them by the king of Allada was intercepted by the Whydah forces (Bosman 1705:332).

Dahomey, despite its situation in the interior which cut it off from direct access to the European trade, was relatively quick to adopt the use of imported firearms. There is no contemporary documentation of the weaponry of the Dahomian army before its conquest of the coastal region in the 1720s, but tradition current in the late eighteenth century held that prior to their adoption of firearms the Dahomians had used clubs (pre-sumably throwing-clubs, as in Whydah) and bows and arrows (Dalzel 1793:219); more recently recorded tradition speaks of clubs and slings (Le Herissé 1911:14). It is noteworthy that the traditions mention only missile weapons, suggesting perhaps that early Dahomian tactics placed a greater emphasis upon missile warfare than was the case in the coastal states, where shock combat at close quarters was the dominant mode, and it may be that the Dahomians' greater success in making effective use of firearms was due in part to a preexisting penchant for missile tactics. At any rate, descriptions of Dahomian forces in the 1720s show that they were armed exclusively with muskets and swords (Snelgrave 1734). King Agaja himself declared in 1726 that "Both I and my predecessors were,

and are, great admirers of fire armes, and have allmost intirely left of[f]
the use of bows and arrows"; although the coastal peoples still used "old
fashioned weapons" such as spears and clubs, the Dahomians "think none
better than the gunn, and . . . cutlass" (Law 1990:217).

The Dahomian army's superior standards of discipline and drill enabled it to make much more effective use of these weapons than had been
done in Allada or Whydah, in particular permitting the coordination and
concentration of firepower to maximum effect. A European observer of
Dahomian military exercises in 1727 noted admiringly that they fired "at
least twenty rounds [presumably coordinated salvos] with their small
Arms, in less than two hours time" (Snelgrave 1734:78). By the nineteenth century, if not earlier, Dahomian forces also employed a form of
the countermarch, or firing by ranks, which enabled the maintenance of
a continuous fire despite the long time taken in reloading (Ross 1971:
154). In combination with these organizational improvements, firearms
now became the dominant weapon in Slave Coast warfare, and missile
tactics therefore the decisive mode of combat. Armies were now expected
to break and flee under the impact of Dahomian musketfire, before they
came to close quarters; the cutlasses which the Dahomians still carried
were intended more for the decapitation of already slain (or at least captured) enemies than for hand-to-hand combat. The rise of Dahomey, like
that of Akwamu and Asante in the Gold Coast, was in part a triumph for
the new military technology.

Although thus successfully adopting the use of muskets, the Slave
Coast states made less effective use of European artillery. The six cannon
belonging to the king of Whydah are alleged to have played a decisive
role in a civil war between rival claimants to the throne in 1703, presumably in repulsing an attempt by the defeated party to take possession of
the palace which they guarded (N***** 1719:43). Agaja of Dahomey, as
has been seen, also used cannon, placed behind European-style earthworks, to resist an attack by the cavalry forces of Oyo in 1728. On both
these occasions, the cannon were used in static defense of a fortified position. Cannon were never used on the Slave Coast, however, in a mobile
role in support of armies in the field. This was partly, as was observed of
Whydah in the early eighteenth century, because of the lack of horses or
other suitable animals to draw them (Labat 1731(2):189). But there was
in any case also a general lack of wheeled carriages for the transport of
artillery pieces (Law 1980). Agaja of Dahomey in 1724 was reported to
be constructing carriages for his cannon, but in the event nothing seems
to have come of this project (Smith 1744:182). Later Dahomian kings

normally employed their cannon merely in the firing of salutes, rather than in serious warfare.[7] The only sphere in which cannon were commonly put to any practical military application on the Slave Coast (and elsewhere in West Africa) was in the war canoes operating along the coastal lagoons (Smith 1976:113–14).

MILITARIZATION AND CENTRALIZATION: THE CHANGING POLITICAL ECONOMY OF WAR

Dahomey was a highly militarized society (cf. Maroukis 1974), whose organization and ethos prompted its characterization by one nineteenth-century observer as a "black Sparta" (Burton 1966:322). All important state officials had military functions, so that the political hierarchy reproduced (or was reproduced in) the command structure of the Dahomian army. War was institutionalized, campaigns being undertaken, in principle, every year. Military success was celebrated and advertised by the sacrifice of a portion of the captives taken at public festivals (known as the "Annual Customs") in honor of the deceased kings of the dynasty (Law 1985). The heads of enemies slain in battle or subsequently sacrificed were also preserved for exhibition as trophies at these ceremonies (Law 1989).

The historical origins of this militarization, as noted earlier, have been a matter of controversy since the eighteenth century. Many contemporary observers held that it reflected the impact of the Atlantic slave trade, Dahomey's wars being motivated by the desire to secure captives for export. Abolitionist observers thus tended to dismiss Dahomian wars as mere "slave-hunts" (e.g.; Forbes 1851(1):20; Burton 1966:201).[8] Defenders of the slave trade such as Dalzel, on the other hand, insisted that these wars were ideological rather than commercial in motivation, reflecting a traditional militarism unconnected with the slave trade. In support of this view, Dalzel cited the alleged statement of an eighteenth-century king of Dahomey, Kpengla (1774–89): "In the name of my ancestors and myself I aver, that no Dahoman man ever embarked in war merely for the sake of procuring wherewithal to purchase your [European] commodities" (Dalzel 1793:215). In the context in which it is reported, in an anti-abolitionist polemical work whose central purpose was to refute the argument that the slave trade was a cause of wars in Africa, this statement is bound to be suspect. But there is no need to question its essential accuracy, since there is abundant corroboratory evidence that in Dahomey war was seen as a way of life, requiring no justification beyond itself.

Dahomian traditional history is replete with assertions of the essentially and uniquely military character of Dahomey. Thus the Dahomians were not traders, like the Whydahs; rather, their "only wealth consisted in enemy spoils." Nor were they farmers, like the Oyo; "the kings of Dahomey cultivate only war" (Le Herissé 1911:39–40, 313). But this sort of militaristic ideology is quite compatible with, and indeed was very probably derived from, the economic reality that war was, through the operation of the Atlantic slave trade, a major source of material enrichment. The kings of Dahomey themselves, indeed, were not above conceding the point on other occasions. Thus King Gezo in 1850, for example: "My people are a military people . . . my revenue is the proceeds of the sale of prisoners of war . . . all my nation—all are soldiers, and the Slave Trade feeds them" (Law 1986:253). The ideology of militarism was founded in the political economy of the slave trade.

The question is not so much whether Dahomian militarism *became* inextricably bound up with the slave trade, as whether (or to what degree) it *originated* as a response to the conditions created by the slave trade. On this, there is the powerful circumstantial argument that Allada and Whydah, the powers that preceded Dahomey on the Slave Coast, although not innocent of a warrior ethos (practicing headhunting, for example), were clearly much less systematically militarized than Dahomey later. The question of human sacrifice is illuminating in this connection. In the 1720s, when the Dahomian practice of sacrificing war captives was first recorded by contemporary European observers, Dahomian informants insisted that such sacrifices "had ever been the Custom of their Nation" (Snelgrave 1734:46–47). Perhaps they had, but Dahomey was a recently created state, probably then less than a century old. In Allada and Whydah during the seventeenth century, there is no record of comparable sacrifices of war captives. At the Annual Customs in honor of the deceased kings of Whydah there were no human sacrifices at all (*Relation* n.d.: 67–68). It is difficult to resist the conclusion that the scale of human sacrifice in Dahomey, and the culture of militarism of which it formed a part, were indeed a recent development, which had arisen during the seventeenth and early eighteenth centuries. The inference that this militarization reflected the impact of the Atlantic slave trade remains persuasive (Law 1985).

Dahomey differed from its predecessors not only in the elaboration of its military ethos but also in the degree of central control which the king exercised over military matters. In Whydah earlier, for example, soldiers normally equipped and armed themselves, although the king "sometimes" supplied them with ammunition; whereas in Dahomey, guns, powder, and iron (which was cut up for use as shot) could not be legally sold except to "the King, or to his ministers, for him" (Labat 1731(2):188; Dalzel 1793:208 n.). In Whydah also, the great majority of the prisoners taken were left in the hands of their captors, the king taking only a tithe, and the heads brought back as trophies also remained in the possession of those who took them. But in Dahomey all captives and heads were surrendered to the king, in return for a small cash payment, at the conclusion of the campaign (Labat 1731(2):191; Snelgrave 1734:37–38). The king thus monopolized both military glory and the proceeds of slave dealing. Warfare was not only commercialized, but also centralized.

It perhaps warrants comment that on the Slave Coast, as was also the case on the Gold Coast, the new military state emerged in the interior rather than at the coast, despite the more direct involvement of the coastal communities in the trade with the Europeans and their readier access to supplies of imported firearms. This is explicable by the fact that a sort of division of labor operated within the African section of the slave trade, with coastal communities such as Whydah operating primarily as middlemen, while the actual process of enslavement took place predominantly in the interior. It was slave "production" rather than slave trading that gave rise to the new political order, and this production was the business of hinterland societies such as Dahomey.

In contrast with the experience of many other societies at the frontier of European contact, the political and military power of Dahomey was enhanced rather than undermined by the impact of European trade. Its relative autonomy derived not only from the political and military weakness of the European presence on the Slave Coast but also, and more critically, from the particular form of the international division of labor that operated in the slave trade, which left to Africans the business of forcibly enslaving the victims prior to export. Dahomian expansion thus represented a sort of subimperialism, or *comprador* imperialism, which was able to flourish through its complementarity of interest with European commercial capitalism. This compatibility, however, came to an end in the mid-nineteenth century with the transition from the trade in slaves to that in palm oil. With this shift to agricultural exports, Dahomian militarism came rather to be identified as an *obstacle* to the realization of the region's commercial potential, because the Dahomian warrior ethos involved a disdain for farming, and military operations withdrew labor from agricultural production (Reid 1986). As this contradiction between the character of the Dahomian state and the changed nature of European commercial interests became evident, from the 1850s onward, European-Dahomian relations became increasingly confrontational, culminating in the French conquest in the 1890s.

THE HINTERLAND SLAVING FRONTIER

Dahomey clearly cannot be regarded as a tribal society on the periphery of an expanding colonial state, but was itself an expanding state in the era of the Atlantic slave trade. The impact of the European trade, however, was felt not only in coastal slave-selling societies such as Dahomey, but also in the hinterland. Many of the slaves sold through Dahomey were supplied by Oyo, to the northeast, and Oyo in turn drew some of its slaves from its own northern neighbors (Law 1977). The violence and disorder that the Atlantic slave trade engendered were therefore felt, to some degree, hundreds of miles in the interior of West Africa. Within Dahomey itself (and within other slave-supplying states, such as Oyo), it is also necessary to distinguish between the central core area which was closely administered (and from which the national military forces were raised) and surrounding areas which were subject to a looser military domination. The distinction between "territorial" and "hegemonic" forms of expansion invoked in other cases (e.g., Mattingly and Hassig, this volume) might be applied here, although Dahomey's relations with its neighbors were essentially predatory (involving principally raiding for slaves) rather than strictly hegemonic. While Dahomey at one level constituted a part of the West African periphery of the European-dominated trans-Atlantic trading system, it had its own periphery in the form of the neighboring peoples it raided for slaves. Although the history of these neighboring societies is much less well documented than that of Dahomey, it is clear that they differed significantly from the latter in their military and political organization. It is, indeed, among these victims of Dahomey's expansion, rather than in Dahomey itself, that the closest parallels to the experience of the "tribal" societies studied in other contributions to this volume may be found. In particular, it may be suggested that the process of "tribalization" of peripheral societies under the impact of expanding states which has been analyzed elsewhere (Whitehead, this volume), while not applicable to Dahomey itself, can be traced among those subject to Dahomian slave raiding.

One case for which there is sufficient information to document this process is that of the Mahi, Dahomey's immediate northeastern neighbors, who were subject to continual Dahomian incursions throughout the eighteenth century, until they were formally conquered in the 1830s and 1840s. Dahomey deliberately prohibited the sale of European firearms to interior peoples such as the Mahi in order to maintain its own military advantage, and Mahi warfare therefore continued to be based on the bow and arrow (Duncan 1847(2):111) and did not undergo a firearms-related military revolution. Unlike the Dahomians also, the Mahi remained politically fragmented, divided into many small and autonomous communities. Defense of this political fragmentation, and rejection of the centralizing principles of Dahomey, appears indeed to have formed an element in the Mahi's definition of their distinctive identity. During the 1750s they fought a protracted war in successful resistance to a Dahomian attempt to impose a single ruler over them, on the plea that political unification would facilitate commercial dealings (Dalzel 1793:75–76). The Mahi did nevertheless develop a tradition of military cooperation in resistance to Dahomian attacks: according to tradition, the mechanism that they employed to secure this unity of purpose was the swearing of a mutual "blood pact" (Hazoumé 1937). It was probably this shared experience of Dahomian aggression and resistance to it which gave the Mahi their sense of common identity, since in origin they comprised disparate groups with no single history, culture, or even language (Bergé 1928). Both the existence of the Mahi as an ethnic group and their fragmented "tribal" political organization, therefore, were in some measure a consequence of their resistance to the expansion of the Dahomian state.

——— *Notes* ———

1. Bodleian Library, Oxford: Rawlinson C.746, letter of Edward Jacklin, Whydah, 10 May 1692.

2. Archives Nationales, Paris: C.6/25, Mémoire contre le Sr Gallot, 8 November 1730; letter of [Dupetitval], Whydah, 20 May 1728; letter of Delisle, Dahomey, 31 August 1728.

3. Firearms may also have been brought to the Slave Coast from the interior, since Muslim traders coming from the interior to the coast are reported to have possessed firearms, though they are not said to have traded in them (Labat 1731(2)222). These contacts, however, appear to have postdated the beginnings of the European trade: the Muslim traders are said to have come to Whydah for the first time only in 1704, though they had been trading to Allada for some years before then.

4. Public Record Office, London: T.70/1222, Calculations of Cargoes exported by the Royal African Company of England, 1663–99.

5. Public Record Office, London: T.70/1222, Calculations of Cargoes exported by the Royal African Company of England, 1663–99; Van Dantzig

1978:173; Labat 1731(2):91–92. By 1750, further inflation had taken the price of a slave to 40 guns, or 400 lb. of powder (AN: C.6/25, memorandum of Pruneau and Guestard, Whydah, 18 March 1750).

6. Rawlinson, C.746, Edward Jacklin, Whydah, 10 May 1692.

7. In the mid-nineteenth century, the Dahomians did succeed in constructing workable gun-carriages, and three cannon mounted on locally made carriages were taken on an attack on Abeokuta (to the east, in modern Nigeria) in 1864, but they played no significant role in the action (Law 1980:257).

8. It is possible that "slave-hunts" translated an indigenous idiom, since one modern account asserts that "the word translated as 'war' [in Dahomey] means literally 'man-hunt'" (Argyle 1966:81), but I have been unable to corroborate this supposed etymology locally (and the most usual Dahomian word for war, *ahuan,* certainly does not mean "man-hunt").

Chapter 6

Tribes Make States and States Make Tribes

Warfare and the Creation of Colonial Tribes
and States in Northeastern South America

NEIL L. WHITEHEAD

A NALYSES of the origins of warfare often show special theoretical interest in situations of conflict at the periphery of, or in isolation from, state formations. It is assumed that historical variables—such as the possibility that a particular martial organization is but a response to a prior threat of external force—can largely be held constant and that the archaeological data for warfare can be examined as if warfare were the pristine outgrowth and expression of basic human tendencies to violence (Haas 1990b; Sturtevant 1983).

Such arguments risk being circular because they assume that "warfare" is an identifiable category of behavior that transcends cultural and social context. The notion that "contact," however tenuous, automatically contaminates the evidence preserved in state records, particularly those of the European colonial powers, ignores the truism of all scientific methodology that any act of observation or measurement—archaeology not excepted—implies interaction with the object of analysis.

In fact, the course of European conquest in America has left abundant information about Amerindian societies before the intervention of the state, for the state was slow to be established in many parts of South America, and then sometimes only with the active and willing cooperation of the indigenous population (see also Gledhill 1988b:302). This hiatus between the arrival of Columbus and the maximum expansion of colonial states in this region—the time period 1492 to 1820—provides a window through which we may observe the last flickerings of autochthonous social processes.

THE SYMBIOSIS OF TRIBE AND STATE

It has been argued (Fried 1975) that tribal organization is itself only a particular response to European state contact, with the corollary that this "tribalization" involves the degradation of preexisting political formations, be they chieftaincies or ethnic groups (Gonzalez 1983; Helms 1976; Wolf 1982).

On the basis of ethnohistorical evidence about European colonial expansion, this judgment seems substantially correct. Indeed, a more extensive and detailed reading of this evidence might allow some resolution of current disputes over the origins and characteristics of "tribes" (cf. Shennan 1989). Certainly the lack of any adequate historical perspective in the use of ethnographic data has engendered some false oppositions (summarized in Haas 1990b) between theorists who see warfare as the prime force in tribal formation (Adams 1975; Sahlins 1968; Service 1971) and those who favor explanations that feature intensifying contact and cooperation between autonomous kin groups (Plog and Braun 1983). It is historically evident that both processes have been important, and there is no need to assign a preeminent role to either. One may note, however, that under the particular conditions of European colonial state formation and expansion, the likelihood of armed conflict certainly increased over time—so that "tribes" in Fried's sense are indeed the product of the historical violence of the European occupation, while ethnic formations ("tribes" in the Adams, Service, and Sahlins sense) may occur in many situations and for many more diverse reasons (as in Plog and Braun's view).

It is relevant to ask, however, whether such tribalization is the effect that *any* state formation has on groups external to its immediate control or whether it is a specific effect of European colonialism (Gledhill

1988a:22). We might also question whether or not warfare actually has had a preeminent role to play in this historical process, since state expansion and the formation of colonial enclaves may be engendered as much by commerce as by conquest.

The notion that the European colonial state is not unique in its effects on nonstate societies is suggested by the possibility that, within the long histories of interchange between such groups who were ancestral to state formations (only some of whom later diverge to form states), there was a tendency toward the maintenance of boundaries on the part of both the protostates and the prototribes. In this sense they are the alternative products of a shared history and so counterparts in what might be loosely conceived of as a single social system (see MacNeish 1981:123–54). Wolf (1982:32–34, 49) makes essentially the same points about the long interchange between pastoral nomads and settled villagers in Africa and Asia, as do Fox (1969), Gardener (1966), and Gibson (1990) concerning hunter-gatherers and agrarian states in South and insular Southeast Asia, and as does, more generally, recent work on the category of the hunter-gatherer (Ingold, Riches, and Woodburn 1988). The chapters by Mattingly, Gunawardana, Hassig, and Law in this volume similarly emphasize the potential of all states to create "tribal" ethnic formations.

In this way, "tribes" may be conceptualized as a recurrent and universal residual political phenomenon of both state formation and state expansion, achieving identity and forming boundaries only as a consequence of this external force. As Plog (in Haas 1990b: 172–73) indicates, there are many other kinds of "risk" that can lead to human agglomeration; but the tribe is a form of human agglomeration particularly appropriate to interaction with state organization on an autonomous basis. Nevertheless, the contradiction and instability in this type of ethnic formation (i.e., its dynamic aspect) is that it also risks the loss of its autonomy in the course of that interaction. The history of European colonialism in South America illustrates this very well, as shall be demonstrated below.

This interrelation of tribe and state is not just conceptual but also empirical, and consequently the peoples categorized as "tribals" or "savages" are always found on the borders of states. Whatever definitions of the cultural practices of savagery are used by state ideologies (e.g., cannibalism, polygamy, child sacrifice, sodomy), the key definitional characteristic of savage society is the supposed lack of "polity," such that private force rather than public justice—in other words, anarchy—prevails. This situation is then used as both a premise and a justification for the extension of state control.

By contrast, chieftaincies—historical precursors to the state (after

Carneiro 1981)—are always ringed by "barbarians,"[1] often being those without agriculture. While such groups are thought at least to possess polity, as they too use kin-ordered organization, they still lie outside the particular lineage or network that defines the social space of the chieftaincy. As a consequence, barbarians are ignorant of key cultural techniques and are considered "poor," fit only for affinal incorporation as slaves (see also Wolf 1982:389). Evidence from the northeastern South American region as to the existence of precolonial tribal formations ("barbarians") will be discussed below.

In such a context, one may again question the theoretical validity of the historical and archaeological search for situations of apparently "pristine" contact between state and tribal societies since, empirically, no such situation may ever have existed (Cohen 1981:122). In this case the conduct of a "tribal" mode of life does not represent a failure to develop "higher" state- or chieftainlike social forms but rather an abstention from them (Gibson 1990), especially in those regions that would seem to be favorable to the development of states but where state forms have not been recorded (Cohen 1981:121; MacNeish 1981:153).[2]

For this reason one should expect to find, in situations where states form or expand, that this process is resisted by some sections of an ethnic group and not by others, and that the resistant groups then go on to become (or remain) "tribal," at the periphery of the state. Such a process can indeed be observed directly; for example, during the evangelism of the Amerindians in Venezuela (see below). But as a general consequence it follows that tribalization is *not* a phenomenon unique to European colonialism, as many of the papers in this volume clearly illustrate. Nevertheless, the colonial period of history is a very important arena of debate since the written historical sources permit a complexity of inference that is not available from the archaeological record.

THE WAR OF TRIBE AND STATE

As the means by which the flow of persons between ethnic groups is often regulated, and as a force for radical change, the role of warfare is of particular interest to the study of the processes outlined above. It is by no means the only one, however. Economic dependency, demographic factors, and the political history of intercolonial rivalry are all part of the explanation of the effects of state formation or expansion on ethnic groups. In short, those ethnic formations that lie outside state control at a given point in time are either "tribalized" or destroyed in periods of state formation and expansion. No other outcome is possible if the state itself is to survive, since the state is a political formation under which authority must proceed from a uniform source. In this sense tribal and state organization can be treated as historically symbiotic social forms, culturally antagonistic yet each relying on the presence of the other to become a fully viable mode of human social organization. Anecdotally one might note that the threat of the "savages" on the borders of states has often had an important function in controlling population internal to the state, as in the political philosophy of Thomas Hobbes's *Leviathan,* while in the case of the Roman empire the German tribes actually became integral to its military efficiency (Anderson 1974:109–10; Todd 1975:30–42).

This relationship is also illustrated in state warfare against tribes, since it is in this social moment that the relative effectiveness of each social form is tested; that is, as states form and expand, the problems posed in asserting state control are fully displayed—as is the tribal response. This response need not be military to be successful, for the state may be forced to permit the existence of tribal formations at its frontiers for a lack of ability or resources to "civilize" them. As long as the tribes can be rendered amenable by war, trade, or diplomacy, their interdependency may achieve considerable stability, as in the Roman case. Yet the destruction or capture of the state by the tribes remains a constant historical possibility, as again the Roman case demonstrates (see also Bronson 1988). In the same way, among the tribal formations the correct management of political and economic relations with the state is often critical to successful leadership, as can be seen from the South American case (e.g., McCorkle 1952; Thomas 1982).

Accordingly, tribes may be said to contradict the forms of political allegiance experienced under state organization by means of their ideologies of genealogical and linguistic boundaries, regardless of how those boundaries are defined according to kinship terminology or dialect differences. This means that political alliance beyond the village level is always problematic due to the actual variation in language use and marriage practice. Segmentary lineage organization might represent a globally significant solution to this impasse,[3] since it consistently confers a strategic military advantage in the face of sedentary or state populations (Sahlins 1961; Wolf 1982:33). The presence of age-grades, cults, and other sodalities appears to have had an analogous historical role.

In this manner, sections of one tribe will view other sections as more or less authentic depending (in some situations) on their attitude to the state. The generosity with which "authenticity" is defined will also vary over time. Many modern groups can be clearly shown to be amalgamations of ethnic formations that differed widely in the past; in such situations we can infer many changes in historical definitions of authenticity. In short, boundaries are not generated in abstract but in response to a material threat to the status quo, whatever its particular and contingent definition. For example, despite evidence of warring among the Amerindians at contact and subsequent relationships of antagonism and slaving, indigenous groups of the Venezuelan and Guayana coasts and along the Orinoco and Amazon rivers nonetheless offered a frequently hostile response to the Spanish. They later evolved military alliances, with knowledge of Spanish atrocities in the Caribbean acting as a catalyst in this process of ethnic realignment.[4]

It was, then, the colonial state itself which created such conditions, actively eliciting and sustaining some of these new alignments ("tribes") if they were proved to be amenable to colonial purposes, and thereby providing the ground for future disputes. As Anderson (1974: 108) writes of the German tribes: "Roman diplomacy actively fanned these internecine disputes, by means of subventions and alliances, in order to neutralise barbarian pressures on the frontier and to crystallise a stratum of aristocratic rulers willing to co-operate with Rome." In a similar manner—through armed conflict against the enemies of their favored tribes, such as the Arawaks—the Spanish knocked out the key members of the ancient elites and replaced them with puppet leaders, increasing the economic and political influence of such "reduced" groups by granting them a relative monopoly on the distribution of highly valued European goods.

The hierarchical structures and sodalities that shaped the ancient, precolonial tribes proved to be the greatest source of potential opposition to the establishment and extension of state power: possibly because they most clearly mirrored it. This conclusion is reflected in the extensive debate over the point at which chiefdoms become states (see endnote 2) and in the debate over the role of segmentary lineage organization in the formation of both chieftaincies and states (Fox 1987).

Empirical evidence for this observation is found in the fact that these institutions historically are the first to be swept away by the advent of colonialism; their disappearance is a sign that the creation of colonial tribes has begun. Only in the later stages of state expansion, at the extension of direct administrative control over the tribes, are the subsequent tribal formations completely destroyed and their associated military formations ended by "pacification." Such pacification becomes possible because the dependency of indigenous leaders on the state renders the tribes either incapable or unwilling to resist, and sometimes actively seeking incorporation as citizens of the state.

It is to the demonstration of these processes in early colonial South American history that I now turn.

PRECOLONIAL AND COLONIAL TRIBES

As the Europeans arrived in South America, they searched diligently for signs of "polity" among the Amerindians. Whenever possible, indigenous political structures were recorded, their terminologies noted, and analogies drawn with the political formations of Europe (see *C.D.I.* 1864–84; Colón 1989; Las Casas 1951; Ralegh 1848). Whatever the shortcomings of these descriptions, they nonetheless make it clear that the Europeans in certain areas were confronted with civilizations of at least the complexity and sophistication of their own. As a result, the often low-born *conquistadores* (Gongora 1976) were apt to accept the cultural and political prejudices of the ancient elites they encountered. In the Caribbean-Guayana area this had consequences that continue to echo down the centuries, as the alleged savagery of the *caribes* ("fierce, wild men") and *caniba* ("mainlanders-from-the-south") was specially singled out to provide a moral and legal basis for the military occupation of the New World. As a result, the "cannibals" continue to inhabit the thickets of the European imagination[5] (see Hulme and Whitehead 1992).

Although it is at present uncertain whether or not the more powerful polities of this region were true states, it would seem that groups of a lesser scale and social complexity ("tribes") already existed in the hinterland that often occurred between them.[6] Preeminent among these, according to the Taino kings, were the *caribes* (Whitehead 1988). But the *caribes* were by no means the only group; on the mainland itself, the *aruacas* were held in the same contempt by the ancient elites of the Orinoco mouth. Similarly, the designations *waika* and *guaharibo* have been applied to groups as geographically and culturally disparate as the Kapon (Akawaio) and Yanomami-Sanuma: all groups who at some point have been, or become, marginal to the workings of Amerindian macropolities in this region. A pre-Columbian hierarchy of Amerindian social systems is also implied by the widespread use of the designations *maku* and *poito* on the part of agriculturalists to discriminate themselves from the hunter-gatherer forest-dwellers. Evidence given directly by the remnants of the Lokono ruling elites in the eighteenth century makes it clear that the notion of the *faletti* ("barbarians") was used for more than the simple maintenance of tribal boundaries, *faletti* being a term that was both regional and transethnic in its reference.

Once we understand that the Europeans came to accept these designations as ethnographic fact, we can in part explain both the pattern of European wars of conquest and pacification and the ideological means that were used to justify these conquests. The active involvement of the Europeans in Amerindian political life meant that the tribalization of this old order could begin. The Lokono themselves were reduced to the status of *faletti* by such means. Recognizing this, their modern descendants have told me that "our fathers have been *too* clever in their friendship with you whites."

Such results were often achieved directly by military campaigns of extermination, or more subtly by the formation of tactical alliances with *guatiao* (the Taino category for "friendly") *caciques,* who then provided the political and often military means by which further conquests could be initiated. This process quickly undermined precolonial political structures, which were extremely vulnerable to the mass executions of their ruling elites. The Lokono, for example, were able to extend their distribution in Guayana significantly, and at the expense of indigenous groups, through direct military assistance from the Spanish. The Spanish gave this assistance because Lokono knowledge of the native political geography enabled them to lead Spanish raiding parties which otherwise would have had great difficulty in locating inland settlements (Keymis 1596:4, 8–9). Considerations such as these came to dominate the internal workings of the Amerindian polities, and it was those groups that most successfully adapted to these conditions that emerged as the dominant ethnic force in the colonial period proper. This much is also very evident on a global scale, and it is these adaptive groups that most fully exemplify the "colonial tribe" (after Fried 1975; Wolf 1982).

One might therefore make the following distinctions among the ethnic formations that can be observed during the period of approximately A.D. 1500 to 1800: (1) those tribes that emerged as a direct consequence of the European presence (Caribs); (2) those groups that were aboriginally powerful but (a) failed to negotiate the new conditions of initial European occupation and were reduced to tribal status by direct military campaigns (Warao) or (b) did make such a successful transition but were nevertheless tribalized as a consequence of this political and economic dependency on the Europeans (Lokono, Kalinago, Palikur); and (3) those groups that were created as an indirect consequence of the European presence, but often without any direct contact until the nineteenth century. This last category might be further distinguished as follows: (a) amalgamations/immigrants such as the Trio, Wai-Wai, Yanomami, Wapishana, and Wayapi; (b) marginalized/self-marginalizing (whites-avoiding) groups such as the Taruma, Akuriyo, Waimiri, and Wayana; (c) regional indigenous ethnic networks such as the Soto and Pemon-Kapon that have had varying "tribal" identities (see Colson 1983–84).

In each of these cases, specific tribal identities have been shaped by the slow and tenuous expansion and contraction of the colonial states in the region, notwithstanding their geographical distance or relative isolation from these states (cf. also Schlee 1989). Thus, no modern groups can be seen as exemplifying pre-Columbian patterns of existence, as has sometimes been the rather naive assumption of ethnographers and archaeologists.

The tripartite distinction outlined above may also be reflected in the way in which ethnicity and subsequent tribal identities were derived. In case 1, political authority derived solely from competence in trade and war, genealogical boundaries being commensurately negotiable. In case 2, and befitting those groups who displayed the most complex polities at contact, political authority originally derived from some form of dynastic social charter or genealogical positioning, and genealogical boundaries were more rigid as a result. Such groups came to more closely approximate those in case 1. In case 3, political authority continued to derive from a role in exchange relationships within the surviving indigenous political economy of the region, and "tribalization" was thus only indirect and tenuous. Nevertheless, demographic collapse, predation from martial groups, and repeated immigrations and amalgamations all evince the reality of historical process among these groups.

These distinctions may also be directly related to sociophysical distance from the centers of colonial state expansion and, most importantly, to the incidence of warfare. Before considering this latter phenomenon, however, one further variable needs to be discussed: that is, the differing modes of European contact and colonialism, which decided the rhythm of warfare in the region. As an invasive force, the Europeans held the military initiative; as a colonial enterprise, they became vulnerable to ambush and raid.

PROTOCOLONIAL AND COLONIAL STATES

Just as it has proved possible to make a series of clarifications and qualifications concerning the nature of the social formations that were first encountered in America and their subsequent interaction with the Europeans, so too it is clear that there are important distinctions to be made in the manner of the colonial process, not just as it occurred in geographically distant areas, but also in regard to the objectives of the colonizers themselves.

Equally important are the distinctions, implicit in the deliberate conflation of state formation and state expansion discussed above, between the formation of a colonial state and the expansion of a metropolitan one, as well as between the formation of the colonial state (enclave) and the expansion of that state beyond these initial confines. The historical reality of such distinctions is suggested by a consideration of the Guayana-Caribbean area which, as a zone of intense colonial rivalry from the very inception of European presence, saw the repeated foundation or destruction of colonial enclaves. In turn, the perennial problems metropolitan centers had in asserting their political and economic priority over these enclaves suggests that such colonies should be considered states in their own right. It should be emphasized that although we may speak of, say, the "Spanish," in point of fact the personnel who carried out the first *conquistas* and subsequent settlement were, as in the case of Columbus himself, not necessarily either Castilian or Aragonese. Indeed it is arguable that the American colonial encounter, just as it tribalized indigenous societies, at the same time permitted the construction of nation-states in Europe (see also endnote 3; Gledhill 1988b:303). Without the vast material and intellectual gain that Europe received from the Amerindians, as from other areas of colonial activity, few of the social advances of the seventeenth and eighteenth centuries would have been possible. In this sense also, then, "tribe" and "state" can be seen as symbiotic social phenomena.

Various though colonial encounters were, however, they also display uniformity. Bodley (1982), on the basis of a global survey of European contact situations, has suggested that three phases may be distinguished in the unfolding of the colonial system. These may be summarized as (1) violent, random impact, followed by (2) specific military campaigns to ensure the security of a colonial enclave, and (3) the extension of administrative control by threat or persuasion.

Certainly military action is implicit in all three of these phases, but not to the same degree and with different objectives in different cases. Moreover, as the European experience in Guayana shows, colonial ambitions are themselves highly variable, ranging from purely commercial trade to the establishment of feudal mini-states. Given the small scale of the European military garrisons in this region, however, the pattern of Amerindian warfare often decided the ultimate fate of any colonial enterprise; although this was increasingly less so as the infrastructure of the eighteenth-century colonial states was consolidated and extended, beginning with the missionary campaigns in Colombia and Venezuela. It will be appreciated, therefore, that the progress of colonial state building was very uneven throughout this area, with the frontier between the state and tribal formations retreating as well as advancing, often due to factors outside the control of either. Such an episodic experience of the limits to state power has thus been a distinctive factor in the formation of Amerindian political consciousness. It may well be a reason why ethnicity has remained a potent force into the modern era, even where particularly indigenous modes of living have completely disappeared (see also Friedman 1989).

In light of these considerations, one might extend Bodley's schema to distinguish conquest and plunder from commercial trade in phase 1, and between the feudal appropriation of Amerindian labor (encomiendas) and the use of Amerindians in the plantation system during phase 2. Phase 3 had very specific characteristics in tropical South America, where the importance of missionary evangelism was paramount. But it should be noted that the missionary orders themselves, despite being the political proxies of the Spanish and Portuguese crowns, were frequently antagonistic toward the colonial administration.[7]

Having established both the distinctions drawn in the responses of indigenous groups and the schema for European contact outlined above, it remains to examine how the conduct of warfare by Amerindian groups affected the outcome of contact or the proximity of European state formations in the northeastern South America region.

THE CREATION OF THE TRIBES, 1492–1680

From the early accounts of the Europeans in the New World it is evident that the Amerindians already possessed military capabilities. It is more difficult to determine whether later accounts describe a situation in which the threat of European presence had induced Amerindian groups to extend and refine their military practices, or whether traditional military behavior was being adhered to even in the face of superior European military techniques.

I have argued elsewhere (Whitehead 1990a, 1990b) that in the case of the Caribs, at least, it would seem that there are important contrasts between the initial and later periods. Given nearly three centuries of Carib and European interaction, this is perhaps not surprising. From the point of view of the creation of the Carib polity, the contrasts would seem to support the notion that the European presence induced innovations in military organization where such organization had previously been of a lesser or different social significance. Much the same could be said of many groups other than the Caribs, including the Kalinago (Caraibes) of the Antilles, the Miskito of Honduras, the Aruan of Brazil, and the Ranqueles in Argentina.

But this limited perspective ignores the effect of Amerindian warfare on the military practices of the Europeans. It should be emphasized that neither guns nor horses were of decisive strategic value in this area of the New World, and as a consequence, great reliance was put upon the political and military intelligence of the Amerindians themselves, as is shown by the pattern of European alliance making. It was not until the late colonial period that professional soldiery from Europe was deployed extensively in this region, tribal mercenaries being utilized instead, and it was often those martial tribes that earlier had been deliberately cultivated as mercenaries by the Europeans that were to become the object of these later military campaigns.

Military campaigns thus always implied the political support of some section of the indigenous population, and those groups that could most closely conform to European political and economic expectations had a strong influence on the conduct and object of such campaigns. It is for this reason that the Arawaks (Lokono) on the Orinoco River, the Caribs on the Essequibo, and the Aruan at the mouth of the Amazon supported the colonial ambitions of, respectively, the Spanish, Dutch, and French. As a result, European occupation was also the pretext for settling disputes or gaining social advantage. In certain cases, these "loyal" Amerindians (*guatiao*) were specifically encouraged to "eat out" the aboriginal inhabitants of designated areas, as the Spanish encouraged the Arawaks to do along the Atlantic coast in the early seventeenth century. The threat of the Spanish presence could also occasion the alliance of enemies, and the outcome of these realignments was closely studied and exploited by later colonial arrivals such as Walter Ralegh and Lawrence Keymis.

Nonetheless, the European conquests were always uncertain and, in light of the intercolonial rivalry mentioned above, often counterproductive. For example, the early colonial settlements of Chirivichi, Santo Tomé, San José de Oruña, Cayenne, Surinam, and Tobago were all destroyed by Amerindian flotillas at one time or another; several of them were destroyed a second time by joint European and Amerindian raiding parties during the repeated bouts of intercolonial conflict that characterized the whole of this period. In the situation of unpredictable conflict created by the Europeans, groups that had been accustomed to the relative predictability and stability that seems to characterize traditional feuding relationships took up a more overt military posture.[8] This response is shown by the adoption of permanent or more complex village defenses and by unceasing efforts to induce the Europeans to provide military assistance. Failure to take such measures left Amerindian groups vulnerable to enslavement or dispersion.

As time progressed, Amerindian societies as a whole were necessarily forced to adapt to the exigencies of contact with the colonial state, and the first steps along the road to the creation of modern tribal structures had begun. The widespread ethnic cooperation and alliances that had first greeted the Europeans were then steadily broken down by either direct conquest and exterminations or through policies of preferential trading and military alliance. In the latter case new "tribal" identities emerged very rapidly, since the redistribution of European manufactures was a powerful source of economic and political influence among groups without access to the Europeans.

In either case, both the permeability of group boundaries and the sociogeographical contiguity of settlement that had once underlain it were inhibited and interrupted (cf. Osborn 1989). It is these processes, therefore, that must be accounted fundamental to "tribalization," since it is in these features that there is the greatest contrast between precolonial and colonial tribes. Emphasis on the immediate locality as the only safe sphere of interaction, an increased emphasis on language as a political marker, and the refusal, on the part of the Europeans, to observe indigenous social distinctions therefore encouraged the kind of inward-facing, bounded, and isolated social unit that is classically a modern "tribal" formation. Moreover, the political leadership of such units is of necessity both unstable and incapable of integrating co-ethnics beyond a certain level, as the work of Chagnon (1968) on the Yanomami illustrates.

Here we can see the mutual formation of state and tribe most clearly; for this tendency to identify language and polity was of equal import to the Europeans, who were themselves in the process of creating linguistically exclusive macropolities (i.e., nation-states) on the basis of their American wealth. This meant that there were also powerful international forces encouraging the Amerindian retreat into the immediate kin group. However, limitations in the effectiveness of the strategy of conquest to achieve these results meant this situation did not persist. Among the Dutch and French colonial enclaves of the Guayana coast, for example, a measure of stability had been achieved by the end of the century, the authorities having reached agreements and signed treaties of peace with the various local groups, such as the Arawak and Carib. These groups then emerged as regionally dominant through their privileged contacts with the Europeans, displaying the attributes of "colonial tribes" par excellence.

In the Spanish territories, despite some success in conquering the groups of the open savannas north of the Orinoco, colonial settlements were essentially still limited to the immediate coastal and riverbank areas. As a result, in 1652 the Spanish Crown decreed the end of the *conquista a fuego y sangre* (conquest by fire and blood) and initiated the *conquista de almas* (conquest of souls).

THE REDUCTION TO OBEDIENCE, 1652–1763

Commensurate with their new-found status, such groups as the Carib and Arawak used their preferential relations with the Europeans to consolidate and extend their trade-clientship through trade and raid. Against a background of severe demographic decline in the overall position of the Amerindian during this period, tribal recruitment was in itself evidently critical. This recruitment apparently was more successfully managed by groups that were unencumbered by complex rules of marriage and descent, for there is evidence (Schwerin 1983–84; Henley 1983–84) that such kinship systems were abandoned in response to changed conditions.

In such a context demographic factors played an important role in determining the differential survival of tribes. Ironically, it was those groups that most actively sought contact with the Europeans (thereby often achieving a relative dominance over other groups), in addition to those already reduced to obedience, that were to face the brunt of the epidemics that swept this area in the eighteenth century. The establishment of missions furthered the process of supplanting indigenous authority, since what the *conquistadores* had failed to achieve by force of arms against the independent tribes, the missionaries accomplished indirectly by the economic and political marginalization of regional leaders and traders. The eventual demographic devastation of Amerindian populations undoubtedly facilitated this process. In consequence, Amerindian warfare centered on the missions which held relatives and trade-clients in a state of captivity, thereby undermining the economic and social exchanges that had once supported the autonomous political authority of the *caciques*.

Similarly, as the range of Dutch trade activities with the Amerindians shrunk due to the inception of sugar plantations along the Guayana coast, different tribes competed for the dwindling supply of European goods. Although the colonial authorities did all they could to defuse local conflicts, access to these goods was heavily dependent on a willingness to conform to European expectations. As a result, an informal system of ethnic ranking emerged in regard to the distribution of these goods. Favored Amerindian leaders were also formally "confirmed" in their authority by the colonial administration, who gave them insignia of office.

It becomes increasingly evident in this period that "problem" groups of the interior who were "relatively deprived" (Adas 1987:61–62) in relation to these arrangements were targeted, and punitive expeditions were led against them (see Whitehead 1990b). Significantly, it was among such groups that millenarian movements arose in the aftermath of these campaigns. By targeting problem groups the dependency of loyal groups was increased. Their willingness to act as European proxies ensured that any attempts to form pan-Amerindian alliances independently of the Europeans, as had been done in earlier times, would fail.

THE PRELUDE TO INCORPORATION, 1763–1820

Although by the second half of the eighteenth century the infrastructure of the colonial states was firmly established, the political identity of the administration still experienced occasional changes. It is symptomatic of the increasingly marginal position of even the most powerful colonial tribes, however, that they were less important to these changes than was true at the inception of the colonies. Professional soldiery from Europe or specially formed slave regiments (Buckley 1979; de Groot n.d.) were now frequently used instead of native auxiliaries, especially against the Maroon (rebel slave) colonies of the interior (Stedman 1790).

Nevertheless, within local spheres of influence the police role of certain Amerindian *caciques* was of vital importance, since the Guayana plantations experienced chronic problems in the basic day-to-day control of their black slave populations. Indeed, notwithstanding the assistance of certain Amerindian leaders, Maroon enclaves sprang up throughout the region, particularly in Surinam where the authorities eventually gave them formal recognition and diplomatic status.

In the Spanish territories the evangelization of the Amerindians was nominally complete, but this did not necessarily entail a complete pacification, and sporadic rebellions against the mission regime occurred all over the Orinoco Basin. Nevertheless, the cooperation of Amerindian groups was vital in the achievement of even this limited expansion of state authority, as tribal conflicts were used to augment the effectiveness of missionary reduction. As in earlier times the Europeans became the pretext for the settling of old scores.

The antithesis between state and tribe is very evident in the missionary process, and the contrasting social priorities of each were clearly displayed in the problems that confronted the missionaries. Inducing the Amerindians to settle in one place, to follow a specific labor regime, and to accept the political authority of the missionaries required a judicious blend of military threat and political persuasion. Many missions were accordingly ephemeral, their neophytes preferring the "deceitful freedom of the woods" to the "gloomy" mission huts (Hamilton 1820–21).

Still, at the turn of the century state control in Guayana was at its zenith, and Amerindians in the nineteenth century maintained their political independence only by deepening their retreat into the interior or by choosing a deliberate social isolation, even from others of the same tribe. It was in such a situation that the first ethnographers encountered them.

CONCLUSIONS

A number of questions arising from the foregoing material require specific attention. What are the differences between state and tribal warfare? How is tribal warfare related to different processes of contact? In what way does the conduct of war relate to the social situation and differential survival of groups? On the basis of the general analysis of tribe-state relations and the particular examination of the South American case presented above, the following discussion offers preliminary answers to these questions.

THE CULTURE OF WAR AND THE INTERDEPENDENCE OF ENEMIES

At contact—variable in time though that moment was—it is clear that the purposes of Amerindian and European warfare differed markedly. This was true despite the fact that a limited and contingent coincidence of political interests was to become the basis for the earliest military alliances, such as that between the Spanish and Arawak. For their part, the first Spanish *conquistas* were essentially directed toward securing a base of operations, even if only for the provision of "wood and water"; to make a profit on the cost of *entradas* by the barter or plunder of gold, jewels, pearls, and slaves; and to then transfer this booty to Europe, where it could be used to live the civilized life. But this individual itinerary often ran counter to the Spanish Crown's designs to extend state power over the whole of the American continent, and so the pattern of Spanish warfare was determined by the interplay of these conflicting aims (Gongora 1976). In this early phase the process of colonial state formation is arguably indistinguishable from that of metropolitan state expansion.

By contrast, the aim of Amerindian warfare was still largely defined by the pre-Columbian political economy until it was destroyed during the occupation of the Orinoco and Guayana coasts between 1590 and 1630. Consequently, the capture of women and ritual objects and the pursuit of feuding relationships governed the conduct of indigenous war. The Europeans were certainly perceived as threatening and though they could initially be discouraged by martial display, where the invaders acted in earnest the Amerindians suffered many casualties. So it was that Topiawari, king of the Guayanos at the Orinoco mouth, offered military alliance to Walter Ralegh since the presence of the Spaniards in Margarita, as

Ralegh reported, had caused "these frontiers to grow thin of people and also great numbers [of Indians] are fled to other nations farther off for fear of the Spaniards" (Ralegh 1848:95). This movement of population in advance of Spanish contact itself became a pretext for war, as refugees tried to settle along the Guayana coast. Similarly, the presence of the Dutch colonies later *attracted* Amerindian groups and sparked intergroup conflicts over priority of access to European goods.

Military initiative, the advantage of an invasive force, most often rested with the Spanish. Amerindian groups were usually limited to defending their homes, and they initially feared attacking the Spanish because of their firearms (Keymis 1596:23). Nonetheless, the Spanish were often defeated in the early years. They were then forced to pay ransom for the European and African captives that the Amerindians seized, if they were able to recover them at all. Consequently, although the actual military capabilities of Spanish and Amerindian differed vastly, their military cultures and techniques came to more closely approximate each other due to their intimacy and interdependency as perennial enemies. The Spanish, for example, learned the arts of small-scale ambush and raid, while the Amerindians adopted the art of making elaborate defensive positions, since to offer open battle against European firearms was suicidal.

Still, battles among the Amerindians themselves often continued to be fought in a distinct manner, for only in this way could the symbolic and social purposes of such encounters be properly expressed. The Caraibes, for example, despite the extent to which they had been exposed to European military tactics and had successfully adopted them, when fighting their traditional enemies the Arawak did so "not to become masters of a new country, or to load themselves with the spoils of their enemies; but only the glory of subduing and triumphing over them" (Rochefort 1665:531). So too they continued to consider the Arawak as the only appropriate victims for their anthropophagic rituals, as well as lexically distinguishing "Amerindian" and "European" enemies and the practice of "vengeance" from the conduct of "war" (Breton 1665:222–23, 308, 370; Breton 1666:142; Rochefort 1665:531).

The convergence of state and tribal warfare was the main trend, however, as Amerindian levies were increasingly integrated into colonial military forces and as the native Americans themselves sought military alliances with the Europeans in order to pursue their traditional conflicts. At the same time, the purposes of Amerindian warfare also changed, since the political economy from which pre-Columbian patterns of alliance had evolved was itself changing rapidly, especially as the other European nations began the extensive trade of cloth and steel tools.

MODES OF CONTACT AND MILITARY RESPONSE

The differing modes of contact certainly influenced the types of military behavior that evolved under the colonial political economy. In the Spanish case the *conquistas* most obviously elicited an initial armed response on the part of the Amerindians, but if the Spanish withdrew in the face of this threat they later experienced great difficulty in bringing Amerindian warriors to battle. Yet to be politically effective they required an agreed "victory" over indigenous political structures. They hoped to achieve this first through the capture and control of the ancient elites. Failing in this, they sought political proxies (such as the Arawak) within the Amerindian political economy, who then gave political direction to Spanish military actions. Sources of pan-Amerindian opposition were knocked out, and the tribalization of the remnant groups rendered them at least tractable, if not ready to become "feudal vassals" of the Crown. In this sense the growth of Carib political dominance in the seventeenth century represented an anti-Spanish front across the whole of this region, underwritten by the alliances the Caribs established with the colonial rivals of Spain (Whitehead 1988).

The nature of the first *conquistadores* themselves must also be considered. It has already been suggested that their individual social backgrounds had particular consequences for the political relations they established in the New World, and so it was in the military sphere as well. The inevitable problems of maintaining military discipline, joined with the entrepreneurial nature of their reconnaissances into the hinterland, meant that the larger political designs of establishing "governorships" in the name of the Spanish Crown were often jeopardized or utterly frustrated by the random violence of the *entradas* (see Ojer 1966). Later colonial arrivals such as Lawrence Keymis were fully able to appreciate and avoid the consequences of pointlessly engendering native hostility (Keymis 1596:26). In addition, the fact that the *reconquista* in Spain had been completed in the very year that Columbus stumbled across America meant that there was a ready supply of mercenaries and adventurers to man even the most ill-planned expeditions. At the command level, though, these individuals were in fact the product of a highly developed military tradition, one that later dominated the European theater of war as the Spanish Crown professionalized these early war captains (Lynch 1964(1):76–79; see also endnote 3).

The initial actions of such groups, usually concerned only with short-term gain, elicited suspicion and hostility from the Amerindians who, as a result, either withdrew from the coasts and main rivers or adapted to this threat by seeking new military alliances. However, although both these strategies became widespread, they also became increasingly ineffective as the colonial states definitively established themselves.

For those groups that did not succumb to the first decades of such contact, a more stable relationship with the Spanish was possible. On the part of the Spanish Crown the indiscipline of its representatives necessitated a definition of and distinction between groups that were to be conserved, as part of the possessions of the Crown, and those that might, in order to sustain the individual profitability of the colonial process, be arbitrarily enslaved or plundered. Accordingly the Caribbean and its southern littoral was subject to a survey by the Spanish royal judge, Rodrigo de Figueroa (*C.D.I.*(11): 32), which gave legal basis to the distinction between *caribes* and *guatiao*. Those groups falling into the former category became liable to, and often experienced, slave raids and the destruction of their homes and subsistence sites. This ethnographic exercise by the Spanish Crown was one of the clearest examples of overt state tribalization, since although these were native categories, their application and meaning was given a wholly Spanish interpretation. As a result, "conquests by fire and blood" were a constant feature of relations with the *caribes*, while in the immediate locale of Spanish settlement the *guatiao* were parceled out in *encomiendas* to the Spanish colonizers to whom annual tribute was due. Although the authority of the *encomenderos* might be extremely tenuous, such groups were essentially pacified and their rebellions easily and brutally crushed.

Trade was sometimes established with groups outside the immediate reach of Spanish administration, and its effects foreshadow the more extensive commerce that Spain's colonial rivals were to inaugurate at the beginning of the seventeenth century. Essentially, the Spanish grant of a monopoly on the distribution of European goods was a powerful political tool in the hands of Amerindian leaders. There can be little doubt that without this trade gap, Amerindian responses would have been vastly different; indeed, many groups initially treated the European baubles with contempt. Nevertheless, access to this trade was perceived by both the Amerindians and Spanish as a way of reforming the political leadership in the region. Spanish alliances with the Arawak and Nepoyo, for example, were explicitly justified in these terms (Keymis 1596:20; Ojer 1966:161–235). As a result these new leaders evolved a dependency on the Europeans and vice versa, for the Europeans were utterly dependent on the Amerindians for the supply of foodstuffs and for their knowledge of the vast continent that lay to the south.

With the increasing physical presence of the Dutch, French, and English colonial competitors of Spain, the politics of this preferential trading became very complex indeed; but it is this network of relationships that shaped the pattern of warfare. As the actual items of trade varied, so did the socioeconomic consequences of that trade. For example, one might contrast the trade for gold and pearls that occurred at contact with the slave trade that ensued as the native store of such items was exhausted and the Spanish sought to exploit the mines and pearl beds for themselves. In the former case, the favorable terms of exchange that the Amerindians offered generally supported pacific contacts; in the latter, raid and plunder became the order of the day.

By contrast, during the inception and establishment of the Dutch West India Company's enclave in Essequibo, whose purpose was to manage a profitable trade with the Amerindians rather than lead them into the light of Christian civilization, all was done to steer a middle course between Amerindian disputes so that trade could be as open as possible for all groups that desired it. Such a noncommittal policy certainly ran counter to the ambitions of many different ethnic chieftains, and it is not surprising to learn that the first Dutch governor of Essequibo was soon forced to come to exclusive trading arrangements with the local Caribs. The local Arawak families then moved on to Barbados, where the foundation of an English enclave offered better prospects for exclusive contacts (Handler 1968).

Such was largely the pattern for all the other trading enclaves, but Amerindian conflicts were sometimes so irreconcilable that the authorities agreed to the military dispersal of their trade partners' rivals. For example, by contrast with Essequibo, in Surinam and Berbice it was the Arawak who were finally favored over the Carib, and subsequent tensions between the colonial administrations of Surinam and Essequibo may be partly related to the different trajectories along which these initial Amerindian alliances had propelled them (Whitehead n.d.). Indeed, the necessity of choosing between the Arawaks and Caribs in this area was itself a legacy of the Spanish occupation of the Orinoco. It was Spanish military support and their exchange of European goods for manioc flour that had underwritten the Arawak invasion and settlement of lands west of the Berbice and east of the Corentyn rivers, which included traditional areas of Carib occupation.

As the value of direct trade for Amerindian products fell off, so did the importance of correctly managing relations with the native population. Plantations were established throughout this region and, as the number of black slaves and Maroons increased, both the interior trade and the demographic position of the Amerindians declined. Even in limited numbers, however, they were still useful in policing this black population. At the prompting of the Dutch, Amerindian warfare was often conducted against rebel black colonies or against other Amerindians, who were then used as domestic slaves. In this role both the Caribs and Arawaks were preeminent, and they were also used to police the "wild tribes" of the inland. But the interior tribes themselves, having been integrated into the colonial political economy by the redistribution of European goods, increasingly exemplified Carib or Arawak patterns of warfare, as they too began raiding each other for slaves and hunting down Maroons (Whitehead 1988:91–97, 151–70).

During the eighteenth century, the tribalization of the Guayana groups is shown clearly by the European endorsement of certain Amerindian leaders and rejection of others, a practice that had extended to the interior groups by the turn of the nineteenth century (Hilhouse 1825). Significantly, the characteristic colonial attitude shown in the secondary literature of the eighteenth and nineteenth centuries (e.g., Bancroft 1769; Hartsninck 1770; Stedman 1790; Waterton 1825) no longer looks at the generality of Amerindian life, with ethnic characteristics being treated as a largely political attribute, but rather reflects the results of the unfolding of the colonial process and the stabilization of the colonial state. By this time the Amerindian groups are no longer called "nations" but rather "tribes," and their boundaries are described as being clear and nonnegotiable. Although this certainly was not the full truth of the situation, and of course represents the results of unprofessionalized ethnography, it nonetheless reflects the outlook of those responsible for the management of relations with the Amerindians. Accordingly it was those groups who most closely conformed to these European cultural and political assumptions who were the most successful in their management of relations with the authorities.

Contemporary with these developments in the Dutch and French territories, the Spanish *conquista de almas* induced a different pattern of warfare and alliance. Evangelism was itself often a military process, and where it was successful it exacerbated existing intertribal divisions or even opened new divisions within the discrete tribal structures that had been created by the first phase of conquest and occupation. The missionaries capitalized on this divisive effect and sought to use one section of an evangelized tribe, the *indios reducidos* ("pacified Indians"), against still independent groups, or *indios bravos* ("wild Indians"). The final result was to create warring factions of "Spanish Caribs" and "Dutch Caribs" or "Spanish Arawaks" and "Dutch Arawaks," divisions that persist into the present day. State creation of tribal boundaries could not be better illustrated than in such cases.

The mechanism of missionary work derived its economic base from the exploitation of the labor of the Amerindians, who were paid in European manufactures. As such it directly challenged the basis of tribal leadership, since these distributions by the missionaries were initially of a greater regularity and facility of access than those of Amerindian traders such as the Caribs. In time, as the political and military dominance of the missionaries was further established, the mission labor regime became more and more exploitative, however, and the Amerindian became indistinguishable from the *peon* at the base of the economies of the emergent nation-states of the region. Where the martial traditions of such groups were utilized it was exclusively in the policing of other Amerindians, though use was made of the Caribs during the Venezuelan wars of independence in the early nineteenth century.

TRIBAL SURVIVAL AND THE CONDUCT OF WAR

Preeminent among military factors determining the survival of tribal groups was the way in which firearms found their way into exchange networks. This was less because of the actual usefulness of such weapons for combat in a tropical forest environment (which was universally acknowledged to be minimal) than because their possession was a marker of a group's favorable relations with the Europeans. Even when guns became available they were mostly used for their psychological effect, underlining the point that Amerindian warfare rarely had physical extermination as its object. The dispersion of enemy villages was considered sufficient grounds for victory. But as the military technology of the Europeans improved, so did the desirability of such weapons. By the late eighteenth century the Europeans were extremely alarmed that "unscrupulous traders" were freely trading guns into the hands of the Amerindians in order to encourage raiding for slaves. At this point very small parties of well-armed individuals became extremely effective militarily, and traditional social constraints on the scope of raiding and feuding were loosened accordingly (Whitehead 1990a; see also endnote 8).

In earlier times the native use of arrow poison had certainly alarmed the Spanish (who therefore retained body armor), but its strategic significance declined as the Amerindians rarely continued to offer open battle. As has been mentioned, this refusal to offer combat, along with the deliberate secretion of habitation and garden sites, led to a direct reliance on an Amerindian "fifth column" if military victories were to be achieved. In turn, ever more severe strategies of retreat were needed if groups were to remain undetected; this led inevitably to fights between refugees and indigenous populations in the areas of retreat. Alternatively, some groups, such as the Akuriyo (Kloos 1977), took up a nomadic existence and dropped out of Amerindian regional networks entirely.[9]

On the part of the Europeans the decision to embark upon military campaigns that appeared desirable was invariably influenced by the chronic lack of military resources and trained personnel prior to the eighteenth century; hence the extensive use of Amerindian levies where possible. The specific tribal affiliation of these levies, or ethnic soldiers (Whitehead 1990b), also tended to channel military activity toward groups that were the particular enemies of these indigenous allies of the Europeans. When European soldiery and weaponry was available, the colonial authorities were capable of delivering overwhelming armed force, suggesting that where Amerindian independence persisted it was less a product of their military effectiveness than of the relative political priority that was assigned to their conquest.

The manner in which groups were finally assimilated can thus be seen as the net result of the factors outlined above. Tribe-by-tribe analysis of such factors will then show us the specific interplay of the "structure and conjuncture" (Bourdieu 1977:78), or the material and the ideological, that has occurred during this general historical process. But it is in the communality of that colonial history, which is now as much a part of Amerindian heritage as it is of our own, that a basic anthropological rule of human grouping is demonstrated: Tribes make states and states make tribes.

Notes
---

1. This semantic distinction between "savage" and "barbarian" has some historical and etymological justification, since these terms may be distinguished as meaning "wild" and "foreigner," respectively (Oxford English Dictionary).

2. This apparent absence of state formations may relate only to criteria employed when defining the state, and some "states" might have been no more than chieftaincies politically. By displaying great social inertia or continuity, caused by the transmission of a repetitive ethnic identity through time, such chieftaincies may nonetheless come to be identified archaeologically and ethnohistorically as monarchical states. Such a state of affairs cannot be realized or be historically recognized until there is no living memory of the inception of the original chieftaincy, and its existence has become a fact of the world into which subsequent generations are born (cf. Gledhill 1988a:13–14; Gledhill 1989:120–21; Salomon 1986).

3. Segmentary lineage organization also seems to be important in the transition to statehood proper, as in the Maya case (Fox 1987). It is striking that the expansion of European feudalism from the eleventh century on was, in fact, not the work of "nations," kingdoms, or states so much as that of spontaneously

organized bands or groups of warriors. This is classically the case for Norman expansion into Europe and the Mediterranean, and for the Crusades. In Spain, despite the central role played by the crowns of Aragon and Castile, much of the task of regaining national territory was actually left to autonomous military units, such as the Iberian orders of Santiago, Alcantara, and Montesa, and the international ones such as the Templars and Hospitallers (Gongora 1976).

4. That these groups were not intractably warlike is demonstrated by the fact that the Dutch and English were able to make peaceful contacts with the same groups. Contact with the Spanish had already, by the 1630s, "tribalized" these groups to some degree, but the resulting hostilities only crystalized into intractable tribal divisions as the new European arrivals exploited and reinforced such conflicts.

5. Although, following Columbus, *caniba* has been directly glossed as "cannibal," de Goeje (1939) suggests that the meaning actually may have been a more mundane geographical reference. It is interesting to note that Sanday (1986) suggests a symbolically strong relationship between cannibalism and the direction south, in the Fijian Islands case.

6. Some (DeBoer 1981) have interpreted these dead zones as buffer areas between chieftaincies, and this may well have been an outcome of the growth of such chieftaincies to the limits of their circumscription (after Carneiro 1981). However, it would still have to be shown that such chieftaincies had the potential to encompass other polities, or the desire to do so, before the apparent lack of contiguity in indigenous settlement can be given this interpretation.

7. This conflict between church and state led, in 1767, to the expulsion of the entire Jesuit order from the New World. The Jesuits in Paraguay, for example, had organized Amerindian labor so effectively that their missions formed a virtually independent state, as did the Capuchins' missions in the cattle-ranching areas south of the Orinoco (Whitehead 1988: 131–50).

8. Perhaps because of the participants' ability to make precise calculations concerning the effect of a raid, evinced by the intentional selectivity with which opponents are killed, such feuding relationships show a tendency to long-term stability—at least until factors such as access to new military techniques open the vista of a higher-order victory.

9. The Akuriyo became known as the "Di-Di" by the black prospectors who entered the interior in the nineteenth century, and they were earnestly sought by anthropologists as possible examples of protohominids that had survived to the modern age. Charles Darwin thought the Tierra del Fuegans were similar "survivals."

Chapter 7

Beavers and Muskets

Iroquois Military Fortunes
in the Face of European Colonization

THOMAS S. ABLER

I T has long been an axiom in the voluminous ethnohistorical literature relating to the wars of the Iroquois Confederacy that the expansion of European states into North America, and particularly the
involvement of members of the Iroquois Confederacy in the fur trade, was
crucial to the military and diplomatic activities of members of the confederacy (see McIlwain 1915; Hunt 1940; Fenton 1940; Trelease 1962; Trigger 1978; Wesler 1983). In this chapter I build upon and reflect these
ethnohistorical analyses of the Iroquois wars, but I also hope to provide
some original refinements and additions to the current scholarly consensus. While giving passing attention to prehistoric warfare among the Iroquois and their neighbors, I focus on Iroquois conflict from the time of
contact with Europeans (ca. A.D. 1600) until the establishment of reserve
and reservation communities following the American Revolution. Several
themes common to other papers in the volume are emphasized, among
them issues of demography and ethnogenesis, the importance of trade

and trade goods, the impact of more advanced military technology on the practice of war, and the involvement of indigenous populations as allies (or "ethnic soldiers") in expansionist wars of empire.

In examining Iroquois diplomacy and warfare in the historic period it is important to remember that the Iroquois were a confederacy of (originally) five nations: Mohawk, Oneida, Onondaga, Cayuga, and Seneca. They may have been either an egalitarian society or a nonstratified rank society as modeled by Fried (1967), who denies the existence of so-called tribes except as "secondary" phenomena triggered by the expansion of a state (Fried 1975). The Iroquois Confederacy does fit well the notion of "tribe" developed by Sahlins (1961) and Service (1962), however Sahlins (1961:325) emphasizes the fragmentary nature of "tribes" in which economically independent local segments are tenuously held together "by pan-tribal institutions, such as a system of intermarrying clans, of age-grades, or military or religious societies, which cross-cut primary segments."

For both the Iroquois proper and their neighbors the primary tribal segment was the village, each one composed of a number of matrilineages. In ordinary times, these agricultural villages were self-sustaining, and they often acted independently in matters of politics and war. A source of unity among them was a matriclan structure which transcended village boundaries. There also was for the Iroquois a Confederacy Council with hereditary positions representing each of the five nations, but this is best viewed as a pan-tribal institution whose political ritual emphasized symbolic unity (Abler 1988:7). In political reality it could do little to formulate common policy (for similar views, see Richter 1987). Fenton (1951: 52) long ago emphasized the importance of the village community in Iroquois life, asserting that despite the presence and structure of the Confederacy Council, "power remained in the hands of local chiefs."

One should not write of "Iroquois" history, then, but rather of the histories of the component members—at the village and nation level—of the Iroquois Confederacy. Unfortunately the quality of primary sources sometimes obscures the identity of these components, but the careful student will find that the history makes a good deal more sense if one eschews the category "Iroquois" and looks for local origins and motivations for policies and actions of members of the confederacy.

PREHISTORIC WARFARE

War did not come with Europeans to Iroquoia. Oral tradition describes the time of strife prior to the formation (likely in prehistoric times) of the Iroquois Confederacy:

> Everywhere there was peril and everywhere mourning. Men
> were ragged with sacrifice and the women scarred with the
> flints, so everywhere there was misery. Feuds with outer
> nations, feuds with brother nations, feuds of sister towns and
> feuds of families and of clans made every warrior a stealthy man
> who liked to kill. (Parker 1916:17)

The legendary lawgiver Deganawida established the Great Peace
among the five Iroquois nations and set up a council of 50 hereditary
positions. But since the blessings of the metaphorical Tree of Peace which
Deganawida planted at the initial meeting of the council extended only to
those who sat under its branches, war continued. The eagle Deganawida
placed atop the Tree of Peace is symbolic of the militancy necessary
among members of the confederacy to maintain peace (see Wallace 1946;
Tooker 1978a).

Archaeological evidence confirms the presence of prehistoric conflict:
skeletal remains show violent death, torture, and cannibalism (Molto,
Spence, and Fox 1986; Jamieson 1983; see also Abler and Logan 1988:
10–11). Settlement system data also suggest warfare. Nucleation of villages with the introduction of domesticates may initially have been the
result of a more productive and predictable economy (Trigger 1981:
33–36), but later consolidation into larger villages was for defensive advantages (Tuck 1971:213; Bond 1985:37; Bibeau 1980).

The presence of prehistoric warfare appears to be based upon conflict
over vital resources. Abundant agricultural lands were available, but, as
Gramly (1977, 1988) has pointed out, deer hides were essential to these
farming populations for clothing. Gramly's modeling of aboriginal requirements suggests there was excessive human pressure on the herds
(see also Turner and Stantley 1979; Starna and Relethford 1985). These
arguments led Abler and Logan (1988:10) to conclude that "Northern
Iroquoian warfare . . . was essential for securing productive hunting territories, something vital to those involved."

As Newcomb (1960:332) observed, it is important to bring "the distinction between the reasons why individuals fight in wars and the causes
of their culture's wars . . . clearly into focus." Goldschmidt (1989:16)
emphasizes that "tribal warfare is usually serious *economic* business" (ital-
ics his), but he explores additional "inducement to military participation"
in a sample of "tribal communities and preliterate state systems."

It is appropriate here to discuss Richter's (1983) application of Smith's
(1951) concept of "mourning war" to Iroquois behavior. Richter was
working from historical data, but there is every reason to suppose that
the practice derives from prehistory.[1] With the mourning war, the death
of a kinsman impels his clansmen to go to war and replace him with a

war captive or a scalp. Women played an important role in urging their brothers and sons to action. But I would argue against the mourning war as a *cause* of conflict (for a contrary view, see Blick 1988). As Ferguson (1989c: 564) has noted vis-à-vis the Yanomami, "the decision to retaliate is a tactical one, a part of the process of war, rather than its cause." Among the Iroquois, when there was the political will to suppress blood revenge, it usually was suppressed. I see the mourning war as an example of Goldschmidt's (1989:25) "inducement to military participation."

ST. LAWRENCE IROQUOIANS: DISPERSAL AND DISEASE

One final topic must be discussed prior to consideration of the historic wars of the Iroquois. When Jacques Cartier sailed up the St. Lawrence River in 1534 he encountered Iroquoian-speaking populations at Quebec City and Montreal. These appear to have represented two separate ethnic entities, usually called Stadaconans and Hochelagans (Trigger and Pendergast 1978). Sometime in the sixteenth century these populations disappeared, and it is suggested they were already in retreat in 1534, having abandoned the area previously occupied west of Montreal (Trigger 1985:144–45). The disappearance of the St. Lawrence Iroquoians has been attributed to warfare with the Huron (Ramsden 1977; Wright 1979), warfare with the Iroquois (Trigger 1972), warfare with both (Trigger 1985:144), or to European diseases (Fenton 1940:175; Dobyns 1989). Speculation that all this warfare was an attempt by interior peoples to remove a St. Lawrence Iroquoian blockade which denied access to European trade goods (Ramsden 1977, 1978) may lack foundation, for St. Lawrence Iroquoians were in retreat prior to evidence of European trade in their villages (Trigger 1984, 1985:144–51). Trigger (1985:151) concedes that "the wars between the Hurons and St. Lawrence Iroquoians began and were largely, if not wholly, fought during the late prehistoric periods." He does feel there was likely a later Mohawk–St. Lawrence Iroquoian war, occurring in the last decades of the sixteenth century, motivated by the desire of the former to capture steel axes (Trigger 1985:147).

The disease hypothesis remains unproven. Dobyns (1983) argues that there was a massive depopulation of the Americas as a whole in the sixteenth century—a result of Old World pathogens introduced by colonial Spanish in Mexico and the Caribbean. For no apparent reason, Dobyns sees epidemic diseases as the sole cause of the periodic relocation of Seneca villages in the sixteenth and seventeenth centuries (Dobyns 1983: 313–18; for discussion of Iroquoian village relocation see Abler 1970: 22–24; Heidenreich 1971:180–87; Starna, Hamell, and Butts 1984;

Snow and Lanphear 1988:21). Dobyns "correlates" the dates of village removal (which, in any case, were estimates [Wray and Schoff 1953; Wray 1983] with a considerable margin of error) with a chronology of epidemics in Florida which he perceives (this has come under attack; see Henige 1986a, 1986b) and with a Narragansett chronology of *earthquakes!* Since Narragansetts "mentally associated earthquakes with pestilence" (Dobyns 1983:318), Narragansett oral traditions of past earthquakes became to Dobyns "a chronology of episodes of epidemic disease." Small wonder that Henige (1986b:311) concluded that "Dobyns's discussion of 'disease' among the Iroquois is one of the most extraordinary of the entire work."

In a reply to his critics, Dobyns (1989) takes up the issue of St. Lawrence Iroquoians. He argues "that the 1535 epidemic so weakened them that they migrated not long after Cartier sailed for France, or that later sixteenth-century disease so weakened them that they moved from the river valley" (Dobyns 1989:289). Both Henige (1989) and Snow and Lanphear (1989:302) deny that Cartier's observation of sick and dying Indians at Hochelaga proves a 1535 pandemic, and the latter point out that the St. Lawrence Iroquoian retreat had begun before 1492.

It should be added that Ramenofsky (1987), clearly in sympathy with the hypothesized (or better, hypothetical) epidemics argued by Dobyns, fails to find sufficient archaeological evidence in central New York to support a dramatic sixteenth-century population decline there. Detailed consideration by Snow and Lanphear (1988, 1989) convincingly rejects the arguments of Dobyns and dates the first epidemic in the Northeast at 1616.

INITIAL IROQUOIS CONTACTS WITH EUROPEANS

When French explorer Samuel de Champlain sailed up the St. Lawrence in the first decade of the seventeenth century, he found that Algonquian speakers of Quebec and the Ottawa Valley were allied with the Huron of Georgian Bay (which Desrosiers [1947:31] terms the *Coalition laurentienne*) and at war with the Mohawks (see fig. 7.1). The Mohawks traveled north through Lake George, Lake Champlain, and down the Richelieu River to raid members of the *Coalition laurentienne*. Their goal appears to have been, at least in part, piracy. Through war the Mohawk gained access to trade goods, especially metal weapons.

In 1609, a Mohawk[2] war party of 200 encountered a force of Montagnais, Algonquin, and Huron on the shores of Lake Champlain. The Mohawks responded in the traditional action in prehistoric conflict: they constructed a temporary fortification and inside its walls danced and sang

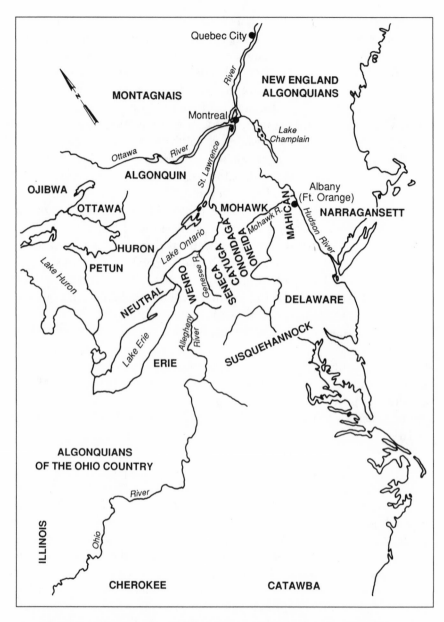

Figure 7.1. The Iroquois and their enemies. This map does not show the location of groups (in uppercase letters) at any single point in time, but rather places them in their locale when they play their most prominent part in the narrative presented.

war songs through the night. The next morning they put on their armor (made of interlaced wooden rods) and marched out, probably expecting to engage in a relatively bloodless archery battle. Out of the ranks of the Algonquians stepped Champlain, who fired his arquebus and killed three Mohawk leaders (he had loaded four bullets in his weapon). When another Frenchman fired, the Mohawks fled[3] (Biggar 1922–36(2):95–105).

The next summer Champlain participated in an even more decisive Mohawk defeat. A party of 400 (largely Montagnais and Algonquins) encountered a Mohawk party of 100 barricaded in its temporary fortification at the mouth of the Richelieu River. The fortification was pulled down and Champlain asserts that except for 15 taken captive all the Mohawk were slain in the fort or while fleeing.

Two defeats in consecutive years likely made the Mohawk rethink their strategy of raiding the St. Lawrence for trade goods[4]: after all, their enemies in the region now had French allies armed with matchlocks. Mohawk war parties did not return to the St. Lawrence until 1634 (Desrosiers 1947:47). As important as French arms, though, was the fact that establishment of the Dutch, English, and Swedish colonies in eastern North America provided alternative sources of trade goods for peoples south of the St. Lawrence (see Trigger 1978:348).

THE MAHICAN WAR

With Mahican permission, the Mohawk could trade with the Dutch on the Hudson. It appears the Mahicans, like other groups astride trade routes, could demand gifts from persons passing through their country for the purposes of trade. Relations between Mohawk and Mahican seem to have deteriorated after 1620, however, and since hostility on two fronts was undesirable, the Mohawk established formal peace with the French and the *Coalition laurentienne* in 1624 (Desrosiers 1947:89; Trigger 1971: 279). Open warfare then flared between Mohawk and Mahican. The Dutch reestablished themselves on the site of Albany, New York, this same year, naming their post Fort Orange (Trelease 1960:35), and the Mohawk sought direct access to this post (Trigger 1971:278; Hunt 1940:35; Bachman 1969:93–94).

The war between the Mohawks and Mahicans was fierce. A Mohawk village was burned by the Mahicans in 1626. For a time the Dutch supported the Mahicans, but after a defeat of a Mahican-Dutch force in which four Dutch were killed, the Dutch reestablished their neutrality (Trigger 1971:279). One of the Dutch casualties, Tymen Bouwensz, was "well roasted," providing the Mohawk with their first taste of Europeans

(Jameson 1909:84–85). After the Dutch withdrawal of support the tide turned, and by August 1628 the Mahican had been driven from lands west of Fort Orange (Trigger 1971:281). For 30 years thereafter Mohawks and Mahicans remained at peace and wampum flowed through the Mahican to the Mohawk (Brasser 1978a).

BEAVERS, EPIDEMICS, AND FIREARMS

If in fact warfare in late prehistoric times was generated by competition for deer-hunting territory, then one could expect such conflict to decrease with the onset of the fully developed fur trade. European textiles became an important part of that trade, and they rapidly supplemented or replaced deer hides for all items of clothing except moccasins. Thus deer became much less important in the economies of the agricultural peoples of northeastern North America. Beaver pelts were required for the new fur trade, however, and beaver were susceptible to local extinction through overhunting. A group that had exhausted its supply of beaver could obtain pelts through trade, raid, or the conquest of new hunting territories. Pursuit of these last two alternatives meant that warfare was intensified in the Northeast by the development of the fur trade (Abler and Logan 1988; Gramly 1988).

It was George T. Hunt (1940) who in a remarkable publication called attention to the depletion of beaver in the Iroquois country and its impact on Iroquois warfare. Hunt also brought attention to the Huron trading empire and the Huron role as middlemen in the trade with New France. I would echo the judgment of Francis Jennings (1984:42): "a remarkable book for its challenge to assumptions of primitive savagery, . . . it [has] forced rethinking about Indian economics." Hunt was wrong in his hypothesis that the Iroquois intended to replace the Huron as "middlemen," a point later scholars have emphasized (Trelease 1962; Trigger 1976, 1978), but he was correct that the depletion of beavers in their own territories brought the Iroquois into conflict with their neighbors.

In the 1640s, with no pelts to trade and with firearms playing an increasingly important role in warfare, it was crucial for the Iroquois to somehow gain access to beaver.[5] To this end, the Mohawk appear to have relied primarily on piracy, ambushing canoe fleets in Canada and bringing stolen pelts south to trade for European goods, including flintlock muskets (see Puype 1985; Abler 1989a; see also Malone 1973). The Upper Iroquois, though probably not so well armed as the Mohawk, still possessed state-of-the-art flintlock weaponry (Puype 1985; Bradley 1987: 142–45), and it seems likely that these Iroquois viewed expansion of their hunting territory as a solution to the problem of a shortage of beaver. The Seneca drove the Wenro from their territory (possibly the Oak Orchard Swamp in western New York) in 1638 (White 1978a:409).

If depletion of local supplies of beaver was prompting the various Iroquois groups to go to war in the 1640s, another important factor in those wars was the impact of European diseases in the region. The Iroquois nations, their Huron enemies, and, indeed, most peoples in the Northeast were first struck by a major epidemic (probably smallpox) in 1633–34 (Trigger 1985:230; Snow and Lanphear 1988:23). Snow and Starna estimate a pre-epidemic Mohawk population of not less than 8,100 and possibly as high as 10,570. Epidemics reduced them to "a population of no more than 3,200 in 1644" (Snow and Starna 1989:147). Losses of similar magnitude are suggested for all groups in the region (Trigger 1981; Snow and Lanphear 1988; Johnston 1987; Schlesier 1976).

Captives, when not sacrificed in war ritual, were adopted into Iroquois matrilineages and incorporated into the Iroquois community. Thus warfare was utilized to offset the severe population losses caused by European diseases. A major goal of Iroquois warfare and diplomacy through both the seventeenth and eighteenth centuries was to replenish the populations of Iroquois communities with war captives and refugees. Their success is indicated by generally stable population statistics throughout this time period (Michelson 1977).

The imported epidemics were important in one other respect. They most likely destroyed the morale of affected populations and very probably removed the oldest generation, the repository of ritual and knowledge (Trigger 1976, 1985). Although this impact would have been experienced by both the Iroquois nations and their enemies, it did mean that if one side succeeded in striking a formidable blow, the impact of the blow would be multiplied.

If the Mohawks and other Iroquois were short of homegrown beaver in the 1640s, they still through piracy acquired sufficient quantities of pelts to arm themselves with firearms. The introduction of firearms led to a revolutionary change in aboriginal warfare (Otterbein 1964; see also Fausz 1979; Malone 1973). Admittedly the mid-seventeenth-century flintlock and later muskets were less accurate than a bow in the hands of a well-trained archer (Abler 1989a; Given 1981:91–92). Elsewhere (Abler 1989a), I have argued that dodging missiles is a common tactic found among archers engaged in formal battles, and that this tactic is ineffective against muskets. Their adoption was thus a rational decision on the part of native North Americans. Once muskets were used, the formal battle became a thing of the past.

Earnest trade in firearms between Mohawk and Dutch began in the 1640s (see Hunt 1940: 165–72), influenced by the fact that the Mohawks would go to Connecticut to trade with the English if they could not get firearms from the Dutch. By 1643 the French claimed Dutch arms gave Mohawks military superiority: "The settlement of the Dutch is near them; they go thither to carry on their trades, especially in arquebuses; they have at present three hundred of these, and use them with skill and boldness" (JR 24:271). In contrast, "the Hurons who come down [to the St. Lawrence] . . . having not one Arquebus . . . have no other defense than flight" (JR 24:271–73). Some scholars have questioned the importance of the flow of arms from New Netherland to Iroquoia (Given 1981) or have pointed to the volume of French trade in firearms to Christian converts among their Indian allies (Hunt 1940:173–75). However, the weight of current scholarly judgment is that at the middle of the seventeenth century the imbalance in firearms was the significant factor in Iroquois victories (see Tooker 1963:117; Trigger 1976:629; Jennings 1984:81).

DISPERSAL OF THE HURON

In the 1640s both the Mohawk and Seneca failed to gain access to beaver pelts through diplomatic means. The Huron, on their part, attempted to isolate the Mohawk and Seneca by courting an active alliance with the Onondaga. But Mohawk actions cut communications between the Huron and Onondaga, and the Seneca and Mohawk increased their pressure on the Huron, who were weakened by losses to European disease and rent by strife between pro-Christian and anti-Christian factions.

In 1647–48 three villages on the frontiers of Huronia were destroyed by the allied Seneca and Mohawk. An armed Seneca-Mohawk force of some 1,000 men hunted in southern Ontario during the winter of 1648–49, and at dawn on March 16, 1649, they struck the village of St. Ignace. Only three of its 400 residents escaped to warn the next town, St. Louis. Eighty warriors of St. Louis remained to confront the invaders while the remaining 500 village residents fled. The major portion of the Seneca-Mohawk army attacked St. Louis, breached its walls, and captured the town. The French at the fortified mission station of Sainte-Marie saw the smoke of the burning St. Louis at 9:00 that morning.

On March 17, a Huron counterattacking force took refuge in the charred ruins of St. Louis. The ensuing battle lasted into the night and the Seneca-Mohawk prevailed, but at great cost. On May 19, 1649, after withdrawing to St. Ignace and resting a day, they began the return journey to Iroquoia, carrying with them both booty (beaver pelts and trade goods) and captives (see Otterbein 1979).

Casualties were heavy on both sides, the Huron suffering at most 50 percent higher casualties than their invaders. But the Huron panicked, and within two weeks they had burned their own villages and fled. Some took refuge among Petun or Neutral neighbors; others settled on Christian Island, hoping there to escape the summer invasions of Huronia by small, lethal war parties. The following winter on Christian Island proved to be one of famine and starvation cannibalism. A group of 300 survivors settled near Quebec City; a large portion of the rest settled in Iroquoia and were incorporated into the social system of their former enemies.

CONQUEST OF BEAVER LANDS

As the Huron starved on Christian Island, the Petun in turn received the focus of Iroquois hostility. The nature of Iroquois-Petun relations before the winter of 1649–50 is unclear (Garrad and Heidenreich 1978:396). If they were not already enemies, aid given by Petun to the Huron may have stimulated Iroquois ill will. A major Petun village was destroyed by Iroquois on December 7, 1649, and the Petun fled to their Ottawa allies on Manitoulin Island. Later, along with refugee Huron who joined them, they became known as Wyandot in various settlements in the upper Great Lakes (JR 35:109–19; Hunt 1940:95; Tooker 1978b).

The Neutral Confederacy, concentrated at the western end of Lake Ontario, had for a time enjoyed peace with both the Iroquois Confederacy and that of the Huron. After the Wenro dispersal, however, Neutral-Seneca relations became tense. The Seneca burned a Neutral village in 1647, supposedly because of the slaying of a Seneca in Neutral territory by a Huron or Petun (Trigger 1978:355; White 1978a:410). The Neutral apparently did not then retaliate, but war between Neutral and Seneca did break out in 1650, although there is no record of who was the aggressor. Trigger (1976:791) points out that the Seneca coveted "the rich beaver grounds around Lake St. Clair and along the Thames and Sydenham Rivers."

There were no observers close to the scene to report this clash, so information is incomplete and distorted. A Neutral village fell in the autumn of 1650 to a Seneca-Mohawk force numbering between 600 and 1500 (JR 36:119–21); possibly a counterattack on this force or an attack on a Seneca town led to the reported loss of 200 men. The Seneca women fled east to the Cayuga for safety. The principal Neutral town fell that winter when 1,200 Iroquois struck. Many prisoners were brought back to

Iroquoia, and the Neutral abandoned the country (for divergent scholarly interpretations compare Hunt 1940:97; White 1978a:410; Trigger 1976: 791). By 1652 southern Ontario was open to exploitation by Seneca beaver hunters. It also became a route toward further expansion of beaver-hunting territory, when the Seneca drove the Algonquians from Michigan's lower peninsula.

Possibly because expansion westward continued as a Seneca goal, tensions developed with yet another Iroquoian people, the Erie, who lived south of the lake bearing their name. Stories of the intensification of Upper Iroquois-Erie war, however, are couched in the ideology of blood revenge. An embassy from the Erie to the Seneca was slaughtered after one of the ambassadors killed a Seneca, reportedly by accident. More important, however, the Onondaga and the remainder of the Upper Iroquois were drawn into the fray. A prominent Onondaga chief, Annenraes, fell into Erie hands and was given to a woman to replace her brother. As was her right, she chose to have him executed. He is reported to have exclaimed that as he perished the entire Erie nation would perish in flames (JR 41:81).

The entrance of the Onondaga into the Erie war was probably of some import, since unlike the Seneca they had not had their manpower reduced by the Huron, Petun, and Neutral wars. It is possible they suffered some losses in the continual Iroquois war with the Susquehannock, although it is far from certain that the Susquehannock targeted all the Iroquois in their aggressive action. It is also possible, even likely, that some individual Onondaga accompanied the Seneca and Mohawk armies. It would appear, though, that the Onondaga could contribute a large body of fresh fighting men to the Erie war.[6]

The Upper Iroquois were unwilling to pursue the Erie war while at war with the French and their Algonquian allies. It is also possible that they wished to avoid duties charged for passing through Mohawk lands to trade at Fort Orange. Peace and direct trade links were sought with the French.

In the fall of 1654 a large army of Upper Iroquois (estimates range from 1,200 to 1,800) invaded the Erie country, destroyed Erie towns, and successfully attacked an Erie fortification by using canoes as ladders to scale its walls. The Erie war dragged on for possibly three more years, with French Jesuits, established in a mission among the Onondaga, witnessing the steady return of war parties and captives. In the end the Erie were refugees, some fleeing to Chesapeake Bay. A generation later these Erie refugees joined the Iroquois.

Most authors have emphasized the difficulties the Iroquois had with the Susquehannock (and with the French) following the dispersal of the

Erie. What was probably more significant, however, were the Iroquois raids driving Algonquians out of Ohio and southern Michigan and again securing rich beaver lands for exploitation by Iroquois trappers (Wilson 1956).

THE IROQUOIS EMPIRE

When the English conquered New Netherland in 1664, renaming it New York, the Iroquois Confederacy was at the apex of its power, at least in terms of territory. Southern Ontario and Michigan as well as the Ohio country were beaver-hunting grounds of the western Iroquois, and colonies had been established on the northern shore of Lake Ontario (Konrad 1981, 1987). Wampum continued to flow into Iroquoia through the Mohawks from "tributary" peoples to the south and east.

It must be emphasized, however, that the wars of the seventeenth century did not cause the Iroquois to evolve into a state. They remained a tribal society with constituent elements (nations or even villages or individuals) participating in war or peace as they saw fit. Armies were raised on an ad hoc basis and appear to have had no formal command structure. The Confederacy Council did not determine policy, and there was great danger of a Seneca-Mohawk, or intra-Iroquois, war in 1657.

The incorporation of captives and refugees served at least partially to stem the population loss caused by European diseases. Adult male captives were successfully incorporated, and the Seneca were reported to have 11 nations represented within their population (JR 43:265) while the Oneida had more foreigners than natives in their country (JR 51:123). This process can be likened to the process of "ethnogenesis" described elsewhere in this volume (see "The Violent Edge of Empire," Gunawardana, etc.). Formerly diverse peoples (including Europeans) were amalgamated into undoubtedly changing ethnic units in western New York. That the Iroquois were skilled at socializing prisoners and refugees into Iroquois men and women is certainly true (see Axtell 1975), but it is equally certain that Iroquoian communities of 1675, 1700, and 1750 were different from those of earlier decades because of the incorporation of foreign peoples.

THE SUSQUEHANNOCKS

While the Upper Iroquois enjoyed success against Indian nations to the west, the Susquehannock to the south proved to be more troublesome. Unlike many peoples dispersed by the Iroquois, the Susquehannock had ready access to arms. Moreover, through portaging the west branch of the

Susquehanna River, they had entrée into the Ohio country and its furs, which placed them in direct competition with the Seneca. Another advantage enjoyed by the Susquehannock was the flow of their rivers: Iroquois raiding against their villages had to retreat upstream and thus were vulnerable to counterattack, whereas their own raiding parties into Iroquoia could reach the Susquehanna drainage with relative ease, allowing a quick withdrawal to the safety of their homeland.

An invading Upper Iroquois (mainly Seneca) army of 800 was repulsed in 1663 in an attempt to destroy the major Susquehannock town, which was defended by bastions and cannon (see Abler 1989a:277–78). The literature is filled with references to defeats of the Upper Iroquois by Susquehannocks, and the Mohawk, possibly because of hostility verging on open war with the Seneca, withdrew from conflict with the Susquehannock.

Sometime around 1675 fortunes turned against the Susquehannock. Some historians have attributed their destruction to Upper Iroquois victories, but evidence supports the hypothesis that Maryland and Virginia militia inflicted the *coup de grace* (Jennings 1968, 1978, 1984, 1987; Washburn 1957; for contrary views see Tooker 1984; Webb 1984). The Iroquois, whatever their role in the political destruction of Susquehannock, were anxious to welcome Susquehannock refugees to their country. In 1677 a large portion of the surviving Susquehannocks were escorted to Iroquoia.

THE NEW ENGLAND ALGONQUIANS

Salisbury (1987:61) declares "Mohawk relations with the Algonquian speakers of southern New England" constitute "of all the boundaries of Iroquoia, the least studied and least understood." The arena appears to have been strictly a Mohawk sphere of interest, but the Mohawk had also to contend with the French and their allies to the north and to some extent the Susquehannocks to the south.

Wampum—cylindrical white and purple shell beads made from whelk and quahog shells, respectively (Salwen 1978:166)—appears to have been a major motivation for Mohawk activity in the New England area. Although of prehistoric origin, wampum was manufactured in large quantities only after the introduction of iron drills. For English and Dutch colonists it took the place of scarce coinage (Salisbury 1987); for the Iroquois it was not a general-purpose money, but had a sacred character. Holding a string of wampum demonstrated the sincerity of a speaker, and belts of wampum were exchanged at treaty negotiations and retained as a record of the words spoken. Gifts of wampum could turn aside the threat of blood revenge (on wampum see Tooker 1978a:422–24; Fenton 1971; Foster 1985; Ceci 1982).

Demand for wampum rose with its supply, and the desire for wampum drew the Mohawk into a series of wars in New England. The shifting pattern saw the Mohawk initially allied to the Narragansett—a source of wampum—and serving as allies against Narragansett enemies. A wampum payment from the Narragansett precipitated the Mohawk delivery of a Pequot sachem's scalp and hands to the Narragansett's English allies in 1637 (Salisbury 1987:62). As Narragansett-English relations endured periodic crises in the next two decades, the flow of wampum kept the Mohawks in line as allies to the Narragansett.

The Algonquians of southern New England withdrew from their alliance with the Mohawks in the 1660s, possibly yielding to influences of more northerly Algonquian speakers, such as the Abenaki, who were being drawn into the French orbit (Salisbury 1987:66). Other factors may have been Mohawk ties to "the universally detested Mohegans of Connecticut" (Salisbury 1987:67) and the fact that manufacture of wampum was passing from the hands of coastal Algonquians to English colonials, so Mohawks perceived that their interest lay toward that vector of power in the region. The Algonquians twice attacked Mohawk towns, in 1662 and 1669, but both attacks met with failure. The Mohawk found their revenge in the aftermath of King Philip's War, 1675–76, when they descended upon refugee Algonquians (Salisbury 1987:70–71; Washburn 1978:94).

PEACE AND MIGRATION TO THE ST. LAWRENCE

The Susquehannock war led the Upper Iroquois to seek peace with the French, while the destruction of four of their towns by French regulars under de Tracy in 1666 induced the Mohawk to follow a similar course (the Mohawk had suffered no casualties, but their food supply was destroyed) (Lamontagne 1966). With the peace Jesuits again entered Iroquoia. Over the next decade they converted a substantial number of Iroquois (Richter [1985:8] estimates 20 percent) and persuaded them to migrate to Caughnawaga on the St. Lawrence, a settlement established near Montreal. Most of these converts were Mohawk, so many that in 1673 the Mohawk population on the St. Lawrence outnumbered that in the Mohawk Valley (Fenton and Tooker 1978:469–70).

This migration, another example of ethnogenesis as a result of European expansion, considerably weakened the Mohawk and strengthened the French. Mohawk converts to Catholicism were soon in the field beside the French and their other allies, even invading Iroquoia. New England was to receive their repeated attacks in the French-English wars of the next century.

A second aspect to this migration was perhaps unanticipated by the French. The Mohawk settlers retained their ties to the south and served as a conduit for an illicit north-south trade that brought furs from France's Indian allies to Albany.

THE IROQUOIS RETREAT

In both the north and the west Iroquois dominance came to be challenged. There opened in the 1680s "a renewal of the Beaver Wars" (Richter 1987:24), which Aquila (1983) has aptly if imprecisely named "the Twenty Years' War"—a war in which the Iroquois did not fare well.

This phase of Iroquois military history begins with Seneca aggression into the Illinois country. It had become clear that French activity above Niagara Falls, such as the construction of a sailing ship, the *Griffon,* in 1679 (see Quimby 1966), would lead to extensive French trade in the upper Great Lakes. The Seneca feared that the populations they had driven westward would be armed by the French. By mid-September 1680 an army of 500 was in the Illinois country. This initial foray was victorious, but as Hunt (1940:151) concluded, "this invasion was the last successful advance of the Iroquois into the Illinois country, and a poor enough triumph it was."

French aggression against the Iroquois, however, proved a failure. La Barre, recently installed as governor of New France, was convinced that military action could divert the Iroquois trade from Albany to Montreal (La Roque de Roquebrune 1966:444). He assembled an army at Fort Frontenac (now Kingston, Ontario) and marched toward Iroquoia, but his army was devastated by illness (Jennings 1984:184) and he treated for peace instead. The Onondaga orator, Garangula (see Grassman 1966), expressed Iroquois contempt:

> He [the French governor, known as Yonnondio] says that he only came to the Lake to smoke on the great Calumet with the Onnondagas. But Garangula says, that he sees the Contrary, that it was to knock them on the head, if Sickness had not weakened the Arms of the French. I see Yonnondio Raving in a Camp of sick men, who's Lives the great Spirit has saved, by Inflicting the Sickness on them. (Colden 1958:54)

He also warned the French about using Fort Frontenac for military purposes: "Take care for the future, that so great a Number of Soldiers as appear here do not choak the Tree of Peace planted in so small a Fort" (Colden 1958:56).

Three years later another French army, commanded by Denonville, La Barre's replacement, enjoyed greater success. His army may have numbered over 2,000, including 1,600 soldiers and habitants (French Canadian settlers) and numerous Indian allies, among them Mohawks from Caughnawaga. On July 13, 1687, the invading force was ambushed by the badly outnumbered Seneca (Denonville estimated their strength as 800), who were forced to leave the field but inflicted sufficient losses on the French to cause Denonville's army to pause a day to lick its wounds (Denonville 1848:177–78).

After this defeat the Seneca burned their villages and fled into the forest. Two old men, too enfeebled to flee, "were cut into Pieces and boyled to make Soop" for the French allies (Colden 1958:64). Denonville's army spent a week burning the fields of maize they found surrounding the Seneca towns, Denonville reporting the destruction of 350,000 minots of green corn and 50,000 minots of old corn (*NYCD* 9:367–68). The French commander had been warned by a Catholic Mohawk not to overturn the wasps' nest without killing the wasps, and this is exactly what he had done (Parkman 1901:156).

Denonville then retreated, after establishing a blockhouse with a garrison of 100 at the mouth of the Niagara River (Eccles 1969:102). These troops found themselves surrounded by Seneca, and unable to venture out of their fortification, 89 of them died of scurvy. At Fort Frontenac 100 of the besieged garrison perished (Eccles 1969:102). In 1689 an Iroquois force reputed to be 1,500 strong, aware that England and France were now at war, struck at the French settlement of Lachine, within miles of Montreal. Fifty-six houses were burned, 24 persons were killed, and another 80 or so were taken prisoner. Although the actual loss was small, as Eccles (1969:103) notes, "the sudden ferocity of the attack was a devastating blow."

The Iroquois thus enjoyed relative success against the French. It is true that the Mohawk country was invaded in 1693 and its villages burned (Fenton and Tooker 1978:473), and the principal village of the Onondaga was burned in the face of an invading army in 1696 (Blau, Campisi, and Tooker 1978: 493–94). But although these expeditions destroyed the housing and crops of individual Iroquois nations, shelter and sustenance could always be obtained from neighbors.

More severe losses probably came in battles to defend beaver-hunting lands that had been conquered earlier in the century. An elaborate tale has been put forward of the Ojibwa conquest of southern Ontario (Eid 1979; Schmalz 1984), its details based on Ojibwa "oral traditions" set down by literate, bilingual Ojibwa in the nineteenth century. Although some of the details are dubious, such as accounts of the "Skull Mound" or the "naval" battle in which Ojibwa in birch canoes defeated Seneca in dugouts, the conquest did take place. It is quite likely that the drastic decline in Iroquois fighting strength between 1680 and 1700 (see Michelson 1977) was due to warfare in Ontario and in the Illinois-Ohio country.

A POLICY OF NEUTRALITY

Pressure by Indians in the west and north coupled with the conclusion of King William's War (the peace treaty of Ryswick was signed in 1697) led the Iroquois nations to seek peace with New France and her allies. Hunt (1940:157) suggests that the Iroquois also perceived as an advantage the possibility of trading at either Albany or Montreal. Competition might bring better prices.

Neutrality was achieved in independent conferences with the English and French in 1701 (Wallace 1957). Trelease notes that both the French and the English felt they had reaped diplomatic victories at these conferences. "The real victory, however, lay with the Indians themselves" (Trelease 1960:363). Richter (1983:535) has noted that Iroquois diplomats secured "rights to hunting in the west; potentially profitable trade with western Indians passing through Iroquoia to sell furs at Albany; [and] access to markets in New France and Pennsylvania as well as New York."

It must be mentioned that "presents" were very much a factor in frontier diplomacy (see Jacobs 1949, 1950). Wampum belts commemorated the words being spoken, but other gifts of less symbolic and more practical worth were also given at councils. As neutrals in a setting in which frequent conferences with both sides were necessary, the Iroquois were able to convert diplomatic skills into economic gains.

The economy of the Iroquois was also diversifying. As traders established posts in the interior, both the Senecas (at Niagara) and the Oneida (en route to Oswego) found employment as porters. The Mohawks at Caughnawaga and from the Mohawk Valley found similar employment in the illicit trade between Albany and Montreal.

EIGHTEENTH-CENTURY IMPERIAL WARFARE

The first half of the eighteenth century saw the movement of some Seneca and other Five Nations tribes into the Ohio country. Here they remained, mixing with Algonquian peoples and perhaps with refugees of the Iroquoians dispersed the previous century by the Five Nations. These Ohio Iroquois came to be known as Mingoes. It is usually suggested that these

Mingo were "under" the Five Nations council at Onondaga, but in reality they were virtually independent.

The general upheaval caused by continually expanding white settlement on the coast brought refugees to the Iroquois. Most prominent were the Tuscarora, an Iroquoian-speaking people driven from their Carolina home by the whites. They became the "sixth nation" of the Iroquois, although they never had the political rights of the original five. The Tuscarora are not in the least unusual, as the territory of the Iroquois increasingly became a refuge for homeless Indians.

Although the Iroquois consciously attempted to avoid involvement in the colonial wars, warfare continued, along with hunting, as an important element in Iroquois life. War parties now traveled the warrior's path to hunt the Cherokee and Catawba (see Merrell 1987; Perdue 1987). The need for defense of hunting territories to the south and west may have motivated the Seneca in these conflicts.

CONTINUED DIVISION WITHIN THE CONFEDERACY

The first 60 years of the eighteenth century found the Iroquois attempting to maintain their neutrality, for the most part, against the increasingly intense struggles between France and England on the North American continent. The nations of the confederacy varied in their devotion to neutrality, however, and the geographical proximity to sources of trade led some warriors to take the field in support of one or the other of the two European powers. The Mohawk, closest to Albany, were the firmest allies of England. The Seneca, most distant from that post, most often supported the French, though they were divided into pro-French and pro-English factions (Fenton 1955:339).

The western Seneca were drawn into the French orbit by trade links. The elder Joncaire (see Zoltvany 1969; MacLeod 1974; Dunn 1979) had been captured and adopted as a youth by the Seneca. He continued to be regarded as a kinsman, and he negotiated permission in 1720 to build a "house" for the conduct of trade at the mouth of the Niagara River, one of the most strategic locations in North America. This heavily fortified trading post grew through the years into Fort Niagara; from it, he and his two sons exerted considerable influence over their Seneca neighbors who dwelt on the Genesee (those Seneca further to the east, on Seneca Lake, were less amiable toward New France).

Some Seneca moved to the south and west, into the Allegheny River drainage. This upland is less amenable to agriculture than the region they left, and the purpose of the move was to exploit beaver-hunting grounds and alternate sources of trade from Albany. The Allegheny was a highway to the Ohio country and provided access to Pennsylvania and to French traders who were penetrating that region. Again, these Seneca often supported French interests.

For their part, the English in New York valued the Mohawk alliance and attempted to keep the Iroquois aggressively neutral if not actively on their side. Three Mohawks and one Mahican chief were sent to London in 1710 to impress the Indians, and more especially the home government, of the importance of the New York–Iroquois alliance (Garratt 1985). Cadwallader Colden published volumes of Iroquois history in 1727 and 1747 (Colden 1958) with the same political end in mind. Finally Sir William Johnson, Superintendent of Indian Affairs for the Northern Department, was able to use his knowledge of Mohawk culture and kin ties (his Indian wife, Molly Brant, was a prominent Mohawk matron) to consolidate links between the Crown and the Mohawk members of the Iroquois Confederacy.

It is worth noting that both the British and the Iroquois had strong motivation for emphasizing the strength and antiquity of the links that bound them together (the "Covenant Chain").[7] Both also, then, had reason to exaggerate past Iroquois conquests and contemporary Iroquois domination of other groups (see Jones 1982; Jennings 1984). This mutual misrepresentation of the real political situation in North America acted as a counter to French claims, serving British interests while encouraging the hopes of Mohawks and other Iroquois that British support and British arms could help them turn some of their claims to empire into reality.

PARTICIPATION IN THE 1763 UPRISING

The eventual triumph of the English over the French brought difficulties for the Indians, no matter whose allies they were. With the danger of Indian alliances with the French removed, presents, the grease of Indian diplomacy (see Jacobs 1950), no longer flowed freely. The result of this economy measure on the part of the English authorities was the so-called Pontiac rebellion (Peckham 1947). The Seneca, alone of all the Iroquois, participated in this uprising, capturing forts at Venango, Le Boeuf, and Presqu'ile (Abler 1989b:30) and massacring a British column at the battle of Devil's Hole on the Niagara River. This last battle was "the worst drubbing of the war to British arms" (Peckham 1947:226).

It is worthy of note that at the very time western Seneca at Devil's Hole were throwing Redcoats into the Niagara gorge, "six Senecas from two villages which had hesitated to follow the bloody trail of their brethren" were in attendance at a peace conference at the home of Sir William Johnson in the Mohawk Valley (Peckham 1947:225). Again the importance of the local group in the politics of the Iroquois is shown.

The western Seneca who fought at Devil's Hole were leaders rather than simply participants in the 1763 uprising. A prominent Seneca chief, active in intertribal diplomacy, was Kayásotha?, and a contemporary document refers to the war as the "Kiyasuta and Pontiac war" (Peckham 1947:107n; see Abler 1979).

The 1763 uprising, as successful as it was in its initial stages, could not be long-lived. The native forces had no second European power to serve as a source of arms and ammunition, and when Bouquet attempted to quell the uprising in the Ohio country in 1764, the second year of the war, he found the population reduced to using bows and arrows for hunting.

THE AMERICAN REVOLUTION

It is often stated that the American Revolution was the downfall of the Iroquois Confederacy, for it saw the Oneida and some of the Tuscarora take up arms against their brethren in the confederacy. This view, expounded by Morgan (1851:28) and others, ignores the amount of Iroquois blood shed by Iroquois throughout the seventeenth and eighteenth centuries.

The Mohawk had close ties to the Crown and its Indian Department; the Mohawks also were Anglicans. The Oneida, however, had accepted a New England missionary (New England was the heart of the rebellion), Samuel Kirkland, and his influence drew them into the rebel camp. Some of the Tuscarora joined them.

The other Iroquois, like most native North Americans, eventually became allies of the Crown. The Crown had several advantages over the rebellious colonies. Their economic strength meant they could continue the practice of giving presents and could support warriors in the field and their families at home. The experienced Indian Department was able to use knowledge of native cultures and social networks built up over decades to deal with native politics. Probably most important was the fact that the Crown represented a barrier to expansion into native lands, or at least the orderly regulation of that expansion (see Abler 1975).

The British did not seek Iroquois aid until 1777. The Seneca and Cayuga joined the Mohawk as British-Loyalist allies, while the Onondaga appear to have remained neutral. The initial commitment of the major portion of the Iroquois to battle occurred when they accepted an invitation to accompany Lieutenant Colonel St. Leger in his attempt to capture Fort Stanwix (now Rome, New York). The fort did not fall, but an American relief column under General Herkimer was cut to pieces in a ravine at Oriskany, suffering some 400 killed including its commander. The Mohawk Joseph Brant had selected the site of the battle, and the Indians bore the brunt of the fighting.

Most Mohawks abandoned their Mohawk Valley homes in 1777, but the Indians and their Loyalist allies gained an impressive series of victories—notably at Wyoming and Cherry Valley. The rebels responded by committing a major portion of their meager military resources to invading the Cayuga and Seneca country. In the late summer of 1779, the major thrust was led by Major General John Sullivan, while Brodhead burned Seneca towns on the Allegheny and troops from Fort Stanwix destroyed the town of the previously neutral Onondaga.

The Iroquois suffered hardships that winter, but their military power was not broken. In July 1780, 830 Iroquois warriors, of an estimated total of 1,200, were out raiding, and the Iroquois-Loyalist Schoharie Valley campaign "virtually wiped out all white settlement in the Mohawk Valley west of the environs of Schenectady" (Wallace 1970:146). Fort Stanwix was abandoned by the Americans in 1781. The remainder of the war found the Iroquois continually in the field and continually victorious, but the war was decided on fields other than New York; eventually the British made peace, abandoning their loyal and effective allies (on Iroquois in the Revolution see Graymont 1972; Wallace 1970; Abler 1989b).

At the close of the Revolution the bulk of the Iroquois were living on the Niagara frontier, with scattered settlements on the Genesee and the Allegheny. Joseph Brant, the influential Mohawk leader, obtained a land grant on the Grand River in Upper Canada to which he led his Mohawks, along with portions of the Cayuga and Onondaga and a few Seneca and Tuscarora (Johnston 1964). Other Mohawks followed Captain John Deseronto to a reserve on the Bay of Quinte (Fenton and Tooker 1978: 476). Those who remained on lands recognized (by the British) as part of the United States made peace with the new American republic, much to the disgust of the former "subservient" peoples in the Ohio country, who for another decade fought a bloody war to halt American expansion.

CONCLUSIONS

Iroquois warfare in the colonial era was not simply the blind continuation of hostilities that existed prior to European entry onto the continent, but the presence of European traders and trade goods was central to wars in the historic era. Wars were fought to gain access to points of trade, to pirate trade goods or beaver pelts from other groups, and to secure access to beaver-hunting grounds. In addition, it became important to deny one's enemies access to the trade, for European arms had become a vital part of war. Once tied to the trade, Indians were subject to pressures to serve major trading partners as "ethnic soldiers" in European imperial wars.

Epidemic diseases from Europe were also a factor in this warfare. A clear goal of Iroquoian war and diplomacy was to incorporate sufficient numbers of captives and refugees to counterbalance losses to disease. Depopulation probably also reduced stability in the region, since groups were made more vulnerable when subjected to a military blow. Well-armed Iroquois warriors had the impact they did because they were making war on peoples who had recently lost major portions of their population.

In all of these actions the Iroquois functioned not as a unitary state but as a tribal society (in the sense of Sahlins 1961). Seldom, if ever, did fighting men from all segments of the confederacy contribute to the pursuit of a common military goal. The student of Iroquois history would do well to use the term Iroquois as seldom as possible.

The lack of intertribal unity continued to be demonstrated in the latter portion of the colonial era, when segments of the Iroquois fought for Britain or for France, depending upon the strength of trade links. In the American Revolution, too, Iroquois warriors fought for each side.

Armed with Dutch and English weapons, the Iroquois warriors made vast territorial gains in beaver-hunting lands. Once their enemies became equally well armed some of these lands were lost, but by no means all. The Iroquois controlled far more territory in the latter part of the eighteenth century than they had at the beginning of the seventeenth. This territory was conquered using muskets obtained for beaver pelts; it was conquered to increase the supply of beaver pelts; and it was defended with Iroquois lives to maintain that supply of beaver.

------- Notes -------

1. Champlain's observations of elaborate ritual treatment of Iroquois scalps brought to the St. Lawrence by their Montagnais enemies in 1609 convinces one that blood revenge, scalping, and war ritual were strongly developed among the Iroquoians and their Algonquian neighbors of the St. Lawrence region (Biggar 1922–36(2):106).

2. Champlain used the word "Iroquois" but at that point in time Iroquois designated only the easternmost member of the confederacy in Champlain's vocabulary.

3. Trigger has set the number of Iroquois dead at "about fifty" (Trigger

1985:176; see also Trigger 1976:254). The source of Trigger's discussion of this battle is the writings of Champlain (Biggar 1922–36). Champlain, however, describes killing three Mohawk with the first shot and goes on to claim that he himself killed "still more of them" (*"i'en fis demeurer encores d'autres"*) and that "Our Indians also killed several" (*"Nos sauuages en tuerent aussi plusiers"*). This wording leaves me to believe 50 is too high an estimate. Given Iroquoian demography, the death of as many as 50 warriors in a single battle would have been significant indeed.

4. Even making allowances for exaggeration in the accounts of Champlain, Mohawk losses relative to their population were considerable. Champlain suggests at least 25 Mohawk were taken prisoner and close to 100 were killed. Michelson (1977:4) found no estimate in the historic record of more than 700 Mohawk warriors, but even if Starna's (1980) high estimates of a pre-epidemic Mohawk population are correct a loss of 125 would constitute 5 percent of Mohawk fighting men.

5. Trigger (1981:27) argues that for the Huron, "depletion of beaver stocks was underway, or complete, prior to the epidemics of 1634–40," and "while it is uncertain whether or not beaver had been eliminated within the hunting territories of the Five Nations Iroquois by 1640, the furs that could be taken from these territories clearly no longer sufficed to purchase all of the European goods that the Iroquois wished to obtain."

6. Little consideration in the ethnohistorical literature is given to the psychological factors of combat, although admittedly data are not strong in this area. Authors tend to see North American Indians either as having an insatiable desire for war (in a somewhat ambiguous passage, even the arch antiracist historian Francis Jennings [1984:64] seems to class Indians as "warlike peoples") or as having no stomach for pitched battle (see Wise 1970). The latter view is contrary to the evidence, as examination of Indian participation in battle shows (see Abler 1989b, or, for that matter, the two centuries of warfare described here), while the former ignores the fact that even elite military units break and run and that long periods of combat increase the likelihood of this happening.

7. Historian Francis Jennings is fond of writing of a "Covenant Chain Confederation" (see Jennings 1984). I see the so-called Covenant Chain as simply a metaphor for an alliance (and often a very tenuous alliance) between the nations of the Iroquois Confederacy and the British Crown. One must recognize the importance of metaphor in Iroquois speeches and diplomacy, but I feel it overstates the case to write of a Covenant Chain confederacy.

Chapter 8

Tribe and State in a Frontier Mosaic

The Asháninka of Eastern Peru

MICHAEL F. BROWN AND EDUARDO FERNANDEZ

ROM the seventeenth century onward, Spanish chroniclers in Peru had frequent cause to lament the ferocity of an Amazonian people whom they called "the Campa tribe," now more accurately called Asháninka. In the course of three centuries, Asháninka warriors martyred more than a score of Franciscan missionaries. Stories of violent encounters with Asháninkas and accounts of homicidal raiding within Asháninka society itself became the stock-in-trade of Amazonian adventurers beginning in the nineteenth century. Leonard Clark, an explorer whose book *The Rivers Ran East* was read by thousands of adolescent boys in the 1950s and 1960s, devotes page after page to lurid descriptions of Asháninka savagery, the following passage being fairly typical:

> We caught the movement of hundreds of vultures circling in the sky; others were perched in the taller trees along the banks . . .

> All this was an indication to our Indians of death, of stinking
> bodies lying in the underbrush, the grim tally of the internecine
> wars of the Campas. (Clark 1953:151)

Clark's narrative is easy to dismiss as feverish hyperbole, yet his tale echoes stories of Asháninka belligerence that circulated widely in Peru at the time of the author's expedition.

On the face of it, the Asháninka would appear to illustrate the processes that Marvin Harris (1984) sees as endemic among tribal populations of Amazonia: high levels of warfare ultimately caused by competition for areas rich in game animals. In this chapter, however, our goal is not to make a contribution to what has come to be called the Great Protein Debate, which seeks to explain tribal violence in ecological terms.[1] Our observations instead register the links between warfare and contact with larger polities, most notably colonial and postcolonial states. In this respect our work parallels that of Robert Murphy (1960) among the Brazilian Mundurucú, Jane Bennett Ross's study of the Ecuadorian Achuará (1984), and Brian Ferguson's reanalysis of the Yanomami case (this volume), all of which show how the influence of distant powers and their local representatives shapes the form and frequency of conflict in apparently pristine Amazonian settings.

At the heart of any assessment of Asháninka history must be a careful look at the nature of the state with which the Indians were drawn into contact. In the literature on colonialism there is a tendency to reify the state, as if it were a well-integrated social unit following a consistent, rational policy of domination.[2] While a degree of coherence might be found in the imperial policies of some modern nations, most native peoples have found their contacts with colonial powers to be characterized by contradiction. Missionaries importune them with one set of demands, administrators with another, traders and labor recruiters with yet a third. Official policies can change overnight according to the political currents that prevail in distant capitals. Moreover, the interest of the state in frontier regions such as the Upper Amazon is typically spasmodic, growing and ebbing in response to large-scale economic processes in the metropole.

By reviewing in a schematic way the history of a native people on the frontier of the Latin American state, our principal aim is to expose how the frontier's changing nature and its own inconsistencies affected Asháninka attempts to maintain a degree of political and cultural autonomy. The rich historical evidence shows that Asháninkas, as shrewd social actors, responded to the stresses and opportunities of contact in various and sometimes conflicting ways: accommodation, resistance, flight, increased intratribal warfare and banditry, and millenarian revitalization. Indeed, during four centuries of contact history, the internal contradictions of the state created multiple political spaces that native populations could occupy and exploit, depending on their assessment of the advantages and disadvantages of each. This undoubtedly contributed to internal differentiation within Asháninka society that may in some instances have inhibited collective action in defense of tribal sovereignty (Fernández 1988: 31). But the sociopolitical mosaic that emerged in eastern Peru also made the Indians harder to organize and classify, and therefore to control. The Asháninkas' skill at finding and exploiting these differentiating spaces helps to account for the persistence of Indian social identity in a region with the longest history of contact in the Peruvian Amazon.

CULTURAL BASELINE: THE PRECONTACT PERIOD

Contemporary Asháninka communities are found in the sizable region defined by the Perené, Pachitea, Ene, Tambo, Apurímac, and Ucayali rivers (fig. 8.1). Estimates of the contemporary Asháninka population range widely, from a low figure of 28,000 to a high of 45,000 (Hvalkof 1989: 145). "Traditional" Asháninka communities have been defined as "dispersed neighborhoods" led by male leaders who correspond in certain respects to Melanesian big-men (Bodley 1971:79).

Although information about prehistoric Asháninka society is scarce, we now know that the eastern forests of Peru were more cosmopolitan than once thought. The various regional Asháninka subgroups comprised a population of many thousands of Indians who lived in close proximity to other native groups, including such related Arawakan peoples as the Machiguenga, Nomatsiguenga, Yanesha (Amuesha), and Piro.[3] It is likely that Asháninkas were also in contact with Panoan populations on the Ucayali River, including the Conibo, Cashibo, and Shipibo. The Machiguenga and Piro engaged in raiding and trading relations with Andean peoples during the Inca empire, links that may date to the Tiahuanaco state early in the first millennium A.D. (Camino 1977; Lathrap 1973). By extension, one can infer that Asháninkas sustained similar contacts with highland polities, most notably the Inca, though no Andean state was able to impose its political institutions on the peoples of Peru's tropical forest.

The prehistoric development of long-distance trading relations between Andean polities and Amazonian populations—the key feature of pre-Conquest Peru's "internal frontier" (cf. Kopytoff 1987b)—may have changed native settlement patterns and institutions, perhaps fostering

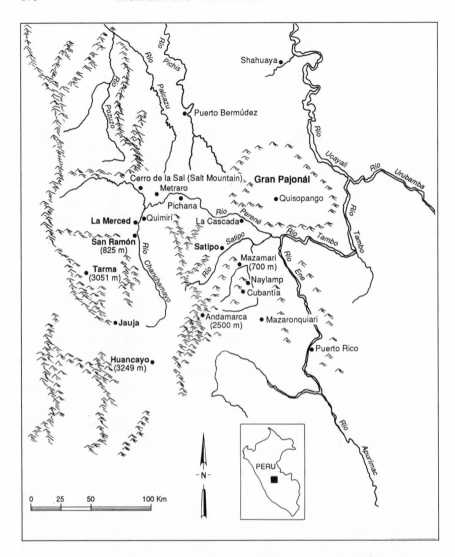

Figure 8.1. Central jungle region of Peru, including sites mentioned in the text. Altitudes (in meters) are noted in parentheses. (Drawing by Katrina Lasko)

conflict between Asháninkas and their neighbors, though it is just as likely to have produced a network of peaceful trade. It is, however, reasonable to assume that internal feuding was a part of Asháninka life long before the arrival of outsiders.

Prehistoric Asháninkas shared with their modern descendants a mixed subsistence regime of horticulture, hunting, and fishing. Leadership roles, most significantly, that of *curaca* or *cacique* (local leader, "chief"), fell to senior men with acknowledged competence in hunting, diplomacy, and warfare. So far as we know, there is no evidence to suggest that Asháninka constituted a "tribe"—that is, a circumscribed, corporate, ethnolinguistic group—in any meaningful sense prior to European contact.

EUROPEAN CONTACT

Even before Spain established permanent settlements in the tropical forests of eastern Peru, the Spanish conquest of Peru's coastal and Andean regions may have changed the Asháninka world in significant ways. There is tantalizing but still controversial evidence that highland Indians escaping Spanish oppression made their way to Asháninka territory in the seventeenth century. One refugee community, Pucutuguaru, was rumored to have a population of six thousand or more (Lehnertz 1974:45–48). These settlers may have affected Asháninka settlement patterns and health status, especially if the refugees carried European diseases.

The first recorded European contact with Asháninkas was made by the Jesuit missionaries Juan Font and Nicolás Mastrillo during an expedition that began late in 1595. Padre Font was impressed by the Asháninkas' apparent interest in the Christian faith, but he fretted about what he saw as a lack of centralized leadership, complaining that "one cannot make much progress with them, principally for being so few and so scattered, without authority or leader" (quoted in Varese 1973:125).

The Spaniards' inability to identify the proper scale of indigenous political units led them to oscillate wildly between over- and under-specificity in naming jungle peoples. Asháninkas, for instance, were referred to generically as *chunchos*, a broad term for jungle Indians, or by the inevitable labels "infidel" and "savage." Yet during the same period and in the same general region, travelers alluded to contacts with a score of specifically named "tribes"—for example, Andes, Amages, Pilcozones, Canparites, Anapatis, Pangoas, and Satipos—most of whom were probably local groups of Asháninkas. These "tribal" designations were often based on place-names or the name of a local *cacique* known to Spanish authorities (Fernández 1987:337).

A sustained missionary effort among the Asháninka began with the ministry of Fray Jerónimo Jiménez, a Franciscan who in 1635 founded the mission at Quimirí, near the site of the present-day town of La Merced. Quimirí had strategic importance because of its proximity to Cerro de la Sal, or Salt Mountain. Located just north of the junction of the Chanchamayo and Perené rivers, Salt Mountain is veined with mineral salt that was exploited by several different Amazonian peoples, including the Asháninka, Yanesha, Conibo, and Piro, as well as by Indians from nearby Andean communities. Trade in salt tied into a regional network that included commerce in cotton cloth, metal tools (from the Andes), vanilla pods, feathers, and animal pelts. The missionaries concluded that the site would offer them access to a captive audience drawn from all the heathen tribes of the region.

Fray Jiménez and a fellow priest became the first martyrs to the cause of Asháninka conversion when they were murdered in 1637 on the Río Perené—evidence, according to the Franciscan historian Bernardino Izaguirre, of what the Indians' "barbarous breasts could conceive and their inhuman arms could undertake" (Izaguirre 1922 (book 2):163). The issue leading to the martyrdom was one that became a persistent source of Franciscan-Asháninka friction: the Church's opposition to the polygamous marriages of Asháninka headmen.

Both the Franciscans and the Dominicans, who had also established missions in the region, fell victim to the inconsistency of Spanish colonial policy in the mid-seventeenth century. Although the viceroy supported the friars' efforts to gather Indians into Christian settlements, he also approved military expeditions that negated years of diligent missionary work. One such expedition was that of Pedro Bohórquez Girón in the late 1640s. An Andalusian soldier of fortune, Bohórquez obtained Dominican support for an expedition to Salt Mountain in search of gold. During the months that he and his band of freebooters controlled Quimirí, they rustled cattle from nearby highland communities, murdered a native headman, abused the wives of Asháninka converts, and abducted Indian children for use as servants. Their behavior became so intolerable that all of the Asháninka converts fled the mission (Santos 1986).

The Franciscans endeavored to reestablish a stable mission system in 1671 but were thwarted in 1674 by a bloody revolt in Pichana. They tried again in 1709 with missions along the Perené River and, about 15 years later, in a remote grassland called the Gran Pajonál. Another Asháninka uprising in 1737 proved that the mission system was still only precariously rooted.

Why did the Asháninka resist the missions so resolutely? After all, the actual area controlled by the stations of the late seventeenth and early eighteenth centuries was small—so small, in fact, that the historian Jay Lehnertz (1974:63) observes a process of "progressive encystment" among the missions of the 1720s and 1730s. Lehnertz reports that the largest number of residents for the nine missions of the *conversión* of Tarma was recorded in 1718, when there were 1,287 Indians. (This figure apparently includes significant numbers of Quechua Indians brought from the highlands to provide military security and expertise in essential crafts.) Figures for later years are considerably lower, reaching as few as 605 in 1730 (Lehnertz 1974:390). Mission records reveal a high turnover rate within this population. Many more Indians may have had direct contact with stations, at least for brief periods, than the census would imply, but few were thoroughly integrated into the mission world.[4]

The Asháninka response to the mission system oscillated between accommodation and avoidance. Trade goods were the principal pull factor; push factors included epidemics, corporal punishment, the uncongenial discipline of mission life, assertions of control over Indian children, and relentless hectoring by monks. The Franciscans also aroused Asháninka ire by using members of enemy tribes as guides during their expeditions in Asháninka country. The warlike Conibos, whose seventeenth-century settlements were apparently concentrated along the upper reaches of the Río Ucayali, supported Franciscans on their explorations of the Perené, Tambo, and Ene rivers. Padre Huerta, for instance, notes in his description of a 1686 expedition: "On the second day of the *entrada* to the Ene, we came ashore to shelter ourselves from the sun; following some human footprints for a short stretch, the [Conibos] came upon some Campa houses and, after surrounding them, they sacked the settlement, kidnapping women and children and taking whatever else was there" (quoted in Varese 1973:146).

As Huerta's account shows, the Asháninka had come to be known as "Campa" by the late seventeenth century, mostly owing to the influence of the Franciscan explorer and missionary Manuel de Biedma (Varese 1973:135). Nevertheless, local "tribal" names were used with considerable frequency well into the nineteenth century.

Mission documents emphasize that local headmen often brokered mass conversions and the establishment of mission stations. Lehnertz (1974:99) found that friars attempting to convert Indians in the Gran Pajonál had "distributed iron tools to the area's *cananbiri* [headmen], and presumably that distribution was part of an ongoing exchange which was carried on between the two zones." The "inconstancy" of the Asháninka headmen, about which the Franciscans frequently complained, may have been caused by the missions' failure to supply trade goods in quantities sufficient to sustain the headmen's ambition.

THE REVOLT OF 1742–1752

In late May of 1742, Asháninka converts suddenly deserted the Perené missions. When asked by the friars why they were leaving, the Indians replied that they were traveling to the Gran Pajonál to see "Lord Inca," who had come to a place called Quisopango. Under the protection of the local *cacique*, this Inca was holding court and promising to oversee the creation of a new world order.

The mysterious visitor came to be known as Juan Santos Atahualpa.[5] A wanderer from the Andes, Juan Santos proclaimed a spiritual message that was nativistic in emphasis. He sought the removal of Spaniards from Peru, Indian control of Christian worship, and reestablishment of a native empire over which he was to reign as monarch. As we have seen, a vigorous tradition of Asháninka resistance had taken root long before Juan Santos's appearance. What remains enigmatic about his movement is why this new gospel—which in its allusions to the Inca empire was as alien to Asháninka political practice as the teachings of the Franciscans—appealed to Asháninkas at all. Here was a political vision that was hierarchical in the extreme, that drew on memories of an empire with which Asháninkas were largely unfamiliar. Nor does it seem likely that Asháninkas felt much of a commitment to Christian worship, even if it were in Indian hands. One early description of Juan Santos's encampment hints at the different goals of messiah and followers. Two blacks who visited the rebels testified that the "Amajes, Andes, Conibos, Sepibos, and Simirinchis" who rendered obedience to Juan Santos shouted that "they wanted no priests, that they did not want to be Christians." But we are told that "the Inca opposed all this and spoke to them in reprimands; the Indians, both Christians and infidels, do much dancing and they are quite content with their new king" (Castro Arenas 1973:11).

Who was Juan Santos? We know that he had benefited from a formal education, probably from the Jesuit order in Cuzco. Most scholars believe he was attached to a Jesuit priest as a servant or novice. He may well have traveled to Europe, and his revolutionary ideas seem to have been inspired by his visit to Catholic missions in Africa, where black priests regularly said mass.

The incompatibility of Andean and Amazonian world views leads at least one historian, Jay Lehnertz (1972, 1974), to question the Asháninka role in the rebellion. The real support for Juan Santos, he asserts, came from escaped black slaves and highland Indians who had experienced the full brunt of Spanish oppression. Nevertheless, all of the documents related to the revolt mention the involvement of *chunchos*—jungle Indians—in battles against Spanish forces. Nor is it likely that highland Indians could have survived in such a difficult landscape without the active support of Asháninkas. Although there is no reason to think that all or even most Asháninkas were active in the rebellion, there is little question that Asháninka populations played an important part in the struggle.

When hostilities eventually broke out, Asháninka bowmen engaged Spanish forces in areas as far apart as Quimirí, the Apurímac Valley, and the highland village of Andamarca, suggesting broad Indian support for the rebellion. Repeated Spanish attempts to exploit divisions within Asháninka society in such a way as to produce Juan Santos's betrayal harvested only failure. Colonial documents also attest to the movement's ability to cross ethnic lines: Conibo, Piro, and Yanesha communities joined in the uprising.

Spanish attempts to crush the rebellion and capture Juan Santos were demoralizing failures. The last major engagement was in 1752, when rebel forces moved from the jungle into the highlands to capture and occupy the town of Andamarca for three days. This caused widespread panic in Peru, but the rebels proved unable to consolidate their victory. The Spanish settled on a policy of containment rather than reconquest; from the jungle came only silence. By the 1760s the Spanish realized that the new Lord Inca had disappeared as inexplicably as he had arrived.

Predictably, there are contesting versions of the death of Juan Santos Atahualpa. In 1766, a Franciscan heard from some Conibos that Juan Santos died in Metraro, after which his body disappeared in a cloud of smoke (Castro Arenas 1973: 148). A late nineteenth-century expedition reported that Juan Santos died during a drunken feast when an Asháninka, doubting the messiah's godlike status, hurled a stone at Juan Santos's head to see if he would feel pain (Izaguirre 1922 (book 3): 182–83).

The very success of the rebellion prevents us from understanding the internal political changes it may have produced within Asháninka society. So far as we know, no Spanish documents exist that would shed light on Asháninka institutions between the early 1740s and the mid-nineteenth century. The most conservative assessment is that the large-scale political links forged in the crucible of revolt did not survive peacetime. The ideological impact of the revolt should not be underestimated, however. Franciscans who cautiously reentered the region in the nineteenth century found the Indians sullen and unwilling to cooperate. More important may have been the spread of a belief in Inkarrí, the Inca king, a myth of native renewal that played a role in later Andean revolts and, in a modified form, captured the imagination of Asháninkas.[6]

Asháninka stories explain that Inca controlled the creation of all important goods: cloth, metal tools, firearms, machinery, and metal cooking pots. Through the sinful behavior of Inca's son, the *viracochas* (Europeans in general, though in this context specifically the Spaniards) emerged from a jungle lake and began a campaign of extermination against the Asháninka people. The Spanish captured Inca and decapitated him. Some variants of the myth conclude by explaining that the *viracochas* now own

Inca's head or entire body, which lives on, providing them with all the valuable goods Asháninkas lack. Asháninkas will be rich once again when Inca returns to them.

Although the myth of Inca has indigenous roots, its spread among Asháninkas was probably aided by the teachings of the Franciscans, many of whom held millenarian views themselves (Phelan 1970). In the words of Félix Alvarez Sáenz (1989:16), the apocalyptic and millenarian Christianity of the Franciscans furnished the Indians with a "discourse more than a faith"—a discourse that alloyed itself with Andean and Amazonian beliefs in the cauldron of the colonial experience to support faith in an imminent apocalyptic transformation that would result in a reversal of the Asháninkas' fortunes and the end of the oppressive rule of outsiders.

NINETEENTH- AND TWENTIETH-CENTURY CONTACT

Documentary sources on the Asháninka reappear after the construction of a government garrison at San Ramón in 1847. The American explorers William Herndon and Lardner Gibbon (1854:85), sent by the U.S. Department of the Navy to survey the Amazon, observed that the Indians were "determined to dispute the passage of the rivers and any attempt at further conquest." Nineteenth-century travelers navigating the Río Perené's treacherous currents often found themselves the target of Asháninka arrows en route. Nevertheless, this stalwart resistance failed to stem the large-scale forces undermining the Indians' isolation and autonomy. The formal apparatus of state control was weak in the Amazon, often nonexistent. At the same time, the Peruvian government encouraged entrepreneurial rapine by foreign and domestic economic interests as well as by individual settlers. Even the humblest farmer could afford a repeating rifle that gave him a generous advantage in firepower over Indians still equipped with bows and arrows.

In 1891, the Peruvian government ceded an immense tract of land along the Perené to the Peruvian Corporation, Ltd., an enterprise based in London (Barclay 1989). By 1913, 500 Asháninkas worked the plantation's coffee groves. In 1938 the figure was closer to 2,000, if one counts temporary Indian laborers hired for the harvest season (Bodley 1971:10; Manrique 1982:39). Although the Perené Colony, as the British concession came to be known, was the best organized effort to settle the region, piecemeal appropriation of Indian lands quickened elsewhere as well: in the Chanchamayo Valley (where by 1907 there reportedly were 14,000 colonists), along the Apurímac, in the valley of the Pichis, and later near Satipo (Bodley 1971:10–15; Elick 1969; Shoemaker 1981).

The advance of the agricultural frontier was overshadowed by the explosive growth of rubber tapping that began in the 1870s. Although the rubber boom of Peru's central jungle was less violent than its counterpart on the Río Putumayo to the northeast (Taussig 1987), it was just as dependent on forms of debt servitude. Coveted trade goods—firearms, ammunition, coarse cotton cloth, metal pots, decorative trifles—were advanced to the Indians against future latex production. Merchants fixed the value of the goods and of the latex, and Indians never produced enough to cancel the debt. Flight was futile: traders watched the rivers for tappers attempting escape. Punishment for attempted desertion was harsh, sometimes unspeakably brutal.

The period also saw the growth of commerce in human beings. On his expedition to the Gran Pajonál in 1896, the Franciscan priest Gabriel Sala found that even whites of modest means commonly bought and sold Asháninka children:

> From the highest authority to the lowest farm hand or merchant, all want to have a *chuncho* boy or girl in service; and if they don't have one, they ask somebody to go among the *chunchos* or to stage a raid; and once they've obtained their *chuncho*, they thank [the slaver] very much and then pay him. (Sala 1897:66)

Another traveler in the region reported that "a boy of ten or twelve years is normally worth five hundred *soles*, and if it's a Campa quite a bit more . . . The children come to forget their savage customs, learn Spanish, and prove useful to their patrons—that is, if they live" (quoted in Fernández 1986b:57).

Stefano Varese (1973:246) explains that the rubber barons encouraged the traffic in captives by playing off one native group against another. "The method was simple," he writes. "Winchesters were delivered to the Conibo, to be paid off with Campa slaves, after which Winchesters were delivered to the Campa to be paid off with Conibo or Amuesha [Yanesha] slaves." Nevertheless, raids took place within tribes as well as between them, implying a political complexity lost in Varese's formulation.

Asháninka *caciques* or *curacas*, acting as intermediaries between merchants and the general Indian population, often carried out forced "recruitment" of rubber workers and the outright capture of slaves. Padre Sala provides a portrait of a *curaca* named Venancio: "There suddenly appeared four canoes with twenty-five men (*chunchos*) well armed with rifles and led by the *curaca* Venancio. He entered in a routine way, with a black parasol, a hat, and a scarf at his neck." On two other occasions Sala

Figure 8.2. Portrait of Asháninkas published in F. A. Stahl's 1932 memoir,
In the Amazon Jungles. *Stahl's original caption identifies the subjects as "a*
band of murderers . . . organized for the purpose of stealing children, after
killing the parents." (Reprinted with kind permission of Grace and Orlando
Robins)

meets Asháninka parties sent by Venancio to conscript Indians from the
Gran Pajonál for rubber tapping on the Río Manú. "The merchant who
knows how to play with his *curacas* grows like the foam on a whirlpool
of dirty water," the priest observes (Sala 1897:96, 99).

The preeminent rubber baron of the Asháninkas' part of the jungle
was Carlos Fermín Fitzcarrald.[7] The memoirs of Fitzcarrald's associate,
Zacarías Valdez Lozano, trace the alliances between Indians and Fitzcarrald's representatives that came to define Asháninka political realities during the height of the rubber frenzy. On the left bank of the Urubamba,
for example, Fitzcarrald had in his employ four Piro Indian *curacas*: a
supreme chief named Curaca Agustín, and three lesser chiefs named
Francisco, Jacinto, and Ronquino, who answered to Agustín. The Asháninkas of the Ucayali and Tambo were balkanized into warring groups
under the control of traders of Peruvian, Spanish, and Chinese origin, all
of whom eventually came to work for Fitzcarrald (Valdez Lozano 1944:
13–14).

The full extent of the violence associated with slave raiding was still
evident when John H. Bodley conducted his field research in the 1960s.
He reports that more than 30 percent of adults interviewed at the Sha-

huaya mission stated that they or one of their parents or grandparents had been captured by raiders (Bodley 1971:106). Since raiders killed adult men whenever possible, taking as captives only women and children, this rate of enslavement is an index of high mortality among male defenders (fig. 8.2).

Even Franciscan priests were drawn into the local traffic in children. Monsignor Irazola, who established the twentieth-century mission in Satipo, "found it prudent," as he put it, to acquire kidnapped children from Asháninka slave raiders who came to the mission. He saw these children "as a gift of the Providence that perhaps in this way seeks to instill and propagate the faith among these infidels" (quoted in Fernández 1988:32).

Commerce in Asháninka children continued in some areas until the early 1960s. In 1984, a man named Chimanca recalled with chilling clarity the raids organized in the 1940s by Shora, a "chief" appointed by Spanish-speaking authorities of the area:

> Shora was made chief by a colonist named Antenor. He was named because he was Antenor's *compadre*. Just as boys and girls were traded before, this Antenor traded them for cotton cloth. He asked Shora to bring him girls and boys so that he could raise them, so that they would work for him without pay. They were only given food, sometimes clothes—but old clothes, the poor children! He had plenty of them! Antenor also asked for children to be sent to his mother in Lima . . .
>
> You delivered a child and they gave you a piece of cloth. "Bring me a child," they said to Shora, and they gave him cloth. So Shora, since he was a warrior, was able to take them from over there, from the Río Ene. He killed the parents and took the children. They arrived here and they were given to the one who had paid him with cloth. (Fernández 1986a:139–40).

MILLENARIANISM

Out of this sanguinary period of Asháninka history there emerged stories of a new messiah. The most believable report comes from Gabriel Sala's diary of his expedition to Gran Pajonál. In the entry dated March 10, 1897, Sala recorded his meeting with an Asháninka man who told him that "in Chanchamayo the Campas and the whites are fighting, and that there has appeared again the *Amachegua*, descended from heaven, to help us in the combat" (Sala 1897:127). The *Amachegua* to which Sala refers—more properly, Amachenga or Amachenka—denotes a class of mythical saviors (Weiss 1975:258). Sala later states that one such Amachenga was none other than the rubber baron Carlos Fitzcarrald, who Sala believes manipulated Asháninka spiritual beliefs to conscript rubber tappers.

A more firmly documented Asháninka crisis cult arose in the late 1920s, when Fernando A. Stahl, a Seventh-Day Adventist, established a mission on the Río Perené. Stahl's efforts produced little progress at first, but eventually Asháninkas began to show glimmerings of interest. Stahl's visits to communities along the Perené attracted large groups of Indians waiting to be baptized: "Suddenly we came in view of an open valley, and as we entered the valley we were met by hundreds of Campa Indians, who greeted us warmly" (Stahl 1932:86). The photographs that accompany Stahl's memoirs show scores of Asháninkas standing stiffly beside the missionary.

In his research on the impact of Stahl's mission, John Bodley (1972) found that Asháninka enthusiasm for Stahl's message had achieved a life of its own, in many cases even before Stahl had contacted specific communities. Stahl preached of the imminent return of Christ, who would destroy those who failed to respect the Word of God. Asháninkas elaborated their own interpretation of his teachings, including a belief that Christ would appear within a matter of weeks, bringing about a cataclysmic transition to a world without sickness and death.

Hundreds of Asháninkas—perhaps as many as two thousand—assembled spontaneously to await the predicted millennium. In areas where the movement took hold, the sudden disappearance of Asháninka workers enraged white landowners. They organized reprisals against native catechists, including the murder of one on the Río Shahuaya. Most Asháninkas eventually dispersed when Christ failed to appear, but two hundred or more adherents remained in communities organized by native leaders at Las Cascadas and Tambo (Bodley 1972:224–26).

From the 1920s onward, hundreds of Asháninkas chose to escape the threat of slave raids or the burdensome demands of landowners by moving to the mission communities that sprang up across the region. In the 1960s, John Bodley found 38 mission settlements functioning in their territory, mostly under the aegis of Protestant denominations (Bodley 1971:147–48).

Asháninka converts proved as wayward in the twentieth century as their ancestors had in the eighteenth. Commenting on the negligible impact of 20 years of Protestant missionary work at the Cahuapanas mission, John Elick, an anthropologist and missionary who lived with the Asháninka for seven years, notes that many Asháninkas exhibited "a gradual rejection of what apparently comes to be an unsatisfying way of life and a return to the old Campa ways" (Elick 1969:16).

However volatile the Asháninka commitment to Christianity, the missions offered undeniable attractions: a degree of protection from outsiders, medical care and education, trade goods, livestock, and the drama of radio communications and airplane landings. The material plenty associated with mission life also gave rise to beliefs reminiscent of the messianism observed by Padre Sala in the nineteenth century. One such case occurred in the late 1950s or early 1960s, when a Protestant missionary attracted a significant Asháninka following at a site called Puerto Rico on the Río Ene. A woman interviewed by Eduardo Fernández recalled that people spoke of this mysterious gringo as a messiah:

> At that time we were living there in my village [Mazaronquiari], and I heard people who spoke this way: "Upcountry there is a gringo, a little gringo who is a brother, who is a god. He is white." He was white. The people said: "You ought to believe it! He's the sun, our god!" . . . The people believed that he was Itómi Pavá, Son of the Sun. That's the way it was! He was an evangelical. I don't remember his name, but I got a good look at him. My people believed that he was Itómi Pavá. Yes! They said: "Our god comes from Lima in an airplane." "Let's go to the Río Ene," said the gringo. "Let's go to the Ene," they answered him.

By the 1960s, colonization of Peru's central jungle region by immigrants from the Andes had reduced the Asháninka to a minority population along parts of the Río Perené, the Río Chanchamayo, around the town of Satipo, and in other sections of their traditional territory. In these densely colonized areas, Asháninkas maintained tenuous control of lands that were woefully inadequate for the subsistence needs of their families—as little as 3.4 hectares per family around Satipo (Shoemaker 1981:168). Although more land was available in refuge areas along the Ene and Tambo rivers and in the Gran Pajonál, Asháninkas living there lacked ready access to the trade goods and medical care that they now considered essential for their survival. Tensions between the Indians and local landowners along the Río Perené grew markedly in the early 1960s.

In 1965, a group of leftist guerrillas belonging to the Movement of the Revolutionary Left (MIR), a Castroite party determined to overthrow the Peruvian oligarchy through an act of "revolutionary audacity," made contact with Asháninka settlements around Cubantía in Satipo Province. Some Indians in the contacted villages joined the guerrillas as combatants and guides in the ensuing months, until units of the Peruvian armed forces had succeeded in liquidating most of the MIR leadership by January 1966.[8] During the course of the counterinsurgency, Peruvian fighter bombers napalmed and strafed Asháninka villages.

Oral histories reveal that some Indians regarded the local MIR commander, Guillermo Lobatón, as a messiah who would lead them in the destruction of colonist society and a redistribution of land and trade goods. In this sense, Lobatón seems to have walked unawares into a symbolic role occupied formerly by Juan Santos Atahualpa, F. A. Stahl, and possibly Carlos Fitzcarrald, all charismatic outsiders who inspired millennial enthusiasm among Asháninkas. Lobatón was black, which would have made him especially marked as an "other" from the Asháninka point of view. Pedro Kintaro (a pseudonym), who served time in prison for allegedly collaborating with the guerrillas, remembers the debate over Lobatón's identity as the Son of the Sun:

> Ernesto, a shaman, said: "These guerrillas are going to defend us, they are going to help the Indians. We have to believe them." Some believed that Lobatón was Itómi Pavá, that he was the Son of the Sun. Sure, but there were others who didn't believe it. "How could the Son of the Sun appear as a human being?" they asked.

The MIR's campaign was of such brief duration, and the government repression so fierce, that we cannot say whether or not the rebellion would have spread to include those skeptical about the arrival of the Son of the Sun. In any event, our research suggests that pro- and antiguerrilla factions among the Asháninka formed along lines of long-standing political rivalries. Coercion by Peruvian soldiers also led some Asháninkas to work as guides for the counterinsurgency forces.

Although the revolutionary struggle of the MIR was a failure and Asháninkas sustained significant casualties, the violence did lead some landowners to moderate their demands on Indian workers and tenants. The exposure of Peruvian army officers to the desperate social conditions in the countryside helped to inspire a leftist military coup in 1968 and the subsequent enactment of a progressive Native Communities Law that promised land titles to Asháninkas and other Amazonian Indians. Here again, the internal contradictions of the Peruvian state asserted themselves. While employees of the government agency dedicated to "social mobilization," mainly reform-minded young people from Lima, attempted to issue land titles to Indians, local settlers and provincial officials lost no opportunity to oppose the formal titling of native communities.[9] Land titles were, in any case, of little use to Indians living in areas of heavy colonization, for there was no unoccupied land left to be claimed.

Since the guerrilla struggle of 1965, Asháninkas have directed their political energy to the creation of intervillage organizations, which are allied to native federations at the national and international level. To a lesser extent, they have also tried to forge links to Peru's political parties by presenting Asháninka candidates for local elective office.

Yet even as Asháninkas formalize their links to the state, the state's power to control events in the central jungle region has ebbed. Asháninka lands are under increasing pressure from colonists eager to cash in on the growing world demand for cocaine by growing coca. Meanwhile, two Marxist guerrilla groups—the Túpac Amaru Revolutionary Movement (MRTA) and the Shining Path—have become major political forces in parts of eastern Peru. Beginning with widely spaced and selective assassinations of Asháninka leaders, the Shining Path has recently launched attacks against entire Asháninka communities that refuse to obey the guerrillas' directives. In April of 1990, as many as 40 people were killed when a Shining Path column assaulted the Asháninka village of Naylamp in Satipo Province.

The Asháninka encounter with the MRTA took a sharp turn late in 1989, when guerrillas executed a prominent Asháninka leader named Alejandro Calderón Espinoza. Asháninka reaction to the killing was explosive: in the words of the popular press, the Indians "declared war on the MRTA." In late December of 1989, hundreds of Asháninka men stormed the town of Puerto Bermúdez, detained the town officials, and rounded up dozens of MRTA suspects. Press reports from Puerto Bermúdez claimed that the Indians subjected a score of guerrillas to "popular justice," including execution. The Peruvian government was slow to send army units to restore civil control or to take custody of the alleged MRTA suspects in Asháninka hands, apparently because it was happy to have the burden of the conflict borne by Indians rather than by the army.[10] In sum, state control of some parts of Asháninka territory has declined to levels comparable to the era of the rubber boom, and Asháninkas are once again forced to depend on their own wits to survive in a dangerously unstable social environment.

DISCUSSION

Let us now analyze this complex history in light of the links between state expansion and violence. The central issues can, we believe, be distilled to four distinct but interrelated questions.

Did the expansion of the Spanish, and later, the Peruvian state increase levels of violence within Asháninka society? The answer to this question is an unequivocal "yes," though the proximal causes and specific shape of violence have changed through time. During the early contact period (1595–1742), Spanish mission stations became a significant political factor in Peru's central jungle region. Fragmentary evidence from Franciscan missions in Peru, as well as comparative data from other parts of the New World, suggests that headmen increased their power by redistributing valuable trade goods, especially steel tools, provided to them by missionaries in exchange for compliance with the missionaries' efforts. Competition for access to mission resources promoted intercommunity conflict, both within Asháninka society and between Asháninkas and their neighbors. The Spanish use of native mercenaries (e.g., Conibos) contributed to higher levels of violence between ethnic groups that may formerly have engaged only in sporadic conflict. A dramatic exception to this pattern was the interethnic solidarity inspired in 1742 by the rebel messiah Juan Santos Atahualpa, whose uprising cleared the region of settlers for nearly a century.

When interest in colonizing the jungle revived in the mid- to late-nineteenth century, landowners and rubber barons learned to manipulate traditional raiding and trading patterns to their own advantage (Chevalier 1982:204). There is overwhelming evidence that this strategy increased local violence to unprecedented levels, especially when it included the distribution of repeating rifles to Asháninka slave raiders, making combat much more lethal than in the precontact era. White merchants destroyed traditional Indian trading networks to foster Asháninka dependency, a tactic that incited Indians desperately in need of basic goods (salt, for instance) to raid their more prosperous neighbors.

The violence engendered by colonization of the jungle was not always in the immediate interests of the state that fostered it. As the world market for rubber collapsed, for example, rubber merchants in the Pichis Valley attempted to squeeze every last *centavo* from their Asháninka workers. The situation eventually exploded: beginning in December of 1913, Asháninka warriors raided white settlements, cut telegraph wires, killed 150 settlers, and closed the Pichis Trail linking the region to the Perené Valley and the Peruvian coast (Bodley 1971:109–10; Elick 1969:14–15).

What strategies did the Asháninka devise to adapt to higher levels of violence? Obviously, some Asháninkas were willing to modify precontact feuding and raiding patterns to take advantage of the new circumstances in which they found themselves. Ambitious headmen, such as Carlos Fitzcarrald's henchman Venancio, used predatory violence to increase their personal power and the size of their retinues. In 1900, Colonel Pedro Portillo visited Venancio's village on the Río Tambo, a place called Washington. "Washington is like a military plaza or an impregnable fortress . . . of five hundred inhabitants, subject to Venancio," Portillo reported. "From the months of June to November they are in continuous journeys to extract *caucho* and *sheringa* [types of latex] from the region of Sepahua, Cuja, and Purús" (Portillo 1901:40).

Indians who wished to avoid forced labor recruitment by *caciques* such as Venancio either fled to remote corners of the jungle or joined together in large communities (often at missions or plantations) that afforded some protection from attack. The cruel irony is that Asháninkas had to turn to Western institutions to find a safe harbor from the violence spawned by the widening influence of the Western extractive economy. Worse still, high levels of indigenous violence were fixed upon by Peruvian nationals as justification for the forced acculturation of Indians. "Satipo's old-timers often told me that they literally stepped between groups of warring Campas and forced them to disband," writes Robin Shoemaker (1981:165). The national society had become a source of peace in a violent world largely of its own making.

Anthropologists tend to view missions and plantations as places where indigenous people can be brought under control and their culture systematically extinguished. In eastern Peru, however, the competing interests of missionaries, traders, and plantation owners created a complex sociopolitical mosaic that in some respects may actually have impeded control over the native population. Consider the case of missions. Although it is true that missionaries sometimes worked hand-in-hand with colonists (Ortiz 1961:255), on other occasions their aims were in direct conflict. Fernández (1986b:56) observes that some Asháninkas have been attracted to the missions of the Summer Institute of Linguistics (an American organization dedicated to the translation of the Bible into native languages) because the American evangelicals are visibly "other" vis-à-vis Peruvian nationals; in a sense, the Indians see the religion of the Americans as an alternative to the dominant religion of Peruvian national society, Roman Catholicism. More recently, events suggest that at least a few Asháninkas have used the chaos unleashed by guerrilla war to settle personal scores with their enemies—in effect advancing their own agendas by taking advantage of cracks in the edifice of state control.[11]

Asháninkas have used these fields of political and ideological difference as resources to be investigated and exploited. One can see this in the turnover of Asháninka population in the Franciscan missions of the eighteenth century and similar short-term residence at Protestant missions in the twentieth. Asháninka biographies collected by John H. Bodley (1971) in the 1960s reveal how this movement within the frontier mosaic has played itself out in individual lives. A man named Juan Antonio Sharihua, for example, has spent parts of his life as an agricultural peon, as a rubber tapper and gold miner for white patrons, as a cash-crop farmer living next to a Protestant mission, and as a "traditional" householder in independent Asháninka settlements (Bodley 1971:128–29). Bodley's study documents in Asháninka life histories and population movements a slow course from subsistence production to market involvement, but the heterogeneity of the frontier world has allowed Asháninkas to move on that path with a stuttering zigzag rather than in a swift, straight dash.

We are *not* arguing that missions, plantation communities, multinational corporations, or Marxist guerrilla groups have promoted the preservation of traditional Asháninka culture in any direct way; indeed, all of them assert control over Asháninka labor, settlement patterns, or beliefs. Our point is that the internal contradictions of the Peruvian state have given rise to different institutions in the Amazonian frontier and that competition among these institutions provides opportunities for Asháninkas to pursue varying strategies for cultural survival.

What ideological responses have Asháninkas formulated in the face of such dramatic changes? One of the most persistent responses has been the belief that the world in which Indians are subservient to outsiders will be destroyed, to be replaced by one of utopian abundance. Asháninkas, writes Gerald Weiss (1975:407), "anticipate a time when Tasórentsi [God] will destroy the world or, rather, transform it into a new world." "When that occurs," he adds, "sky and earth will again be close together, the earth will speak once again, and its inhabitants will be a new race of humanity knowing nothing of sickness, death, or toil." John Elick found a similar belief among the Asháninkas he studied. "This world, tainted and contaminated by the intrusion of evil forces and beings," they told him, "will also pass away" (Elick 1969:236).

We have no way of knowing whether this apocalyptic vision predates contact with Europeans or evolved in reaction to it. What we can say, however, is that it has helped to propel Asháninka millenarian enthusiasm since the rebellion of Juan Santos Atahualpa in 1742, including the 1965 alliance with the guerrilla fighters of the MIR. Other instances of millenarianism among the Asháninka—for example, the movement inspired by the American missionary F. A. Stahl in the 1920s—have not evoked armed resistance. Yet in each case Asháninkas expressed their unwillingness to endure the status quo. We would not go so far as to suggest that Asháninkas have formulated a true "culture of resistance" of the sort documented among the Saramaka of Surinam (Price 1983), but their willingness to put a millenarian dream into action represents a durable critique of their situation and an ideological resource that Asháninka leaders have drawn on to galvanize a violent response to oppression.

To what extent has contact promoted "tribalism" among Asháninkas? Here the historical record remains equivocal. The increased power of Asháninka headmen in the face of early European contact seems to have produced larger social units in Asháninka society, as did the unifying but short-lived influence of messianic figures. This tendency toward social consolidation was countered by intercommunity conflicts fostered by slave raids, fear of the epidemics associated with large settlements, and competition for access to scarce trade goods. By the late nineteenth century, Europeans came to realize that Asháninka populations represented a single (if in some respects heterogeneous) linguistic group labeled "Campas," but we find little evidence that the Indians conceived of themselves as a cohesive "tribe" with shared interests until recently. By the 1980s, Asháninka leaders had assimilated the rhetoric of ethnic assertion common to native groups elsewhere in Amazonian Peru and had begun to formulate their demands to the government in terms of the needs of "the Asháninka people." Yet even as we write, Asháninkas are divided into eight federations, each representing communities from a single valley or region. Thus far no organization has succeeded in creating stable links to all Asháninka communities.

In conclusion, we trust it is clear that the tidal frontier of the post-Conquest state has had a marked impact on the level of violence experienced by Asháninkas in their daily lives. In our assessment of the effects of frontier expansion, however, we have tried to avoid utopian assumptions about what the Asháninka world might have been like had the Indians not fallen prey to states. An analysis that blames every act of brutality on the pernicious effects of colonialism, as does the glib "post-imperial" anthropology espoused by Edward Said (1989), would reduce the Asháninka to the status of passive victims rather than recognize them as active shapers of their history. There is little question that Asháninkas have been capable of great violence, both within and outside of their own society, and that they have not hesitated to use force in pursuit of ends important to them: self-defense, control of resources, personal ambition, revenge. By aggressively exploiting the discontinuities and contradictions in the state's hold on their territory, Asháninkas have fashioned a culture of survival.

——— *Notes* ———

1. The research on which this chapter is based was made possible by the financial support of the National Endowment for the Humanities, the School of American Research, the Wenner-Gren Foundation for Anthropological Research,

Williams College, and the Harry Frank Guggenheim Foundation. The authors wish to express their gratitude to these organizations, to the other participants in the School of American Research advanced seminar, and to John H. Bodley, who was kind enough to comment on an earlier draft of our essay.

2. The work of Eric Wolf (1982) is exceptional in showing how European colonial states were rife with contradictory tendencies, largely related to the transition from a "tributary mode of production" to a capitalist one. Wolf observes that this transition took place at different times, and in distinct economic sectors, in each country; the shifting fortunes of competing modes of production had a profound influence on colonial policy in different places.

3. In this essay we do not analyze regional differences within the Asháninka population as a whole. Weiss (1975), for instance, makes a distinction between the River Campa—the population along the Apurímac, Ene, Perené, and Tambo rivers—and the Pajonál Campa, who live in the area known as Gran Pajonál. He and other authorities believe the Nomatsiguenga, who live surrounded by Asháninka communities, to be a Machiguenga population, though they are culturally almost indistinguishable from their Asháninka neighbors.

4. Zarzar (1989:26) provides much higher totals for Franciscan mission populations in the central jungle region, but we judge Lehnertz's detailed analysis of census data to be more reliable.

5. Principal sources for the following discussion of the rebellion of 1742 are Castro Arenas (1973), Lehnertz (1972), Loayza (1942), Stern (1987), and Varese (1973). Two recent publications that include information about Juan Santos, by Flores Galindo (1988) and Zarzar (1989), came into our hands too late to be fully integrated into the analysis. In any event, they assess the rebellion from an Andeanist perspective and shed little light on its possible meaning to tropical forest peoples such as the Asháninka.

6. For details of the Inkarrí theme, see Bierhorst (1988), Fernández (1987), Flores Galindo (1988), Ossio (1973), Stern (1987), and Weiss (1986). Weiss argues persuasively that some aspects of the Inkarrí myth may have an Amazonian rather than an Andean origin.

7. The life of Fitzcarrald was the inspiration for Werner Herzog's film *Fitzcarraldo*. Allegations that Fitzcarrald's activities among the Indians had a messianic dimension are made by Reyna (1942) but strongly denied by Valdez Lozano (1944:5–6), Fitzcarrald's former associate.

8. For background on the MIR guerrilla campaign, see Ministerio de Guerra (1966) and Gott (1973). Brown and Fernández (1991) provide the most detailed analysis of the Asháninka-MIR alliance and its significance.

9. As recently as the 1980s, the Peruvian government found itself under pressure from the World Bank to issue titles to Asháninka communities, but footdragging at the local level and in some of the national ministries prevented the issuance of significant numbers of titles.

10. The struggle between Asháninkas and the MRTA was front-page news in Peru during the first weeks of 1990, and the sources we have used to prepare

this brief summary are too numerous to mention here. Benavides (1990) presents a review and analysis of the struggle through July 1990.

11. See, for example, a communiqué by the Central de Comunidades de la Selva Central (CECONSEC), an Asháninka intercommunity federation, published in the Lima newspaper *La República* on July 22, 1990. The statement alleges that the president of a rival Asháninka organization killed several CECONSEC members using arms provided by local military authorities. It also denounces a group of "Asháninkas and colonists" who it contends were demanding protection money from travelers in exchange for safe-conduct passes (*cupos*), a tactic commonly used by both the MRTA and the Shining Path in zones where the guerrillas operate.

Chapter 9

A Savage Encounter

Western Contact and the Yanomami War Complex

R. BRIAN FERGUSON

THE lives of the Yanomami of the Orinoco-Mavaca river confluence of southern Venezuela have been presented in the works of Napoleon Chagnon as a kind of morality play. Embroiled in seemingly endless violence fueled by sexual competition, status rivalry, and revenge, the Yanomami are held to exemplify the Hobbesian condition of " 'Warre'—the chronic disposition to do battle, to oppose and dispose of one's sovereign neighbors" (Chagnon 1974:77; see Bennett Ross 1980). Moreover, their lifeways are said to represent "a truly primitive cultural adaptation . . . before it was altered or destroyed by our culture" (Chagnon 1977:xi). Their warfare is portrayed not as aberrant or unusual, but as the normal state of existence for sovereign tribal peoples, seeming atypical only because other war patterns have been suppressed by colonialism (Chagnon 1977:163). It is "an expected form of political behavior and no more requires special explanations than do religion or economy" (Chagnon 1983:213). The conditions Chagnon describes are said to resemble those at the dawn of agriculture (Chagnon 1983:30). The Yanomami are "our contemporary ancestors" (Chagnon 1983:214); thus, understanding their "quality of life . . . can help us understand a large fraction of our own history and behavior" (Chagnon 1983:213). The same insecurities that create Warre among the Yanomami account for warfare among modern nation-states, and the same inference is to be drawn: "the best defense is a good offense" (Chagnon 1974:195).

Chagnon's portrayal is persuasive and has been widely accepted. In the Foreword to his Yạnomamö: The Fierce People, one of the most widely read texts in the history of anthropology, the series editors write that the "sovereign tribal" politics of these Yanomami is "a product of long-term sociocultural evolution without intervention from outside alien populations and life ways" (Spindler and Spindler 1983:vii). Even scholars who have been the most attentive to the violence-provoking possibilities of Western contact accept the Yanomami's relatively "pristine" character (Fried 1974; Service 1967). Students of the Yanomami have been more skeptical, many pointing out that the Orinoco-Mavaca area has undergone extensive contact-related changes (e.g., Bennett Ross 1971; Davis 1976; Good 1989; Lizot 1976; Smole 1976). None of the critics, however, has shown in any systematic way how those changes relate to observed patterns of violence.

The seminar for which this paper was written was intended to explore exactly those relationships, and to challenge the idea that any ethnographic case of indigenous warfare is fully understandable apart from the historical circumstances of contact with an expanding state. The Yanomami of the Orinoco-Mavaca area provide a crucial test of this assertion. I will not dispute that they are less disrupted and transformed by Western contact than most of the peoples for whom we have ethnographic information. Nevertheless, I will argue that after centuries of sporadic contact with outsiders, Orinoco-Mavaca society was undergoing massive change for some two decades prior to Chagnon's arrival, and that this process of change accelerated during the time period described in Chagnon's monographs (1964–72). His statement that "it is not true, as a few of my colleagues believe, that the Yanomamo were described at a particularly 'turbulent' period of their history" (Chagnon 1977:163) is unsupportable. The "fierce people" immortalized by Chagnon represent a moment in history in which Yanomami culture was pushed into an extreme conflict mode by circumstances related to the intensifying Western presence. Their warfare and other conflicts are manifestations of this larger situation. Where Chagnon tells us that the Yanomami provide "an intimate glimpse beyond history, whither we came" (Chagnon 1977:xii), I maintain that they will remain a baffling chimera until they are seen in the light of their own history.

This paper is one of two studies of Yanomami warfare. In them my objectives, though complementary, are quite different. My other study is a monograph (Ferguson n.d.a) that addresses a very specific question: how can we understand the occurrence and patterning of actual incidents of warfare, or why war happens? In that work, every reported case of actual or threatened war involving all Yanomami, not just those of the Orinoco-Mavaca area, is explained with reference to a general model that centers on the basic proposition that war among the Yanomami is a result of antagonistic interests regarding access to or control over trade in Western manufactured goods. That explanation of the occurrence of war is incorporated in the current essay (below, under "Political Organization"), but my focus here is on other aspects of social violence and Western contact.

In this chapter I look at war less as an act than as a condition or state of society, a total social fact that is shaped by and shapes other aspects of social life. To analyze such a "war complex," I use a model (Ferguson 1990b, n.d.b) developed for a previous School of American Research advanced seminar (Haas 1990a), which posits a nested hierarchy of progressively more limiting constraints. The model begins with infrastructural parameters of demography, ecology, and technology; moves on to structural factors of economics, kinship, and politics; and culminates in superstructural variables of psychology and belief. Indeed, this essay was conceived as a test of that model, and specifically of its ability to elucidate changes associated with contact (Ferguson 1990b:51–54).

In the context of the contact experience, this chapter will explore secondary contributing factors and various social consequences of war, along with parallel developments that further heighten or reflect the climate of interpersonal violence. All of these taken together affect the threshold where antagonism turns into combat, making a particular people "peaceable" or "warlike." This is relevant to the aims of my companion monograph explaining the occurrence of war (Ferguson n.d.a): in the Orinoco-Mavaca area, it took much less to start the blood flowing in 1966 than it did in 1946. However, the basic nature of the antagonisms remained the same, or at least within the parameters of the same model. For the current study, these contact-related correlates of war are used to explain the other manifestations of aggression that are so striking in Chagnon's descriptions. Although much interpersonal violence is set apart from the processes of war, examining such belligerence enables us to understand the unusual "fierceness" of the Orinoco-Mavaca Yanomami.

Topics in this chapter which are detailed and documented in my longer monograph (Ferguson n.d.a) will be summarized here, without source citations. This applies mostly to discussions about Western goods, the exchange relations that grow up around them, and the application of force to affect exchange patterns; that is, to the elements of the explanation of the occurrence of war. The summaries will suffice to show how these factors connect to other elements of the war complex. Also detailed in the monograph is the political history of the Yanomami of the Orinoco-Mavaca area (n.d.a:part 3); the following very brief overview merely provides some context for subsequent discussions.

LOCAL HISTORY

The ancestors of the Yanomami were raided by slavers, in varying intensity, from probably the mid-seventeenth century to about 1850. The raids drove them deep into the Parima highlands, although some still came down to the rivers to trade. The rubber boom of the latter nineteenth century reached into mountain areas and was accompanied by wars and migrations for the recent ancestors of the Orinoco-Mavaca people. The collapse of rubber production left the region more isolated from Westerners from around 1920 until 1940, a brief interlude which has been misconstrued as a primeval state. For the Orinoco-Mavaca people, this was a time of peace.

Sporadic, sometimes violent, contact began in the area around 1940 and intensified over the decade. The captive woman Helena Valero (Biocca 1971) was in this area, and she describes the intensifying conflicts as new tools and diseases began to filter in. In the late 1940s the Namowei-teri, the population cluster later to host Chagnon's field research, divided into hostile western and eastern (Patanowa-teri) groups. Then, in 1950, the establishment of the first mission near Mahekodo-teri on the Orinoco was followed almost immediately by the slaughter of a western Namowei-teri trading party by the more isolated Shamatari. Interior groups continued to harry the wealthier villages around the Orinoco until, in 1955, the latter demonstrated their military superiority. During the relatively peaceful half decade to follow, a second mission was established by Iyewei-teri at the mouth of the Ocamo River. The Iyewei-teri are an important contrast to other local groups (see Cocco 1972): although only a few hours by launch downstream from Chagnon's field site, they had a more stable and wealthy Western power base than any upstream village, and enjoyed almost unbroken peace while the upriver villages endured several wars.

In 1958, a government malaria control station was set up at the mouth of the Mavaca River. The Bisaasi-teri, the larger of the western Namowei-teri groups, accepted an invitation to settle by the post. (The other western group, the closely allied Monou-teri, was located a short distance up the Mavaca.) Almost immediately, the missionaries at Mahe-kodo-teri moved their main operation to Bisaasi-teri. The Bisaasi-teri and Monou-teri then set out to establish beneficial alliances with Shamatari groups up the Mavaca, and in one instance demonstrated their willingness to use force against potential adversaries. For the next several years, Bisaasi-teri would be the metropolitan center of the far upper Orinoco, especially in late 1964 to early 1966, when Chagnon lived there, and when another mission was attempting to establish itself directly across the Orinoco. But those years also saw the western Namowei-teri beleaguered by internal factionalism and external enemies. This was the extraordinary fighting described in *Yąnomamö: The Fierce People* (1968). Information is limited after 1966, but it seems that in the next six years, violent conflict diminished and moved away from Bisaasi-teri to more active contact fronts farther up the Orinoco and the Mavaca. After the early 1970s, very little historical information is available at all.

INFRASTRUCTURE

Western contact brings epidemic diseases. In the Orinoco-Mavaca area, epidemics began to occur around 1940, and they continued with devastating frequency (Chagnon 1966:153; Chagnon and Melancon 1983; Ferguson n.d.a:chaps. 9, 10; and see Ramos and Taylor 1979). A major outbreak of malaria in 1960 killed an estimated 10 percent of the area population (Smole 1976:50), and another outbreak is indicated for 1963 (Lizot 1977:503). Chagnon's initial census established the cause of death of 240 individuals: 130 are attributed to malaria and epidemics, and another 25 to "sorcery" (Chagnon 1966:62). A measles epidemic swept through the area in 1968 (Chagnon 1977:146–47; Cocco 1972:176, 417). Among deaths recorded by Chagnon for 1970 to 1974, 82 (69 percent) were due to all infectious diseases (including "magic") (Melancon 1982:42). In a different sample gathered at Mavaca for 1969 to 1979, 53 (39.6 percent) were due to malaria (Flores et al. in Colchester and Semba 1985:26).

A single influenza epidemic that hit three remote villages in 1973 shows how terrible the impact can be. One hundred six people died,

27.4 percent of the combined population (Chagnon and Melancon 1983: 59–61). One village lost 40 percent (Chagnon 1977:147). In this epidemic, and presumably in all of them (Cocco 1972:481), the young and old died in disproportionate numbers. The contagion apparently was transmitted by men coming back from a trip downstream to obtain machetes (Chagnon 1977:147; and see Chagnon et al. 1970:343–44).[1] Added to these are war deaths, which take mostly adult men. In Chagnon's (1966:62) original census, 37 adults had died in war. In a later estimate, 25 percent of adult male Namowei-teri died in war, and 30 percent of adult male Shamatari (Chagnon 1983:79). Lizot (1989:30) reports a comparable figure, 24 percent of adult male deaths in war, in his sample just east and north of Chagnon's. These figures are much higher than those reported for other Yanomami areas (Cocco 1972:393; Ken Good, personal communication, 1989; Lizot 1989:30).

In sum, in the Orinoco-Mavaca area, a great many families were disrupted by death during the contact period. Only about one-quarter of the children there have both parents alive and coresident by the time they reach the age of 15 (Chagnon 1982:299). For the Yanomami, family, economy, and polity are one, and this many deaths tears at the fabric of society. The immediate consequence of observed epidemics is disruption of the system of provisioning, and hunger which can cause more deaths than the infectious agent (Chagnon and Melancon 1983:69–70; Cocco 1972:176; Neel 1973:172–73; and see Colchester 1985:65, 69; Rice 1928:355). The longer-term consequences are described by Chagnon and Melancon (1982:73):

> Disruption of village life and the resulting coalescence or fusion shatters the social organization and creates chaos, conflict and disorder in the newly-constituted village(s). This is so because whatever integration and order existed in the independent local villages before the epidemic, was enmeshed in the kinship, marriage and leadership patterns. The development of these kinship ties and marriage alliances takes years of inter- and intra-group social promises and actual exchanges, and is a complex, difficult process in even the most demographically advantageous circumstances. Forging a new order out of the chaos generated by epidemics and depopulation is all the more difficult in composite villages, and what emerges is usually quite a different system entirely.

A second major impact of Western contact is ecological depletion (see Colchester 1981). The posited linkage between game depletion and warfare is examined elsewhere (Ferguson 1989a). Evidence from numerous

Amazonian populations shows that a sizable village population will indeed deplete game in its immediate vicinity, but this problem is typically dealt with by relocation rather than war. Less acculturated Yanomami maintain an adequate protein intake by extended deep-forest hunting treks and relocation of villages (Good 1989; Lizot 1971:40; Ramos 1972:36–37). Among some Yanomami of the Orinoco-Mavaca area, the movement option is greatly reduced by the political imperative to remain close to the sources of Western manufactures, and the missionaries actively discourage people from absenting themselves for extended hunts (Lizot 1976:12). Whereas visitors to relatively remote villages frequently find them completely empty (Good 1989:6; Ramos 1972:18; Smole 1976:86), there is no suggestion that Bisaasi-teri or Mahekodo-teri is ever left vacant. The Salesian mission village Iyewei-teri is noted as not having gone on a hunting trek for at least a decade (Colchester 1984:299).

The situation is complicated by the unknown dietary contribution of mission-provided food (Cocco 1972:176); an increased danger of catastrophic crop failure in large, sedentary river villages (Cocco 1972:176, 419; Lizot in Colchester 1984:299); and the use of new (for the Yanomami) river resources (Cocco 1972:174, 378; Colchester 1984:299; Good 1989:64; Lizot 1977:509). Nevertheless it is clear that game depletion has occurred over the contact period. Lizot (1976:13), writing from the perspective of 1975, observes that

> over a decade, the Upper Orinoco, the lower and middle Mavaca and the Ocamo have witnessed the irrevocable disappearance of animals which used to populate their banks. Species which move around only a little are exterminated; such has been the case with some large birds, hogs, agoutis, tapirs and pacas, these animals represent an important part of those habitually eaten by the Yanomami. Other animals, terrified, move further away.

Chagnon (1977:148), commenting about the same time, noted that even the remote upper Mavaca had been "turned into a near desert. Now, not a single otter can be seen along its entire course, and many other species of common game animals are almost nonexistent."

Both Lizot and Chagnon are emphatic in attributing these depletions to conditions associated with the resident Westerners.[2] Given what we know about ecological adaptation in Amazonia (Ferguson 1989a), they are undoubtedly correct. But the anchoring effect of Western outposts goes back to the 1950s or even earlier, and research throughout Amazonia (Ferguson 1989a:188–91) and in several other Yanomami areas (Colchester and Semba 1985:17; Good 1983:7–9; Good 1989; Saffirio and Hames 1983:37–38; Saffirio and Scaglion 1982; Shapiro 1972:57;

Smole 1976:181) indicates that depletion would have begun soon after villages located permanently near the Western outposts. As Chagnon (1977:33) himself wrote, prior to the development of the protein controversy (see Sponsel 1983:206), "Game animals are not abundant, and an area is rapidly hunted out."[3] Lizot (1976:27) acknowledges that by 1975 some villagers may have been experiencing dietary protein deficiency.[4] It seems this was a problem for some time. Records of deaths at Mavaca beginning with 1969 show two deaths from malnutrition in both 1969 and 1970 (Flores et al. in Colchester and Semba 1985:26).

Long before it got this bad, game depletion would have had serious social consequences. Among the less sedentary, forest-dwelling Yanomami, wide sharing of meat is a fundamental basis of village solidarity (Good 1983:12–14; Good 1989:131–40; Peters 1973:79; Taylor 1972), as is the case all over Amazonia (Ferguson 1988b:144). Good (1989: 135–40) finds that failure to share leads to gradually widening social rifts, culminating in village fissioning. Helena Valero describes strict rules of sharing among pre-mission Namowei-teri (Biocca 1971:159–60; and see Cocco 1972:62), but I could find no indication of this generalized sharing among the Namowei-teri of Chagnon's time. Instead, game seems to have been kept and consumed within individual families (Chagnon 1977:91–92). In the Iyewei-teri, according to Cocco (1972:365), the community has no claim to a share of meat or fish, which is kept or distributed according to the whim of the procurer.[5]

Although game scarcity seems largely inadequate as an explanation of warfare (Ferguson 1989a), it does seem reasonable to conclude that increasing game scarcity has led to diminishing reciprocity between families in settled villages throughout the contact period. As Malinowski observed (1982:23), daily reciprocity is an important basis of social control. Less well bound by sharing, these villagers are primed for atomization and anomie, and for the instrumental use of interpersonal violence.

A third major infrastructural consequence of contact is technological change. Of paramount importance is the introduction of steel cutting tools (for details and documentation, see Ferguson n.d.a:chap. 2), which are up to ten times more efficient than stone.[6] As with other Amazonian peoples (Ferguson 1990a), Yanomami have gone to great lengths to obtain these tools, relocating villages, sending trading parties on long and hazardous journeys, and raiding vulnerable possessors of steel. All known Yanomami had obtained some metal tools long before any anthropologist visited them, yet these highly valued items remained scarce until very recently. And steel tools are only the beginning. New needs develop rapidly for a range of Western manufactures, in a process that can lead to assimilation into the lowest stratum of the expanding state. In the Orinoco-Mavaca area, those with greatest access to Westerners are seen by other Yanomami as having "turned white" (Cocco 1972:377).

Machetes, axes, and knives are unlike anything in the indigenous economy. At least at first, their utility and scarcity makes them more precious than items of native manufacture. Furthermore, they are unequally available, their sources restricted to a few points of Western presence, so procurement is the key problem. It is commonly acknowledged that Yanomami villages have moved out of the Parima highlands in order to provide closer access to sources of steel, and that in the Orinoco-Mavaca area, this is why Yanomami moved from the highlands to the insect-infested rivers. And there is more to it than movement.

> Thus there grew up two types of community—those holding manufactured goods acquired directly at source, and those (isolated ones) which were deprived of them. The entire map of economic and matrimonial circuits, along with political alliances, was transformed and flagrant imbalances appeared. Gradually, though scarcely within twenty years . . . the economy was disrupted, the society menaced at its roots, and dysfunctional attitudes developed. (Lizot 1976:8–9)

In later discussions, I will describe how contradictory interests in the quest for manufactures lead to violence.

Other significant technological changes are the introduction of shotguns and of medical treatments for wounds (Ferguson n.d.a:chap. 2). Hassig, Law, Whitehead, and Abler (this volume) have shown the limited effectiveness of early firearms, but in this regard the Yanomami more closely resemble the Papua New Guinean situation described by Strathern: shotguns clearly confer a great advantage in combat. Villages with shotguns, even if they are possessed only by the resident Westerners, are more secure against attack and more effective in retaliation. The spread of shotguns since the mid-1960s led to a rash of new killings. If an outpost village does engage in war, the medicine and medical care provided by the resident Westerner means that more of the wounded will recover (Barker 1959:163). Furthermore, outpost villages have more cutting tools and thus find it easier to construct palisades and clear forest around the settlement, both of which are important defensive tactics; and canoe transport provided by resident Westerners can aid in maneuvering, as can traded canoes provided by missionaries. The result of all these technological changes is that outpost villages have major tactical advantages over more isolated villages.

These advantages combine with the primary benefit of access to Western manufactures to anchor outpost villages in place. As noted above, this is what leads to problems with game supply, but there is another even more important consequence of this anchoring. One of the most significant factors acting to prevent or minimize war in Amazonia is the fact that most peoples are able and willing to move, to relocate their villages, when they are raided or even threatened (Ferguson 1989a:196). Settlement around Western outposts eliminates this pacific option.[7]

In addition to the anchoring effect, the primary social implications of the infrastructural changes associated with contact can be summarized as follows: deaths from disease and war scramble existing social organization; game depletion weakens social cohesion; and access to Western technology provides a new source of conflict, a new principal for ordering society, and a significantly enhanced ability to wage war for outpost villages. In the next section, we will follow some of the violent ramifications of these basic changes.

STRUCTURE

The structural effects of contact on war are here separated into three conventional topics: economics, kinship, and political organization.

ECONOMICS

A central problem for all Yanomami economies is how to obtain Western manufactured goods (Ferguson n.d.a:chap. 2). In different Yanomami areas, these have been obtained by hunting for pelts, traveling to work as farmhands, or producing manioc flour or bananas for sale or trade. In the Orinoco-Mavaca area, the way to obtain Western goods has been to work for the Westerners who come there to live or visit. Missionaries and other resident Westerners regularly give away substantial quantities of manufactures. They make large presentations on special occasions, such as visits to more remote villages, but normally give the manufactures as payment for goods (garden products, meat, firewood), for services (as guides, ground clearers, housebuilders, translators, maids, informants, etc.), and in some instances, for local manufactures with external sale potential. Very few details are available about employment and payments, but one obvious point has important consequences for understanding patterns of conflict: to work for the Westerners in most of these capacities requires that one live close to them.

Before following out the implications of this spatial inequality for understanding war, another aspect of working for Westerners should be mentioned, which will be significant for a later discussion of male violence against women. Most of the work done for Westerners is done by men, rather than women. This applies even to the production of garden products, as the Yanomami are unusual among Amazonian cultivators in that men do most garden work (Chagnon 1977:90; Good 1989:48; Smole 1976:106). Other changes are evident concerning the relative labor contribution of women. Firewood, an absolute necessity for the Yanomami, becomes depleted around the outpost settlements, and women spend many hours each day finding and carrying firewood. That and hauling water appear to be their main procurement tasks (Chagnon 1977:81–82, 91; Chagnon 1983:68). By contrast, Shirishana Yanomami women start gathering wood late in the day, and find most of it in the vicinity of the settlement (Peters 1973:79); and among the mobile Yanomami just east of the study area, wood gathering requires an average of only 0.6 hours per day (Good 1989:49, 122–23). The latter population illustrates another change: among mobile Yanomami, gathering done by women provides crucial foods during the time when new gardens are being established (Good 1989:120). This task ends when villages become anchored to Western outposts. Wood gathering and water hauling are essential tasks, but they are not subject to the same concern and respect that goes to male specialities of hunting, war, and procuring Western manufactures.

To return to the question of access to Western manufactures (see Ferguson n.d.a:chap. 2), the Yanomami generally make great efforts to monopolize access to the Western provider, using pleas, threats, and deceptions to keep the distribution of goods within their local group. Beyond the source point, Western manufactures are passed along from village to village through networks of kinship. Often the people in one village use a tool for some time, then pass it along to the next village when they get a new one. The quantities in exchange can only be guessed, but that guess must be high. An incomplete listing of goods distributed from the Catholic mission at Iyewei-teri for 1960 to 1972 includes 3,850 machetes, 620 axes, 2,850 pots, 759,000 fishhooks, and large quantities of other items (Cocco 1972:378). Most of these goods were traded to more remote villages.

Nevertheless, some villages separated from Western sources by two or three intervening villages are reported as receiving only poor remnants of manufactures. The Shamatari village Mishimishimabowei-teri, about 12 days and three middlemen south of Bisaasi-teri, in 1968 had broken blades that were "usually unrecognizable as machetes" (Chagnon 1974:35) and "two of the most miserable 'axes' I have ever seen . . . worn down by years—perhaps decades—of heavy use" to a third of their original size (Chagnon 1983:39).

Most reports indicate that the exchange of Western manufactures is usually without overt contention. A request for an item is made, and that item is given, on the promise of some future compensation. On the other hand, Lizot (1985:184) reports that "the bargaining, however, does not procede without bitter disputes. The partners stay at the brink of rupture." Even the smooth transactions may mask tensions, and the major trading that occurs at feasts is often preceded or followed by violent confrontations. Veiled and not-so-veiled threats are made, as when a man "named the men he had killed on various raids—just before demanding a machete" from Chagnon (1974:1). "In some communities, to declare, 'I will not give anything' or 'I will not give what you are asking' is to risk a clubbing" (Lizot 1985:184). Both parties to an exchange generally express dissatisfaction with its terms. Dialogue reported during trading contains insistent demands for machetes. The Namowei-teri complain generally about the "extravagance and sharpness" (Chagnon 1974:165) of Shamatari requests. If most exchanges go smoothly, it is only because a man generally will ask only for what he can expect to receive. The terms of trade are understood.

In exchange for Western manufactures, more isolated Yanomami make and trade local manufactures. Consistent with the earlier quotation from Lizot, this has led to a clear division of labor between Yanomami communities. All the villages around missions have specialized in the trade of Western items; residents of villages without such access have become specialists in producing specific local commodities, which they trade to the mission villages. Thus in Iyewei-teri, men obtain Western goods by working for the mission, then exchange these goods for bows, quivers, curare arrowpoints, cotton, hammocks, manioc strainers, manioc cakes, tapioca, plantains, and other items, from a total of 12 villages (Cocco 1972:376–78).

But does this general pattern apply to the Bisaasi-teri? Admittedly, it would be difficult to infer its existence from reading *The Fierce People*. Cocco (1972:205), however, like Lizot, describes the pattern as applying to all mission villages in the area, which would include Bisaasi-teri. In a letter written during his initial fieldwork, Chagnon (1972a:66) reports the same pattern: "Some villages specialize in making one or another object; others who have special sources of access purvey axes or machetes and pots to the rest." The pattern is also suggested by the captions of two photographs from the same trading session: "Kaobawa trading his steel tools to Shamatari allies" (Chagnon 1974:11), and "Kaobawa . . . trading with his Shamatari allies for arrows, baskets, hammocks, and dogs" (Chagnon 1983:6); and it is implied in a passing mention of "steel tools and aluminum pots" being the trade specialization of "several contacted villages" (Chagnon 1977:100). But Chagnon follows this point immediately with a discussion that downplays the utilitarian aspect of trade in local manufactures, arguing that trade specialization is to be understood as a gambit to create political alliances. People "forget" or "remember" how to make certain things in order to create a basis for reciprocal exchange (Chagnon 1967:121; Chagnon 1977:100–101).

I have been unable to locate a report of such collective amnesia in any other ethnographer's writings on the Yanomami. Moreover, the material interest in Bisaasi-teri trade is apparent in regard to cotton and hammocks. Woven by men in this area (see Ramos 1972:36; cf. Peters 1973: 196–97), cotton hammocks are scarce and very valuable. They are traded widely, even into the Parima highlands (Biocca 1971:108; Chagnon 1983: 66; Smole 1976:30, 124, 225, n. 110).

> The Bisaasi-tedi obtain much of their spun cotton and curare arrow points from their Shamatari allies. It takes considerable time and labor to accumulate these items. When the Shamatari are visited by the Bisaasi-tedi, the latter make known their desire to have these items, and their hosts promise to produce them. When the items are accumulated, the Shamatari visit the Bisaasi-tedi to inform them their cotton and arrow points are ready. A feast is arranged and the items are given over to the Bisaasi-tedi after the celebration terminates. The Shamatari then request specific items from their hosts, and the cycle continues. (Chagnon 1966:95)

The Bisaasi-teri export this cotton yarn to another ally, and it is then "brought back in the form of manufactured hammocks, the importer merely contributing labor to the process" (Chagnon 1977:101). In other words, the Bisaasi-teri come to possess a quantity of a very valuable trade item without expending any labor in its production. Curare arrowpoints, not incidentally, are listed by Cocco (1972:378) as the item Bisaasi-teri uses when trading at Iyewei-teri.

In sum, Yanomami with direct access to sources of Western manufactures make great efforts to monopolize them, sharp tensions surround the exchange of Western items, the quality and quantity of Western manufactures diminishes markedly at each step in the exchange network, and outpost villages acquire large quantities of various local, labor-intensive manufactures. My inference is that those groups who control sources of

Western manufactures exploit more isolated peoples who depend on them for metal tools. This inference is reinforced by the more obvious exploitation by middlemen in the realm of marriage relationships, discussed in the next section. Later, we will see how all these factors generate warfare.

KINSHIP

The main focus of this section is marriage patterns and the much-debated "fighting over women." But first, there are issues to be considered concerning village composition and size. Both are strongly affected in the Orinoco-Mavaca area by the intensity of war during the contact period.

Throughout Amazonia, postmarital residence is influenced by combined circumstances of production and conflict (Ferguson 1988b). In the case of the Orinoco-Mavaca Yanomami, production is essentially neutral in regard to residence. Absent are those conditions, such as commercial manioc flour production, which elsewhere favor cooperative female work groups and uxorilocality. (Other Yanomami who do produce farina demonstrate a strong tendency toward uxorilocality [Barandiaran and Walalam 1983:108, 193; Ramos 1972:32, 57].) Also absent is the conflict situation that favors uxorilocality: external war against collective enemies.

What is present in this area is intense local conflict. Hostilities which pit neighbors, even coresidents, against each other make uxorilocality difficult to maintain. At the same time, the substitution of Western manufactures for bride service (discussed below) makes it easier to keep married sons at home. The result is a strong virilocal tendency among the Orinoco-Mavaca people (Chagnon 1977:68; Lizot 1971:39). This is in marked contrast to other Yanomami areas, where bilocal or uxorilocal residence are most frequent (Barandiaran and Walalam 1983; Peters 1973; Ramos 1972). Even in the nearby community of Iyewei-teri, an absence of warfare is accompanied by uxorilocality (Cocco 1972:215).

The facility with which Orinoco-Mavaca Yanomami mobilize as conflict groups is consistent with fraternal interest group theory (Otterbein 1977). What is unanticipated by that theory (see Ferguson 1988b:140), however, is the fact that mobilization is not along strictly fraternal lines. Instead, it involves two intermarrying lines of brothers, sometimes lined up against their own agnatic kin (Chagnon 1966:104; Chagnon 1977:66). This variation can be attributed to the basic Dravidian organization common to all Yanomami (Peters 1973:71; Ramos 1972; Shapiro 1972:72–82) and indeed most northern Amazonian peoples (see Arhem 1981; Riviere 1984).

Village size is also affected by the intense conflicts of the contact period. The danger of war sets a minimum size for a viable village, which Chagnon estimates at 40 people, or 10 to 15 warriors. Above that minimum, there is strength in numbers, and villages in the Orinoco-Mavaca area are much larger than those in areas with little war, with an average of 76 (versus 53) inhabitants, and a maximum of 250 (versus 100) (Chagnon 1973:134–35).[8] In this area, the largest villages, such as Patanowateri and Mishimishimabowei-teri, are located inland, and as noted earlier, their people are relatively mobile. The villages along the Orinoco are considerably smaller (Chagnon 1974:136; Chagnon 1977:74). The ecological limitations described above put a cap on the size of the more sedentary river groups: "The jungle simply does not produce enough wild foods to sustain larger groups, and the threat of warfare is such that smaller groups would soon be discovered by their enemies and exterminated" (Chagnon 1977:98).

But this relationship has an additional twist. As argued elsewhere (Ferguson 1989a:185–86; and see Ross 1978:5–8, 31), village size is a major factor determining whether or not local hunting will lead to game depletion. Small residential groups remain in one place for long periods without wiping out their meat supply, so the decimation of local game noted by Lizot and Chagnon is due not only to new Western hunting techniques and increased sedentism, but to the war-influenced size of local villages.

In sum, the basic parameters of coresidence respond to the exigencies of violent conflict, and because of that, coresidents are easily and rapidly organized into effective fighting forces. In the following discussion, I will argue that the formation of families is shaped by access to sources of Western manufactures, and so family units are very sensitive to changes in their availability. This brings us to the subject of marriage, and to another discussion which summarizes topics detailed and documented elsewhere (Ferguson n.d.a:chap.2).

One of the paramount concerns of a senior man is to find wives for his sons, younger brothers, and other coresident agnates. These men comprise his political supporters. But marriage makers are also vitally concerned with the question of bride service. In terms that are negotiated in advance, a groom is required to live with and labor for his wife's parents for a certain period after marriage, usually one to four years in the Orinoco-Mavaca area, before returning to the husband's village. The main duty of a son-in-law is to hunt, but other obligations are involved, including support of the father-in-law in war. The centrality of marriage arrangements is summed up by Lizot (1985:143): "The highest cleverness consists in acquiring wives for one's sons by negotiating the briefest possible marital service and in seeking for one's daughters husbands who agree to settle permanently in the community."

Negotiation of marriage arrangements is made far more difficult by the circumstances of Western contact. In the Orinoco-Mavaca area, there is a well-known scarcity of marriageable females. I argue elsewhere (Ferguson 1989b:253–55) that current evidence supports Chagnon's (1972b:273–74) original observation that the intensity of female infanticide is associated with the intensity of warfare, despite his later assertion that sex ratio is skewed at birth (Chagnon, Flinn, and Melancon 1979). The local scarcity of marriageable women is aggravated by the relative predominance of polygyny. The actual incidence of polygyny is unclear. Some of Chagnon's generalizations, such as "a successful man may have had up to a dozen or more different wives, but rarely more than six wives simultaneously" (Chagnon 1988:239), appear exaggerated. Lizot (1989:31), in contrast, reports that only one in ten marriages is polygynous, and that it is rare for a man to have more than two wives at once.[9] At any rate, it is clear that polygyny is more pronounced here than in some other Yanomami areas, where polyandry is commonplace. Again, the local intensity of war seems to be a contributing factor: particularly aggressive men clearly do sometimes appropriate women as wives, as both Chagnon and Harris have always maintained (see Ferguson 1989a:180, 195).

This relative scarcity of women would make finding a mate for a young man very difficult, and choosing a mate for daughters very political under the best of circumstances. The Yanomami do not live in the best of circumstances. As noted earlier, marriage arrangements are built up over years of negotiations, and they are reduced to chaos by the death waves of epidemics. Many disrupted families must be reconstituted, and arranging new marriages becomes even more difficult when the youngest generation of women dies off (Chagnon and Melancon 1983:74).

Simultaneously, the new ordering principle of access to Western goods enters in. Studies of some eastern Yanomami demonstrate a partial substitution of gifts of Western manufactures for actual bride service (see Ferguson n.d.a:chap. 2). The exchange is not a one-time payment. A man who has access to Western goods is expected to obtain them regularly for the wife-giver family. Although most marriages are village-endogamous, intervillage marriages are the firmest basis of alliance. Intermarriage, trade, and political support are all woven together. As noted earlier, the entire map of matrimonial, trade, and alliance networks was redrawn after the introduction of Western manufactures. The basis for this transformation is clear: women flow toward mission and other Western outpost villages. Among the eastern, Brazilian Yanomami, Peters (1973) and others describe a dramatic increase in village exogamy, with women going to the mission residents who could make bride payment with Western manufac-

tures. In the northern reaches of their territory, Yanomami seeking Western manufactures from their well-supplied neighbors the Yekuana, gain
access by a one-way ceding of women as brides or sexual partners.

All these general changes hold true for the Orinoco-Mavaca area. In
1969, Karohi-teri, with regular access to Westerners, had 23 males to 23
females, while a more remote village had 30 males to 21 females (Lizot
1971:42). Cocco makes the generalization that "the increase of women
in mission villages is an incontestable fact" (Cocco 1972:210, my translation). The case of the Iyewei-teri headman shows how this occurs. At
the founding of the mission, he had one wife. The next year, he obtained
another, making an initial bride payment of one hatchet, one pot, and one
machete. A third wife was obtained later, from a father who wanted to
move to the Iyewei-teri village (Cocco 1972:212–13).

The alliance between Chagnon's main field location, Bisaasi-teri, and
its Shamatari trade-partners to the south is perhaps the best illustration
of this general pattern. In the four or five years after it moved to the
government malaria station, Bisaasi-teri managed to obtain from the Shamatari "two dozen or so women . . . while having given or promised only
a half-dozen in return" (Chagnon 1977:80). The chain of trading villages
leading out from Bisaasi-teri exhibits a "cline in sex ratios": 0.8, 1.1, 1.2,
1.6 (Chagnon 1966:57–58). Bisaasi-teri has an unusually high rate of
exogamic marriages, 53 percent, compared to 15 percent in Patanowa-
teri (Chagnon 1972b:272); and the majority of exogamic marriages in at
least one of Bisaasi-teri's two divisions are through alliances, while most
of Patanowa-teri's are through abductions of women (Chagnon 1977:73).

Bisaasi-teri has been equally privileged in terms of bride service.

> The men who have obtained Shamatari wives have, as well, man-
> aged to cut short their period of bride service in the Shamatari
> village. Conversely, Shamatari men who have been promised
> women of Kaobawa's group are pressed into very lengthy bride
> service. (Chagnon 1977:79; and see Cocco 1972:211)

The bride service of these Shamatari seems particularly difficult. Chagnon
(1974:13–14) describes one young man who was "expected to do all
manner of onerous tasks . . . [and] was subject to a considerable amount
of ridicule and harsh treatment." His "father-in-law was particularly un-
pleasant to him. He denied Wakarabewa sexual access to the girl while at
the same time he allowed the young men of the natal village to enjoy
these privileges."[10]

Viewing access to Western manufactures as the key to obtaining
women from allies is a different perspective than that argued by Chagnon,

who has consistently attributed success in obtaining wives to physically aggressive measures (e.g., Chagnon 1966:6–10, 198–99; Chagnon 1977:98; Chagnon 1988:239). The relevance of the Western manufactures-for-women connection is, however, indicated in a brief comment at the start of his thesis: "the disposition of desirable trade goods may affect the balance in the exchange of women between two villages" (Chagnon 1966:6). Also, in a coauthored article based on team research in another Yanomami area, Chagnon et al. (1970:343) note that control over steel tools gives Makiratare (Yekuana) the ability to "demand and usually obtain sexual access to Yanomama women," both in affairs and as marriage partners.

POLITICAL ORGANIZATION

Having examined the unequal trade and marital relationships that develop on the basis of unequal access to steel tools and other Western items, we can now understand the nature of the antagonisms that lead to war and other political conflicts in the Orinoco-Mavaca area. Steel tools are essential means of production. In the Orinoco-Mavaca area during the period under discussion, they were available from a few source points. Compared to villages dependent on Yanomami middlemen, those with monopolistic access to Westerners received: (1) more Western items, (2) better quality Western items, (3) many local manufactures, (4) more wives, and (5) better bride service terms. Furthermore, as noted in the infrastructure section, those located at the Western outposts enjoyed, if after some time, heightened military security.

How is force applicable in this context? (See Ferguson n.d.a:chap. 3, and parts 2 and 3.) The most direct application of force is that aimed at obtaining Western manufactures through plunder. That has been done by Yanomami, as by many Amazonian peoples (Ferguson 1990a:243–45), but it is a high-risk endeavor, and unusual within the Orinoco-Mavaca area. Force is more routinely applied to affect the flow of Western items beyond their source points. This occurs in several ways. Ambush or the threat of ambush is used to discourage travel that would circumvent a middleman village, or raids and surprise attacks at feasts are used to make a village relocate. The latter course can be used by a trade controller against a village that is attempting to move closer to the source of Western goods, and by those without good access to Westerners, in an attempt to make the controlling villages abandon their monopolistic position. Finally, club fights and other violent confrontations are used within established exchange relationships in order to direct the distribution of scarce items, and (more hypothetically) to influence the implicit rates of exchange of Western goods for other valuables.

The Yanomami do not appear at all unusual in this patterning of violence. Very similar considerations shape warfare on the Pacific Northwest Coast (Ferguson 1984b), and also may be discerned in several of the other studies in this volume. Conflict over access to Western manufactures fosters intense political conflict not just because of the importance of steel, but because unequal access creates a structured, collective conflict of interest between villages or factions. One man may benefit by capturing a wife, but a whole community benefits by an enhanced flow of machetes, axes, and pots. But turning a community of interest into an action group prepared to do violence is a difficult task, requiring great leadership skills. That brings us to the topic of leaders, and how they too have changed in the circumstances of contact.

Leadership among the Yanomami (Chagnon 1966:43–44; Chagnon 1974:137, 161–67; Chagnon 1977:14–16, 93–96; Lizot 1985:61, 142–43; and see Barandiaran and Walalam 1983:97–98; Peters 1973:144–45; Ramos 1972:78–81; Smole 1976:69–70) falls squarely within the general pattern for all recently described Amazonian societies (Ferguson n.d.c). The headman represents his coresident kin, either a separate settlement or a recognizable cluster of families within a larger village, in interactions with outsiders. He is more likely than other men to be polygynous, and his status relative to other headmen largely depends upon the size of his kin group. In a sense, the group makes the leader, but the leader also makes the group. By his manipulation of marriages and other movements of people, he can gain or lose followers. The headman is the capstone of coresidential group organization, and those groups often dissolve on his death.

Leadership also responds to the changes associated with contact, however. Headmen are the main recipients of Western goods, especially in the more remote villages.

> There was a characteristic pattern regarding the relationship between me, trade goods, and the members of any given village. At first contact with the new village I would bring a quantity of assorted trade goods for the known leaders and important men in the village. In this I followed Yanomamo precedent. (Chagnon 1974:164)

The impact of this practice may be guessed from the one case for which Chagnon provides figures. The very remote village of Iwahikoroba-teri had one "dull and badly worn" machete when he arrived. On his departure,

Chagnon gave the village headman 25 new machetes, "earmarking one of them for ... the leader of a splinter group" (Chagnon 1974:177, 180; and see Rice 1928:351–52; Seitz 1963:136, 144, 165, 193). Over time, Chagnon (1974:165) notes, he would establish relationships with more men and give out tools more widely. But the intensifying conflicts he encountered while working with the Shamatari were due to the unrelenting efforts of Moawa, the Mishimishimabowei-teri headman, to possess all of Chagnon's trade goods, or at least direct their distribution to his followers exclusively (Chagnon 1974:165–71, 185–93).

The role of headmen in channeling Western manufactures in outpost villages is less clear, but there are indications that they continue to have special access (Chagnon 1974:167; Chagnon 1977:13). To the east, at the Catrimani mission, each mission payment to an individual had to be approved first by the headman (Shapiro 1972:31). Furthermore, headmen often enjoy the very substantial benefit of explicit backing by resident Westerners (Lizot 1976:16; and see Saffirio 1985:168; Seitz 1963:165). Ultimately, however, the changes introduced by the Westerners undermine the traditional bases of leadership, as has occurred in more acculturated Brazilian Yanomami communities (Peters 1973:115–17, 146–50; Shapiro 1972:31). It is not clear if that had begun in the Orinoco-Mavaca area prior to 1972.

Another contact-related factor affecting the status of headmen is the intensity of conflict. Increasing danger of war brings an immediate, palpable increase in the authority and jurisdiction of headmen (Chagnon 1966:44; Chagnon 1974:162; Cocco 1972:387; and see Migliazza 1972:415). In a politically charged environment, a leader can be peremptory, even tyrannical, using violence against those who do not obey his orders (Chagnon 1974:161–62).

During peaceful times, the need for leadership is limited, but during war and other periods of high tension, the headman has two major responsibilities. One is tending to the necessities of combat, such as organizing raiding parties or checking village perimeters for signs of raiders (Biocca 1971:30; Chagnon 1977:96, 126; Lizot 1985:4–5). This is not an easy job. Despite the Orinoco-Mavaca Yanomami's reputation for ferocity, their efforts to organize war parties meet with resistance, counterarguments, and a high rate of "deserters" (Biocca 1971:218; Chagnon 1977:115, 130; Lizot 1985:182–83).

The other responsibility is managing alliances. During peaceful times, political alliances between villages are of limited development and importance. During wartime, they are essential. Allies are needed for survival and success in war, providing both warriors on raids and vital places of refuge (Barker 1953:475; Chagnon 1967:120; Chagnon 1977:77–80, 97–99; Chagnon 1979:92). There are often substantial tensions between allies, which the headman must keep under control. Management of alliances has two aspects of concern here.

One aspect of managing an alliance is sponsoring feasts. Feasts are the main political event, where alliances are cemented and understandings created (Chagnon 1977:97, 101–17; Cocco 1972:326, 339). Feasts occur among other Yanomami (Barandiaran and Walalam 1983:225–26; Smole 1976:96), but without the intensity evident in the Orinoco-Mavaca area (Chagnon 1967:114). Less-contacted and more peaceful villages just east of the study area attended a feast an average of every 17 months (Good 1984:5), whereas the Bisaasi-teri were involved in at least three major feasts in less than four months (Chagnon 1977:4–5, 104–5). The protection of a resident Westerner may allow more of the men to leave the village to attend a feast (Cocco 1972:339).

Feasts require a large amount of food, and sponsoring frequent feasts extends headmen's control into the area of subsistence production. Headmen have larger gardens than other men (Chagnon 1967:114; Chagnon 1977:34, 96, 107; Chagnon 1983:67; Lizot 1985:142; and see Migliazza 1972:397; Saffirio 1985:69). They also must have men who can be sent on deep-forest hunts to procure meat (Biocca 1971:53–54; Chagnon 1966:184; Chagnon 1977:105–7; Cocco 1972:341–42; Lizot 1977: 507; Lizot 1985:142–43; and see Migliazza 1972:401; Shapiro 1972: 147–48). Both requirements rely on male labor.[11] Heightened feast activity thus represents an intensification of production. Intervillage distribution of game taken in deep-forest hunts may enhance dietary standards in the Orinoco-Mavaca area. (Eating meat seems to be one of the main interests of those attending a feast [Chagnon 1974:189–91; Chagnon 1977: 102].) Sharing here is not just symbolic, it creates a significant community of interests. However, the driving imperative behind feasts is not ecological but political. And in sponsoring these feasts, the headmen of the Orinoco-Mavaca area come to seem more like incipient big-men.

The other aspect of alliance is managing chest-pounding matches (see Ferguson n.d.a:chap. 3), which often take place during a feast. These duels are reported all over Yanomami territory, and clearly have an ancient basis in Yanomami culture. But the duels reported for the Orinoco-Mavaca area differ from the others in that the matches are primarily confrontations between large groups, rather than between a few individuals, and in that they have a pronounced tendency to escalate to more serious forms of violence.

Chest-pounding matches and more serious confrontations such as club or axe fights are precipitated by a variety of offenses concerning gossip, food, trade, women, and so on. The possible role of pounding matches in establishing terms of trade has already been noted, and their significance as a form of status testing is discussed later. Here the point is that headmen play a major role in the conduct of pounding matches. They stand aside, cajoling the reluctant young men to take part, but ready to intercede if things get out of hand. A well-managed pounding match is an important part of a feast, clearing the air of petty animosities and making a stronger alliance. Without the heightened leadership of Orinoco-Mavaca headmen, it is doubtful that such collective confrontations could be used so constructively.

Given the role of the headman as the capstone of the coresidential group, and his centrality in relation to the practice of war and alliance, it is easy to understand a tactic of Yanomami warfare: targeting the headman. Headmen are frequently reported as the intended targets or actual victims of raiders (Biocca 1971:37, 56, 185, 194; Chagnon 1977:122; Cocco 1972:112, 398–400; and see Saffirio 1985:66; Seitz 1963:185). The effectiveness of this tactic is illustrated by the plight of Monou-teri in 1965, when the killing of their headman by raiders left them adrift and dependent on the leadership of self-interested neighbors (Chagnon 1977: 126–37).

SUPERSTRUCTURE

Consideration of the beliefs and attitudes associated with violence in the Orinoco-Mavaca area begins with the related topic of status; specifically, with differences in the status of men and women. Chagnon (1977:81) reports that "Yanomamo society is decidedly masculine." Women have little say in political affairs and are frequently brutalized by their husbands, who frequently club them and may even cut off their ears or shoot them with arrows (Chagnon 1966:189; Chagnon 1977:81–84; Cocco 1972:213, 216; Lizot 1985:71). This extraordinary, almost casual brutality is one of the most striking images in Chagnon's reports. But woman's lot as described by Helena Valero for the 1940s is less miserable—women resist the assaults of men, and they play an active role in political decision making (Biocca 1971:114–15, 132, 157, 161–62, 168–71, 176, 219, 243, 273–74, 306; and see Smole 1976:70).

Four factors, already explained in this paper as related to contact, can be identified as contributing to the remarkably low status of women in Chagnon's descriptions. First is the division of labor. Motherhood notwithstanding, the wood gathering that takes up so much of women's time is not likely to generate the same respect as the hunting, warring, and Western-goods procuring that men do. Second is the marked local viri-locality (after bride service), which keeps fathers and brothers together, separates women from their natal families, and facilitates the incorpora-tion of female captives (see Ferguson 1988b:149–50). Third is the un-usual number of inmarried women in Bisaasi-teri, Chagnon's main base of observation, and other Western outpost villages. A woman who marries into a village away from her brothers has no one to defend her, and is far more likely to be subject to abuse (Chagnon 1977:69, 83; and see Sha-piro 1972:116–19, 180–82).

A fourth factor is the intensity of warfare. As Chagnon (1972b:180–82) notes and Divale and Harris (1976) emphasize, war increases the value of men, especially aggressive men. The latter authors (and see Harris 1977:42–43, 63–64) also argue that sex is employed socially as a reward for aggressive behavior, and Chagnon (1988:989) does assert that war-riors (*unokais*) (cf. Albert 1989; Chagnon 1990) have more wives than less aggressive men (and see Barandarian and Walalam 1983:101; cf. Lizot 1989:31). Even women have a stake in this system, which increases their security against outside raiders (Biocca 1971:162; Chagnon 1977:83–84; Lizot 1985:155–56). The low status of women engendered by these four factors underwrites the capture and use of women as political pawns by men, which in turn reinforces their low status.

Another point at which status differences enter into conflict patterns is in relations between different groups. Chagnon, after describing esca-lating tensions during his work in Mishimishimabowei-teri, asserts that they were not really about material possessions: the "real reasons" for fighting "have to do with the status system" (Chagnon 1974:194). In the reported confrontations, however, what was at issue was the distribution of Western manufactures (see Ferguson n.d.a:chap. 12). I do not see ma-terial and status considerations as opposed here, or even separable.

Two factors are involved in status differences between political group-ings (see Ferguson n.d.a:chap. 2). One is access to Western manufactures, which in itself confers status (see Peters 1973:143, 151; Saffirio and Hames 1983:26; Soares Diniz 1969:4). "In addition to having real, prac-tical value, the trade goods often, but not invariably, reflected, when they passed from one person to another, a kind of pecking order and hierar-chy" (Chagnon 1974:164; also see Lizot 1985:184). The other factor is ability to apply force. Those who cannot match force with force are treated with open contempt (Chagnon 1977:128; and below). The chest-pounding matches and other confrontations that occur so frequently are public demonstrations of the ability to use force.

These two factors come together in the contrast of "generosity" and "extortion." A valuable gift freely given raises the relative status of the giver and creates an obligation to him. The same valuable obtained by intimidating its owner lowers his status and makes future abuses more likely (Chagnon 1967:132; Chagnon 1974:164). As Peters (1973:138– 39) observes in reference to the exchange of Western items, "the article itself is often considered an extension of the personality of both the giver as well as the owner." So I can agree with Chagnon that in one sense fighting is about status, but understanding how and why that is so requires placing the status contests into the contact situation.

A second superstructural concern is the etiology of belligerence. As Chagnon observes in the third paragraph of his famous monograph, "The thing that impressed me most was the importance of aggression in their culture" (Chagnon 1977:2). It must be stressed that this is truly an extreme case. For example: a man comes home to find that his son has eaten some of his bananas without asking permission. The father rips a pole out of the house and begins to pound on the son. The son does the same, and soon others join in on both sides (Chagnon 1977:119). One can search the literature on Amazonia and find little that compares to this. Why are the Orinoco-Mavaca Yanomami so violent?

Our answer begins with the infrastructural changes described earlier. Disease and war break up many existing families, and game depletion decreases reciprocity between families, thus creating tendencies toward social fragmentation and atomization. At the same time, the introduction of Western manufactures eliminates the traditional way of dealing with social conflict—moving away from it—and creates a new and extreme kind of competition, which we have seen manifested in all aspects of social organization. With all this, one should expect a breakdown in social control, an anomic situation evocative of the Hobbesian war of all against all.

In such an environment, security against the depredations of others may come from one's reputation of using force, of being *waiteri* ("fierce") (Chagnon 1966:109; Chagnon 1967:124–26; cf. Ramos 1987:286). Individual fierceness is socially encouraged. Male children are taught to be aggressive, to strike out (Chagnon 1967:130; Chagnon 1977:84, 132; Lizot 1985:74), and a young man who establishes his fierceness gains respect and women (Biocca 1971:66; Chagnon 1972b:274; Lizot 1985: 183). Some exceptionally violent men rise to great political prominence, such as Moawa of Mishimishimabowei-teri (Chagnon 1974:162–66, 196). But this emphasis on fierceness should not be overestimated. Another exceptionally fierce man, Helena Valero's husband Fusiwe, ultimately found himself isolated and abandoned by kin because of his aggressiveness (Biocca 1971:196–244). As noted earlier, efforts to organize war parties meet resistance. "Some men never go on raids" (Chagnon 1988: 987), and 38 percent of the men over 41 years old in Chagnon's sample had never participated in a killing (Chagnon 1988:989) Even those who do kill appear to feel a deep ambivalence, manifested in what in our society might be called neurotic symptoms of internal decomposition (Biocca 1971:63–66; Lizot 1985:5; and see Barandiaran and Walalam 1983:102–3).

Fierceness is embodied in a commitment to take revenge, in cultivating an image that retaliation *will* follow any killing (Chagnon 1967: 130–32; Chagnon 1988; Lizot 1985:74, 155–56). As Fusiwe reportedly told potential enemies: "We are in this world to avenge ourselves; if you do it to me, I will do it to you" (Biocca 1971:158). This image has obvious defensive value. In a climate of ongoing wars, the failure to retaliate for a hostile act creates the appearance of weakness, and this can encourage future attacks (Chagnon 1977:41; Cocco 1972:398–400; Lizot 1985: 123, 183). But it is necessary to distinguish the tactical value of retaliation from the idea that wars are propelled forward by sentiments of blood revenge (see Ferguson 1984b:308; Ferguson 1988c:ii-iii). In a recent publication, Chagnon (1988:985–87) places great emphasis on blood revenge as a factor itself responsible for raiding and other violence. In a commentary on that article, I argue that the vengeance motivation itself is highly malleable, manipulated to suit political needs (Ferguson 1989c:564).

Chagnon's cases provide ample evidence of the malleability of the need for revenge. Bisaasi-teri's need to avenge itself against Mishimishimabowei-teri for its participation in a slaughter in 1950 was genealogically manipulated out of existence when Chagnon began to travel regularly between the two villages, and it was suddenly "remembered" when Chagnon decided not to return to the Shamatari village (Chagnon 1974:70, 172, 194). The main shooting war during Chagnon's fieldwork began when Patanowa-teri succeeded in retrieving, without any shooting, five of the seven women that Monou-teri had abducted the day before. When Monou-teri raided Patanowa-teri some time later, it was allegedly because "Yanomamo canons of ferocity dictated that this loss would have to be avenged" (Chagnon 1966:177): that is, getting only two women instead of seven called for revenge.[12] The case used by Chagnon (1988:986) to indicate the long duration of revenge motivation, of one village raiding another in 1975 to avenge the killing of a headman in 1965, becomes quite problematic when one looks at earlier writings on that conflict. The headman of the raiding village had declared himself avenged after a retaliatory killing back in 1965 (Chagnon 1983:186). Moreover, according to the body count from that conflict, it was the village being raided, not those doing the raiding, that had an outstanding blood debt to pay (Chagnon 1983: 189). The list could be extended. Revenge simply does not explain variations in the actual practice of violence.

A final topic to be considered here is the cognitive effort to make the tragedy of intense warfare more intelligible. This effort occurs on both general and specific levels. On the general level, the Yanomami of the Orinoco-Mavaca area have an origin myth in which the falling blood of a wounded moon explains their propensity to violence (Chagnon 1977: 47–48; Cocco 1972:468). A similar myth is found among Sanema Yanomami to the north, who also have experienced a great deal of recent warfare (Barandiaran and Walalam 1983:9ff.). The myth is not found in other, more peaceful areas of Yanomami territory (Chagnon 1967:127; Migliazza 1972:426–27).

In regard to specific conflicts, intensifying hostility between political groups is conceptualized in terms of spirit battles, controlled by their respective shamans. An accusation of witchcraft often precedes combat, so that it may appear that these beliefs are the cause of war (Chagnon 1977:49; Cocco 1972:386; Lizot 1985:114–23; Lizot 1989:31–32; and see Albert 1988; Barandiaran and Walalam 1983; Migliazza 1972: 416; Saffirio 1985:66, 94; Smole 1976:50). But it has been a consistent finding of witchcraft studies in other parts of the world (Marwick 1970) that accusations of witchcraft *express* existing hostilities rather than cause them. Here too, bad relations lead to suspicions of sorcery (Chagnon 1977:118), and villages "linked by trade and feasting ties ... rarely accuse each other of practicing harmful magic" (Chagnon 1977:98). Barandiaran and Walalam (1983:103) provide a nice illustration of this, in which the diagnosis of witchcraft that precedes an attack follows a breakdown in the flow of Western trade goods. However, a partial exception to this generalization may be needed in a particular circumstance: the unprecedented catastrophe of first experience with epidemic disease (see Albert 1988:95). It is certainly believable that the killing of a visiting man soon after the first epidemic was encouraged by suspicions of witchcraft, as the Yanomami informants explain (Chagnon 1966:153).

The sources cited above indicate that the attribution of a death to sorcery is accompanied by a felt need for blood revenge. It may be that witchcraft and revenge are two sides of a coin. Witch beliefs confirm the malevolence of particular outsiders ("them"); vengeance beliefs emphasize the solidarity of the local group ("versus us"). Together, they make up an effective ideological system for the difficult task of mobilizing people for collective violence.[13]

CONCLUSIONS

This paper has examined the multiple, interacting effects of Western contact on the war complex of Yanomami of the Orinoco-Mavaca area. Contact both generated war, primarily through conflicting interests in Western manufactures, and led to pervasive reorganization of society and culture, such that all of life became oriented toward violent conflict. Comparing these Yanomami to Yanomami elsewhere, one cannot doubt that they share a fundamental cultural identity. But the "fierce people" represent Yanomami culture in an extreme conflict mode, a mode that is clearly attributable to the exogenous factors of Western contact. These people cannot be taken as "our contemporary ancestors." They do not represent a phase in sociocultural evolution.

No one can say if the Yanomami ancestors made war before they felt any effects of European contact. But their *known* wars are clearly products of the contact situation, and more specifically, of the infrastructural changes wrought by contact, played out through a changing structure and superstructure. If villages were not anchored to outposts but were able to move freely, if long-established marital alliances were not disturbed by massive mortality, if communal sharing of meat were still the norm, and above all, if necessary technology were widely and equally available, my theoretical expectation is that there would be little collective violence among the Yanomami.[14]

This essay has been an application of a theoretical model which attempts to explain a war complex as a total social system, in interaction with agents of another social system, at a particular moment in history. But it is only a moment, a brief quarter century. The history of Yanomami interaction with Western agents and other indigenous polities goes back for centuries at least (Ferguson n.d.a:chap. 4; Whitehead, this volume), and it continues beyond 1972. The period discussed here is one of great disruption and often violent internal divisions. But it is also a period of ethnogenesis, when the regionally diverse Yanomami came to be generally recognized as a single cultural entity (Chagnon 1966:26-29, 45-49; Migliazza 1972:5-9, 352-447; and see Ferguson n.d.a:chap. 4).

In the 1990s, the Yanomami are under assault, especially in Brazil, by combined economic and military interests (*Cultural Survival Quarterly*

1989). The outcome remains uncertain. Physical or cultural extinction of many regional village clusters is a frightening possibility. But it is also possible that the interests will be checked by worldwide political pressure. If greater social stability were made possible by a general availability of those Western goods which the Yanomami deem necessities, and by medical care sufficient to prevent massive mortality, the Yanomami might develop political institutions of unification and representation, capable of defending their culture and interests (see Yanomami 1989). Some day soon, the Yanomami could become a tribe.

——— *Notes* ———

I would like to thank Jane Bennett Ross, Leslie Sponsel, and Robert Murphy, and all the participants in the School of American Research advanced seminar, especially Neil Whitehead, for constructive commentary. Leslie Farragher assisted me in various ways. Research, writing, and revision were supported by the Harry Frank Guggenheim Foundation, and especially by a New Jersey Governor's Fellowship in the Humanities.

1. These data support arguments by Whitehead and Abler in this volume that the spread of Western diseases in nonresistant populations is not an automatic process, but is shaped by the character of the contact situation.

2. Lizot (1977:508–12) has solid data indicating adequate protein intake at one point in Karohi-teri.

3. It is not clear how long after Karohi-teri's founding in 1968 (Lizot 1971: 41) Lizot measured its game intake, but it already took the residents of that village roughly one-third more time to locate game than it did the residents of a more interior village (Lizot 1977:508).

4. Colchester and Semba (1985:17) report protein deficiency as a major problem in other areas.

5. Saffirio and Scaglion (1982:39–41) document a major decline in meat sharing between families in villages along the Brazilian perimetral highway (and see Seitz 1963:141–43).

6. Moreover, there is some question whether all pre-steel Yanomami even had stone axes (Ferguson n.d.a:chap. 4).

7. Chagnon (1973:136) has extended Carneiro's (1970:735) concept of "circumscription" to the case of the Yanomami, arguing that they are "socially circumscribed" by surrounding enemies. While this may apply to some Yanomami, most of the villages described by Chagnon are located at the very edge of Yanomami territory, next to unoccupied forest (Ferguson 1989a:196). If these groups are socially circumscribed, it is by the nature of the Western presence.

8. When the threat of war markedly diminished around 1984, all of the larger villages in the area fissioned into at least two parts (Lizot 1989:29–30).

9. I have not found any actual observation of a man with more than five wives at one time (Biocca 1971:129).

10. Chagnon (1967:123) also notes, but without specifying place, that head-men of particularly strong villages "may even have the bride service waived."

11. Apparently, women make little special contribution to the preparations for a feast (see Shapiro 1972:153).

12. I explain this raid as a result of sharply contradictory trade interests (Ferguson n.d.a:chap. 11).

13. The fact that witchcraft suspicions so frequently precede raiding suggests the potential for combining witchcraft and warfare studies.

14. It must be added that changing circumstances in later contact periods can lead to new forms of interpersonal violence—see chapter 1, endnote 19; and Strathern, this volume.

Chapter 10

Let the Bow Go Down

ANDREW STRATHERN

I N this chapter,[1] I approach the theme of the relationship between tribes and states in two ways: first, by discussing the situation created when tribes are encapsulated within a new state through pacification, and second, by describing the contemporary political circumstances in the Western Highlands Province of the Independent State of Papua New Guinea. After an initial period of pacification, warfare became resurgent in the Western Highlands, and it has recently been exacerbated by the introduction of guns. Hence the chapter title, "Let the bow go down," taken from a young warrior's comment on the shift from bows and arrows to firearms since 1986.

HISTORY AND SOCIAL STRUCTURE

The modern state of Papua New Guinea is an amalgam carved out of a larger geographical and historical entity, the island of New Guinea. The western half of this land mass was formerly a Dutch colony, and since the 1960s it has been a province of the Indonesian Republic. Papua New Guinea, the eastern half of the island, comprises the old British colony of Papua and, to its north, the former German colony of New Guinea. The two territories effectively came under Australian administration after the end of the first World War, and they were formally joined together as an independent nation in 1975. Coastal and inland areas were explored first; the Highlands region, within which my case study is located, was "discovered" only in the 1930s—first by explorers seeking gold, and swiftly thereafter by missionaries and colonial officials. Social change in the Highlands has been rapid, accelerating since 1945 and particularly since 1975. Today, the region is one of the most populous and economically advanced within the new state. The earlier colonial plantation economy (in coffee and tea) has largely given way to smallholder activity and the development of secondary businesses such as hauling, merchandizing, and management services. The urban center of Mount Hagen, around which live the "tribal" peoples whom I have been studying since 1964, has a population of approximately 10,000; it possesses supermarkets, banks, hotels, government offices, and a coffee factory. On the face of it, then, we might wish to argue that a process of "detribalization" is occurring in this area. But though this is correct in certain respects, it is incorrect at the political level, where new power blocs are emerging in ways that are more accurately described as "tribalization."

The term "tribalization" here refers to the continuous re-creation of political identities that has resulted from the incorporation of the Mount Hagen people into a centralized national state. I do not intend to imply that such identities were previously absent. In earlier publications (e.g., Strathern 1971), I have shown that social groups in Hagen display an elaborate array of segmentary identities, and I have used the term "tribe" to designate one of the broader identities involved in local politics. Since pacification, even broader identities have been fashioned, partly out of administrative units set up in colonial times, and partly out of business coalitions centering on relatively new economic enterprises such as coffee plantations (Strathern 1974, 1982). The so-called tribes that form a part of my accounts of Hagen politics are, then, named groups with some potential political cohesion. They vary in size from a few hundred to several thousand people, and are subdivided into clans. Tribes are also usually paired to form wider units of alliance, and alliances at all levels of the social structure are expressed not only by military assistance, but also by intermarriage and ceremonial exchanges of wealth goods, pigs, valuable shells, or money.

Such exchanges are particularly highly elaborated in Hagen, where they have crystalized into a specific institutional form known as the *moka*, in which groups and individuals attempt to repay gifts at a higher level than those received previously. This has introduced a pervasive process of competition for prestige, and those individuals most successful at *moka* emerge as "big-men," or leaders of factions, networks, and at times even segmentary groups. Far from disappearing as a result of social change, *moka* exchanges have tended to effloresce and ramify. They have made their own contribution to the widening of spheres of political action in contemporary society. Part of the rationale for the *moka* is the establishment of peace between warring groups, and after colonial pacification, *moka* exchanges brought about a positive switch away from warfare—but only for a while (Strathern 1971, 1976).

PACIFICATION

Pacification throughout the Highlands region was achieved with the aid of guns, access to which was originally denied to those pacified, for obvious reasons. The overall picture of pacification in Melanesia has been described exhaustively by Rodman and others in a volume devoted to this topic (Rodman and Cooper 1983). In parts of island Melanesia such as the Solomons there was a long history of labor recruitment prior to actual pacification, recruitment that was stimulated by the desire of colonials to establish a plantation economy. Subsequently, indigenous groups in coastal areas voluntarily brought themselves within colonial rule either when they needed military protection or when they wanted to gain a foothold in the cash-cropping economy in some role other than as suppliers of labor.

In the Highlands of Papua New Guinea, these patterns were compressed in time. In the first place, pacification came much later than it did elsewhere in Melanesia, during a time when colonial policies were already under surveillance from the United Nations. Second, in the Highlands, pacification was perceived as the prerequisite for other forms of development, including labor recruitment. As Rodman notes, "Highlanders neither benefited nor suffered from the long period of linkages primarily at the level of exchange between natives and Whites that had characterized nineteenth-century relations elsewhere in Melanesia" (Rodman

1983:9). Instead, after an initial period of improvised and minimal administration prior to World War II, there was an extremely rapid expansion of effort by the Australian administration to instigate almost simultaneously changes on all fronts, political and economic. Roads and airstrips were constructed, plantations were established, and indigenous farmers were encouraged to grow coffee and vegetables, and later to raise cattle for sale. Local government councils were set up from the 1950s onward, and these were used as a forum for further political education with the aim of eventually setting up a parliamentary form of national government. In this way, the indigenous state was gradually formed under the umbrella of an elaborate administration structured like the Australian Public Service.

A flood of mission activity also followed the opening of the frontier. At first, dating from pre-war times, there were Lutheran and Catholic missions; from the 1950s and 1960s on, there was an influx of Protestant fundamentalist and charismatic sects. By the middle to late 1960s, when my fieldwork in the Western and Southern Highlands began, it looked as though social, economic, and political transformations were leading the people inexorably toward an acculturated, Western way of life. The late 1980s, however, have seen severe complications, if not reversals, in this trend. Serious fighting has defined and redefined groups in such a way as to recreate, in part, an earlier tribal structure—a structure uncomfortably at odds with its own national government and strengthened by the adoption of guns into the pattern of fighting itself. This pattern of violence is by no means restricted to Mount Hagen, but is found widely throughout the Highlands, perhaps especially in the Western Highlands and Enga provinces (Balakau 1978; Brown 1982a, 1982b; Gordon 1983; Gordon and Meggitt 1985; Kerpi 1976; Mackellar 1975; Meggitt 1977; Moses 1978; Oram 1973; Orken 1974; Podolefsky 1984; Reay 1987; Standish 1973, 1979; Wormsley n.d.; Zorn 1976).

If we may return briefly at this point to the earliest, "improvised" period of contact, we shall be able to see the seeds both of early success and of later failure in "pacification." Pacification certainly depended from time to time on the use of guns by explorers and government officers. In fact, the Highlands of Papua New Guinea were opened up initially not so much by colonial officers as by the gold miners Michael, James, and Danny Leahy. Although their quest for gold was entirely enigmatic to the local people, their possession of the valuable "gold-lip" pearl shell, an important prestige item in the native systems of exchange and bridewealth, was immediately recognized as advantageous and was the major reason these intruders were accepted at all. In most cases, the foreign explorers were also considered to be either the Sky People of local mythology (an attribution undoubtedly influenced by their possession of airplanes) or spirits of the indigenous dead, which gave them some limited immunity from attack.

At a slightly later stage, when administrative officers took over and began to assert their power by constructing a jail and requiring people to work on roads, guns were used as a direct instrument of control. They were often employed by detachments of indigenous police from coastal areas rather than directly by the government officers, or "Kiaps," themselves. On the whole, it is remarkable that the amount of actual force that had to be exerted by the administration at this time in order to bring fighting between groups to a halt was relatively modest. The lure of wealth goods, which could be used to enhance local exchange practices, was a significant incentive for people to accept the otherwise irritating rules of the incomers. And the power of the gun and the fear of being jailed stood behind this process as a negative sanction of last resort. Again, the contrast with the contemporary situation is stark. Today, more and more force has to be exerted by the police against recalcitrant fighters, and exasperated politicians (either elected members of Papua New Guinea's National Parliament or else members similarly elected to provincial-level assemblies) from time to time have requested that the army be brought in, a move that would be in violation of the country's constitution.

How this contemporary situation has come about is the focus of the discussion that follows.

GUNS IN FIGHTING TODAY

In 1977, I published an article reviewing tribal fighting in the Mount Hagen area, and remarked that guns had not as yet been made a regular part of such combats. I found this interesting because it suggested a conscious or unconscious agreement on the limitation of weapons. If so, it was a phenomenon of the same general order as other "ritualizations" that have enabled a movement from war to peace to take place in Hagen; for example, displays of mourning behavior, which are used to persuade the responsible group to pay compensation for killings. The transformation of anger into a show of grief acts in effect as an appeal to the compassion of the other side, with an undercurrent of suggestion that if such an appeal should fail feelings will switch back to anger and violence will be resumed (Strathern 1977, n.d.).

At the end of 1986, the Kawelka tribe in Hagen became embroiled in serious fighting against their enemies in the Minembi tribe. It soon became clear that the "rule" against using guns—if it ever had been articulated as a rule—was now being broken. I became aware before long that not only did some warriors on both sides have access to guns through various illegal channels, but that many of the younger men were busy manufacturing their own guns.[2] Guns of both kinds were used with deadly effect in the new phase of fighting, and the Kawelka viewed this development as a decisive change, comparable to their earlier switch from pearl shells to cash in *moka* exchanges (Strathern 1979). The Kawelka also saw the change as irreversible: "Now the bow will go down." This recrudescence of warfare brought with it a revival of knowledge of the tactics used in fighting, developed for the bow and arrow or spear, and now adapted to the special new capabilities of the gun.

The problems here are two: first, to explain why warfare has reemerged within the framework of the state; and second, to explain why guns have now penetrated into this "tribal" or "tribalized" context. In approaching both problems, a number of factors must be considered in turn.

FACTORS AND PROCESSES AT WORK

The relationships I am going to explore here are (1) the widening spheres of political competition in general, (2) the growth of business activities and the concomitant rise of *raskal* gangs, and (3) the situation of authority and leadership within clans. Taken together, factors arising out of these spheres help explain why an escalation of killings in violent encounters has taken place. It is necessary also to understand some of the details of the earlier imposition of colonial control in the area and of more recent politico-administrative changes, in particular the role of the local police force.

Indigenous policemen have always carried, and often used, firearms, and numbers of Highlanders have been employed in either the army or the police force, where they gain adequate training in the use and maintenance of guns. On retirement or on dropping out of the force, they carry this knowledge back to their villages, where it may become used in new ways. Highland men also have regularly obtained shotgun licenses for hunting. Both the introduction of firearms and the knowledge of how to use them, then, considerably preceded their extensive introduction into tribal fighting. Those Hageners who did obtain guns, however, genuinely wanted them in order to shoot game, protect their business investments

(e.g., trade-stores), or both. In neither case were they likely to risk confis-
cation of their weapons by using them in local warfare. Factors that have
recently come into play and contributed to a change in this situation are
an increase in the number of illicit firearms entering the hands of tribesmen and the discovery of how to build homemade guns. Both innovations
are due largely to the activities of criminals.

Tribal fighting itself, of course, is not a new problem in the Highlands.
Prior to colonial control, which effectively came about in the 1940s, warfare was endemic (Berndt 1962, 1964; Brookfield and Brown 1963; Donaldson 1982; Feil 1987; Glasse 1968; Hanser 1985; Hayano 1974; Koch
1974; Langness 1972; Lindenbaum 1979; Reay 1959; Sillitoe 1977;
Strathern 1972, 1977; Vayda 1971; Watson 1967, 1983). There followed
the period of pacification from about 1945 to 1965, during which Australian administration officials acted as powerful agents of law and order
whose pronouncements were widely respected by Highlanders. From the
mid-1960s onward, with the dismantling of the portmanteau of powers
these officials carried and the dispersal of power among magistrates, police, and numerous government departments, the respect of the people
for state authority decreased. Fighting began again, in some places over
land and in others over killings that had occurred in earlier times or over
unpaid compensations. Alcohol consumption exacerbated the situation,
leading to brawls and fatal traffic accidents. Special squads of riot police
armed with tear gas were called in to disperse fighters when they could.
Ceremonies of peacemaking were held, then forgotten. The national government wavered between putting control and responsibility back into
the hands of the people (with local-level Village Courts and Trouble Committees) and giving more powers instead to the police. The police had
superiority in weapons but were inferior in mobility; they took to punish-
ing whole settlements by confiscating goods, burning houses, and arresting relatives of fighters. At the same time, the general crime rate in urban
areas continued to grow, giving police more to do.

During the 1970s there were only sporadic uses of guns in tribal fighting, but their use in criminal robberies became common. The police on
more than one occasion called in all firearms and proposed that there
should be *no* gun licenses granted to ordinary citizens. Unfortunately,
the execution of this operation left much to be desired. Confiscated guns
were kept in police stations, but they tended to disappear mysteriously.
Sometimes the stations themselves were broken into and weapons stolen.
The overall result has been an increase of guns in the hands of criminals
and semi-criminals. In some instances, these people now have better guns
than the police themselves, and some of these guns have certainly reached

the rural areas through networks of kinship ties. Ammunition is brought from coastal towns where there is no well-enforced ban on sales. The police are now sometimes afraid to go into an area because the people are rumored to have long-range weapons.

The three general factors that have accompanied or influenced the accelerated entry of guns into Highland warfare in 1986 are now discussed in turn.

POLITICAL COMPETITION

The range of political networks has been continually expanding since initial pacification began in the 1930s and 1940s. Dei Council, to which the Kawelka belong, is a Local Government Council area and an electorate for a single member of Parliament. When electorates were introduced in the 1960s, Dei was combined with the neighboring Mul Council. Violence severed this connection, and the two areas became separate electorates after an attempt on the life of the Dei M.P. (Strathern 1974). But networks do not necessarily end at electorate borders. M.P.s belong to political parties, some of which are in government and some in opposition. Each M.P. therefore has a set of friends and a set of enemies, and each attempts to gain benefits from his party and the political bosses in power. A wide range of people therefore have an interest in the reelection—or defeat—of a sitting M.P.

Within Dei, there is an established "traditional" division between the Tipuka-Kawelka pair of tribes and the Kombukla-Minembi. It was precisely along this major rift that serious fighting broke out at the end of 1986. However, the latest bout of fighting does not stop at the traditional division. Groups have been pulled in from the neighboring Mul Council, and Mul-Dei has been constructed as a new political field of relations (fig. 10.1). This widening of the political field is associated with the use of guns.

The reason for the association between guns and politics is as follows: It can be assumed that differential possession of guns could lead to a breakdown in the relatively egalitarian structure of political relations between groups. A group under pressure therefore seeks to involve other groups, and the process spreads outward as the pressure increases. Engagement of an ally almost automatically brings with it the possibility of another enemy, that ally's own enemy. If my enemy's enemies are my allies, my ally's enemies are also mine. In this way, enmities and alliances can form in a chainlike manner, generating wider political fields. In just

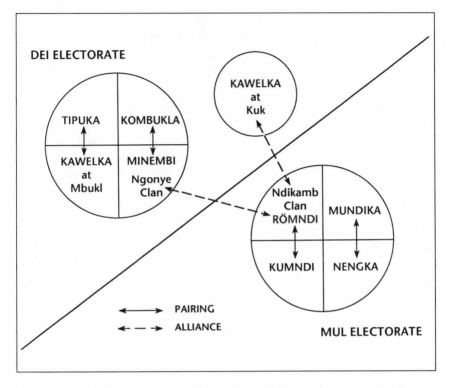

Figure 10.1. The expanded field of warfare and alliances between Mul and Dei councils in 1986.

this way, gun warfare has crossed the divide of relationships between the Mul and Dei councils.

Throughout these chains of escalation in involvement, a crucial role is played by groups that occupy ambiguous or interstitial positions. They serve as transmitters of hostility, linking what in previous contexts had been separate cells or fields of action.[3] The whole process is intensified when guns are introduced, both because of the greater risk of defeat and because certain groups, by reason of their earlier involvement in education or out-migration, have built up larger numbers of guns than others. These factors, then, worked in concert at the end of 1986 to produce a widening sphere of warfare and an effective "tribalization" of Mul-Dei political relations, made even sharper by the fact that individual M.P.s also appear to have had an interest in the outcome of the fighting.

The significant points here, briefly, are two. First, within Dei the major political line of cleavage since precolonial times has been between two pair-clusters of tribes. The long-standing M.P. in Dei came from one of these pairs (Tipuka-Kawelka), but he also wished to retain, or even gain, political support in one half of the opposed pair, since in its other half a candidate was standing against him and the votes from his own pair were not sufficient to ensure victory in the 1987 elections. His own pair, Tipuka-Kawelka, has approximately 5,000 people in all, of whom some 3,500 are in his immediate group, the Tipuka, and about 1,500 are Kawelka. In the opposed pair, some 5,000 at least are in the Minembi tribe alone; perhaps another 3,000 are in the Kombukla tribe, which was putting up a candidate against him. The M.P. clearly needed Minembi votes in order to win, yet the Minembi were the chief enemies of his own chief allies, the Kawelka. He was thus caught between the old political obligation to support his allies and the new political advantage of seeking the votes of his enemies. This predicament explains the form his reaction to the fighting took. He sent from the national capital city, Port Moresby, a number of flags of the nation, apparently as a symbolic protest against the flouting of state power which the fighting represented. The move can be taken as an attempt to distance himself from his tribal identities and align himself with the state government, from which the M.P. draws his salary. Asserting a further alignment with the Minembi, he flew to Hagen in December 1986 and took part in a ceremony in which the Minembi tribesmen burnt their weapons (bows and arrows, not guns). These actions illustrate the M.P.'s effort to make a bridgehead into the opposite tribal faction because of its superior numbers, and his use of state ideological apparatus to achieve this aim. (He was not successful, however, and lost the election to the Kombukla candidate.)

The second point regarding M.P.s and their role relates to the Mul electorate. Here, various groups were drawn into the main arena of conflict in Dei, and it was rumored (whether correctly or not) that the Mul M.P., who is also a businessman, was acting as an arms broker to his faction in the electorate in order to consolidate his own future political support. This example, if true, indicates that guns can become a political commodity and that votes may be obtained with them. Again, if the rumors were correct, the implication is that M.P.s, while officially condemning warfare, may in terms of *Realpolitik* have reasons for fostering and even extending it, especially if the main theater of conflict is thrown outside the ambit of their own support network, as was the case in this instance. Both of the points made here regarding M.P.s also underline the "intertwining" process that goes on today between levels and contexts of political action.

THE ROLES OF BUSINESSMEN AND THE RISE OF RASKAL

"Business," in the Highlands, means inequality, and since the 1960s resentment has focused on businessmen who achieve an unusual degree of success. Such men live in fear of both physical violence and sorcery attacks. If not politicians themselves, businessmen can help buy votes for those who are, and major business groups have created wide-scale divisions and strong competition between groups for valuable land resources. These linkages extend to the national level. In Dei, for example, the most prominent businessman by far is a man who used his Lutheran-mission-sponsored education with superb skill to build a small empire of interests in plantation holdings in the North Wahgi area, which includes the Tipuka-Kawelka section of Dei Council to which he himself belongs. He is also a director of the government-sponsored Kumul Kopi coffee-buying company. Tie-ups of this kind, always strengthened by the use of money and other forms of politico-economic advantage or protection, are accurately diagnosed and assessed by those on the opposite side of the political fence. They can be used to discourage competitors; conversely, they can provoke more vigorous competition. Such a context only increases tension between groups whose men identify with different business leaders, and this contributes in turn to a greater likelihood of armed conflict.

There is in the Highlands another factor that works in the same direction. While businessmen grow rich, other Highlanders conspire to remove their riches from them through violence. These are the *raskal*, "rascals" or gang members who form part of a rapidly growing criminal class. *Raskal* are recruited largely from the ranks of high school-educated young men. Their style is influenced by cowboy and gangster films, and by patterns of freewheeling and pimpery which they pick up in the coastal cities of Lae and Port Moresby. Their aim is to get cars, money, food, girls, and—increasingly—guns to further their acquisition of goods by theft. Their numbers grew markedly in the 1980s. At first, their operations were separate from those of tribal fighters, and one could distinguish between the *raskal* problem and the problem of tribal fights. This separation no longer holds. In the bouts of fighting in 1986, for example, there were persistent rumors that *raskal* gangs had been hired to conduct raids, assassinations, acts of arson, and damaging thefts. While the gangs have arisen as a negative and dialectical response to the growth of business and the penetration of money into the economy, they have now, in a sense, been at least partially reintegrated into the neotraditional political system. Guns are the primary issue: *raskal* members have guns, and they know how to repair and use them. They also know how to steal weapons or bribe police to obtain them.

The *raskal* situation is by no means peculiar to Mount Hagen. It is widespread in the Sepik Province of Papua New Guinea and all the areas near the main Highlands Highway from Lae to Wabag, including the mid-Wahgi area—especially the town of Minj—just east of Hagen itself. Young *raskal* men now challenge the older and more established men for leadership positions in Minj (Reay 1987), and no one can afford to ignore the threat of *raskal* activity. How are we to situate the latest tribal fighting in relation to this matter? Guns, supplied by both *raskal* and businessmen, have entered the fights, and I have noted an overall rise in tensions that is fueled both economically and politically. These observations prompt us to consider more directly leadership within the clan, as Reay (1987) has for Minj.

INTERNAL PATTERNS OF LEADERSHIP

A dispute that occurred at the end of 1985 offers a good index of patterns of change among the Kawelka. Ongka is a leader of preeminent standing, who has been at the forefront of Kawelka public affairs for some forty years. Now well into his sixties, Ongka still vigorously sets the pace when a matter to do with ceremonial exchange is at issue. The hearing of disputes and other things to do with "government," however, he leaves to his younger successor of the same subclan as himself, Yap-Roklpa. Yap is a Local Government Councillor and a member of the Dei Council Trouble Committee, which tries to arrange compensation payments following intergroup fights; he is also active in business, being associated with the Dei Development Company and having planted some five acres of his own with cardamom trees. But when it comes to *moka*, Ongka is still a significant force. It was a shock to the whole group, then, when he was attacked violently by young men of Kawelka itself at a ceremonial ground on October 18, 1985. These young men, who were in league with *raskal* of a neighboring group, had stolen a car from the nearby government agricultural research station at Kuk. To their surprise, the plantation people found where the car had been concealed, many miles away to the north in the other territory of the Kawelka. The thieves suspected that Ongka's son Namba had tipped off the station personnel, and they chose the public occasion of a *moka* to humiliate and injure both father and son. Such a pattern of behavior was well outside the norms of both custom and the introduced law. It stems instead from the *raskal* context, and as such, it provoked universal condemnation. The attackers were forced to pay compensation to Ongka and his group, which they did reluctantly. Tribal norms and Ongka's status were revalidated, but in a sense they were also permanently shaken by these events. A division is growing between *raskal* and the rest of tribal society.

In December of 1986 solidarity was achieved again as a result of warfare against the Minembi, which threatened all the Kawelka. The older leaders, including Ongka, were once more at the heart of political activities. Ongka harangued his men, trying to make them laugh, and encouraging visiting allies (who included another younger man who had his eyes set on candidacy in the 1987 elections). But at the same time, he tried to make people aware of how serious their situation was. Next day, Yap returned to report that the Trouble Committee's attempts at mediation had failed and that five Kawelka men had been ambushed in their house early one morning and killed—with spears, arrows, and bullets. The contrast with the previous day's lengthy speeches was remarkable. One leader simply said, "Remember that the police operate a road block after 2 A.M." Another said, and his order was taken up by many, "Eat sweet potato." By this was meant, "Eat now and go quickly to the battle site, remember that food supplies down there are uncertain." Men dispersed rapidly to the fight, marching overnight by a roundabout route; many also did not go, including some of the clan which had just lost men.

Clearly, the older leaders were very much in command, though by and large it was the younger men who actually went. Ongka was on tenterhooks: he wanted to be there to encourage his men, but he was too old and too important to be risked. Those middle-aged men who did go were greatly esteemed, and it was clear that they went in a representative capacity. But Ongka was held back by the more significant task of holding together the group at Kuk. *Raskal* men, however, neither went nor had any honorable part to play in the discussions.

In these new battles, younger men come to the fore, not as *raskal*, but as "good citizens" ready to fight and die for their tribe. The advent of guns provided a further incentive for the prominent involvement of young men. They can make guns for a purpose which, while still illegal from the viewpoint of the law, gains the approval of their elders. And in the actual fighting younger men take over the strategy of killing, because they can usually handle guns better than the older men. In 1986 shields were apparently used as defense against guns, and daytime fighting was confined to particular agreed-upon places; but nighttime-to-dawn ambushes were also a feature. In one move, the young men crept at night through a precipitous forest territory of the Minembi and took up their post at the back of a mountain settlement. They instructed the older men to follow a short time later with shields, and to make their way frontally to the settlement from the opposite direction. The Minembi awoke to see the men with shields near them; they prepared to defend themselves, and then were shot by guns from behind. One of those killed was a son of an important big-man who in the past had been an exchange partner of one of the Kawelka's greatest leaders in *moka*, Ndamba. The power of pigs had been replaced by the power of bullets.

The foregoing episode illustrates how patterns of activity and leadership shifted with the introduction of guns into fighting. Older men retained a role as advisers and organizers, but younger men took over the actual process of fighting. In the course of these events, positive alliances created through *moka* exchanges by the older leaders in the 1960s broke down and were replaced by hostility.

DISCUSSION

It is in the light of these events that we must interpret the statement "Let the bow go down." Until 1986, warfare had been seen as an "old-time" activity. With guns it has become "new time," and younger men take prominence in it. In this respect, the switch from bows to guns does indeed resemble the earlier switch from shells to money; and money in fact is dominant here too, because it takes money to buy the most powerful guns. But whereas money cannot successfully be counterfeited, guns can be made at home. Monopolization is therefore to some extent counterbalanced by popular manufacture. Still, the best guns, which cost the most, give a considerable advantage, to such an extent that the police themselves have recognized that some of the weapons used are superior to their own and have appealed to the government to give them more firepower. The state's only alternative is to call in the army, a putative clandestine source of some of these weapons, to confiscate the tribesmen's guns.

What we see at work here is a kind of re-creation of the old through the new. Instead of a "modernized traditional" society, we have in a sense a "traditionalized modern" one, in which the actual impetus for change comes from objective alterations in political and economic structure, but the response pattern to these changes turns the society around again. In the 1970s the switch to money in *moka* turned Highland society to a re-creation of exchange. Now, the switch to guns has turned it to violence.

These two patterns, exchange and violence, thus continue their dialectical interplay. Despite their undeniable influence on it, politico-economic changes have not abolished this dialectic.

In more obvious political terms, and without appealing to any metaphysical level of argument, we can see good reasons why, once the change to guns occurred, it occurred swiftly. The simple fact is that guns give an advantage to those who have them. Others will therefore strenuously attempt to "get equal" again—and speedily, because of the cultural desire to avenge the killing of kin. The Kawelka were placed somewhat at a disadvantage by their relative lack of access to powerful guns in the 1986 fighting, and this was one reason why they accepted help from allies in Mul, who were rumored to possess numbers of the .404 rifles used by the police. The search for weapons itself stretched political networks. As Vayda has noted for Maori warfare, the relevant factor became numbers of guns, not numbers of warriors (Vayda 1976:90); and guns had to be solicited or hired from diverse sources. The diversity of losses which resulted from the expanded scale of fighting also placed a heavy burden on the Kawelka for the future, and in that sense actually placed a limit on their willingness to pursue the war itself. Finally, the *raskal's* technical innovation of producing homemade guns was rapidly adopted in order to maintain the necessary balance of power between the Kawelka and their enemies. It can safely be assumed that the Minembi manufactured homemade guns as well, but they *also* had the best guns, and at the end of 1986 it looked as though they might upset the "equal" pattern of fighting and establish dominance. Their tactic of burning their traditional weapons and indicating a desire for peace was probably based on the fact that at that moment they had killed more of their enemies than they had themselves lost. Accepting police intervention meant that they could present an image of being amenable to law, while maintaining an advantage in terms of killings. The Minembi certainly did not yield their guns to the state, and one could, therefore, only assume that at least another round remained to be fought later, whenever a further pretext for hostilities should present itself. This assumption proved correct, since by mid-1988 the area was again embroiled in warfare, and in mid-1989 the pattern was exacerbated further by new killings. Compensation payments for these were arranged, but created at best an uneasy truce punctuated by rumors of further impending violence.

This case study of contemporary group fighting in the New Guinea Highlands can be conceptualized in terms of "warfare," as I have done here; that is, in terms of the levels of groups mobilized, widening and

changing political spheres, and technological changes stemming from activities of a new marginal class in the society. But if one examines the
inner wellspring of motivation involved in the fighting, it is hard to avoid
the conclusion that what we are seeing is also a kind of "expanded feuding" based on the ethic, or perhaps the emotion, of blood revenge. What
is the purpose of this fighting? We do not have to furnish it with a rational
purpose, of course, but still, some purpose is required—a purpose that
must be considered within a context of change. This leads us back to
politics and economics.

To repay violence with violence is not a problematic response for Hageners. Violence is usually followed by atonement and appeasement, so
there is even a paradoxical kind of safety in it, a belief that it will not get
completely out of hand, that a way of switching out of it can always be
found. But while violence proceeds, its duration is unpredictable, and the
balance of killings has always been an important factor. The introduction
of guns certainly had an influence on the periodicity of fighting, one that
no one could be clear about. An inequality in firepower could result either in domination or in desperate retaliation. Having just one powerful
gun in hand could encourage a group to continue fighting in the hope of
evening the score. An imbalance could be registered quickly, followed by
a tactical declaration of peace when the score was in one's favor. But this
would scarcely be acceptable to the other side. The absolute escalation in
numbers of deaths would also slow the possibilities of making compensation payments, and to that extent effective peacemaking would be jeopardized. Suppressive action by the police could occur randomly with
respect to the state of play between participants, and as a result resurgence
would always be possible. Predictably, large-scale fighting subsided in
1987 into a more definite feuding pattern, in which attempts were made
individually to kill enemies, exploiting the fact that people leave their
villages, traveling in vehicles to work or to school or university in town.
Today, the network of revenge potentially covers the whole country. Thus,
feuding reduces the intensity of fighting but increases its extent (cf. Keiser
1986).

The revenge mentality in Hagen dates from precolonial times and has
remained strong, however overlaid it was in the 1960s by proclamations
of the brave new colonial fiction of law and order. But it is true that, for
a time, colonial rule began to alter the construction of feelings, largely
because it gave relatively free rein to the practice of *moka* exchange. The
highly creative way in which big-men expanded these exchanges in the
1960s to include their former major enemies must now be looked on

as an extraordinarily favorable development. But why the reversal and deconstruction of this fabric of exchanges, built so exuberantly twenty years ago?

The intensity of shock felt by Hageners over the new killings, and their reaction of desire for revenge, is probably heightened by the fact that there *was* a period of intermission in intertribal fighting. When fighting with guns began in 1986, the initial response was disbelief, followed by a feeling of profound discomfort as all notions of security were stripped away, and finally by a hardening of decision about what must be done. As young men were being killed by guns, so other young men came to the fore to kill in revenge by the same weapons.

Keiser, following Averill's book on anger as a cultural emotion (Averill 1982), distinguishes between action and passion as modes of emotional conduct. Where a response is defined as central to being, it will be experienced as a passion, an emotion that cannot be controlled. This distinction can be paralleled by linguistic usages in Melpa, the language spoken by Hageners. *Popokl*, anger which can include revenge anger, is said to be experienced in the *noman* ("mind" or "will"); but different verbal constructions are employed in conjunction with the idea. Where a passion in Averill's sense is involved, the verb *iti*, "to make," is used impersonally; thus *popokl itim*, "it made popokl." Where there is more conscious control and the issue is not so serious, a personal construction, with the verb *mondui*, "to make to be," is found; thus *popokl mondonom*, "she or he is making *popokl*." In revenge killing, the first verb form—*iti*—is regularly employed. The only sense in which "self-interest" is involved is that what is at stake is the very definition of the "self."

In practical terms, of course, there is a stage of decision making for action too. Some Kawelka went to fight, and others stayed out of it. The main point, however, is that in feuding societies blood revenge constitutes itself as a specific emotion, albeit one which through its linkage with the ideas of the self may be historically variable. Young men in Hagen *are* redefining themselves through use of the gun. "Rascals" certainly do so. Coming in from the margins of society, they have brought technical innovations that are redefining larger spheres of social relationships. The creation, or self-invention, of this class is having some rather unexpected results within Highland society. Explanations of the new pattern of violence have to be sought, then, in certain external changes *cycled through* indigenous cultural concepts.

I have stressed the roles of two new classes, businessmen and criminals, in allegedly supplying guns to fighters and fostering violence. The

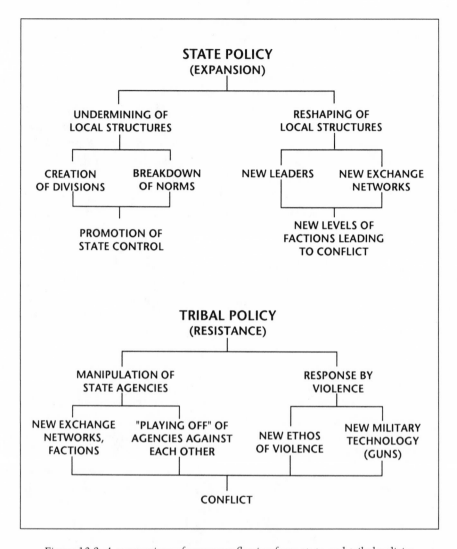

Figure 10.2. A comparison of processes flowing from state and tribal policies in Highland Papua New Guinea.

impetus to killing thus comes from two groups that are actually opposed in the new social formation: criminals, who predate on those who are successful, and the successful businessmen and politicians who spend much of their time denouncing these criminals as well as the tribesmen who are gripped by the actual fighting.

COMPARATIVE IMPLICATIONS

In this case study, I have been concerned with the theme of tribe-state relations in an involute way. Other studies in this volume deal with the frontier between states and tribes and the mutual political influences flowing across this frontier in the context of longer-term changes, or with earlier stages of contact between states and the tribes within the purview of their colonial interests. I have been looking at a later historical stage, however, that of encapsulation of indigenous groups within a new state apparatus. In this stage the "frontier" becomes harder to discern and is greatly permeated, but as intergroup fighting clearly shows, it still exists. Political and economic changes foster turbulence as much as they are predicated on its exclusion, and the overall outcome is indeed neatly expressed by the concept of tribalization that I have taken from Neil Whitehead's chapter in this volume. The technological switch-over to guns has further triggered a set of responses that have greatly widened the fields of these "tribalized" forms of political interaction. Even the national political system is in interaction with this sphere, since politicians manipulate political fields in order to secure votes for their reelection to Parliament. In terms of formal state policy, these tribalized patterns of activity clearly represent a threat to state rule; yet they also are in part a result of processes set in motion, intentionally or otherwise, by earlier state agencies. At the risk of implying too great an intentionality on either side, one can speak of "state policy" versus "tribal policy"; and for Mount Hagen one can delineate the possible outcomes as shown in figure 10.2. It is evident that the general tendency of these outcomes is not simply in the direction of modernization and the elimination of the traditional structures. Rather, as I have argued, development contains within itself its own nemesis of conflict, generated from the interplay of material and ideological factors.

UPDATE: APRIL 1991

In February 1991 the Papua New Guinea government sponsored a national crime seminar in Port Moresby, attended by politicians, public servants, church workers, academics, and business people. Out of this seminar there emerged a resolve to combat the problems of "law and order" with fresh energy. One result has been the mounting of special police operations in the Highlands and in the coastal cities of Lae and Port Moresby. For the first time the army has also been permitted to assist the police, and an 8 P.M. to 5 A.M. curfew has been instituted, with strict surveillance of the main highways and areas surrounding the towns. The government has consolidated police powers, and consequently the police can enter and search houses and confiscate property believed to be stolen. Their operations have on the whole been greeted with approval by ordinary Highlanders, and the fear of police reprisals has lowered both the crime rate and the incidence of tribal fighting, making it possible for people to travel about again in reasonable safety.

Concomitantly, however, fears of sorcery killings have risen, as they tend always to do in periods of truce. Kawelka men consider that seven packages of sorcery substance or "poison" have been brought into their territory recently by in-married women whose natal groups are of the enemy Minembi tribe. One man is said to have died already, and the woman responsible is declared to have confessed to the act. She had originally planned to kill her own husband, but instead administered the substance to his sister's husband. She herself is from the Minembi Engambo clan, long-standing enemies of her husband's clan, the Kawelka Kundumbo. As the man who actually died is the son of a big-man of Membo clan in Kawelka, the incident has set up an ambiguous feeling between the Kundumbo and Membo clansmen and has delayed the preparations being made by all the Kawelka clans to give compensation to a wide range of allies who assisted them in the 1986–89 fighting. This collective payment was originally scheduled for April 1991, but now May or June is being cited as the likely month. It is uncertain whether it will be preceded by any internal gifts associated with the recent death. Meanwhile, both raskal and tribal fighters are staying quiet, though the former are reported to be migrating to other parts of the country not affected by the curfew, and the latter are said to be simply waiting until the period of the police special operation expires.

In analytical terms, what we see then is a recognizable phase, in which the dampening down of physical conflict is accompanied by a heightened fear of sorcery attacks. Paranoia is greatest among the young men who distinguished themselves in the gun fighting earlier, and is made worse by the widespread understanding that the lethal substances involved in sorcery are no longer of a traditional kind but are simply "white man's poisons," obtained in stores. The police are doing their best to round up criminals, some of whom are actually walking back into jail after having broken out, in order to protect their relatives from police reprisals. There's even an ex-criminals' task force: reformed criminals who work to persuade existing criminals to hand over their guns to police and begin a normal life again. The task force is assisted by an adviser from the Catholic church in Hagen, and claims to have over 3,000 members in the province.

The overall scene has therefore shifted, at least temporarily, from overt conflict to a phase of settlement negotiations and government attempts to bring the situation under control. Underlying enmities, however, remain, and will be able to reassert themselves at a later stage unless a more lasting version of peace is brought about between the enemy groups involved and not just between allies, as is currently planned by the Kawelka. The state has regained coercive control for the time being, but a genuine peace has yet to be engineered between the Kawelka and the Minembi, as the current epidemic of sorcery fears clearly indicates.

Notes

1. Versions of this chapter have been given at seminars in the Department of Anthropology, University of Pittsburgh, and at the American Anthropological Association's annual meeting in Phoenix in November 1988, as well as at the School of American Research advanced seminar itself. I thank all those who have provided me with helpful comments and suggestions, particularly Neil Whitehead and Brian Ferguson. My especial thanks to Ross Hassig for struggling with my paper as its commentator in Santa Fe, and to Gabriele Stürzenhofecker for her perspectives on the implications of the introduction of firearms for the ethos of fighting in Mount Hagen. All errors remain mine.

2. These guns are similar to the "zipguns" used in New York by street criminals. Barrels are made from any kind of metal pipe, to which a carved wooden stock is fitted and a triggering mechanism set up by means of a spring into which a nail or pin is set. The spring is often taken from an old umbrella. Each man makes a gun for himself, using whatever materials come to hand. In 1986 there were no specialists. By 1989 the use of these zipguns had declined in favor of a greater supply of more powerful weapons obtained through networks of political patronage, a process discussed in the paper and already underway by 1986.

3. The Kundumbo clan of Kawelka, for example, have long been interstitial between Kawelka and Minembi. Between the 1950s and the 1960s, the Kundumbo built up friendly exchange ties with their former enemies among the Minembi, especially with two clans, Papeke and Engambo. This achievement in turn had much to do with the efforts of a single Kundumbo big-man, Ndamba, and reciprocally individual big-men among the Minembi. However, living with these Minembi there are Ngonye men. The Ngonye in turn have links with the Kumndi of Mul Council. They are enemies of Kundumbo. When the Kundumbo began fighting the Ngonye in 1984 this meant a much larger disturbance than the involvement of these two clans alone. There was a backwards-linking effect to pull

in allies from the Tipuka-Kawelka complex; and since the fighting was primarily against the Ngonye, their Kumndi friends were implicated. Enemies of the Kumndi include some Nengka and some Römndi tribesmen, and with the Römndi tribesmen, the circle closes, because these are also friendly with many of the Kawelka who live at Kuk, far from the main body of the Kundumbo. At this point differential access to guns becomes relevant again, since these Römndi are said to possess many guns and to have scores of their own to pay off in relation to the Minembi clans who live nearby.

Provisional Diagrams from the Advanced Seminar

R. BRIAN FERGUSON AND NEIL L. WHITEHEAD

The intent of the School of American Research advanced seminar that generated this volume was to open up a new field for investigation. On the last day of the seminar, the participants attempted to synthesize their main ideas. From a long list of variables and relationships suggested during the week, together we developed a few schematic drawings. We present them here not as the considered position of any individual member of the seminar, but as starting points toward a more rigorous conceptualization of the relationships between expanding states and indigenous warfare.

Our first diagram (below) is of the "frontier zone," which differs from Ferguson and Whitehead's concept of a "tribal zone" in being restricted to the area of direct interaction between state and tribe. The tribal zone, by contrast, extends indefinitely outward through indirect contact. The diagram maps the major elements that shape the strategic and tactical decisions of both state agents and indigenous people. It applies to a given situation (Time 1), and by the interaction of factors gives rise to a subsequent situation (Time 2). The diagram highlights the larger structuring forces that shape any historical pattern and keep it in constant transformation; at the same time, it calls attention to the active participation of both state agents and indigenous people in making local history.

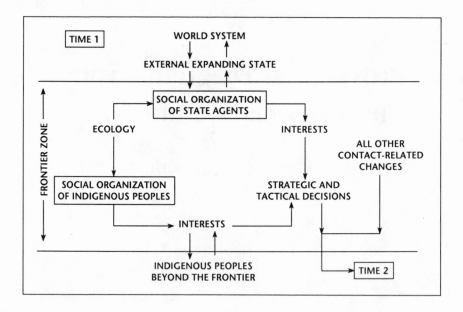

The second diagram concerns the interaction of new inducements to indigenous warfare with the broader process of acculturation associated with state contact. The "new war complexes" that result are often taken, in ahistorical studies of tribal warfare, to represent the pristine indigenous warfare pattern. The "space for agency" block on the diagram acknowledges that even individual decisions at crucial junctures in this interaction can have a significant effect on later developments.

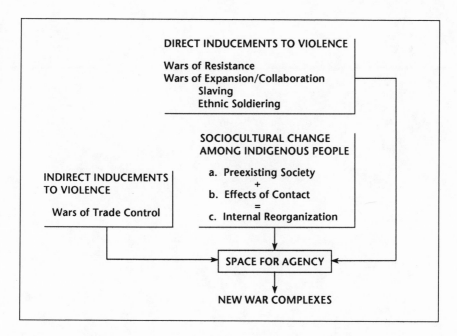

Our final diagram outlines the major options available to indigenous peoples facing state expansionism; the political situations attendant on those choices; and the possibilities of new forms of violence after loss of sovereignty to the state. Developments at any point along these trajectories can be accompanied by the processes of ethnogenesis or tribalization.

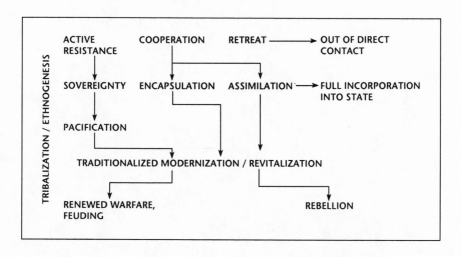

References

Abler, Thomas
   1970   Longhouse and palisade: Northeastern Iroquoian villages of the seventeenth century. *Ontario History* 62:17–40.
   1975   Presents, merchants, and the Indian Department: Economic aspects of the American revolutionary frontier, Canadian Ethnology Society Proceedings. *National Museum of Man Canadian Ethnology Service Mercury Series* 28(2):608–15.
   1979   Kayahsota?. *Dictionary of Canadian Biography* 4:408–10.
   1988   *The Iroquois*. Canada's Visual History 78. Ottawa: Canadian Museum of Civilization, National Film Board of Canada.
   1989a   European technology and the art of war in Iroquoia. In *Cultures in Conflict: Current Archaeological Perspectives*, D. C. Tkaczuk and B. C. Vivian, eds., pp. 273–82. Calgary: University of Calgary Archaeological Association.
   1989b   (Ed.) *Chainbreaker: The Revolutionary War Memoirs of Governor Blacksnake*. Lincoln: University of Nebraska Press.
Abler, Thomas, and Michael Logan
   1988   The florescence and demise of Iroquoian cannibalism: Human sacrifice and Malinowski's hypothesis. *Man in the Northeast* 35:1–26.
Abraham, Meera
   1988   *Two Medieval Merchant Guilds of South India*. New Delhi: Manohar.
Acuña, René, ed.
   1982–   *Relaciones Geográficas del Siglo XVI*. 9 vols. Mexico City: Universidad Nacional
   1987   Autónoma de México.
Adas, Michael
   1987   *Prophets of Rebellion: Millenarian Protest Movements against the European Colonial Order*. Cambridge: Cambridge University Press.
   1989   *Machines as the Measure of Men: Science, Technology, and Ideologies of Western Dominance*. Ithaca: Cornell University Press.
Adams, R. N.
   1975   *Energy and Structure: A Theory of Social Power*. Austin: University of Texas Press.
Akinjogbin, I. A.
   1967   *Dahomey and Its Neighbours 1708–1818*. Cambridge: Cambridge University Press.
Albert, Bruce
   1988   La fumée du métal: Histoire et représentations du contact chez les Yanomami (Brésil). *L'Homme* 28(2–3):87–119.
   1989   On Yanomami "violence": Inclusive fitness or ethnographer's representation? *Current Anthropology* 30:637–40.

Algaze, Guillermo
1989   The Uruk expansion: Cross-cultural exchange in early Mesopotamian civilization. *Current Anthropology* 30:571–608.
d'Almeida-Topor, Hélène
1984   *Les Amazones: Une Armée de Femmes dans l'Afrique Précoloniale.* Paris: Editions Rochevignes.
Alvarez Sáenz, Félix
1989   El Milenarismo Franciscano: Una Aproximación. Manuscript. Lima.
Anderson, P.
1974   *Passages from Antiquity to Feudalism.* London: New Left Books.
Apte, V. S.
1978   *The Practical Sanskrit-English Dictionary.* Kyoto: Rinsen.
Aquila, Richard
1983   *The Iroquois Restoration: Iroquois Diplomacy on the Colonial Frontier, 1701–1754.* Detroit: Wayne State University Press.
Archivo General de la Nación. Ramo de Reales Cedulas Duplicadas. Mexico City.
Argyle, W. J.
1966   *The Fon of Dahomey: A History and Ethnography of the Old Kingdom.* Oxford: Clarendon Press.
Arhem, Kaj
1981   *Makuna Social Organization. A Study in Descent, Alliance, and the Formation of Corporate Groups in the North-Western Amazon.* Stockholm: Uppsala University.
Arthaśāstra
1951   R. Shamasastry, ed. Mysore: Raghuvir.
Asad, Talal
1973   *Anthropology and the Colonial Encounter.* Atlantic Highlands, New Jersey: Humanities Press.
Averill, J. R.
1982   *Anger and Aggression: An Essay on Emotion.* New York: Springer Verlag.
Axtell, James
1975   The white Indians of colonial America. *William and Mary Quarterly* (3rd ser.) 32:55–88.
Bachman, Van Cleaf
1969   *Peltries or Plantations: The Economic Policies of the Dutch West India Company in New Netherland 1623–1639.* Baltimore: Johns Hopkins University Press.
Bailey, L. R.
1973   *Indian Slave Trade in the Southwest.* Los Angeles: Westernlore Press.
Balakau, M.
1978   A perspective on Enga violence. *Yagl-Ambu* 5(2):189–98.
Balée, William
1988   The Ka'apor Indian wars of lower Amazonia, ca. 1825–1928. In *Dialectics and Gender: Anthropological Approaches*, R. Randolph, D. Schneider, and M. Diaz, eds., pp. 155–69. Boulder, Colorado: Westview Press.
Bancroft, E.
1769   *An Essay on the Natural History of Guiana.* London.
Baradez, J.
1949   *Vue Aérienne de l'Organisation Romaine dans le Sud-Algérienne. Fossatum Africae.* Paris: Arts et Metiers Graphiques.
Barandiaran, Daniel de, and Aushi Walalam
1983   *Hijos de la Luna: Monografía Antropológica sobre los Indios Sanemá-Yanoama.* Caracas: Editorial Arte.
Barbot, Jean
1732   *A Description of the Coasts of North and South Guinea.* London.

Barclay, Frederica
1989   *La Colonia del Perené: Capital Inglés y Economía Cafetalera en la Configuración de la Región de Chanchamayo*. Iquitos, Peru: Centro de Estudios Teológicos de la Amazonía.

Barfield, Thomas
1989   *The Perilous Frontier*. Oxford: Blackwell.

Barker, G. W. W., and G. D. B. Jones
1982   The UNESCO Libyan Valleys Survey 1979–1981: Palaeoeconomy and environmental archaeology in the pre-desert. *Libyan Studies* 13:1–34.
1984   The UNESCO Libyan Valleys Survey VI: Investigations of a Romano-Libyan farm, part 1. *Libyan Studies* 15:1–45.

Barker, James
1953   Memoria sobre la cultura de los Guaika. *Boletín Indigenista Venezolano* 1: 433–89.
1959   Las incursiones entre los Guaika. *Boletín Indigenista Venezolano* 7:151–67.

Barrett, J. C., A. P. Fitzpatrick, and L. Macinnes, eds.
1989   *Barbarians and Romans in North-West Europe*. Oxford: British Archaeological Reports International Series 471.

Bartel, B.
1980   Colonialism and cultural responses: Problems related to Roman provincial analysis. *World Archaeology* 12(1):11–26.

Barth, Frederick, ed.
1969   *Ethnic Groups and Boundaries: The Social Organization of Cultural Differences*. London: Allen and Unwin.

Bates, O.
1914   *The Eastern Libyans*. London: Cass. 1970.

Belich, James
1989   *The Victorian Interpretation of Racial Conflict: The Maori, the British, and the New Zealand Wars*. Montreal: McGill-Queens University Press.

Benabou, M.
1976   *La Résistance Africaine à la Romanisation*. Paris: Maspero.

Benavides, Margarita
1990   Levantamiento de los Asháninka del río Pichis: ¿Organización nativa contra guerrilla del MRTA? *Página Libre*, 11 July 1990:11–33. Lima.

Benedict, Francis, and Morris Steggerda
1937   *The Food of the Present-Day Maya Indians of the Yucatan*. Carnegie Institution of Washington Publication 456. Washington, D.C.: Carnegie Institution.

Benezet, Anthony
1789   *Some Historical Account of Guinea*, 2nd ed. London: Frank Cass. 1968.

Bennett Ross, Jane
1971   Aggression as adaptation: The Yanomamo case. Manuscript.
1980   Ecology and the problem of tribe: A critique of the Hobbesian model of pre-industrial warfare. In *Beyond the Myths of Culture: Essays in Cultural Materialism*, E. Ross, ed., pp. 33–60. New York: Academic Press.
1984   Effects of contact on revenge hostilities among the Achuarä Jívaro. In *Warfare, Culture, and Environment*, R. B. Ferguson, ed., pp. 83–109. Orlando: Academic Press.

Bergé, J. A. M. A. R.
1928   Etude sur le pays Mahi. *Bulletin du Comité d'Etudes Historiques et Scientifiques de l'A.O.F.* 11:708–55.

Berkhofer, Robert
1978   *The White Man's Indian: Images of the Indian from Columbus to the Present*. New York: Alfred Knopf.

Berndt, R. M.
  1962   Excess and Restraint: Social Control among a New Guinea Mountain People. Chi-
         cago: Chicago University Press.
  1964   Warfare in the New Guinea Highlands. American Anthropologist 66(4)pt. 2:
         183–203.
Bibeau, Pierre
  1980   Les palissades des sites Iroquois. Recherches Amerindiennes au Quebec 10:
         189–97.
Bierhorst, John
  1988   The Mythology of South America. New York: William Morrow and Company.
Biggar, H. P., ed.
  1922– The Works of Samuel de Champlain. 6 vols. Toronto: Champlain Society.
  1936
Biocca, Ettore
  1971   Yanoáma: The Narrative of a White Girl Kidnapped by Amazonian Indians. New
         York: E. P. Dutton.
Biolsi, Thomas
  1984   Ecological and cultural factors in Plains Indians warfare. In Warfare, Culture,
         and Environment, R. B. Ferguson, ed., pp. 141–68. Orlando: Academic Press.
Birley, A. R.
  1988   The African Emperor: Septimius Severus. London: Batsford.
Black-Michaud, Jacob
  1975   Cohesive Force: Feud in the Mediterranean and the Middle East. New York: St.
         Martin's Press.
Blau, Harold, Jack Campisi, and Elisabeth Tooker
  1978   Onondaga. In Handbook of North American Indians. Vol. 15, Northeast, B. G.
         Trigger, ed., pp. 491–99. Washington, D.C.: Smithsonian Institution Press.
Blick, Jeffrey
  1988   Genocidal warfare in tribal societies as a result of European-induced culture
         conflict. Man 23:654–70.
Bloch, Maurice
  1986   From Blessing to Violence: History and Ideology in the Circumcision Ritual of the
         Merina of Madagascar. Cambridge Studies in Social Anthropology 61. Cam-
         bridge: Cambridge University Press.
Bodley, John
  1971   Campa socio-economic adaptation. Ph.D. dissertation, University of Oregon.
         Ann Arbor: University Microfilms.
  1972   A transformative movement among the Campa of eastern Peru. Anthropos
         67:220–28.
  1982   Victims of Progress, 2nd ed. Palo Alto: Mayfield Publishing.
Boehm, Christopher
  1984   Blood Revenge: The Anthropology of Feuding in Montenegro and Other Tribal So-
         cieties. Lawrence: University Press of Kansas.
Bohannan, P., and F. Plog, eds.
  1967   Beyond the Frontier: Social Process and Culture Change. New York: Natural His-
         tory Press.
Boletín
  1940   Archivo General de la Nación, Boletín. Mexico City: Archivo General de la
         Nación.
Bond, Stanley, Jr.
  1985   The relationship between soils and settlement patterns in the Mohawk Valley.
         In The Mohawk Valley Project: 1982 Field Season Report, D. R. Snow, ed.,
         pp. 17–40. Albany: Institute for Northeast Anthropology.

Borah, Woodrow, and Sherburne Cook
    1963   The aboriginal population of central Mexico on the eve of the Spanish conquest. *Ibero-Americana* 45.

Bosman, William
    1705   *A New and Accurate Description of the Coast of Guinea*. London: Frank Cass. 1967.

Bourdieu, Pierre
    1977   *Outline of a Theory of Practice*. Cambridge Studies in Social Anthropology 16. Cambridge: Cambridge University Press.

Bovill, E. W.
    1970   *The Golden Trade of the Moors*. Oxford: Oxford University Press.

Bradley, James
    1987   *Evolution of the Onondaga Iroquois: Accommodating Change, 1550–1655*. Syracuse: Syracuse University Press.

Brasser, T. J.
    1978a   Mahican. In *Handbook of North American Indians*. Vol. 15, *Northeast*, B. G. Trigger, ed., pp. 198–212. Washington, D.C.: Smithsonian Institution Press.
    1978b   Early Indian-European contacts. In *Handbook of North American Indians*. Vol. 15, *Northeast*, B. G. Trigger, ed., pp. 78–88. Washington, D.C.: Smithsonian Institution Press.

Braudel, Fernand
    1973   *The Mediterranean and the Mediterranean World in the Age of Philip II*, vol. 1, S. Reynolds, trans. London: Fontana.
    1977   *Afterthoughts on Material Civilization and Capitalism*, P. M. Ranum, trans. Baltimore: Johns Hopkins University Press.

Braund, D. C.
    1984   *Rome and the Friendly King. The Character of Client Kingship*. Beckenham: Croom Helm.

Bray, Warwick
    1968   *Everyday Life of the Aztecs*. New York: G. P. Putnam's Sons.

Breton, R.
    1665–   *Dictionnaire Caraïbe-Francois/Francois-Caraïbe*. 2 vols. Auxerre.
    1666

Brogan, O.
    1975   Inscriptions in the Libyan alphabet from Tripolitania and some notes on the tribes of the region. In *Hamito-Semitica*, J. Bynon and T. Bynon, eds., pp. 267–89. The Hague: Mouton.

Brogan, O., and D. J. Smith
    1985   *Ghirza: A Romano-Libyan Settlement in Tripolitania*. Tripoli: Libyan Antiquities Series 1.

Bronson, Bennet
    1988   The role of barbarians in the fall of states. In *The Collapse of Ancient States and Civilizations*, N. Yoffee and G. Cowgill, eds., pp. 196–218. Tucson: University of Arizona Press.

Brookfield, H., and P. Brown
    1963   *Struggle for Land: Agriculture and Group Territories among the Chimbu*. Melbourne: Oxford University Press.

Brow, James
    1978   *Vedda Villages of Anurādhapura: The Historical Anthropology of a Community in Sri Lanka*. Seattle: University of Washington Press.

Brown, David
    1989   Ethnic revival: Perspectives on state and society. *Third World Quarterly*, October: 1–17.

Brown, Michael F., and Eduardo Fernández
1991   *War of Shadows: The Struggle for Utopia in the Peruvian Amazon.* Berkeley: University of California Press.
Brown, P.
1982a   Conflict in the New Guinea Highlands. *Journal of Conflict Resolution* 26(3): 525–46.
1982b   Chimbu disorder: Tribal fighting in newly independent Papua New Guinea. *Pacific Viewpoint* 22:1–21.
Brundage, Burr
1972   *A Rain of Darts: The Mexica Aztecs.* Austin: University of Texas Press.
Buck, D. J.
1984   The role of states in the eastern Maghreb, 500 B.C.–A.D. 500. *The Maghreb Review* 9(1–2):1–11.
1985   Frontier processes in Roman Tripolitania. In *Town and Country in Roman Tripolitania. Papers in Honour of Olwen Hackett*, D. J. Buck and D. J. Mattingly, eds., pp. 179–90. Oxford: British Archaeological Reports International Series 274.
Buckley, R. N.
1979   *Slaves in Red Coats: The British West India Regiments, 1795–1815.* New Haven: Yale University Press.
Bunker, Stephen
1988   *Underdeveloping the Amazon: Extraction, Unequal Exchange, and the Failure of the Modern State.* Chicago: University of Chicago Press.
Burton, Richard
1966   *A Mission to Gelele, King of Dahomey*, C. W. Newbury, ed. London: Routledge and Kegan Paul.
Camino, Alejandro
1977   Trueque, correrías e intercambios entre los Quechuas andinas y los Piro y Machiguenga de la montaña Peruana. *Amazonía Peruana* 2:123–42.
Campbell, J. B.
1984   *The Emperor and the Roman Army.* Oxford: Oxford University Press.
Camps, G.
1960   Massinissa ou les débuts de l'histoire. *Libyca* 8(1):1–320.
1974   Le Gour, mausolée Berbère du VIIIe siècle. *Antiquités Africaines* 8:191–208.
1980   *Berbères: Aux Marges de l'Histoire.* Toulouse: Editions des Hesperides.
1984   Avertissement. *Encylopédie Berbère* 1:1–48. Aix-en-Provence: Edisud.
Canny, N., and A. Padgen
1989   *Colonial Identity in the Atlantic World 1500–1800.* Princeton: Princeton University Press.
Canseco Vincourt, Jorge
1966   *La Guerra Sagrada.* Mexico City: Instituto Nacional de Antropología e Historia.
Carneiro, Robert
1970   A theory of the origin of the state. *Science* 169:733–38.
1979a   Forest clearance among the Yanomamö, observations and implications. *Antropológica* 52:39–76.
1979b   Tree felling with the stone ax: An experiment carried out among the Yanomamö Indians of southern Venezuela. In *Ethnoarchaeology*, C. Kramer, ed., pp. 21–58. New York: Columbia University Press.
1981   The chiefdom: Precusor of the state. In *The Transition to Statehood in the New World*, G. Jones and R. Krautz, eds., pp. 37–79. Cambridge: Cambridge University Press.
Carrasco, Pedro
1984   Royal marriages in ancient Mexico. In *Explorations in Ethnohistory: Indians of Central Mexico in the Sixteenth Century*, H. R. Harvey and H. J. Prem, eds., pp. 41–81. Albuquerque: University of New Mexico Press.

Castro Arenas, Mario
    1973   La Rebelión de Juan Santos. Lima: Carlos Milla Batres.
C.D.I.
    1864–   See Colección de Documentos Inéditos . . .
    1884
Ceci, Lynn
    1982   The value of wampum among the New York Iroquois: A case study in artifact analysis. Journal of Anthropological Research 38:97–107.
Chagnon, Napoleon
    1966   Yąnomamö warfare, social organization and marriage alliances. Ph.D. dissertation, Department of Anthropology, University of Michigan.
    1967   Yąnomamö social organization and warfare. In War: The Anthropology of Armed Conflict and Aggression, M. Fried, M. Harris, and R. Murphy, eds., pp. 109–59. Garden City, New York: Natural History Press.
    1968   Yąnomamö: The Fierce People. New York: Holt, Rinehart and Winston.
    1972a   Untitled (letters from the field). In The Human Condition in Latin America, by E. Wolf and E. Hansen, pp. 65–69. New York: Oxford University Press.
    1972b   Tribal social oganization and genetic microdifferentiation. In The Structure of Human Populations, G. Harrison and A. Boyce, eds., pp. 252–82. Oxford: Clarendon Press.
    1973   The culture-ecology of shifting (pioneering) cultivation among the Yąnomamö Indians. In Peoples and Cultures of Native South America, D. Gross, ed., pp. 126–44. Garden City, New York: Doubleday.
    1974   Studying the Yąnomamö. New York: Holt, Rinehart and Winston.
    1977   Yąnomamö: The Fierce People, 2nd ed. New York: Holt, Rinehart and Winston.
    1979   Mate competition, favoring close kin, and village fissioning among the Yąnomamö Indians. In Evolutionary Biology and Human Social Behavior: An Anthropological Perspective, N. Chagnon and W. Irons, eds., pp. 86–132. North Scituate, Massachusetts: Duxbury.
    1982   Sociodemographic attributes of nepotism in tribal populations: Man the rulebreaker. In Current Problems in Sociobiology, King's College Sociobiology Group, eds., pp. 291–318. Cambridge: Cambridge University Press.
    1983   Yąnomamö: The Fierce People, 3rd ed. New York: Holt, Rinehart and Winston.
    1988   Life histories, blood revenge, and warfare in a tribal population. Science 239: 985–92.
    1990   On Yąnomamö violence: Reply to Albert. Current Anthropology 31:49–53.
Chagnon, Napoleon, M. Flinn, and T. Melancon
    1979   Sex-ratio variation among the Yąnomamö Indians. In Evolutionary Biology and Human Social Behavior: An Anthropological Perspective, N. Chagnon and W. Irons, eds., pp. 290–320. North Scituate, Massachusetts: Duxbury.
Chagnon, Napoleon, and Thomas Melancon
    1983   Epidemics in a tribal population. In The Impact of Contact: Two Yanomamo Case Studies, J. Clay, ed., pp. 53–78. Cambridge: Cultural Survival and Bennington College.
Chagnon, Napoleon, James Neel, Lowell Weitkamp, Henry Gershowitz, and Manuel Ayres
    1970   The influence of cultural factors on the demography and pattern of gene flow from the Makiratare to the Yanomama Indians. American Journal of Physical Anthropology 32:339–49.
Chang, Kwang-chih
    1986   The Archaeology of Ancient China, 4th ed. New Haven: Yale University Press.
Cherry, J.
    1987   Power in space: Archaeological studies of the state. In Landscape and Culture: Geographical and Archaeological Perspectives, J. M. Wagstaff, ed., pp. 146–73. Oxford: Blackwell.

Chevalier, Jacques
1982   Civilization and the Stolen Gift: Capital, Kin, and Cult in Eastern Peru. Toronto: University of Toronto Press.
Chimalpahin, Francisco de San Anton Muñón
1965   Relaciones Originales de Chalco Amaquemecan. Mexico City: Fondo de Cultura Económica.
Christol, M.
1988   Rome et les tribus indigenes en Mauretanie Tingitaine. L'Africa Romana 5: 305–37.
CIL = Corpus Inscriptionum Latinarum
1881f   Berlin: De Gruyter.
Cipolla, Carlo
1965   Guns, Sails and Empires: Technological Innovation and the Early Phases of European Expansion 1400–1700. New York: Minerva Press.
Claessen, Henri, and Peter Skalnik, eds.
1978   The Early State. The Hague: Mouton.
Claessen, Henri, and Pieter van de Velde, eds.
1987   Early State Dynamics. Leiden: E. J. Brill.
Clark, James, ed.
1938   Codex Mendoza: The Mexican Manuscript Known as the Collection of Mendoza and Preserved in the Bodleian Library, Oxford, 3 vols. London: Waterlow and Sons.
Clark, Leonard
1953   The Rivers Ran East. New York: Funk and Wagnalls Company.
Clausewitz, Carl von
1943   On War. O. J. Matthijs, trans. New York: Random House.
1968   On War. London: Penguin.
Cocco, Luis
1972   Iyëwei-Teri: Quince Años entre los Yanomamos. Caracas, Venezuela: Escuela Tecnica Popular Don Bosco.
Códice Ramírez
1975   In Crónica Mexicana y Códice Ramírez, H. Alvarado Tezozomoc, ed., pp. 17–149. Mexico City: Porrúa.
Códice Tudela
1980   Madrid: Ediciones Cultural Hispanica del Instituto de Cooperación Iberoamericana.
Cohen, Mark
1981   The ecological basis for new world state formation: General and local model building. In The Transition to Statehood in the New World, G. Jones and R. Krautz, eds., pp. 105–22. Cambridge: Cambridge University Press.
Cohen, Ronald
1985   Warfare and state formation. In Development and Decline: The Evolution of Sociopolitical Organization, H. J. Claessen, P. van de Velde, and M. E. Smith, eds., pp. 276–89. South Hadley, Massachusetts: Bergin and Garvey.
Cohn, Bernard
1980   History and anthropology: The state of play. Comparative Studies in Society and History 22: 198–221.
Colchester, Marcus
1981   Ecological modelling and indigenous systems of resource use: Some examples from the Amazon of South Venezuela. Antropológica 55: 51–72.
1984   Rethinking Stone Age economics: Some speculations concerning the pre-Columbian Yanoama economy. Human Ecology 12: 291–314.
1985   The Venezuelan Ninam (North Eastern Yanoama): Their health and survival. In The Health and Survival of the Venezuelan Yanoama, M. Colchester, ed.,

pp. 59–72. Copenhagen: Anthropology Resource Center/International Work Group for Indigenous Affairs/Survival International.

Colchester, Marcus, and Richard Semba
1985   Health and survival among the Yanoama Indians. In *The Health and Survival of the Venezuelan Yanoama*, M. Colchester, ed., pp. 13–30. Copenhagen: Anthropology Resource Center/International Work Group for Indigenous Affairs/Survival International.

Colden, Cadwallader
1727 and 1747   *The History of the Five Indian Nations Depending on the Province of New-York in America*. Ithaca: Cornell University Press. 1958.

Colección de Documentos Inéditos Relativos al Descubrimiento, Conquista y Organización de las Antiguas Posesiones Españoles de América y Oceania
1864–   42 vols. Madrid.
1884

Colón, C.
1989   *Textos y Documentos Completos*. C. Varela, ed. Madrid: Alianza Editorial.

Colson, A.
1983–   The spatial component in the political structure of Carib speakers in the Guiana highlands. *Antropológica* 59–62:73–124.
1984

Connolly, Bob, and Robin Anderson
1988   *First Contact: New Guinea's Highlanders Encounter the Outside World*. New York: Penguin Books.

Conrad, Geoffrey, and Arthur Demarest
1984   *Religion and Empire: The Dynamics of Aztec and Inca Expansion*. New York: Cambridge University Press.

Cook, Sherburne
1973   Interracial warfare and population decline among the New England Indians. *Ethnohistory* 20:1–24.

Cooper, Frederick, and Ann Stoler
1989   Tensions of empire: Colonial control and visions of rule. *American Ethnologist* 16:609–21.

Cortés, Hernan
1971   *Hernan Cortes: Letters from Mexico*, A. R. Pagden, trans. New York: Grossman Publishers.

Cosmas Indicopleustes
1909   *The Christian Topography*, F. O. Winstedt, ed. Oxford: Oxford University Press.

Creamer, Winifred, and Jonathan Haas
1985   Tribe versus chiefdom in lower Central America. *American Antiquity* 50(4): 738–54.

Creveld, Martin van
1989   *Technology and War: From 2000 BC to the Present*. New York: The Free Press.

Crone, Patricia
1986   The tribe and the state. In *States in History*, J. Hall, ed., pp. 48–77. New York: Basil Blackwell.

Crónica Mexicana
1975   In *Crónica Mexicana y Códice Ramírez*, H. Alvarado Tezozomoc, ed., pp. 233–701. Mexico City: Porrúa.

Cronon, William
1983   *Changes in the Land: Indians, Colonists, and the Ecology of New England*. New York: Hill and Wang.

Crosby, Alfred
1986   *Ecological Imperialism: The Biological Expansion of Europe, 900–1900*. Cambridge: Cambridge University Press.

Crowder, Michael, ed.
    1971   *West African Resistance: The Military Response to Colonial Occupation*. London: Hutchinson.

Cuevas, P. Mariano, ed.
    1975   *Documentos Inéditos del Siglo XVI para la Historia de México*. Mexico City: Porrúa.

Cūlavaṃsa
    1925   Vol. 1. W. Geiger, ed. London: Pali Text Society.

Cultural Survival Quarterly
    1987a   Militarization and indigenous peoples, part 1. The Americas and the Pacific. *Cultural Survival Quarterly* 11(3).
    1987b   Militarization and indigenous peoples, part 2. Africa, Asia and the Middle East. *Cultural Survival Quarterly* 11(4).
    1989   Brazil: Who pays for development? *Cultural Survival Quarterly* 13(4).

Curtin, Philip
    1984   *Cross-Cultural Trade in World History*. Cambridge: Cambridge University Press.

Dalzel, Archibald
    1793   *The History of Dahomy, an Inland Kingdom of Africa*. London: Frank Cass. 1967.

Daniels, C. M.
    1970   *The Garamantes of Southern Libya*. London: Oleander.
    1975   An ancient people of the Libyan Sahara. In *Hamito-Semitica*, J. Bynon and T. Bynon, eds., pp. 249–65. The Hague: Mouton.
    1987   Africa. In *The Roman World*, vol. 1. J. Wacher, ed., pp. 223–65. London: Routledge and Kegan Paul.

Dapper, Olfert
    1668   *Naukeurige Beschrijvinge der Afrikaensche Gewesten*. Amsterdam.

Daumas, E.
    1968   *The Horses of the Sahara*, S. M. Ohlendorf, trans. Austin: University of Texas Press.
    1971   *The Ways of the Desert*, S. M. Ohlendorf, trans. Austin: University of Texas Press.

Davies, Nigel
    1974   *The Aztecs: A History*. New York: G. P. Putnam's Sons.

Davis, J.
    1977   *People of the Mediterranean: An Essay in Comparative Social Anthropology*. London: Routledge and Kegan Paul.

Davis, Shelton
    1976   The Yanomamo: Ethnographic images and anthropological responsibilities. In *The Geological Imperative: Anthropology and Development in the Amazon Basin*, S. Davis and R. Mathews, eds., pp. 7–23. Cambridge: Anthropology Resource Center.
    1977   *Victims of the Miracle: Development and the Indians of Brazil*. Cambridge: Cambridge University Press.

Deagan, Kathleen
    1985   Spanish-Indian interaction in sixteenth-century Florida. In *Cultures in Contact: The European Impact on Native Cultural Institutions in Eastern North America, A.D. 1000–1800*, W. Fitzhugh, ed., pp. 281–318. Washington, D.C.: Smithsonian Institution Press.

DeBoer, W.
    1981   Buffer zones in the cultural ecology of aboriginal Amazonia: An ethnohistorical approach. *American Antiquity* 46:364–77.

De la Chapelle, F.
    1934   L'expédition de Suetonius Paulinus dans le sud-est du Maroc. *Hesperis* 19: 107–24.

Delbée
1671   Journal du voyage du Sieur Delbée. In *Relation de ce qui s'Est Passé dan les Isles et Terre-Ferme de l'Amérique*, vol. 2, J. de Clodoré, ed., pp. 347–558. Paris.

Delbruck, Hans
1990   *The Barbarian Invasions. History of the Art of War*, vol. 2, W. Renfroe, trans. Lincoln: University of Nebraska Press.

Denonville, Jacques-Rene de Brisay de
1848   Narrative of the expedition of the Marquis de Nonville [sic] against the Senecas, in 1687. *New York Historical Society Collections* (2nd ser.) 2:149–92.

Desanges, J.
1957   Le triomphe de Cornelius Balbus (19 B.C.). *Revue Africaine* 101:5–43.
1962   *Catalogue des Tribus Africaines de l'Antiquité Classique à l'Ouest du Nil*. Dakar: University of Dakar.
1978   *Recherches sur l'Activité des Méditerranéens aux Confins de l'Afrique*. Rome: Collection de l'École Française a Rome.

Desrosiers, Leo-Paul
1947   *Iroquoisie*. Vol. 1, 1534–1646. Montreal: Etudes de l'Institut d'Histoire de l'Amérique Francaise.

Dhātuvaṃsa
1939   M. Kumaratunga, ed. Colombo: Gunasena.

Díaz del Castillo, Bernal
1908–   *The True History of the Conquest of New Spain*, 5 vols., A. P. Maudslay, trans.
1916   London: Hakluyt Society.

Dincauze, Dena, and Robert Hasenstab
1989   Explaining the Iroquois: Tribalization on a prehistoric periphery. In *Centre and Periphery: Comparative Studies in Archaeology*, T. Champion, ed., pp. 67–87. London: Unwin Hyman.

Dīpavaṃsa
1879   Hermann Oldenberg, ed. London: William and Norgate.

Divale, William, and Marvin Harris
1976   Population, warfare, and the male supremacist complex. *American Anthropologist* 78:521–38.

Di Vita, A.
1982   Gli emporia di Tripolitania dall'età di Massinissa a Diocleziano: Un profilo storicoistituzionale. *Aufstieg und Niedergang der Römischen Welt II. Principat* 10(2):515–95.

Dobyns, Henry
1972   Military transculturation of Northern Piman Indians, 1782–1821. *Ethnohistory* 19:323–43.
1983   *Their Number Become Thinned: Native American Population Dynamics in Eastern North America*. Knoxville: University of Tennessee Press.
1989   More methodological perspectives on historical demography. *Ethnohistory* 36:285–99.

Donald, Leland
1987   Slave raiding on the North Pacific Coast. In *Native People, Native Lands*, B. Alden, ed., pp. 161–72. Ottawa: Carleton University Press.

Donaldson, M.
1982   Contradiction, mediation and hegemony in pre-capitalist New Guinea: Warfare, production and sexual antagonism in the Eastern Highlands. In *Melanesia: Beyond Diversity*, R. J. May and H. Nelson, eds., pp. 435–60. Canberra: Australian National University Press.

Doublet, Jean
1883   *Journal du Corsaire Jean Doublet de Honfleur*, C. Bréard, ed. Paris: Charavay Frères.

Douglas, Mary
  1989   Distinguished lecture: The Hotel Kwilu—model of models. *American Anthropologist* 91:855–65.
Duncan, John
  1847   *Travels in Western Africa*. London: Frank Cass. 1968.
Dunn, R. E.
  1977   *Resistance in the Desert*. Beckenham: Croom Helm.
Dunn, Walter, Jr. (in collaboration)
  1979   Chabert de Joncaire de Claussone, Daniel-Marie. *Dictionary of Canadian Biography* 4:137–38.
Durán, Diego
  1967   *Historia de las Indias de Nueva España e Islas de la Tierra Firma*, 2 vols. Mexico City: Porrúa.
Dyson, S. L.
  1975   Native revolt patterns in the Roman Empire. *Aufstieg und Niedergang der Römischen Welt. Principat* 11(3):138–75.
Eccles, W. J.
  1969   Brisay de Denonville, Jacques-Rene de. *Dictionary of Canadian Biography* 2: 98–105.
Eder, James
  1987   *On the Road to Tribal Extinction: Depopulation, Deculturation and Adaptive Well-Being among the Batak of the Philippines*. Berkeley: University of California Press.
Eid, Leroy
  1979   The Ojibwa-Iroquois war: The war the Five Nations did not win. *Ethnohistory* 26:297–324.
Elick, John
  1969   An Ethnography of the Pichis Valley Campa of eastern Peru. Ph.D. dissertation, University of California, Los Angeles. Ann Arbor: University Microfilms.
Ellis, John
  1975   *The Social History of the Machine Gun*. New York: Pantheon.
Encyclopédie Berbère
  1984   Aix-en-Provence: Edisud.
Engelbrecht, William
  1985   New York Iroquois political development. In *Cultures in Contact: The European Impact on Native Cultural Institutions in Eastern North America, A.D. 1000–1800*, W. Fitzhugh, ed., pp. 163–83. Washington, D.C.: Smithsonian Institution Press.
Engels, Donald
  1978   *Alexander the Great and the Logistics of the Macedonian Army*. Berkeley and Los Angeles: University of California Press.
Euzennat, M.
  1984   Les troubles de Maurétanie. *Comptes Rendues à l'Academie des Insriptions et Belles-Lettres* 1984:372–93.
Evans, Peter, Dietrich Rueschemeyer, and Theda Skocpol, eds.
  1985   *Bringing the State Back In*. Cambridge: Cambridge University Press.
Ewers, John
  1980   *The Horse in Blackfoot Indian Culture*. Washington, D.C.: Smithsonian Institution Press.
Fardon, Richard
  1988   *Raiders and Refugees: Trends in Chamba Political Development 1750 to 1950*. Washington, D.C.: Smithsonian Institution Press.
Faulkner, R. O.
  1953   Egyptian military organization. *Journal of Egyptian Archaeology* 39:32–47.

Fausz, Frederick
1979 Fighting "fire" with firearms: The Anglo-Powhattan arms race in early Virginia. *American Indian Culture and Research Journal* 3:33–50.
1985 Patterns of Anglo-Indian aggression and accommodation along the Mid-Atlantic Coast, 1584–1634. In *Cultures in Contact: The European Impact on Native Cultural Institutions in Eastern North America, A.D. 1000–1800*, W. Fitzhugh, ed., pp. 225–68. Washington, D.C.: Smithsonian Institution Press.

Feil, D. K.
1987 *The Evolution of Highland New Guinea Societies*. Cambridge: Cambridge University Press.

Fenton, William
1940 Problems arising from the historic northeastern position of the Iroquois. *Smithsonian Miscellaneous Collections* 100:159–252.
1949 Collecting materials for a political history of the Six Nations. *Proceedings of the American Philosophical Society* 93:233–38.
1951 Locality as a basic factor in the development of Iroquois social structure. *Bureau of American Ethnology Bulletin* 149:35–54.
1955 Factionalism in American Indian society. *Actes du IVe Congrès International des Sciences Anthropologiques et Ethnologiques* 2:330–40. Vienna.
1971 The New York State wampum collection: The case for the integrity of cultural treasures. *Proceedings of the American Philosophical Society* 115:437–61.

Fenton, William, and Elisabeth Tooker
1978 Mohawk. In *Handbook of North American Indians*. Vol. 15, *Northeast*, B. G. Trigger, ed., pp. 466–80. Washington, D.C.: Smithsonian Institution Press.

Fentress, E. W. B.
1979 *Numidia and the Roman Army: Social, Military and Economic Aspects of the Frontier Zone*. Oxford: British Archaeological Reports International Series 53.
1982 Tribe and faction: The case of the Gaetuli. *Mélanges de l'Ecole Français de Rome, Antiquités* 94(1):325–34.

Ferguson, R. Brian
1984a Introduction: Studying war. In *Warfare, Culture, and Environment*, R. B. Ferguson, ed., pp. 1–81. Orlando: Academic Press.
1984b A reexamination of the causes of Northwest Coast warfare. In *Warfare, Culture, and Environment*, R. B. Ferguson, ed., pp. 267–328. Orlando: Academic Press.
1988a Class transformations in Puerto Rico. Ph.D. dissertation, Department of Anthropology, Columbia University. Ann Arbor: University Microfilms.
1988b War and the sexes in Amazonia. In *Dialectics and Gender: Anthropological Approaches*, R. Randolph, D. Schneider, and M. Diaz, eds., pp. 136–54. Boulder, Colorado: Westview Press.
1988c Introduction: Progress and problems in the anthropology of war. In *The Anthropology of War: A Bibliography*, by R. B. Ferguson with L. E. Farragher, pp. i-viii. New York: The Harry Frank Guggenheim Foundation.
1989a Game wars? Ecology and conflict in Amazonia. *Journal of Anthropological Research* 45:179–206.
1989b Ecological consequences of Amazonian warfare. *Ethnology* 28:249–64.
1989c Do Yanomamo killers have more kids? *American Ethnologist* 16:564–65.
1990a Blood of the Leviathan: Western contact and warfare in Amazonia. *American Ethnologist* 17:237–57.
1990b Explaining war. In *The Anthropology of War*, J. Haas, ed., pp. 26–55. Cambridge: Cambridge University Press.
n.d.a *An Analytic History of Yanomami Warfare*. Santa Fe: School of American Research Press, in press.
n.d.b Infrastructural causality. Paper presented at the annual meeting of the American Anthropological Association, New Orleans, November 1990.

n.d.c   Re-Fried Amazonia: A political theory reconsidered. Paper presented at the Columbia University Seminar of Ecological Systems and Cultural Evolution, New York, April 1990.

Ferguson, R. Brian, with Leslie Farragher
1988   *The Anthropology of War: A Bibliography.* Occasional Paper 1. New York: The Harry Frank Guggenheim Foundation.

Ferguson, Yale, and Richard Mansbach
1989   *The State, Conceptual Chaos, and the Future of International Relations Theory.* Boulder, Colorado: Lynne Reinner.

Fernández, Eduardo
1986a   *Para que Nuestra Historia no se Pierda: Testimonios de los Asháninca y Nomatsiguenga sobre la Colonización.* Lima: Centro de Investigactión y Promoción Amazónica.
1986b   El científico ante los problemas de la Amazonía. In *Culturas Indígenas de la Amazonía,* pp. 51–59. Madrid: Comisíon Nacional del V Centenario.
1987   Los Asháninca y los Incas: Historia y mitos. *Anthropologica* 5:334–56. Lima.
1988   El territorio Ashaninca en su frontera sur: Distribución y límites. *Extracta* 7:23–33. Lima.

Ferrill, Arther
1986   *The Fall of the Roman Empire: The Military Explanation.* London: Thames and Hudson.

Fishwick, D.
1971   The annexation of Mauretania. *Historia* 20:467–87.

Fitzhugh, William, ed.
1985   *Cultures in Contact: The European Impact on Native Cultural Institutions in Eastern North America, A.D. 1000–1800.* Washington, D.C.: Smithsonian Institution Press.

Flannery, Kent
1983   Major Monte Albán V sites: Zaachila, Xoxocotlán, Cuilapan, Yagul, and Abasolo. In *The Cloud People: Divergent Evolution of the Zapotec and Mixtec Civilization,* K. V. Flannery and J. Marcus, eds., pp. 290–95. New York: Academic Press.

Flannery, Kent, and Joyce Marcus
1983a   The changing politics of A.D. 600–900: Editors' introduction. In *The Cloud People: Divergent Evolution of the Zapotec and Mixtec Civilization,* K. V. Flannery and J. Marcus, eds., pp. 183–85. New York: Academic Press.
1983b   An editorial opinion on the Mixtec impact. In *The Cloud People: Divergent Evolution of the Zapotec and Mixtec Civilization,* K. V. Flannery and J. Marcus, eds., pp. 277–79. New York: Academic Press.

Flores Galindo, Alberto
1988   *Buscando un Inca,* 3rd ed. Lima: Editorial Horizonte.

Forbes, Frederick
1851   *Dahomey and the Dahomans.* London: Frank Cass. 1966.

Forbes, Jack
1965   *Warriors of the Colorado: The Yumas of the Quechan Nation and Their Neighbors.* Norman: University of Oklahoma Press.

Foster, Michael
1985   Another look at the function of wampum in Iroquois-White councils. In *The History and Culture of Iroquois Diplomacy: An Interdisciplinary Guide to the Treaties of the Six Nations and their League,* F. Jennings et al., eds., pp. 99–114. Syracuse: Syracuse University Press.

Fox, J. W.
1987   *Maya Postclassic State Formation.* Cambridge: Cambridge University Press.

Fox, R. G.
1969   Professional primitives: Hunters and gatherers of nuclear South Asia. *Man in India* 49:136–60.

Frezouls, E.
1957   Les Baquates et la Province Romaine de Tingitaine. *Bulletin d'Archéologie Marocaine* 2:65–116.
1980   Rome et la Maurétanie Tingitane: Un constat d'échec? *Antiquités Africaines* 16:65–93.

Fried, Morton
1967   *The Evolution of Political Society: An Essay in Political Anthropology.* New York: Random House.
1968   The concepts of "tribe" and "tribal society." In *Essays on the Problem of Tribe: Proceedings of the 1967 Annual Spring Meeting of the American Ethnological Society*, J. Helm, ed., pp. 3–20. Seattle: University of Washington Press.
1974   Preface. In *Studying the Yanomamo*, by N. Chagnon, pp. viii-ix. New York: Holt, Rinehart and Winston.
1975   *The Notion of Tribe.* Menlo Park, California: Cummings Publishing.
1979   Economic theory and first contact. In *New Directions in Political Economy: An Approach from Anthropology*, M. Leons and F. Rothstein, eds., pp. 3–17. Westport, Connecticut: Greenwood Press.

Friedman, Jonathan
1975   Tribes, states, and transformations. In *Marxist Analyses and Social Anthropology*, M. Bloch, ed., pp. 161–202. London: Malaby.
1989   Culture, identity and world process. In *Domination and Resistance*, D. Miller, M. Rowlands, and C. Tilley, eds., pp. 246–60. One World Archaeology (3). London: Unwin-Hyman.

Gamst, Frederick
1986   Conflict in the Horn of Africa. In *Peace and War: Cross-Cultural Perspectives*, M. L. Foster and R. Rubinstein, eds., pp. 133–51. New Brunswick, New Jersey: Transaction Press.

García Icazbalceta, Joaquin, ed.
1891   *Nueva Colección de Documentos para la Historia de México.* 3 vols. Mexico City.

Gardener, P. M.
1966   Symmetric respect and memorate knowledge: The structure and ecology of individualistic culture. *Southwestern Journal of Anthropology* 22:389–415.

Garnsey, P. D. A.
1978   Rome's African empire under the Principate. In *Imperialism in the Ancient World*, P. D. A. Garnsey and C. R. Whittaker, eds., pp. 223–54. Cambridge: Cambridge University Press.

Garrad, Charles, and Conrad Heidenreich
1978   Khionontateronon (Petun). In *Handbook of North American Indians.* Vol. 15, *Northeast*, B. G. Trigger, ed., pp. 394–97. Washington, D.C.: Smithsonian Institution Press.

Garratt, John
1985   *The Four Indian Kings.* Ottawa: Public Archives Canada.

Garraty, John, and Peter Gay, eds.
1981   *The Columbia History of the World.* New York: Harper and Row.

Gascou, J.
1972   *La Politique Municipale de l'Empire Romain en Afrique Proconsulaire de Trajan à Septima Sévère.* Rome: Collection École Français de Rome.

Gautier, E. F.
1952   *Le Passé de l'Afrique du Nord*, 2nd ed. Paris: Payot.

Gellner, E. F.
 1969   *Saints of the Atlas.* London: Weidenfeld and Nicolson.
 1973   Patterns of rural rebellion in Morocco during the early years of independence. In *Arabs and Berbers: From Tribe to Nation in North Africa,* E. Gellner and C. Micaud, eds., pp. 361–74. London: Duckworth.

Gellner, E., and C. Micaud, eds.
 1973   *Arabs and Berbers: From Tribe to Nation in North Africa.* London: Duckworth.

Gerhard, Peter
 1972   *A Guide to the Historical Geography of New Spain.* Cambridge: Cambridge University Press.

Gibson, Thomas
 1990   Raiding, trading and tribal autonomy in insular Southeast Asia. In *The Anthropology of War,* J. Haas, ed., pp. 125–45. Cambridge: Cambridge University Press.

Giddens, Anthony
 1985   *The Nation-State and Violence: Volume Two of a Contemporary Critique of Historical Materialism.* Berkeley: University of California Press.

Given, Brian
 1981   The Iroquois wars and native firearms, Canadian Ethnology Society Papers from the Sixth Annual Congress, 1979. *National Museum of Man Mercury Series Canadian Ethnology Service Paper* 78:84–94.

Glasse, R. M.
 1968   *Huli of Papua: A Cognatic Descent System.* Paris: Mouton.

Gledhill, J.
 1988a   Introduction. In *State and Society,* J. Gledhill, B. Bender, and M. Larsen, eds., pp. 1–29. One World Archaeology (4). London: Unwin Hyman.
 1988b   Legacies of empire: Political centralization and class formation in the Hispanic-American world. In *State and Society,* J. Gledhill, B. Bender, and M. Larsen, eds., pp. 302–19. One World Archaeology (4). London: Unwin Hyman.
 1989   The imperial form and universal history: Some reflections on relativism and generalization. In *Domination and Resistance,* D. Miller, M. Rowlands, and C. Tilley, eds., pp. 108–26. One World Archaeology (3). London: Unwin Hyman.

Goeje, C. H. de
 1939   Nouvel examinen des langues des Antilles. *Journal de la Société des Américanistes* 30:1–120.

Goldberg, Neil, and Frank Findlow
 1984   A quantitative analysis of Roman military aggression in Britain, circa A.D. 43–238. In *Warfare, Culture, and Environment,* R. B. Ferguson, ed., pp. 359–85. Orlando: Academic Press.

Golden, Peter
 1991   Aspects of the nomadic factor in the economic development of Kievan Rus'. In *Ukrainian Economic History: Interpretive Essays,* I. Koropecky, ed. Cambridge: Harvard Ukranian Research Institute.

Goldschmidt, Walter
 1989   Inducement to military participation in tribal societies. In *The Anthropology of War and Peace: Perspectives on the Nuclear Age,* P. R. Turner and D. Pitt, eds., pp. 15–31. Granby: Bergin and Garvey.

Gomez de Orozco, Frederico
 1945   Costumbres, fiestas, enterramientos y diversas formas de proceder de los Indios de Nuevan España. *Tlalocan* 2:37–63.

Gongora, A.
 1976   *Studies in the Colonial History of Spanish America.* Cambridge: Cambridge University Press.

Gonzalez, Nancie
  1983 New evidence on the origin of the Black Carib. *Nieuwe West-Indische Gids* 57:143–72.
  1989 Conflict, migration, and the expression of ethnicity: Introduction. In *Conflict, Migration, and the Expression of Ethnicity*, N. Gonzalez and C. McCommon, eds., pp. 1–10. Boulder, Colorado: Westview Press.

Good, Kenneth
  1983 Limiting factors in Amazonian ecology. Paper prepared for the Wenner-Gren symposium on Food Preferences and Aversions, Cedar Cove, Cedar Key, Florida, October.
  1984 Demography and land use among the Yanomami of the Orinoco-Siapa block in Amazon Territory, Venezuela. Manuscript.
  1989 Yanomami hunting patterns: Trekking and garden relocation as an adaptation to game availability in Amazonia, Venezuela. Ph.D. dissertation, Department of Anthropology, University of Florida, Gainesville.

Goodwin, Grenville, and Keith Basso
  1971 *Western Apache Raiding and Warfare*. Tucson: University of Arizona Press.

Goody, Jack
  1971 *Technology, Tradition and the State in Africa*. London: International African Institute.

Gordon, R. J.
  1983 The decline of the kiapdom and the resurgence of tribal fighting. *Oceania* 53(3):205–23.

Gordon, R. J. and M. J. Meggitt
  1985 *Law and Order in the New Guinea Highlands*. Hanover and London: University Press of New England.

Gott, Richard
  1973 *Rural Guerrillas in Latin America*. Harmondsworth: Penguin.

Gottwald, Norman
  1979 *The Tribes of Yahweh: A Sociology of the Religion of Liberated Israel, 1250–1050 B.C.E.* New York: Orbis.

Gramly, Richard
  1977 Deerskins and hunting territories: Competition for scarce resources in the Northeastern Woodlands. *American Antiquity* 42:601–5.
  1988 Conflict and defense in the Eastern Woodlands. In *Interpretations of Culture Change in the Eastern Woodlands during the Late Woodland Period*, R. Yerkes, ed., pp. 86–97. Columbus: Ohio State University Department of Anthropology.

Grassman, Thomas
  1966 Otreouti. *Dictionary of Canadian Biography* 1:525–26.

Graymont, Barbara
  1972 *The Iroquois in the American Revolution*. Syracuse: Syracuse University Press.

Griffen, William
  1988 *Apaches at War and Peace: The Janos Presidio, 1750–1858*. Albuquerque: University of New Mexico Press.

Groot, S. de
  1988 A corp of black chasseurs in Surinam: Collaboration and rebellion. Symposium paper, 46th International Congress of Americanists, Amsterdam.

Grove, David
  1987 Chalcatzingo in a broader perspective. In *Ancient Chalcatzingo*, D. C. Grove, ed., pp. 434–42. Austin: University of Texas Press.

Gsell, S.
  1913–29 *Histoire Ancienne de l'Afrique du Nord*, vols. 1–8. Paris: Hachette.

Gunawardana, R. A. L. H.
1978   The kinsmen of the Buddha: Myth as political charter in ancient and early medieval kingdoms of Sri Lanka. In *Religion and Legitimation of Political Power in Sri Lanka*, B. L. Smith, ed., pp. 96–106. Chambersburg: Anima.
1979a   *Robe and Plough: Monasticism and Economic Interest in Early Medieval Sri Lanka*. Tucson: University of Arizona Press.
1979b   The People of the Lion: The Sinhala identity and ideology in history and historiography. *The Sri Lanka Journal of the Humanities* 5:1–36.
1982   Prelude to the state. *The Sri Lanka Journal of the Humanities* 8:1–39.
1984   Intersocietal transfer of hydraulic technology in precolonial South Asia: Some reflections based on a preliminary investigation. *Southeast Asian Studies* 22(2): 115–42.
1987   Changing patterns of navigation in the Indian Ocean and their impact on precolonial Sri Lanka. In *The Indian Ocean: Explorations in History, Commerce and Politics*, S. Chandra, ed., pp. 54–89. New Delhi: Sage.
1989   Anurādhapura: Ritual, power and resistance in a precolonial South Asia City. In *Domination and Resistance*, D. Miller, M. Rowlands, and C. Tilley, eds., pp. 155–78. One World Archaeology (3). London: Unwin Hyman.
Haas, Jonathan
1982   *The Evolution of the Prehistoric State*. New York: Columbia University Press.
1990a   (Ed.) *The Anthropology of War*. Cambridge: Cambridge University Press.
1990b   Warfare and tribalization in the prehistoric Southwest. In *The Anthropology of War*, J. Haas, ed., pp. 171–89. Cambridge: Cambridge University Press.
Hamilton, J.
1820–   Journal of a trip from Sto. Thomé de Angostura to the Capuchin missions of
1821   the Caroni. *Quarterly Journal of Science, Literature and Arts* 8:260–98; 9: 1–32.
Handler, J.
1968   The Amerindian slave population of Barbados in the 17th and early-18th centuries. *Caribbean Studies* 8:38–64.
Hanson, Jeffery
1988   Age-set theory and Plains Indian age-grading: A critical review and revision. *American Ethnologist* 15:349–64.
Hanser, P.
1985   *Krieg und Recht: Wesen und Ursachen Kollektives Gewaltanwendung in den Stammesgesellschafter Neuguineas*. Berlin: Dietrich Reimer Verlag.
Haring, Clarence
1947   *The Spanish Empire in America*. New York: Harcourt.
Harner, Michael
1973   *The Jívaro: People of the Sacred Waterfall*. Garden City, New York: Natural History Press.
Harris, Marvin
1977   *Cannibals and Kings: The Origins of Cultures*. New York: Random House.
1984   A cultural materialist theory of band and village warfare: The Yanomamo test. In *Warfare, Culture, and Environment*, R. B. Ferguson, ed., pp. 111–40. Orlando: Academic Press.
Hart, D. M.
1973   The tribe in modern Morocco: Two case studies. In *Arabs and Berbers: From Tribe to Nation in North Africa*, E. Gellner and C. Micaud, eds., pp. 25–58. London: Duckworth.
Hartsninck, J. J
1770   *Beschrijiving van Guiana*. Amsterdam.

Hassig, Ross
   1985   *Trade, Tribute, and Transportation: The Sixteenth-Century Political Economy of the Valley of Mexico*. Norman: University of Oklahoma Press.
   1988   *Aztec Warfare: Imperial Expansion and Political Control*. Norman: University of Oklahoma Press.

Hayano, D. M.
   1974   Marriage, alliance and warfare: A view from the New Guinea Highlands. *American Ethnologist* 1(2):281–93.

Hazoumé, Paul
   1937   *Le Pacte de Sang au Dahomey*. Paris: Institut d'Ethnologie.

Headland, Thomas, and Lawrence Reid
   1989   Hunter-gatherers and their neighbors from prehistory to the present. *Current Anthropology* 30:43–66.

Headrick, Daniel
   1981   *Tools of Empire: Technology and European Imperialism in the Nineteenth Century*. Oxford: Oxford University Press.

Hedeager, Lotte
   1987   Empire, frontier and the barbarian hinterland: Rome and northern Europe from AD 1–400. In *Centre and Periphery in the Ancient World*, M. Rowlands, M. Larsen, and K. Kristiansen, eds., pp. 125–40. Cambridge: Cambridge University Press.

Heidenreich, Conrad
   1971   *Huronia: A History and Geography of the Huron Indians 1600–1650*. Toronto: McClelland and Stewart.

Helm, June, ed.
   1968   *Essays on the Problem of Tribe: Proceedings of the 1967 Annual Spring Meeting of the American Ethnological Society*. Seattle: University of Washington Press.

Helms, M.
   1976   *Ancient Panama: Chiefs in Search of Power*. Austin: University of Texas Press.

Hemming, John
   1978   *Red Gold: The Conquest of the Brazilian Indians*. Cambridge: Harvard University Press.
   1987   *Amazon Frontier: The Defeat of the Brazilian Indians*. Cambridge: Harvard University Press.

Henige, David
   1986a   If pigs could fly: Timucan population and Native American historical demography. *Journal of Interdisciplinary History* 16:701–20.
   1986b   Primary source by primary source? On the role of epidemics in New World depopulation. *Ethnohistory* 33:293–313.
   1989   On the current devaluation of the notion of evidence: A rejoinder to Dobyns. *Ethnohistory* 36:304–7.

Henley, Paul
   1978   Os Indios e a Civilização: A critical appreciation. *Cambridge Anthropology* 4:88–111.
   1983–   A survey of intergenerational marriage in the Guianas. *Antropológica* 59–
   1984   62:176–81.

Herndon, William, and Larner Gibbon
   1854   *Exploration of the Valley of the Amazon, Made under the Direction of the Navy Department*. Washington, D.C.: Robert Armstrong, Public Printer.

Hicks, Frederic
   1979   "Flowery war" in Aztec history. *American Ethnologist* 6:87–92.

Hilhouse, W.
   1825   *Indian Notices*. Demerara (private publication).

Hill, Jonathan, ed.
  1988   Rethinking History and Myth: Indigenous South American Perspectives on the Past.
         Urbana: University of Illinois Press.
Hobbes, Thomas
  1651   Leviathan, parts 1 and 2. Indianapolis: Bobbs-Merrill. 1958.
Hoebel, E. Adamson
  1978   The Cheyennes: Indians of the Great Plains, 2nd ed. New York: Holt, Rinehart
         and Winston.
Holt, P. M., and M. W. Daly
  1979   The History of the Sudan: From the Coming of Islam to the Present Day, 3rd ed.
         London: Weidenfeld and Nicolson.
Horn, H. G., and C. B. Ruger
  1979   Die Numider. Bonn: Reinischen Landesmuseums.
Horne, A.
  1977   A Savage War of Peace: Algeria 1954–1962. New York: Viking.
Hulme, P.
  1986   Colonial Encounters: Europe and the Native Caribbean 1492–1797. London:
         Methuen.
Hulme, P., and N. L. Whitehead, eds.
  1992   Wild Majesty: Encounters with Caribs from Columbus to the Present Day. Oxford:
         Oxford University Press. In press.
Hunt, George
  1940   The Wars of the Iroquois: A Study of Intertribal Trade Relations. Madison: Univer-
         sity of Wisconsin.
Hvalkof, Søren
  1989   The nature of development: Native and settler views in Gran Pajonál, Peruvian
         Amazon. Folk 21:125–50.
IAM = Inscriptions Antiques de Maroc. Vol. 2, Inscriptions Latines
  1982   Paris: Centre National de Recherche Scientifique.
Ingold, T., D. Riches, and J. Woodburn, eds.
  1988   Hunters and Gatherers, 2 vols. Oxford: Berg Press.
Isaac, B.
  1990   The Limits of Empire: The Roman Army in the East. Oxford: Oxford University
         Press.
Isaac, Barry
  1983   The Aztec "flowery war": A geopolitical explanation. Journal of Anthropological
         Research 39:415–32.
Izaguirre, Padre Fray Bernardino
  1922   Historia de las Misiones Franciscanas y Narración de los Progresos de la Geografía
         en el Oriente del Perú. Lima: Talleres Tipográficos de la Penitenciaría.
Jablow, Jacob
  1950   The Cheyenne in Plains Indians Trade Relations. American Ethnological Society
         Monograph 19. Seattle: University of Washington Press.
Jacobs, Wilbur
  1949   Wampum, the protocol of Indian diplomacy. William and Mary Quarterly (3rd
         ser.) 4:596–604.
  1950   Diplomacy and Indian Gifts: Anglo-French Rivalry along the Ohio and Northwest
         Frontiers, 1748–1763. Stanford: Stanford University Press.
Jagchid, Sechin, and Van Jay Symons
  1989   Peace, War, and Trade along the Great Wall. Bloomington: Indiana University
         Press.
Jameson, J. Franklin, ed.
  1909   Narratives of New Netherland 1609–1664. New York: Charles Scribner's Sons.

Jamieson, J. B.
　1983　An examination of prisoner-sacrifice and cannibalism at the St. Lawrence Iroquoian Roebuck site. *Canadian Journal of Archaeology* 7:159–75.
Jennings, Francis
　1968　Glory, death, and transfiguration: The Susquehannock Indians in the seventeenth century. *Proceedings of the American Philosophical Society* 112:15–53.
　1978　Susquehannock. In *Handbook of North American Indians*. Vol. 15, *Northeast*, B. G. Trigger, ed., pp. 362–67. Washington, D.C.: Smithsonian Institution Press.
　1984　*The Ambiguous Iroquois Empire: The Covenant Chain Confederation of Indian Tribes from its Beginnings to the Lancaster Treaty of 1744*. New York: Norton.
　1987　"Pennsylvania Indians" and the Iroquois. In *Beyond the Covenant Chain: The Iroquois and Their Neighbors in Indian North America, 1600–1800*, D. K. Richter and J. H. Merrell, eds., pp. 75–91. Syracuse: Syracuse University Press.
Johnston, Charles, ed.
　1964　*The Valley of the Six Nations: A Collection of Documents on the Indian Lands of the Grand River*. Toronto: Champlain Society.
Johnston, Susan
　1987　Epidemics: The forgotten factor in seventeenth century native warfare in the St. Lawrence region. In *Native People, Native Lands: Canadian Inuit and Metis*, B. A. Cox, ed., pp. 14–31. Ottawa: Carleton University Press.
Jones, Dorothy
　1982　*License for Empire: Colonialism by Treaty in Early America*. Chicago: University of Chicago Press.
Jones, G. D. B.
　1978　Concept and development in Roman frontiers. *Bulletin of the John Rylands Library*, 1978:115–44.
　1985　The Libyan Valleys Survey: The development of settlement survey. In *Town and Country in Roman Tripolitania. Papers in Honour of Olwen Hackett*, D. J. Buck and D. J. Mattingly, eds., pp. 263–89. Oxford: British Archaeological Reports International Series 274.
JR = Thwaites, Ruben, ed.
　1896–　*The Jesuit Relations and Allied Documents: Travel and Explorations of the Jesuit*
　1901　*Missionaries in New France*, 73 vols. Cleveland: Burrows Brothers.
Katz, Friedrich
　1974　*The Ancient American Civilizations*. New York: Praeger Publishers.
Kea, Ray
　1971　Firearms and warfare on the Gold and Slave Coast from the sixteenth to the nineteenth centuries. *Journal of African History* 12(2):185–213.
　1982　*Settlements, Trade and Polities in the Seventeenth-Century Gold Coast*. Baltimore: Johns Hopkins Press.
　1986　"I am here to plunder on the general road": Bandits and banditry in the pre-nineteenth century Gold Coast. In *Banditry, Rebellion and Social Protest in Africa*, D. Crummey, ed., pp. 109–32. London: James Currey.
Keiser, Lincoln
　1986　Death enmity in Thull: Organized vengeance and social change in a Kohistani community. *American Ethnologist* 13:489–505.
Kelly, Raymond
　1985　*The Nuer Conquest: The Structure and Development of an Expansionist System*. Ann Arbor: University of Michigan Press.
Kerpi, K.
　1976　Strains, tensions and tribesmen: Clan warfare in Kup. *New Guinea* 10(3):2–18.

Keymis, L.
 1596 *A Relation of a Second Voyage to Guiana.* London.

Khazanov, Anatolii
 1984 *Nomads and the Outside World.* Cambridge: Cambridge University Press.

Kiefer, Thomas
 1967 Power, politics and guns in Jolo: The influence of modern weapons on Tao-sug legal and economic institutions. *Philippine Sociological Review* 15:21–29.

Kiernan, V. G.
 1972 *The Lords of Human Kind: European Attitudes to the Outside World in the Imperial Age.* Harmondsworth: Penguin.

Kipp, Rita, and Edward Schortman
 1989 The political impact of trade in chiefdoms. *American Anthropologist* 91: 370–85.

Kirk, W.
 1979 The making and impact of the British imperial north-west frontier in India. In *Invasion and Response: The Case of Roman Britain*, B. Burnham and H. Johnson, eds., pp. 39–55. Oxford: British Archaeological Reports 73.

Kloos, Peter
 1977 The Akuriyo way of death. In *Carib-Speaking Indians*, E. Basso, ed. pp. 114–22. Tucson: University of Arizona Press.

Knauft, Bruce
 1987 Reconsidering violence in simple human societies: Homicide among the Gebusi of New Guinea. *Current Anthropology* 28:457–500.

Knox, Robert
 1911 *An Historical Relation of Ceylon.* Glasgow: MacLehouse.

Knutsen, Torbjorn
 1987 Old, unhappy, far-off things: The new military history of Europe. *Journal of Peace Research* 24:87–98.

Koch, Klaus-Friedrich
 1974 *War and Peace in Jalemo: The Management of Conflict in Highland New Guinea.* Cambridge: Harvard University Press.
 1983 Epilogue. Pacification: Perspectives from conflict theory. In *The Pacification of Melanesia*, M. Rodman and M. Cooper, eds., pp. 199–207. Association for Social Anthropology in Oceania Monograph 7. Lanham, Maryland: University Press of America.

Konrad, Victor
 1981 An Iroquois frontier: The north shore of Lake Ontario during the late seventeenth century. *Journal of Historical Geography* 7:129–44.
 1987 The Iroquois return to their homeland: Military retreat or cultural adjustment. In *A Cultural Geography of North American Indians*, T. E. Ross and T. G. Moore, eds., pp. 191–211. Boulder, Colorado: Westview Press.

Kopytoff, Igor, ed.
 1987a *The African Frontier: The Reproduction of Traditional African Societies.* Bloomington: Indiana University Press.
 1987b The internal African frontier: The making of African political culture. In *The African Frontier: The Reproduction of Traditional African Societies*, I. Kopytoff, ed., pp. 3–84. Bloomington: Indiana University Press.

Kroeber, Clifton, and Bernard Fontana
 1986 *Massacre on the Gila: An Account of the Last Major Battle between American Indians, with Reflections on the Origin of War.* Tucson: University of Arizona Press.

Kuper, Adam
 1988 *The Invention of Primitive Society: Transformations of an Illusion.* London: Routledge.

Labat, Jean-Baptiste
1731   *Voyage du Chevalier des Marchais en Guinée, Isles Voisines, et à Cayenne*, 2nd ed. Amsterdam.
Lamontagne, Leopold
1966   Prouville de Tracy, Alexander de. *Dictionary of Canadian Biography* 1:554–57.
Langness, L. L.
1972   Violence in the New Guinea Highlands. In *Collective Violence*, J. F. Short and M. E. Wolfgang, eds., pp. 171–85. Chicago: Aldine.
La Roque de Roquebrune, Robert
1966   Le Febvre de La Barre, Joseph-Antoine. *Dictionary of Canadian Biography* 1:442–46.
Las Casas, B. de
1951   *Historia de las Indias*. Mexico City: Fondo Cultura Economica.
Lassère, J.-M.
1977   *Ubique Populus*. Paris: Centre National de Recherche Scientifique.
Lathrap, Donald
1973   The antiquity and importance of long distance trade relationships in the moist tropics of pre-Columbian South America. *World Archaeology* 5:170–86.
Lattimore, Owen
1940   *Inner Asian Frontiers of China*. London: Oxford University Press.
1962   *Studies in Frontier History 1928–1958*. London: Oxford University Press.
Law, Robin
1967   The Garamantes and trans-Saharan enterprise in classical times. *Journal of African History* 8(2):181–200.
1975   A West African cavalry state: The kingdom of Oyo. *Journal of African History* 16(1):1–15.
1976   Horses, firearms and political power in pre-colonial West Africa. *Past and Present* 72:112–32.
1977   *The Oyo Empire c. 1600–c. 1836: A West African Imperialism in the Era of the Atlantic Slave Trade*. Oxford: Clarendon Press.
1980   Wheeled transport in pre-colonial West Africa. *Africa* 50(3):249–62.
1985   Human sacrifice in pre-colonial West Africa. *African Affairs* 84(334):53–87.
1986   Dahomey and the slave trade: Reflections on the historiography of the rise of Dahomey. *Journal of African History* 27(2):237–67.
1988   A neglected account of the Dahomian conquest of Wydah (1727): The "Relation de la guerra de Juda" of the Sieur Ringard of Nantes. *History in Africa* 15:321–39.
1989   "My head belongs to the King": On the political and ritual significance of decapitation in pre-colonial Dahomey. *Journal of African History* 30(3):339–415.
1990   Further light on the Bullfinch Lambe and the "Emperor of Pawpaw": King Agaja of Dahomey's letter to King George I of England, 1726. *History in Africa* 17:211–26.
Leach, Edmund
1989   Tribal ethnography: Past, present, future. In *History and Ethnicity*, E. Tonkin, G. Chapman, and M. McDonald, eds., pp. 34–47. Association of Social Anthropologists of the Commonwealth Monograph 27. London: Routledge.
Leers, Arnout
1665   *Pertinente Beschryvinghe van Afrika*. Rotterdam.
Le Herissé, A.
1911   *L'Ancien Royaume du Dahomey*. Paris: Larose.
Lehnertz, Jay
1972   Juan Santos, primitive rebel on the Campa frontier (1742–1752). *Actas y Memorias, XXXIX Congreso Internacional de Americanistas* 4, pp. 111–26. Lima.

1974 Lands of the infidels: The Franciscans in the central Montaña of Peru, 1709–1824. Ph.D. dissertation, University of Wisconsin. Ann Arbor: University Microfilms.

Lepelly, C.
1974 La préfecture de tribu dans l'Afrique du bas empire. *Mélanges d'Histoire Ancienne Offerts à William Seston*, pp. 285–95. Paris: De Boccard.

Leschi, L.
1942 Rome et les nomades du Sahara central. *Travaux de l'Institut de Recherches Sahariennes* 1:447–62.

Leveau, P.
1973 L'Aile II des Thaces, la tibu des Mazices et les 'praefecti gentis' en Afrique du nord. *Antiquités Africaines* 7:153–92.
1984 *Caesarea de Maurétanie: Une Ville Romaine et ses Campagnes*. Rome: Collection de l'École Française de Rome 70.

Levi, Sylvain
1900 Les missions de Wang Hiuen-ts'e dans l'Inde: Ceylan et Chine. *Journal Asiatique* 9:401–68.

Lewis, Oscar
1970 The effects of white contact upon Blackfoot culture. In *Anthropological Essays*, by O. Lewis, pp. 137–212. New York: Random House.

Lindenbaum, S.
1979 *Kuru Sorcery*. Palo Alto: Mayfield Publishing.

Lizot, Jacques
1971 Aspects économiques et sociaux du changement culturel chez les Yanōmamɨ. *L'Homme* 11:32–51.
1976 *The Yanomami in the Face of Ethnocide*. Copenhagen: International Work Group for Indigenous Affairs.
1977 Population, resources and warfare among the Yanomamɨ. *Man* 12:497–517.
1985 *Tales of the Yanomami: Daily Life in the Venezuelan Forest*. Cambridge: Cambridge University Press.
1989 Sobre la guerra: Una respuesta a N. A. Chagnon (*Science*, 1988). *La Iglesia en Amazonas* 44(April):23–34.

Loayza, Francisco A.
1942 *Juan Santos, El Invencible*. Lima: Los Pequeños Grandes Libros de Historia Americana.

Lockhart, James, and Stuart Schwartz
1983 *Early Latin America: A History of Colonial Spanish America and Brazil*. New York: Cambridge University Press.

López de Gómara, Francisco
1965– *Historia General de las Indias*, 2 vols. Barcelona: Obras Maestras.
1966

Louis, A.
1975 *Tunisie du Sud: Ksars et Villages de Crêtes*. Paris: Centre National de Recherche Scientifique.

Lovejoy, Paul
1983 *Transformations in Slavery: A History of Slavery in Africa*. Cambridge: Cambridge University Press.

Luttwak, Edward
1976 *The Grand Strategy of the Roman Empire: From the First Century B.C. to the Third*. Baltimore: Johns Hopkins University Press.

Lynch, J.
1964 *Spain under the Hapsburgs*, 2 vols. Oxford: Basil Blackwell.

MacDonald, George
1979 *Kitwanga Fort National Historic Site, Skeena River, British Columbia: Historical*

Research and Analysis of Structural Remains. Ottawa: National Museum of Man.
1980   The epic of Nekt: The archaeology of metaphor. Banquet address to the 13th annual meeting of the Canadian Archaeology Association, Saskatoon, Saskatchewan.

Mackellar, M.
1975   The Enga Syndrome. *Melanesian Law Journal* 3(2):213–66.

MacLeod, Malcolm
1974   Chabert de Joincaire, Philippe-Thomas. *Dictionary of Canadian Biography* 3: 101–2.

MacNeish, R. S.
1981   The transition to statehood as seen from the mouth of a cave. In *The Transition to Statehood in the New World*, G. Jones and R. Krautz, eds., pp. 123–54. Cambridge: Cambridge University Press.

Mahāvaṃsa
1958   W. Geiger, ed. London: Pali Text Society.

Malinowski, Bronislaw
1982   *Crime and Custom in Savage Society.* Totowa, New Jersey: Littlefield, Adams. Orig. pub. 1926.

Malone, Patrick
1973   Changing military technology among the Indians of southern New England, 1600–1677. *American Quarterly* 25:48–63.

Mann, J. C.
1979   Power, force and the frontiers of the Empire. *Journal of Roman Studies* 69: 175–83.

Mann, Michael
1986   *The Sources of Social Power.* Vol. 1, *A History of Power from the Beginning to A.D. 1760.* Cambridge: Cambridge University Press.

Manning, Patrick
1979   The slave trade in the Bight of Benin, 1640–1890. In *The Uncommon Market: Essays in the Economic History of the Atlantic Slave Trade*, H. A. Gemery and J. S. Hogendorn, eds., pp. 107–41. New York: Academic Press.

Manrique, Manuel
1982   *La Peruvian Corporation en la Selva Central del Perú.* Lima: Centro de Investigación y Promoción Amazónica.

Marcus, Joyce
1976   *Emblem and State in the Classic Maya Lowlands: An Epigraphic Approach to Territorial Organization.* Washington, D.C.: Dumbarton Oaks.
1983a   Stone monuments and tomb murals at Monte Albán IIIa. In *The Cloud People: Divergent Evolution of the Zapotec and Mixtec Civilization*, K. V. Flannery and J. Marcus, eds., pp. 137–43. New York: Academic Press.
1983b   Changing patterns of stone monuments after the fall of Monte Albán, A.D. 600–900. In *The Cloud People: Divergent Evolution of the Zapotec and Mixtec Civilization*, K. V. Flannery and J. Marcus, eds., pp. 191–97. New York: Academic Press.
1983c   Aztec military campaigns against the Zapotecs: The documentary evidence. In *The Cloud People: Divergent Evolution of the Zapotec and Mixtec Civilization*, K. V. Flannery and J. Marcus, eds., pp. 314–18. New York: Academic Press.

Marcus, Joyce, and Kent Flannery
1983   An introduction to the late Postclassic. In *The Cloud People: Divergent Evolution of the Zapotec and Mixtec Civilization*, K. V. Flannery and J. Marcus, eds., pp. 217–26. New York: Academic Press.

Marichal, R.
1979   Les Ostraca de Bu Njem. *Comptes Rendus à l'Académie des Inscriptions et Belles-Lettres* 1979:436–52.

Markakis, John
  1990   *National and Class Conflict in the Horn of Africa*. London: Zed Books.
Maroukis, Thomas
  1974   Warfare and society in the kingdom of Dahomey: 1818–1894. Ph.D. disser-
          tation, Boston University.
Marwick, Max
  1970   Witchcraft as a social strain-gauge. In *Witchcraft and Sorcery*, M. Marwick, ed.,
          pp. 280–95. Harmondsworth: Penguin.
Matthews, J.
  1976   Mauretania in Ammianus and the Notitia. In *Aspects of the Notitia Dignitatum*,
          P. Bartholomew and R. Goodburn, eds., pp. 157–86. Oxford: British Archaeo-
          logical Reports International Series 15.
Mattingly, D. J.
  1983   The Laguatan: A Libyan tribal confederation in the late Roman Empire. *Libyan
          Studies* 14:96–108.
  1984   Tripolitania: A comparative study of a Roman frontier province. Doctoral the-
          sis, University of Manchester.
  1985   Olive oil production in Roman Tripolitania. In *Town and Country in Roman
          Tripolitania: Papers in Honour of Olwen Hackett*, D. J. Buck and D. J. Mattingly,
          eds., pp. 27–46. Oxford: British Archaeological Reports International Series
          274.
  1986   Soldier or civilian? Urbanisation on the frontiers of Roman Africa. *Popular
          Archaeology*, December 1985/January 1986:61–66.
  1987a   Libyans and the "Limes": Culture and society in Roman Tripolitania. *Antiquités
          Africaines* 23:71–94.
  1987b   New perspectives on the agricultural development of Gebel and pre-desert in
          Roman Tripolitania. *Revue de l'Occident Musulman et de la Méditerranée* 41–
          42:45–65.
Maurice, F.
  1930   The size of the army of Xerxes in the invasion of Greece, 480 B.C. *Journal of
          Hellenistic Studies* 50:210–235.
Maybury-Lewis, David
  1974   *Akwē-Shavante Society*. New York: Oxford University Press.
Mazrui, Ali, ed.
  1977   *The Warrior Tradition in Modern Africa*. International Studies in Sociology and
          Social Anthropology 23. Leiden: E. J. Brill.
McCorkle, T.
  1952   The history of the Guayqueri: An approach to the anthropology of N. E. Ven-
          ezuela. *Kroeber Anthropological Papers* 6:60–87.
McCrindle, J. W., ed.
  1901   *Ancient India as Described in Classical Literature*. Westminster: Constable.
McIlwain, Charles
  1915   Introduction. In *An Abridgment of the Indian Affairs . . . Transacted in the Colony
          of New York, from the Year 1678 to the Year 1751*, by Peter Wraxall, pp. ix–
          cxviii. Cambridge: Harvard University Press.
McNeill, William
  1982   *The Pursuit of Power: Technology, Armed Force, and Society since A.D. 1000*. Chi-
          cago: University of Chicago Press.
McNitt, Frank
  1990   *Navajo Wars: Military Campaigns, Slave Raids, and Reprisals*. Albuquerque: Uni-
          versity of New Mexico Press.
Medina, Jose, ed.
  1988   *The Discovery of the Amazon*. New York: Dover.

Meggitt, M. J.
  1977   *Blood Is Their Argument*. Palo Alto: Mayfield Publishing.
Mekeel, Scudder
  1943   A short history of the Teton-Dakota. *North Dakota Historical Quarterly* 10: 137–205.
Melancon, Thomas
  1982   Marriage and reproduction among the Yanomamo Indians of Venezuela. Ph.D. dissertation, Department of Anthropology, Pennsylvania State University.
Menezes, M. N.
  1977   *British Policy towards the Amerindians in British Guiana 1803–1873*. Oxford: Clarendon Press.
Mercer, Patricia
  1971   Shilluk trade and politics from the mid-seventeenth century to 1861. *Journal of African History* 12:407–26.
Merrell, James
  1987   "Their very bones shall fight": The Catawba-Iroquois wars. In *Beyond the Covenant Chain: The Iroquois and Their Neighbors in Indian North America, 1600–1800*. D. K. Richter and J. H. Merrell, eds., pp. 115–33. Syracuse: Syracuse University Press.
Michelson, Gunther
  1977   Iroquois population estimates. *Man in the Northeast* 14:3–17.
Migliazza, Ernest Cesar
  1972   Yanomama grammar and intelligibility. Ph.D. dissertation, Indiana University. Ann Arbor: University Microfilms.
Millar, F. G. B.
  1968   Local cultures in the Roman Empire: Libyan, Punic and Latin in Roman Africa. *Journal of Roman Studies* 58:126–34.
  1977   *The Emperor in the Roman World*. London: Duckworth.
  1982   Emperors, frontiers and foreign relations. *Britannia* 13:1–23.
Milloy, John
  1988   *The Plains Cree: Trade, Diplomacy and War, 1790 to 1870*. Winnipeg: University of Manitoba Press.
Ministerio de Guerra
  1966   *Las Guerrillas en el Perú y su Represión*. Lima.
Mitchell, Donald
  1984   Predatory warfare, social status, and the North Pacific slave trade. *Ethnology* 23:39–48.
Moerman, Michael
  1968   Being Lue: Uses and abuses of ethnic identification. In *Essays on the Problem of Tribe: Proceedings of the 1967 Annual Spring Meeting of the American Ethnological Society*, J. Helm, ed. pp. 153–69. Seattle: University of Washington Press.
Molto, J. E., M. W. Spence, and W. A. Fox
  1986   The Van Oordt site: A case study in salvage osteology. *Canadian Review of Physical Anthropology* 5(2):49–61.
Monjarás-Ruiz, Jesús
  1976   Panorama general de la guerre entre los Aztecas. *Estudios de Cultura Nahuatl* 12:241–64.
Moorehead, A.
  1967   *The Fatal Impact: An Account of the Invasion of the South Pacific, 1767–1840*. London: Hamish Hamilton/Reprint Society.
Morgan, Lewis
  1851   *League of the Ho-de-no-sau-nee [or] Iroquois*. Rochester: Sage.

Moriarty, James
   1969   Ritual combat. A comparison of the Aztec "war of flowers" and the medieval
          "mèlée." *Miscellaneous Series* 9, Museum of Anthropology, Colorado State Uni-
          versity, Fort Collins.
Morley, Sylvanus, George Brainerd, and Robert Sharer
   1983   *The Ancient Maya.* Stanford: Stanford University Press.
Moses, R. S.
   1978   The people's view of the resurgence of violence. *Yagl-Ambu* 5(2):219–25.
Murphy, Robert
   1960   *Headhunter's Heritage: Social and Economic Change among the Mundurucú Indi-
          ans.* Berkeley: University of California Press.
N***** (Anonymous)
   1719   *Voyages aux Côtes de Guinée et en Amérique.* Amsterdam.
Naylor, Thomas, and Charles Polzar
   1986   *The Presidio Militia on the Northern Frontier of New Spain: A Documentary His-
          tory.* Tucson: University of Arizona Press.
Neel, James
   1973   Lessons from a "primitive people." In *Peoples and Cultures of Native South
          America,* D. Gross, ed., pp. 159–82. Garden City, New York: Natural History
          Press.
Neumann, C.
   1971   A note on Alexander's march-rates. *Historia: Journal of Ancient History* 20:
          196–98.
Newcomb, W. W., Jr.
   1960   Toward an understanding of war. In *Essays in the Science of Culture in Honor of
          Leslie A. White,* G. E. Dole and R. L. Carneiro, eds., pp. 317–36. New York:
          Thomas A. Crowell.
Nietschmann, Bernard
   1987   The Third World War. *Cultural Survival Quarterly* 11(2):1–16.
Nissen, Hans
   1988   *The Early History of the Ancient Near East 9000–2000 B.C.,* E. Lutzeier, with
          K. Northcott, trans. Chicago: University of Chicago Press.
NYCD = O'Callaghan, Edmund, ed.
   1853– *Documents Relative to the Colonial History of New York,* 15 vols. Albany: Weed,
   1887   Parsons.
O'Connell, Robert
   1989   *Of Arms and Men: A History of War, Weapons, and Aggression.* New York: Oxford
          University Press.
Ojer, P.
   1966   *La Formación del Oriente Venezolano.* Caracas: Universidad Católica "Andres
          Bello."
Oram, N. D.
   1973   Administration, development and public order. In *Alternative Strategies for
          Papua New Guinea,* A. Clunies-Ross and J. Langmore, eds. Melbourne: Oxford
          University Press.
Orken, M.
   1974   They fight for fun. In *The Problem of Choice,* P. Sack, ed., pp. 141–50. Can-
          berra: Australian National University Press.
Ortiz, Fr. Dionisio
   1961   *Reseña Historica de la Montaña de Pangoa, Gran Pajonál, y Satipo (1673–1960).*
          Lima: Editorial "San Antonio."
Ortner, Sherry
   1984   Theory in anthropology since the sixties. *Comparative Studies in Society and
          History* 26:126–66.

Osborn, A.
 1989   Multiculturalism in the eastern Andes. In *Archaeological Approaches to Cultural Identity*, S. J. Shennan, ed., pp. 141–56. One World Archaeology (10). London: Unwin Hyman.
Ossio, Juan, ed.
 1973   *Ideología Mesiánica del Mundo Andino*. Lima: Ignacio Prado Pastor.
Otterbein, Keith
 1964   Why the Iroquois won: An analysis of Iroquois military tactics. *Ethnohistory* 11:56–63.
 1977   Warfare: A hitherto unrecognized critical variable. *American Behavioral Scientist* 20:693–710.
 1979   Huron vs. Iroquois: A case study in inter-tribal warfare. *Ethnohistory* 26:141–52.
Paddock, John
 1966   Oaxaca in ancient Mesoamerica. In *Ancient Oaxaca: Discoveries in Mexican Archaeology and History*, J. Paddock, ed., pp. 83–240. Stanford: Stanford University Press.
Pagden, Anthony
 1982   *The Fall of Natural Man*. Cambridge: Cambridge University Press.
Paranavitana, S., ed.
 1959   *University of Ceylon History of Ceylon*, vol. 1, pt. 1. Colombo: Ceylon University Press Board.
 1970   *Inscriptions of Ceylon*, vol. 1. Colombo: Department of Archaeology.
 1983. *Inscriptions of Ceylon*, vol. 2, pt. 1. Colombo: Department of Archaeology.
Paranavitana, S., and C. E. Godakumbura, eds.
 1963   *Epigraphia Zeylanica*, vol 5. Colombo: Department of Archaeology.
Parker, Arthur
 1916   *The Constitution of the Five Nations or the Iroquois Book of the Great Law*. New York State Museum Bulletin 184.
Parker, Geoffrey
 1989   *The Military Revolution: Military Innovations and the Rise of the West, 1500–1800*. Cambridge: Cambridge University Press.
Parkman, Francis
 1901   *Count Frontenac and the New France under Louis XIV*. Boston: Little, Brown.
Paso y Troncoso, Francisco del, ed.
 1905– *Papeles de Nueva España*, 9 vols. Madrid and Mexico City.
 1948
 1939– *Epistolario de Nueva España*, 16 vols. Mexico City: Antigua Librería Robredo
 1942   de José Porrúa e Hijos.
Pearce, Roy
 1988   *Savagism and Civilization: A Study of the Indian and the American Mind*. Berkeley: University of California Press.
Peckham, Howard
 1947   *Pontiac and the Indian Uprising*. Chicago: University of Chicago Press.
Peires, J. B, ed.
 1981   *Before and after Shaka: Papers in Nguni History*. Grahamstown, South Africa: Institute of Social and Economic Research, Rhodes University.
Perdue, Theda
 1979   *Slavery and the Evolution of Cherokee Society, 1540–1866*. Knoxville: University of Tennessee Press.
 1987   Cherokee relations with the Iroquois in the eighteenth century. In *Beyond the Covenant Chain: The Iroquois and Their Neighbors in Indian North America, 1600–1800*, D. K. Richter and J. H. Merrell, eds., pp. 135–49. Syracuse: Syracuse University Press.

Peters, John Fred
  1973   The effect of Western material goods upon the social structure of the family
          among the Shirishana. Ph.D. dissertation, Department of Sociology, Western
          Michigan University. Ann Arbor: University Microfilms.
Peterson, Frederick
  1962   *Ancient Mexico: An Introduction to the Pre-Hispanic Cultures.* New York: Capri-
          corn Books.
Phelan, John
  1970   *The Millennial Kingdom of the Franciscans in the New World,* 2nd ed. Berkeley:
          University of California Press.
Phillips, Thomas
  1732   A journal of a voyage made in the Hannibal of London. In *Collection of Voyages
          and Travels,* vol. 5, A. Churchill and J. Churchill, eds., pp. 173–239.
Pieris, Ralph
  1956   *Sinhalese Social Organization.* Colombo: University Press.
Plog, S., and D. Braun
  1983   Some issues in the archaeology of "tribal" social systems. *American Antiquity*
          48:619–25.
Podolefsky, A.
  1984   Contemporary warfare in the New Guinea Highlands. *Ethnology* 23:73–88.
Portillo, Col. Pedro
  1901   *Las Montañas de Ayacucho y los Ríos Apurímac, Mantaro, Ene, Perené, Tambo y
          Alto Ucayali.* Lima: Imprenta del Estado.
Posey, D. A., and W. Balée, eds.
  1989   *Resource Management in Amazonia: Indigenous and Folk Strategies.* The Bronx:
          The New York Botanical Garden.
Powell, Philip
  1952   *Soldiers, Indians and Silver: North America's First Frontier War.* Berkeley and Los
          Angeles: University of California Press.
Price, Barbara
  1978   Secondary state formation: An explanatory model. In *Origins of the State: The
          Anthropology of Political Evolution,* R. Cohen and E. Service, eds., pp. 161–86.
          Philadelphia: Institute for the Study of Human Issues.
Price, Richard
  1983   *First-Time: The Historical Vision of an Afro-American People.* Baltimore: Johns
          Hopkins University Press.
Procopius
  1961   *History of the Wars,* vol. 1, H. B. Dewing trans. The Loeb Classical Library
          Series. London: Heinemann.
Pruneau de Pommegorge
  1789   *Description de la Nigritie.* Amsterdam.
Ptolemaeus, Claudius
  1966   *Geographia.* Sebastian Munster, ed. Amsterdam: Theatrum Orbis Terrarum.
Pūjāvalī
  1961   A. V. Suravira, ed. Colombo: Gunasena.
Purdy, Barbara
  1988   American Indians after A.D. 1492: A case study. *American Anthropologist* 90:
          640–55.
Puype, Jan Piet
  1985   Dutch and other flintlocks from seventeenth century Iroquois sites, Research
          Records 18, pt. 1. Rochester: Museum and Science Center.
Quimby, George
  1966   *Indian Culture and European Trade Goods.* Madison: University of Wisconsin
          Press.

Rachet, M.
  1970   *Rome et les Berbères: Un Probleme Militaire d'August à Diocletian*. Brussels: Latomus.
Ralegh, W.
  1848   *The Discovery of the Large, Rich and Beautiful Empire of Guiana* . . . *Performed in the Year 1595*, R. Schomburgk, ed. Hakluyt Society, 1st ser., no. 3. London.
Ramenofsky, Ann
  1987   *Vectors of Death: The Archaeology of European Contact*. Albuquerque: University of New Mexico Press.
Ramos, Alcida Rita
  1972   The social system of the Sanuma of northern Brazil. Ph.D. dissertation, Department of Anthropology, University of Wisconsin. Ann Arbor: University Microfilms.
  1987   Reflecting on the Yanomami: Ethnographic images and the pursuit of the exotic. *Cultural Anthropology* 2(3):284–304.
Ramos, Alcida, and Kenneth Taylor
  1979   *The Yanoama in Brazil, 1979*. Copenhagen: International Work Group on Indigenous Affairs, Document 37.
Ramsden, Peter
  1977   A refinement of some aspects of Huron ceramic analysis. *National Museum of Man Archaeological Survey of Canada Mercury Series* 63.
  1978   An hypothesis concerning the effects of early European trade among some Ontario Iroquois. *Canadian Journal of Archaeology* 2:101–5.
Randers-Pehrson, Justine
  1983   *Barbarians and Romans: The Birth Struggle of Europe, A.D. 400–700*. Norman: University of Oklahoma Press.
Rappaport, R.
  1968   *Pigs for the Ancestors*. New Haven: Yale University Press.
Reay, M.
  1959   *The Kuma*. Melbourne: Melbourne University Press, for the Australian National University.
  1987.   Laying down the law in their own fashion. In *Anthropology in the High Valleys*, L. L. Langness and T. H. Hays, eds., pp. 73–108. Novato, California: Chandler and Sharp.
Rebuffat, R.
  1971   Note sur les confins de la Maurétanie Tingitaine et de la Maurétanie Caesarienne. *Studi Maghrebini* 4:33–64.
  1979   La frontière romaine en Afrique, Tripolitania et Tingitaine. *Ktema: Civilisations de l'Orient, de la Grèce et de la Rome Antique* 44:225–47.
  1982   Au-déla des camps Romains d'Afrique mineure, renseignement, contrôle, penetration. *Aufsteig und Niedergang der Römischen Welt II. Principat* 10(2):474–513.
Reid, John
  1986   Warrior aristocrats in crisis: The political effects of the transition from the slave trade to palm oil commerce in the nineteenth-century kingdom of Dahomey. Doctoral thesis, University of Stirling.
Relation
  n.d. (ca. 1714)   Relation du Royaume de Judas en Guinée. Manuscript, Archives d'Outre-Mer, Aix-en-Provence: Dépòt des Fortifications des Colonies, Côtes d'Afrique, ms. 104.
Reyna, Ernesto
  1942   *Fitzcarrald, El Rey del Caucho*. Lima: Taller Gráfico de P. Barrantes C.

Reyna, Steven
1990   *Wars without End: The Political Economy of a Pre-Colonial African State*. Hanover: University Press of New England.

Ribeiro, Darcy
1970   *Os Índios e a Civilização: A Integração das Populaçoes Indígenas no Brazil Moderno*. Rio de Janeiro: Civilização Brasileira.

Rice, Hamilton
1928   The Rio Branco, Uraricuera and Parima, pt. 3. *The Geographical Journal* 71:345–56.

Richter, Daniel
1983   War and culture: The Iroquois experience. *William and Mary Quarterly* (3rd ser.) 40:528–59.

1985   Iroquois versus Iroquois: Jesuit missions and Christianity in village politics, 1642–1686. *Ethnohistory* 32:1–16.

1987   Ordeals of the Longhouse: The Five Nations in Early American History. In *Beyond the Covenant Chain: The Iroquois and Their Neighbors in Indian North America, 1600–1800*, D. K. Richter and J. H. Merrell, eds., pp. 5–27. Syracuse: Syracuse University Press.

Rgveda
1896   Vol. 1, *The Hymns of the Rgveda*, R. T. H. Griffiths, trans. Benares: Lazarus.

Ritchey, Tom
1978   Precapitalist to capitalist imperialism. Paper presented to the First International Conference on Marxist Anthropology, Uppsala.

Riviere, Peter
1984   *Individual and Society in Guiana: A Comparative Study of Amerindian Social Organization*. Cambridge: Cambridge University Press.

Rochefort, C. de
1665   *Histoire Naturelle et Morale des Iles Antilles de l'Amérique*, 2nd ed. Rotterdam.

Rodman, Margaret
1983   Introduction. In *The Pacification of Melanesia*, M. Rodman and M. Cooper, eds., pp. 1–23. Association for Social Anthropology in Oceania Monograph 7. Lanham, Maryland: University Press of America.

Rodman, Margaret, and Matthew Cooper, eds.
1983   *The Pacification of Melanesia*. ASAO Monograph 7. Lanham, Maryland: University Press of America.

Rodney, Walter
1972   *How Europe Underdeveloped Africa*. London: Bogle-L'Ouverture Publications.

Romanelli, P.
1962   Le iscrizioni volubitane dei Baquati e i rapporti de Roma con le tribu indigene dell'Africa. *Hommages à A. Grenier*, pp. 1347–66. Brussels: Latomus.

Ronen, Dov
1975   *Traditional Dahomey: A Search for the "State" in Precolonial Africa*. Jerusalem: Hebrew University.

Roper, Marilyn
1975   Evidence of Warfare in the Near East from 10,000–4,300 B.C. In *War, Its Causes and Correlates*, M. Nettleship, R. D. Givens, and A. Nettleship, eds., pp. 299–344. The Hague: Mouton.

Rosaldo, Renato
1980   *Ilongot Headhunting, 1883–1974*. Stanford: Stanford University Press.

Roseberry, William
1988   Political economy. *Annual Review of Anthropology* 17:161–85.

1989   *Anthropologies and Histories: Essays in Culture, History, and Political Economy*. New Brunswick: Rutgers University Press.

Ross, David
1971   Dahomey. In *West African Resistance: The Military Response to Colonial Occupa-
        tion*, M. Crowder, ed., pp. 144–69. London: Hutchinson.
Ross, Eric
1978   Food taboos, diet, and hunting strategy: The adaptation to animals in Amazon
        cultural ecology. *Current Anthropology* 19:1–36.
Rowlands, Michael, Mogens Larsen, and Kristian Kristiansen, eds.
1987   *Centre and Periphery in the Ancient World*. Cambridge: Cambridge University
        Press.
Ruby, Robert, and John Brown
1976   *The Chinook Indians: Traders of the Lower Columbia River*. Norman: University
        of Oklahoma Press.
Saffirio, Giovanni
1985   Ideal and actual kinship terminology among the Yanomama Indians of the
        Catrimani River basin (Brazil). Ph.D. dissertation, University of Pittsburgh.
        Ann Arbor: University Microfilms.
Saffirio, Giovanni, and Raymond Hames
1983   The forest and the highway. In *The Impact of Contact: Two Yanomamo Case
        Studies*, J. Clay, ed., pp. 1–52. Cambridge, Massachusetts: Cultural Survival
        and Bennington College.
Saffirio, Giovanni, and Richard Scaglion
1982   Hunting efficiency in acculturated and unacculturated Yanomama villages.
        Journal of Anthropological Research 38:317–27.
Saggs, H. W. F.
1984   *The Might That Was Assyria*. London: Sidgwick and Jackson.
Sahagún, Bernardino de
1954   *General History of the Things of New Spain: Florentine Codex*. Book 8, *Kings and
        Lords*, A. J. O. Anderson and C. E. Dibble, trans. Salt Lake City: University of
        Utah Press.
1961   *General History of the Things of New Spain: Florentine Codex*. Book 10, *The
        People*, A. J. O. Anderson and C. E. Dibble, trans. Salt Lake City: University of
        Utah Press.
1975   *General History of the Things of New Spain: Florentine Codex*. Book 12, *The
        Conquest of Mexico*, A. J. O. Anderson and C. E. Dibble, trans. Salt Lake City:
        University of Utah Press.
Sahlins, Marshall
1961   The segmentary lineage: An organization of predatory expansion. In *Compara-
        tive Political Systems: Studies in the Politics of Pre-Industrial Societies*. Garden City,
        New York: Natural History Press.
1968   *Tribesmen*. Englewood Cliffs, New Jersey: Prentice-Hall.
1987   *Islands of History*. Chicago: University of Chicago Press.
Said, Edward
1989   Representing the colonized: Anthropology's interlocutors. *Critical Inquiry* 15:
        205–25.
Sala, R. P. Fr. Gabriel
1897   *Exploración de los Rios Pichis, Pachitea, y Alto Ucayali y de la Región del Gran
        Pajonal*. Lima: Imprenta La Industria.
Salisbury, R. F.
1962   *From Stone to Steel: Economic Consequences of a Technological Change in New
        Guinea*. London: Cambridge University Press.
Salisbury, Neal
1987   Toward the Covenant Chain: Iroquois and southern New England Algonqui-
        ans. In *Beyond the Covenant Chain: The Iroquois and Their Neighbors in Indian*

North America, 1600–1800, D. K. Richter and J. H. Merrell, eds., pp. 61–73. Syracuse: Syracuse University Press.

Salomon, Frank
1986   *Native Lords of Quito in the Age of the Incas: The Political Economy of North Andean Chiefdoms.* Cambridge: Cambridge University Press.

Salwen, Bert
1978   Indians of Southern New England and Long Island: Early Period. In *Handbook of North American Indians.* Vol. 15, *Northeast*, B. G. Trigger, ed., pp. 160–76. Washington, D.C.: Smithsonian Institution Press.

Sammohavinodanī
1923   A. P. Buddhadatta, ed. London: Pali Text Society.

Sanday, P. R.
1986   *Divine Hunger: Cannibalism as a Cultural System.* Cambridge: Cambridge University Press.

Sando, Joe
1979   The Pueblo Revolt. In *Handbook of North American Indians.* Vol. 9, *The Southwest*, A. Ortiz, ed., pp. 194–97. Washington, D.C.: Smithsonian Institution Press.

Santos, Fernando
1986   Bohórquez y la conquista espurea del Cerro de la Sal. *Amazonía Peruana* 13:119–34.

Sartre, Jean Paul
1960   *Critique de la Raison Dialectique: Précédé de Question de Méthode.* Paris: Bibliotèque des Idées.

Sastri, H. Krishna
1925   *South Indian Inscriptions*, vol. 5. Madras: Government Press.

Sastri, K. A. Nilakanta
1955   *A History of South India.* London: Oxford University Press.

Śatapatha Brāhmaṇa
1900   Julius Eggeling, trans. Sacred Books of the East, vol. 44. Oxford: Clarendon Press.

Schlee, G.
1989   *Identities on the Move: Clanship and Pastoralism in Northern Kenya.* Manchester: Manchester University Press.

Schlesier, Karl
1976   Epidemics and Indian middlemen: Rethinking the wars of the Iroquois, 1609–1653. *Ethnohistory* 23:129–45.

Schmalz, Peter
1984   The role of the Ojibwa in the conquest of southern Ontario, 1650–1701. *Ontario History* 76:326–52.

Schulman, Alan
1964   *Military Rank, Title, and Organization in the Egyptian New Kingdom.* Münchner Ägyptologische Studien 6.

Schumpeter, Joseph
1951   The sociology of imperialisms. In *Imperialism and Social Classes*, P. M. Sweezy, ed., H. Norden, trans., pp. 3–130. Oxford: Blackwell.

Schwerin, K.
1983–84   The kin-integration system among the Caribs. *Antropológica* 59–62:125–53.

Secoy, Frank
1953   *Changing Military Patterns on the Great Plains.* Monograph 21, American Ethnological Society. Seattle: University of Washington Press.

Seddon, D. J.
1973   Local politics and state intervention: Northeast Morocco from 1870 to 1970. In *Arabs and Berbers: From Tribe to Nation in North Africa*, E. Gellner and C. Micaud, eds., pp. 109–39. London: Duckworth.
Sedaraman, J. E., ed.
1970   *Ähälēpola Varṇṇanāva*. In *Praśasti Kāvya Rasaya*. Colombo: Gunasena.
Seitz, Georg
1963   *People of the Rain-Forests*, Arnold Pomerans, trans. London: Heinemann.
Seligmann, C. G., and B. Z. Seligmann
1911   *The Veddas*. Cambridge: Cambridge University Press.
Service, Elman
1962   *Primitive Social Organization*. New York: Random House.
1967   War and our contemporary ancestors. In *War: The Anthropology of Armed Conflict and Aggression*. M. Fried, M. Harris, and R. Murphy, eds., pp. 160–67. Garden City, New York: Natural History Press.
1971   *Primitive Social Organization: An Evolutionary Perspective*. New York: Random House.
Seston, W., and M. Euzennat
1971   Un dossier de la chancellerie romaine: La "Tabula Banasitana." Etude de Diplomatique. *Comptes Rendus à l'Academie des Inscriptions et Belles-Lettres* 1971: 468–90.
Shapiro, Judith
1972   Sex roles and social structure among the Yanomamo Indians of northern Brazil. Ph.D. dissertation, Department of Anthropology, Columbia University. Ann Arbor: University Microfilms.
Sharp, Lauriston
1974   Steel axes for Stone Age Australians. In *Man in Adaptation: The Cultural Present*, 2nd ed., Y. Cohen, ed., pp. 116–27. Chicago: Aldine.
Shaw, B. D.
1981   Fear and loathing: The nomad menace in Roman Africa. In *Roman Africa/ L'Afrique Romaine: The 1980 Vanier Lectures*, C. M. Wells, ed., pp. 29–50. Ottawa: Ottawa University Press.
1987   Autonomy and tribute: Mountain and plain in Mauretania Tingitana. *Revue de l'Occident Musulman et de la Méditerranée* 41–42:66–89.
Shennan, S. J.
1989   Introduction. In *Archaeological Approaches to Cultural Identity*, S. J. Shennan, ed., pp. 1–32. One World Archaeology (10). London: Unwin Hyman.
Sherwin-White, A. N.
1973   The tabula of Banasa and the "Constitutio Antoniana." *Journal of Roman Studies* 63:86–98.
Shoemaker, Robin
1981   *The Peasants of El Dorado: Conflict and Contradiction in a Peruvian Frontier Settlement*. Ithaca: Cornell University Press.
Sigman, M. C.
1977   The Romans and the indigenous tribes of Mauretania Tingitana. *Historia* 26: 415–39.
Sīhaḷavatthupakaraṇa
1959   P. Buddhadatta, ed. Colombo: Anula Press.
Sillitoe, P.
1977   Land shortage and war in New Guinea. *Ethnology* 16(1):71–81.
1978   Big-men and war in New Guinea. *Man* 13(2):252–71.
Skalnik, Peter
1978a   Early states in the Voltaic Basin. In *The Early State*, H. J. Claessen and P. Skalnik, eds., pp. 469–94. The Hague: Mouton.

1978b   The early state as a process. In *The Early State*, H. J. Claessen and P. Skalnik, eds., pp. 597–618. The Hague: Mouton.

Skocpol, Theda
1985   Bringing the state back in: Strategies of analysis in current research. In *Bringing the State Back In*, P. Evans, D. Rueschemeyer, and T. Skocpol, eds., pp. 3–37. Cambridge: Cambridge University Press.

Smith, James
1987   The Western Woods Cree: Anthropological myth and historical reality. *American Ethnologist* 14:434–48.

Smith, Marian
1951   American Indian warfare. *New York Academy of Sciences Transactions* (2nd ser.) 13:348–65.

Smith, Michael
1986   The role of social stratification in the Aztec Empire: A view from the provinces. *American Anthropologist* 88:70–91.

Smith, Robert
1976   *Warfare and Diplomacy in Pre-Colonial West Africa*. London: Methuen.
1988   *Kingdoms of the Yoruba*, 3rd ed. Madison: University of Wisconsin Press.

Smith, William
1744   *A New Voyage to Guinea*. London: Frank Cass. 1967.

Smole, William
1976   *The Yanoama Indians: A Cultural Geography*. Austin: University of Texas Press.

Snelgrave, William
1734   *A New Account of Some Parts of Guinea and the Slave Trade*. London: Frank Cass. 1971.

Snow, Dean, and Kim Lanphear
1988   European contact and Indian depopulation. *Ethnohistory* 35:15–33.
1989   "More methodological perspectives": A rejoinder to Dobyns. *Ethnohistory* 36:299–304.

Snow, Dean, and William Starna
1989   Sixteenth-century depopulation: A view from the Mohawk Valley. *American Anthropologist* 91:142–49.

Snyderman, George
1948   Behind the Tree of Peace. *Pennsylvania Archaeologist* 18(3–4).

Soares Diniz, Edson
1969   Aspectos das relacoes sociais entre os Yanomamo do Rio Catrimani. *Boletím do Museu Paraense Emilio Goeldi* 39:1–18.

Soustelle, Jacques
1970   *Daily Life of the Aztecs on the Eve of the Spanish Conquest*. Stanford: Stanford University Press.

Spencer, George
1983   *The Politics of Expansion: The Chola Conquest of Sri Lanka and Sri Vijaya*. Madras: New Era Publications.

Spicer, Edward
1962   *Cycles of Conquest: The Impact of Spain, Mexico, and the United States on the Indians of the Southwest, 1533–1960*. Tucson: University of Arizona Press.

Spindler, George, and Louise Spindler
1983   Foreword. In *Yąnomamö: The Fierce People*, 3rd ed. New York: Holt, Rinehart and Winston.

Sponsel, Leslie
1983   Yanomama warfare, protein capture, and cultural ecology: A critical analysis of the arguments of the opponents. *Interciencia* 8:204–10.

Spores, Ronald
1974   Marital alliance in the political integration of Mixtec kingdoms. *American Anthropologist* 76:297–311.

1983 Postclassic Mixtec kingdoms: Ethnohistoric and archaeological evidence. In *The Cloud People: Divergent Evolution of the Zapotec and Mixtec Civilization*, K. Flannery and J. Marcus, eds., pp. 255–60. New York: Academic Press.

Spores, Ronald, and Kent Flannery
1983 Sixteenth-century kinship and social organization. In *The Cloud People: Divergent Evolution of the Zapotec and Mixtec Civilization*, K. Flannery and J. Marcus, eds., pp. 339–42. New York: Academic Press.

Stahl, F. A.
1932 *In the Amazon Jungle*. Mountain View, California: Pacific Press Publishing Association.

Standish, W.
1973 The Highlands. *New Guinea* 8(3):4–30.
1979 *Provincial Government in Papua New Guinea: Early Lessons from Chimbu*. Port Moresby: IASER Monograph 7.

Starna, William
1980 Mohawk Iroquois populations: A revision. *Ethnohistory* 27:371–82.

Starna, William, George Hamell, and William Butts
1984 Northern Iroquoian horticulture and insect infestation: A cause for village removal. *Ethnohistory* 31:197–207.

Starna, William, and John Relethford
1985 Deer densities and population dynamics: A cautionary note. *American Antiquity* 50:825–32.

Stearman, Allyn
1984 The Yuqui connection: Another look at Siriono deculturation. *American Anthropologist* 86:630–50.

Stedman, J. G.
1790 *Narrative of a Five Years Expedition against the Revolted Negroes of Surinam*, R. Price and S. Price, eds. Baltimore: Johns Hopkins University Press. 1988.

Stein, Burton
1980 *Peasant State and Society in Medieval South India*. Delhi: Oxford University Press.

Stern, Steve
1987 The age of Andean insurrection, 1742–1782: A reappraisal. In *Resistance, Rebellion, and Consciousness in the Andean Peasant World, 18th to 20th Centuries*, S. J. Stern, ed., pp. 34–93. Madison: University of Wisconsin Press.

Steward, Julian, Robert Manners, Eric Wolf, Elena Padilla Seda, Sidney Mintz, and Raymond Scheele
1956 *The People of Puerto Rico*. Urbana: University of Illinois Press.

Stocking, George
1987 *Victorian Anthropology*. New York: Free Press.

Strathern, Andrew
1971 *The Rope of Moka*. Cambridge: Cambridge University Press.
1972 *One Father, One Blood. Descent and Group Structure among the Melpa People*. Canberra: Australian National University Press.
1974 When dispute procedures fail. In *Contention and Dispute*, A. L. Epstein ed., pp. 240–70. Canberra: Australian National University Press.
1976 Transactional continuity in Mount Hagen. In *Transaction and Meaning*, B. Kapferer, ed., pp. 277–87. Philadelphia: ISHI Publications.
1977 Contemporary warfare in the New Guinea Highlands: Revival or breakdown? *Yagl-Ambu* 4:135–46.
1979 Gender, ideology and money in Mount Hagen. *Man* n.s. 14:530–48.
1982 (Ed.) *Inequality in New Guinea Highlands Societies*. Cambridge: Cambridge University Press.
n.d. Warfare in the Highlands: An intractable problem? In *Conflict and Control in*

the New Guinea Highlands, W. Wormsley, ed. Ethnology Monograph Series, University of Pittsburgh. In press.

Sturtevant, W. C.
1983   Tribe and state in the 16th and 20th centuries. In *The Development of Political Organization in Native North America*, E. Tooker, ed., pp. 3–16. Washington, D.C.: American Ethnological Society.

Sumaṅgalavilāsinī
1886   Pt. 1. T. W. Rhys Davids and J. E. Carpenter, eds. London: Pali Text Society.

Sumati, R.
1984   Trade and its impact on the early Tamils: The Cola experience. M. Phil. dissertation, Jawaharlal Nehru University, Delhi.

Super, John
1988   *Food, Conquest, and Colonization in Sixteenth Century America*. Albuquerque: University of New Mexico Press.

Szynkiewicz, Slawoj
1989   Interactions between the nomadic cultures of Central Asia and China in the Middle Ages. In *Centre and Periphery: Comparative Studies in Archaeology*, T. Champion, ed., pp. 151–58. London: Unwin Hyman.

Tainter, Joseph
1988   *The Collapse of Complex Societies*. Cambridge: Cambridge University Press.

Taittirīya Saṃhitā
1914   Pt. 2, *The Veda of the Black Yajus School Entitled Taittirīya Saṃhitā*, A. B. Keith, trans. Cambridge: Harvard University Press.

Taussig, Michael
1987   *Shamanism, Colonialism, and the Wild Man: A Study in Terror and Healing*. Chicago: University of Chicago Press.

Taylor, Kenneth
1972   Sanuma (Yanoama) food prohibitions: The multiple classification of society and fauna. Ph.D. dissertation, Department of Anthropology, University of Wisconsin. Ann Arbor: University Microfilms.

Terrell, John Upton
1973   *Pueblos, Gods, and Spaniards*. New York: Dial Press.

Thapar, Romila
1971   The image of the barbarian in early India. *Comparative Studies in Society and History* 13(4):408–36.

Thomas, D. J.
1982   *Order without Government: The Society of the Pemon Indians of Venezuela*. Urbana: University of Illinois Press.

Thomas, Peter
1985   Cultural change on the southern New England frontier, 1630–1665. In *Cultures in Contact: The European Impact on Native Cultural Institutions in Eastern North America, A.D. 1000–1800*, W. Fitzhugh, ed., pp. 131–61. Washington, D.C.: Smithsonian Institution Press.

Thornton, John
1988   The art of war in Angola, 1575–1680. *Comparative Studies in Society and History* 30(2):360–78.

Thurman, Melburn
1989   World systems, prophets, and Plains warfare. Paper presented at the School of American Research Advanced Seminar, "Expanding States and Indigenous Warfare," Santa Fe, April.

Tilly, Charles, ed.
1975   *The Formation of National States in Western Europe*. Princeton: Princeton University Press.
1985   War making and state making as organized crime. In *Bringing the State Back*

In, P. Evans, D. Rueschemeyer, and T. Skocpol, eds., pp. 169–91. Cambridge: Cambridge University Press.

Tissot, C.
1884   *Géographie Comparée de la Province Romaine d'Afrique*, vol. 1. Paris: Imprimerie National.

Todd, Dave
1979   War and peace between the Bodi and Dime of Southwestern Ethiopia. In *Warfare among East African Herders*, K. Fukui and D. Turton, eds., pp. 211–25. Senri Ethnological Studies 3. Osaka: National Museum of Ethnology.

Todd, M.
1975   *The Northern Barbarians, 100 B.C.–A.D. 300*. London: Hutchinson.

Tonkin, E., ed.
1989   *History and Ethnicity*. Association of Social Anthropologists of the Commonwealth Monograph 27. London: Routlege.

Tooker, Elisabeth
1963   The Iroquois defeat of the Huron: A review of the causes. *Pennsylvania Archaeologist* 33(1–2):115–23.
1978a   The League of the Iroquois: Its history, politics, and ritual. In *Handbook of North American Indians*. Vol. 15, *Northeast*, B. G. Trigger, ed., pp. 418–41. Washington, D.C.: Smithsonian Institution Press.
1978b   Wyandot. In *Handbook of North American Indians*. Vol. 15, *Northeast*, B. G. Trigger, ed., pp. 398–406. Washington, D.C.: Smithsonian Institution Press.
1984   The demise of the Susquehannocks: A 17th century mystery. *Pennsylvania Archaeologist* 54:1–10.

Torquemada, Juan de
1975–   *Monarquía Indiana*, 7 vols. Mexico City: Universidad Nacional Autonoma de
1983   Mexico.

Townsend, Joan
1983   Firearms against native arms: A study in comparative efficiencies with an Alaskan example. *Arctic Anthropology* 20(2):1–33.

Trelease, Allen
1960   *Indian Affairs in Colonial New York: The Seventeenth Century*. Ithaca: Cornell University Press.
1962   The Iroquois and the western fur trade: A problem in interpretation. *Mississippi Valley Historical Review* 49:32–51.

Trigger, Bruce
1971   The Mohawk-Mahican war (1624–28): The establishment of a pattern. *Canadian Historical Review* 52:276–86.
1972   Hochelaga: History and ethnohistory. In *Cartier's Hochelaga and the Dawson Site*, J. F. Pendergast and B. G. Trigger, eds., pp. 3–93. Montreal: McGill-Queen's University Press.
1976   *The Children of Aataentsic: A History of the Huron People to 1660*. Montreal: McGill-Queen's University Press.
1978   Early Iroquoian contacts with Europeans. In *Handbook of North American Indians*. Vol. 15, *Northeast*, B. G. Trigger, ed., pp. 344–56. Washington, D.C.: Smithsonian Institution Press.
1981   Ontario native people and the epidemics of 1634–1640. In *Indians, Animals, and the Fur Trade: A Critique of Keepers of the Game*, S. Krech III, ed., pp. 19–38. Athens: University of Georgia Press.
1984   The road to affluence: A reassessment of Huron responses to early European contact. In *Affluence and Cultural Survival: 1981 Proceedings of the American Ethnological Society*, R. F. Salisbury and E. Tooker, eds., pp. 12–25. Washington, D.C.: American Ethnological Society.

1985   *Natives and Newcomers: Canada's "Heroic Age" Reconsidered.* Kingston: McGill-Queen's University Press.

Trigger, Bruce, and James Pendergast
1978   Saint Lawrence Iroquoians. In *Handbook of North American Indians.* Vol. 15, *Northeast,* B. G. Trigger, ed., pp. 357–61. Washington, D.C.: Smithsonian Institution Press.

Trousset, P.
1978   Les bornes du bled segui: Nouveaux aperçus sur la centuriation romaine du sud Tunisie. *Antiquités Africaines* 12:125–78.

1980a   Signification d'une frontière: Nomades et sédentaires dans la zone du "Limes" d'Afrique. In *Roman Frontier Studies 1979: Papers Presented to the 12th International Congress of Roman Frontier Studies,* W. Hanson and L. Keppie, eds., pp. 931–43. Oxford: British Archaeological Reports International Series 71.

1980b   Villes, campagnes et nomadisme dans l'Afrique du nord: Representation et réalités. In *Villes et Campagnes dans l'Empire Romain: Actes de la Table Ronde,* P. A. Fevrier and P. Leveau, eds., pp. 195–203. Aix en Provence: Université de Provence.

1984a   L'Idée de frontière au Sahara et les données archeologiques. In *Enjeux Sahariens: Table Ronde du Centre de Recherches et d'Etudes sur les Societeés Méditerranéennes,* P. Baudel, ed., pp. 47–78. Paris: Centre National de Recherche Scientifique.

1984b   Note sur un type d'ouvrage lineaire du "Limes" d'Afrique. *Bulletin Archeologique du Comité des Travaux Historiques et Scientifiques* n.s. 17B:383–98.

1986   Limes et "frontière climatique." *Histoire et Archéologie de l'Afrique du Nord, 3e Colloque International Montpellier, 1–5 Avril 1985,* pp. 55–84. Paris: Comité des Travaux Historiques et Scientifiques.

Tuck, James
1971   *Onondaga Iroquois Prehistory: A Study in Settlement Archaeology.* Syracuse: Syracuse University Press.

Turner, E. Randolph
1985   Socio-political organization within the Powhatan chiefdom and the effects of European contact, A.D. 1607–1646. In *Cultures in Contact: The European Impact on Native Cultural Institutions in Eastern North America, A.D. 1000–1800,* W. Fitzhugh, ed., pp. 193–224. Washington, D.C.: Smithsonian Institution Press.

Turner, E. Randolph, and Robert Stantley
1979   Deer skins and hunting territories reconsidered. *American Antiquity* 44: 180–86.

Turner, Frederick
1977   *The Character and Influence of the Indian Trade in Wisconsin: A Study of the Trading Post as an Institution.* D. Miller and W. Savage, eds. Norman: University of Oklahoma Press.

Turney-High, Harry
1971   *Primitive War: Its Practice and Concepts.* Columbia: University of South Carolina.

Turton, David
1989   Report on a visit to the Mursi, December 1987. Paper presented at the School of American Research Advanced Seminar, "Expanding States and Indigenous Warfare," Santa Fe, April.

U.S. Army
1971a   *Foot Marches.* Field Manual no. 21–18. Washington, D.C.: Department of the Army.

1971b   *The Infantry Battalions.* Field Manual no. 7–20. Washington, D.C.: Department of the Army.

Utley, Robert, and Wilcomb Washburn
1985   *Indian Wars.* New York: American Heritage.
Vail, Leroy, ed.
1989   *The Creation of Tribalism in Southern Africa.* Berkeley: University of California Press.
Vaillant, George
1966   *Aztecs of Mexico: Origin, Rise, and Fall of the Aztec Nation.* Baltimore: Penguin Books.
Valdez Lozano, Zacarías
1944   *El Verdadero Fitzcarraldo ante la Historia.* Iquitos, Peru.
Vaṃsatthappakāsinī
1977   G. P. Malalsekera, ed. London: Pali Text Society.
Van Dantzig, Albert
1978   *The Dutch and the Guinea Coast 1674–1742: A Collection of Documents from the General State Archive at The Hague.* Accra: Ghana Academy of Arts and Sciences.
Van Goens, Ryckloff
1932   *Memoirs of Ryckloff van Goens*, E. Reimers, trans. Colombo: Government Press.
Varese, Stefano
1973   *La Sal de los Cerros*, 2nd ed. Lima: Retablo de Papel Ediciones.
Vayda, Andrew
1960   *Maori Warfare.* Polynesian Society Maori Monographs 2. Wellington.
1971   Phases of the process of war and peace among the Marings of New Guinea. *Oceania* 42(1): 1–24.
1976   *War in Ecological Perspective: Persistence, Change, and Adaptive Processes in Three Oceanian Societies.* New York: Plenum.
Veen, M. van der
1985   The UNESCO Libyan Valleys Survey X: Botanical evidence for ancient farming in the pre-desert. *Libyan Studies* 16: 15–28.
Venkayya, V., ed.
1913   *South Indian Inscriptions*, vol. 2. Madras: Government Press.
Verger, Pierre
1968   *Flux et Reflux de la Traite des Nègres entre le Golfe de Bénin et Bahia de Todos os Santos du XVIIe au XIXe Siècle.* Paris: Mouton.
Vivó Escoto, Jorge
1964   Weather and climate of Mexico and Central America. In *Handbook of Middle American Indians.* Vol. 1, *Natural Environment and Early Cultures*, R. West, ed., pp. 187–215. Austin: University of Texas Press.
Wallace, Anthony
1957   Origins of Iroquois neutrality: The grand settlement of 1701. *Pennsylvania History* 24: 223–35.
1970   *Death and Rebirth of the Seneca.* New York: Knopf.
Wallace, Paul
1946   *White Roots of Peace.* Philadelphia: University of Pennsylvania Press.
Wallerstein, Immanuel
1974   *The Modern World System*, vol 1: *Capitalist Agriculture and the Origins of the European World-Economy in the Sixteenth Century.* New York: Academic Press.
1980   *The Modern World System*, vol. 2: *Mercantilism and the Consolidation of the European World Economy, 1600–1750.* Orlando: Academic Press.
Warmington, B. H.
1954   *The North African Provinces from Diocletian to the Vandal Conquest.* Cambridge: Cambridge University Press.
Warren, James
1981   *The Sulu Zone 1768–1898.* Singapore: University Press.

1982   Slavery and the impact of external trade: The Sulu sultanate in the 19th century. In *Philippine Social History: Global Trade and Local Transformations*, A. McCoy and C. de Jesus, eds., pp. 415–44. Quezon City: Ateneo de Manila University and Asian Studies Association of Australia.

Washburn, Wilcomb

1957   *The Governor and the Rebel: A History of Bacon's Rebellion in Virginia*. Chapel Hill: University of North Carolina Press.

1978   Seventeenth-century Indian wars. In *Handbook of North American Indians*. Vol. 15, *Northeast*, B. G. Trigger, ed., pp. 89–100. Washington, D.C.: Smithsonian Institution Press.

1988, ed.   *Handbook of North American Indians*. Vol. 4, *History of Indian-White Relations*. Washington, D.C.: Smithsonian Institution Press.

Waterton, C.

1825   *Wanderings in South America*, L. H. Matthews, ed. Oxford: Oxford University Press. 1973.

Watson, J. B.

1967   Tairora: The politics of despotism in a small society. *Anthropological Forum* 2(1):53–104.

1983   *Tairora Culture*. Seattle: University of Washington Press.

Webb, Stephen

1984   *1676: The End of American Independence*. New York: Knopf.

Weiss, Gerald

1975   *Campa Cosmology: The World of a Forest Tribe in South America*. American Museum of Natural History, Anthropological Papers 52(5).

1986   Elements of Inkarrí east of the Andes. In *Myth and the Imaginary in the New World*, E. Magaña and P. Mason, eds., pp. 305–20. Amsterdam: Centre for Latin American Research and Documentation.

Wesler, Kit

1983   Trade politics and native politics in Iroquoia and Asante. *Comparative Studies in Society and History* 25:641–60.

White, Marian

1978a   Neutral and Wenro. In *Handbook of North American Indians*. Vol. 15, *Northeast*, B. G. Trigger, ed., pp. 407–11. Washington, D.C.: Smithsonian Institution Press.

1978b   Erie. In *Handbook of North American Indians*. Vol. 15, *Northeast*, B. G. Trigger, ed., pp. 412–70. Washington, D.C.: Smithsonian Institution Press.

Whitehead, Neil

1988   *Lords of the Tiger Spirit: A History of the Caribs in Colonial Venezuela and Guyana 1498–1820*. Royal Institute of Linguistics and Anthropology, Caribbean Studies Series 10. Dordrecht/Leiden: Foris/KITLV Press.

1989   The ancient Amerindian polities of the Lower Orinoco, Amazon and Guyana Coast: A preliminary analysis of their passage from antiquity to extinction. Paper presented at the Wenner-Gren International Symposium no. 109, "Amazon Synthesis: An Integration of Disciplines, Paradigms, and Methodologies," Nova Friburgo, Brazil (forthcoming).

1990a   The Snake Warriors—Sons of the Tiger's Teeth: A descriptive analysis of Carib warfare ca. 1500–1820. In *The Anthropology of War*, J. Haas, ed., pp. 146–70. Cambridge: Cambridge University Press.

1990b   Carib ethnic soldiering in Venezuela, the Guianas and Antilles: 1492–1820. *Ethnohistory* 37(4):357–85.

n.d.   The transformation of native Surinam, 1499–1681. In *Indianen van Surinam*, P. Kloos, ed. In preparation.

Whittaker, C. R.

1978   Land and labour in North Africa. *Klio* 60(2):331–62.

Whitten, Norman
   1976   *Sacha Runa: Ethnicity and Adaptation of Ecuadorian Jungle Quichua.* Urbana: University of Illinois Press.
   1981   (Ed.) *Cultural Transformations and Ethnicity in Modern Ecuador.* Urbana: University of Illinois Press.
Wilbert, Johannes
   1966   *Indios de la Región Orinoco-Ventuari.* Caracas: Fundación La Salle de Ciencias Naturales.
Wilson, H. Clyde
   1956   A new interpetation of the wild rice district of Wisconsin. *American Anthropologist* 58:1059–64.
Wilson, Stephen
   1981   Conflict and its causes in southern Corsica, 1800–35. *Social History* 6:33–69.
Willis, William, Jr.
   1972   Skeletons in the anthropological closet. In *Reinventing Anthropology*, D. Hymes, ed., pp. 121–52. New York: Pantheon.
Wise, S. F.
   1970   The American Revolution and Indian history. In *Character and Circumstance: Essays in Honour of Donald Grant Creighton*, J. S. Moir, ed., pp. 182–200. Toronto: Macmillan.
Wolf, Eric
   1982   *Europe and the People without History.* Berkeley: University of California Press.
Woolman, D. S.
   1969   *Rebels in the Rif: Abd el-Krim and the Rif Rebellion.* Stanford: Stanford University Press.
Wormsley, W.
   n.d.   The Enga Law and Order Project: Final report. Wabag: Government of Papua New Guinea.
Wray, Charles
   1983   Seneca glass trade beads c. A.D. 1550–1820. In *Proceedings of the 1982 Glass Trade Bead Conference*, C. Hayes III, ed., pp. 41–49. Rochester Museum and Science Center Research Records 16.
Wray, Charles, and Harry Schoff
   1953   A preliminary report on the Seneca sequence in western New York, 1550–1687. *Pennsylvania Archaeologist* 23(2):53–63.
Wright, James
   1979   *Quebec Prehistory.* Toronto: Van Nostrand.
Yanomami, Davi Kopenawa
   1989   Letter to all peoples of the earth. *Cultural Survival Quarterly* 13(4):368–69.
Yoffee, Norman, and George Cowgill, eds.
   1988   *The Collapse of Ancient States and Civilizations.* Tucson: University of Arizona Press.
Zarzar, Alonso
   1989   *Apo Capac Huayana, Jesús Sacramentado: Mito, Utopía, y Milenarismo en el Pensamiento de Juan Santos Atahualpa.* Lima: Centro Amazónico de Antropología y Aplicación Práctica.
Zoltvany, Yves
   1969   Chabert de Joncaire, Louis-Thomas. *Dictionary of Canadian Biography* 2:125–27.
Zorn, J.
   1976   Fighting over land. *Melanesian Law Journal* 4(1):7–36.

Index

Asháninka: firearms and slave trade, 185; first European contact of, 179; intervillage organizations, 191; and Juan Santos rebellion, 181–83; and leftist guerrillas, 189–91; millenarianism, 187–90, 194–95; missionization of, 179–81, 188–89; myths about Inca, 183–84; not a tribe, 195; precontact, 177–79; relation with Andean peoples, 177; reputation for ferocity, 175–76; territory, map of, 178; trade, 179–80; slave raiding and trade, 185–87. See also European state expansion, and the Asháninka; Warfare, Asháninka

Aztec state expansion: and the Chichimecs, 89; and marriage alliance, 93–94, 95; and political development of nonstate peoples, 90; and political instability, 94–95; and religion, 91–93; and social mobility, 92; and trade embargoes, 91; and tribute, 91. See also European state expansion, and the Aztecs; Warfare, Aztec

Captives: incorporation of, by Iroquois, 159, 163; sacrifice of, in Dahomey, 121, 122. See also Slave trade

Chagnon, Napoleon, on the Yanomami: characteristics of, 199–201; exchange of Western goods by, 210–11, 217–18; exchange of women by, 216; revenge warfare of, 223–24; status among, 220–21

Champlain, Samuel de, 155, 157

Chiefdoms, 129–30; in Roman North Africa, 33; in Sri Lanka, 62–63

Culture, and history, 2, 3

Dahomey state, 106–7; European advisors to, 110; European relationships of, 108, 109; and European trade, 123; as a militarized society, 121–23; military conscription by, 117–18; military control of king in, 122–23; origin of, 116; and peripheral societies, 124–25; prohibition of firearms trade to interior, 125; slave trade, ban of, 113. See also European state expansion, in West Africa; Warfare, Dahomey

Disease: and European expansion, 8–9; among the Iroquois, 154–55, 159; among the Yanomami, 203–4

Dutch: in northeastern South America, 140, 146, 150n4; in West Africa, 107, 108, 109, 111, 112

Empire. See State

English: in northeastern South America, 150n4; in West Africa, 107, 108, 109, 110, 111. See also European state expansion, and the Iroquois

Ethnic group, definition of, 15

Ethnogenesis, of Iroquois, 163, 165. See also Tribalization

European state expansion (general): contact situations, types of, 128–29; and disease, 8–9; and ecological change, 9–10; and European national identity, 16, 136; factors favoring, 20–21; and technological change, 10–11; and tribe formation, 128–29; and warfare, xii–xiii, 18–25, 26–27

European state expansion, and the Asháninka: missionization, 179–81, 188–89, 193; Peruvian colonization,

School of American Research Advanced Seminar Series

PUBLISHED BY SAR PRESS

PUBLISHED BY UNIVERSITY OF NEW MEXICO PRESS

RECONSTRUCTING PREHISTORIC PUEBLO
SOCIETIES
  William A. Longacre, ed.

NEW PERSPECTIVES ON THE PUEBLOS
  Alfonso Ortiz, ed.

STRUCTURE AND PROCESS IN LATIN
AMERICA
  Arnold Strickon &
  Sidney M. Greenfield, eds.

THE CLASSIC MAYA COLLAPSE
  T. Patrick Culbert, ed.

METHODS AND THEORIES OF
ANTHROPOLOGICAL GENETICS
  M. H. Crawford & P. L. Workman, eds.

SIXTEENTH-CENTURY MEXICO:
THE WORK OF SAHAGUN
  Munro S. Edmonson, ed.

ANCIENT CIVILIZATION AND TRADE
  Jeremy A. Sabloff &
  C. C. Lamberg-Karlovsky, eds.

PHOTOGRAPHY IN ARCHAEOLOGICAL
RESEARCH
  Elmer Harp, Jr. ed.

MEANING IN ANTHROPOLOGY
  Keith H. Basso & Henry A. Selby, eds.

THE VALLEY OF MEXICO: STUDIES IN
PRE-HISPANIC ECOLOGY AND SOCIETY
  Eric R. Wolf, ed.

DEMOGRAPHIC ANTHROPOLOGY:
QUANTITATIVE APPROACHES
  Ezra B. W. Zubrow, ed.

THE ORIGINS OF MAYA CIVILIZATION
  Richard E. W. Adams, ed.

EXPLANATION OF PREHISTORIC CHANGE
  James N. Hill, ed.

EXPLORATIONS IN ETHNOARCHAEOLOGY
  Richard A. Gould, ed.

ENTREPRENEURS IN CULTURAL CONTEXT
  Sidney M. Greenfield, Arnold Strickon,
  & Robert T. Aubey, eds.

THE DYING COMMUNITY
  Art Gallaher, Jr., &
  Harlan Padfield, eds.

SOUTHWESTERN INDIAN RITUAL DRAMA
  Charlotte J. Frisbie, ed.

LOWLAND MAYA SETTLEMENT PATTERNS
  Wendy Ashmore, ed.

SIMULATIONS IN ARCHAEOLOGY
  Jeremy A. Sabloff, ed.

CHAN CHAN: ANDEAN DESERT CITY
  Michael E. Moseley & Kent C. Day, eds.

SHIPWRECK ANTHROPOLOGY
  Richard A. Gould, ed.

ELITES: ETHNOGRAPHIC ISSUES
  George E. Marcus, ed.

THE ARCHAEOLOGY OF LOWER CENTRAL
AMERICA
  Frederick W. Lange &
  Doris Z. Stone, eds.

LATE LOWLAND MAYA CIVILIZATION:
CLASSIC TO POSTCLASSIC
  Jeremy A. Sabloff &
  E. Wyllys Andrews V, eds.

Participants in the advanced seminar

EXPANDING STATES AND INDIGENOUS WARFARE.

Left to right:

R. Brian Ferguson

Ross Hassig

Karen Colvard

Michael F. Brown

Thomas S. Abler

Melburn Thurman

Andrew Strathern

R. A. L. H. Gunawardana

Robin Law

Neil L. Whitehead

D. J. Mattingly